PERGAMON INTERNATIONAL LIBRARY
of Science, Technology, Engineering and Social Studies

The 1000-volume original paperback library in aid of education,
industrial training and the enjoyment of leisure

Publisher: Robert Maxwell, M.C.

Evaluation in the Planning Process

THE URBAN AND REGIONAL PLANNING SERIES

For a complete list of titles and other titles of interest see the end of this book.

Pergamon Urban and Regional Planning Advisory Committee

Evaluation in the Planning Process

NATHANIEL LICHFIELD, PETER KETTLE,
AND MICHAEL WHITBREAD

PERGAMON PRESS

Oxford · New York · Toronto · Sydney · Paris · Braunschweig

Pergamon Press Offices:

U.K.	Pergamon Press Ltd., Headington Hill Hall, Oxford OX3 0BW, England
U.S.A.	Pergamon Press Inc., Maxwell House, Fairview Park, Elmsford, New York 10523, U.S.A.
CANADA	Pergamon of Canada, Ltd., 207 Queen's Quay West, Toronto 1, Canada
AUSTRALIA	Pergamon Press (Aust.) Pty. Ltd., 19a Boundary Street, Rushcutters Bay, N.S.W. 2011, Australia
FRANCE	Pergamon Press SARL, 24 rue des Ecoles, 75240 Paris, Cedex 05, France
WEST GERMANY	Pergamon Press GMbh, 3300 Braunschweig, Postfach 2923, Burgplatz 1, West Germany

First edition 1975

Library of Congress Cataloging in Publication Data

Lichfield, Nathaniel.
Evaluation in the planning process.

(Urban and regional planning series)
Bibliography: p.
Includes indexes.
1. Cities and towns—Planning—Great Britain—Evalua-
tion. 2. Regional planning—Great Britain—Evaluation.
I. Whitbread, Michael, joint author. II. Kettle, Peter,
joint author. III. Title. IV. Series.
HT169,G7L5   1975   309.2′62′0941   75-4905
ISBN 0-08-017843-X
ISBN 0-08-018243-7 pbk.

Urban and Regional Planning Series
Volume 10

Printed in Great Britain by A. Wheaton & Co., Exeter

Contents

Foreword

THE techniques involved in public planning become more complicated and abstract as we attempt to measure more and more factors that are now seen to be relevant, and find ways of relating one factor to another. On the other hand, the general public are becoming more and more interested in the whole planning process and determined to take part in it.

The dilemma therefore is that whilst people demand that public participation should be an integral part of the process of planning, the information and analysis on which decisions need to be taken becomes more complex and the process more difficult to understand. Unless technicians can make their work comprehensible, the danger is that much valuable work on techniques will simply be ignored, for at the end of the day the public, in one form or another, take the decision. Even those professionally engaged in planning find many new techniques difficult, if not impossible, to understand. Evaluation techniques are likely to be in the public eye more than many other techniques, and widespread understanding of their contribution to good planning is therefore important.

When I was involved with the team preparing the strategic plan for the South-East in 1968/9 we faced the problem of trying to set objectives that made sense in the context of the region and deciding how to work from problems and objectives through to evaluation techniques that would help us produce an acceptable strategy within the time limit set. We were not, of course, wholly satisfied with our techniques, but even today the situation is not so very different—I still read lists of objectives that might just as well not have been written for all the difference they make to the plan.

The central theme of this book is not about how to undertake plan evaluation as such, on which the authors have written elsewhere. Rather, it concerns the role of evaluation in the overall planning process and the implications of this for the organization and management of studies. A book reviewing the present state of play and hopefully pointing the way forward is therefore timely indeed, and one must be grateful that Professor Lichfield and his colleagues were able to undertake this research task. The analysis of work done on evaluation by practising planners doing

ix

their professional job is balanced by theoretical arguments that help to clarify and focus attention on the main difficulties and ideas. The evaluation techniques, so ably set out in this book, may be tools for specialists, but they should also be understood by all planners. The importance of this work may lie less in its presentation of techniques than in its arguments about crucial aspects of planning. What is planning about? Who is it for?

To many people evaluation is a straightforward process of testing alternative plans so as to guide the decision-maker in choosing the one most appropriate in the circumstances. But the plans put forward for evaluation need to contain some that are "good" relative to all possibilities, otherwise inferior choices will be made. Plans should be designed with the criteria of assessment in mind. To make the most effective use of evaluation methods there should also be consistency between the process of evaluation and various other plan-making activities, such as those of data collection and setting objectives. It has thus become important to see evaluation not just as the final operation before selecting a preferred plan, but rather as part of a total planning process which itself must be continuous. Evaluation leads on to monitoring which leads back to objectives. Those involved in the process, including the general public, can then see why certain information is collected, can argue about objectives and weighting, and can participate fully at the appropriate stages of planning rather than reacting—sometimes rather violently—when the technician has done his job and arrived at a preferred solution.

We have to be clear that whatever techniques we use today we cannot measure everything, and wise judgement is still needed in large measure. Indeed, value judgements become even more important when the many variables involved in any planning situation become more fully appreciated. The role of decision-makers in the planning process must therefore be very carefully considered. At what stage should they be involved and how can the work of the technical expert, the decision-maker, and the public be organized to greatest effect?

An important part of the work of Professor Lichfield and his colleagues has been in setting out a way of thinking about planning activities. What is it that we are trying to find out when assessing the relative merits of planning options? What kind of evidence should be produced to aid public decision-making? What sort of planning process best facilitates the debate on, and selection between, the numerous possibilities that invariably exist? It is this way of thinking that has to be explained to, and understoody by, all those who are involved in the planning process. This study will I believe open the mind in this way.

WILFRED BURNS

Preface

THIS book is the outcome of a research project undertaken from October 1970–March 1973 within the Planning Methodology Research Unit of the School of Environmental Studies at University College London, financed by the Social Science Research Council. The research comprised an investigation into the way in which the activity of plan evaluation is in practice—and should be in principle—incorporated into the process of decision-making in urban and regional planning. Attention was focused primarily on identifying and examining those features of contemporary planning procedures in the United Kingdom which have restricted the effectiveness of evaluation as an aid to choice between possible courses of action. This led us to suggest more effective ways of integrating plan evaluation with other related activities within the planning process, such as the formulation of objectives and the design of alternative plans.

During the project we prepared and circulated for comment a series of working papers. These are listed in the Appendix. Virtually all of them have formed the basis of Parts I and II of the book, although revisions have been made in the light of comments received and our own reflections.

This book is intended to fill what appears to be a significant gap in the literature on evaluation. Whereas a number of discussions of the main methods of evaluation for urban and regional planning are now available, in particular on the principles and application of social cost–benefit analysis, little attention has been paid to the relationship of evaluation to other tasks and activities within processes of decision-making in planning. An exception is the research into procedures for metropolitan land-use-transportation studies by David Boyce and colleagues, then at the Regional Science Department of Pennsylvania University. The subject-matter of their work has certain similarities with our own, but their treatment of principal issues is rather different.

Our research investigations, and the material in this book, have been directed at those who are engaged in the task of aiding decisions on urban and regional planning problems, especially those who are concerned with formulating planning processes and with the management of studies. In terms of academic training and experience, this audience is highly heterogeneous. Accordingly, we have tried to explain in full the meaning which we attach to certain key terms and phrases which are in popular usage. This attempt to be clear may be at the expense of some tedium for readers who find nothing unusual or contentious about the meaning of terminology we have adopted.

The team who undertook the research comprised the authors, with invited contributions on specific aspects from three others, Professor Morris Hill, Miss Hazel McKay, and Mr. Robert Sarly. We had a number of discussions with Morris Hill during his stay at our invitation at the School of Environmental Studies in the autumn of 1971, which, with subsequent correspondence, helped greatly in clarifying points of similarity and difference between his goals–achievement method of evaluation and that of the planning balance sheet. Chapter 5 records a number of the views then expressed. He also prepared a working paper on urban development models. Hazel McKay researched and substantially wrote the discussion of the Grangemouth/Falkirk Study, was responsible for some of the research into the Notts–Derby Study and helped to review the literature on threshold analysis. This is reflected in Part II. Robert Sarly reviewed the academic literature on planning procedures, which formed the basis for some of Chapter 2. These contributions have been most welcome.

A number of organizations and individuals have helped us in a variety of important ways. Many people were kind enough to comment on one or more drafts of various sections of the book and on material originally contained in the working papers. We owe them a considerable debt of gratitude for sparing the time to contribute criticisms and suggestions. We list their contributions in chapter order. In Part I Jean Perraton, now of the Botswana Government's Department of Town Planning, commented on the second section of Chapter 1 and on the planning process presented in Chapter 2. Professor J. Parry Lewis of Manchester University commented on the second section of Chapter 4. Michael Batty of Reading University, Robin Carruthers, now of R. Travers Morgan and Partners, and A. D. J. Flowerdew of the London School of Economics commented on the second section of Chapter 6. We also wish to thank Professor Michael Beesley of the London Graduate School of Business Studies who was instrumental in developing a number of ideas presented in the second section of Chapter 6.

Special mention should be made of contributions to our discussions of studies in Part II. These discussions are intended as appraisals, and it was important that they be based on an accurate account of the work of study teams. To this end, those associated with the studies were most generous in the time they gave to considering and commenting on draft material. We are wholly responsible for any errors of fact and interpretation which remain. Richard Bigwood of Edinburgh University, James Hughes of Glasgow University, and Dr. Jerzy Kozlowski of the Warsaw Institute of Architecture and Planning, commented on the discussion of the Grangemouth/Falkirk Study and on a review of threshold analysis. John Moreton, present Director of the West Midland Regional Study, and William Ogden of Lanchester Polytechnic commented on the discussion of the West Midland Study.

Andrew Thorburn, now County Planning Officer of East Sussex County Council, Geoffrey Steeley, now Deputy County Planning Officer of Hertfordshire County Council, J. D. S. Gillis, now Assistant County Planning Officer of Northamptonshire County Council, William Murray, now of the National Capital Development Commission at Canberra, Australia, Robert Relph, Assistant Chief Planner (Transportation Policy) of West Yorkshire County Council, and Michael Batty commented on the discussion of the Notts–Derby Study. Urlan Wannop, now Deputy County Planning Officer of Warwickshire County Council, J. Martin Shaw, now Assistant County Planning Officer of Norfolk County Council, and Ian Turner, now Deputy Director of Planning of Derby County Borough Council, commented on the discussion of the Coventry–Solihull–Warwickshire Study. Roger Pead, Deputy Chief Planner of the Irvine Development Corporation, Professor Haim Ben-Shahar of the International Institute of Urban Studies in Israel, Sir Hugh Wilson and Eric Browning of Messrs. Hugh Wilson and Lewis Womersley, and Jim Palmer, now of the Scottish Development Department, commented on the discussion of the Irvine New Town Study. Professor Alan Walters and A. D. J. Flowerdew of the London School of Economics, Robin Carruthers, and David Pearce of Southampton University commented on the discussion of the siting of the Third London Airport. As a result, virtually all of Part II has benefited from comment by some of those associated with the studies in question. In the case of the Brighton Urban Structure Plan Study pressure of work prevented members of the Team from commenting, but they were very helpful in providing us with unpublished material.

Quite a number of people typed parts of drafts of the manuscript, but we are especially grateful to Mrs. Margaret Shaw and Mrs. Pat Courtney who undertook with tremendous efficiency the great bulk of the work.

Returning to the origin of this work, we would like to acknowledge the contributions of those who have made our rewarding collaboration possible. We are glad to thank the Social Science Research Council for their financial support and their Planning Committee and officers, who were always helpful, and also University College London for excellent accommodation and support services. Finally, we acknowledge the opportunities afforded by the consultancy of Nathaniel Lichfield and Associates, where we developed many of our ideas on evaluation through working on a number of wide-ranging commissions.

April 1974
London

Acknowledgements. The publisher and authors would like to thank the following publishers and organizations who have kindly given permission to reproduce material from their publications: The American Institute of Planners; the Brighton Urban Structure Plan Team; Built Environment; the Coventry/Solihull/Warwickshire Sub-Regional Study; Her Majesty's Stationery Office; The Irvine Corporation; McGraw-Hill Book Company; Macmillan London and Basingstoke; the Notts./Derby Sub-Regional Monitoring and Advisory Unit; the Royal Town Planning Institute; Regional Studies; the University of Pennsylvania Press; the West Midland Regional Study; John Wiley & Sons, Inc.

Introduction

THE topic of evaluation in urban and regional planning has been approached from a particular viewpoint in this book. To introduce the reader to our discussions, we give here an outline of this approach and the reasons for adopting it. For many years now, since an initial formulation,[1] we have been practising plan evaluation through planning balance sheet analysis, which is based on the principles and techniques developed in public enterprise economics under the name of social cost–benefit analysis. Our work in the main has consisted of the application of such analysis to a variety of urban and regional planning problems.

Following initial research exercises, we have applied planning balance sheet analysis as consultants, sometimes within our own wider planning studies and at other times as economic or evaluation consultants to other planning teams. This experience, together with consideration of recent UK planning studies, suggested to us that the scope and reliability of evaluation is often seriously hampered by its poor integration with activities undertaken at other stages of the planning process. Evaluation is frequently treated in practice as a discrete activity, functionally separate from other plan-making activities, with those responsible for undertaking the evaluation work having little or no influence over the nature of preceding work. Alternatively, evaluation is left until too late in the study for it to make an effective contribution to subsequent decision-making procedures. A variety of difficulties may result. For instance, the data available by which to measure the consequences of alternative plans may be only partial in relation to what is required or may not be in a suitable form; the alternative plans put forward for evaluation may contain only relatively "poor" possibilities. In addition, it is common to find that those responsible for a planning study have only a hazy notion as to the nature of evaluation and the purposes it is intended to serve, which has aggravated the difficulties stemming from poor integration with other plan-making activities. All this is not to deny, of course, that there is still a great deal to be done on extending techniques of plan evaluation *per se*, particularly our ability to quantify the impacts of proposals on those affected.

[1] N. Lichfield, Economics of planned development, *Estates Gazette*, London, 1956, part IV.

Our general conclusion was that the planning profession as a whole has been too slow to appreciate the need to generate alternative plans and to select that which is "best" on the basis of some formal evaluation. Furthermore, it has resisted until recently the introduction of a more rigorous approach to decision-making, in particular the approach that economists can bring to bear to this work. As a result, insufficient regard has been paid in practice to the role of evaluation within the planning process, which in turn has affected the contribution made by evaluation exercises. There has been a general reluctance to appreciate that since the purpose of planning is to devise proposals which are advantageous in terms of the interests of groups within the community, there should be from the outset a rigorous attempt to work towards the definition of possibilities and to subject them to an analysis which will bring out the essential advantages and disadvantages to members of the community. This in turn means ensuring that the planning process itself will lead smoothly to the production of such evidence. These conclusions struck us most forcibly when we acted as evaluation consultants to the West Midland Regional Study Team. This was not because the Team were unappreciative of the need for evaluation of alternatives; there was a failure to integrate the evaluation work within the overall planning process. As a result, we submitted a research proposal to the Social Science Research Council with a view to enabling us to pursue this topic.

Our intention in doing the research has been to try to improve the quality of evidence produced by evaluation as to the welfare consequences of the array of plan possibilities, and thus make these consequences both more explicit and better understood. If decision-takers, and those whose well-being is affected by planning policies (and who pass periodic judgement on the performance of governments), are made more aware of the welfare consequences of choosing between different possibilities, the level of debate about options should be raised and thereby more soundly based decisions result. Other things being equal, those decisions are more likely to be based on comprehensive information as to the effects of proposals on the well-being of members of the community.

Two main lines of investigation were undertaken. The first concerned the nature of evaluation and the functions it should fulfil in the urban and regional planning process, and the second the interrelationships which should exist between evaluation and other planning activities. The work was progressed by examination of a number of recent UK studies which have been concerned with "standard" planning problems, such as the location of urban developments within a sub-region, and the formulation of an urban structure plan. These studies were selected to exemplify what we considered to be advanced practice. A review of each was made in terms of the quality of the information generated by the study team to aid the decision. The performance of a study was assessed against our view of the information required for rational decision-making. Particular attention was paid to the generation of a wide set of alternative proposals, the assessment of their comparative social costs and benefits, and the tracing of the incidence of those costs and benefits.

It was necessary to use published reports as the basis for appraising the work of a study team. There were a number of difficulties with their use. Firstly, there is a strong tendency for those who have been engaged on a study (including ourselves) to rationalize what was done after the event. Logical and consistent explanations often mask what was actually done in a rather unplanned and unforeseen manner. Secondly, people are generally reluctant to be critical of their own efforts in report writing. Thirdly, reports tend to be written for a decision-taking body, typically a group of elected representatives, with the emphasis on setting out recommendations and persuasive supporting arguments. As a result, the strengths of alternative courses of action tend to be underplayed, with a lack of technical explanation. One former member of a team whose work we review in Part II argued that any attempt to investigate study documents in an academic manner is bound to prove fruitless. We think this is an overstatement, but the argument certainly has some truth to it.

Whilst we had to rely in the main on published material, it was sometimes possible to use unpublished "internal" documents as a supplement. In addition, and more important, we had communications with some of those who had been directly involved with the studies. A draft working paper was sent to a number of former members of the study team; in most cases this included the director, some others working at senior management level, and some more technically oriented personnel. This was followed up with verbal discussions if possible, or otherwise with correspondence. In general the responses to our desire for discussion were generous and helpful, and the exchanges proved of enormous value to us. Nevertheless, it is inevitable that much of the discussion of case studies in this book should be regarded as our interpretation of the work undertaken and the nature of the planning procedures that were adopted.

These studies are discussed in Part II. Preceding this, in Part I, are several chapters which consider the principles of evaluation method and the role of evaluation in the planning process; this provides a broad conceptual framework for the consideration of the case studies. We attempt foremost to define the linkages which should exist between evaluation and other stages in the planning process. Part I also contains discussions of specific evaluation methods, particularly that of the planning balance sheet which we favour and, as a comparison with the planning balance sheet, the goals–achievement matrix, as two principal methods both claiming comprehensiveness.

In Part III we draw conclusions from the preceding discussions. In starting our work we had hoped that we would be able to prepare some authoritative statement on how plan evaluation should be carried out in practice in a variety of typical plan-making processes; for example, in relation to structure plans or plans for new towns. But within our time-scale this proved too ambitious. We have therefore had to be content with some firm, but generalized, conclusions of the principles and procedures to be followed.

We are conscious of the boundaries we have deliberately set to our investigations with the intention of achieving some depth. We have been concerned with the role of evaluation in the plan-making process, and not with the role of evaluation in the decisions subsequent to plan-making which come under the heading of "implementation" (whether these be by way of control over development or by way of the formulation of projects in fulfilment of the plan). Neither have we entered into the stage where plans are monitored and reviewed and where evaluation may be used to assess the performance of a plan during implementation. Another self-imposed restriction is that of confining our work to urban and regional planning without reference to the closely related area of corporate planning with which local planning authorities are currently faced in the new framework of local government. Because of these limitations we have not digressed as much as we would have liked into allied topics. However, some reflections are made at the close of the book on these matters, hopefully as an indication of future work which might be done.

PART I

Principles Governing the Use of Evaluation in the Planning Process

CHAPTER 1

Evaluation and Planning

1.1. PLANNING AND WELFARE

The implementation of urban and regional planning proposals without question affects the well-being of members of our society. The consequences are frequently of major significance for the welfare of individuals. Moreover, because they affect the lives of large numbers, the cumulative consequences are important. Public planning agencies are established to protect and further the interests of society at large; that is, their concern is with all those who comprise society rather than with the interests of particular groups to the exclusion of the interests of others. Accordingly, the merits of planning proposals should be judged by their potential effect on all members of society. We argue that planning proposals should be subject to some kind of formal "welfare test".[1] In principle, no affected persons should be ignored in such an assessment.

Urban and regional planning has, in the past, been predominantly concerned with the social consequences of the development and use of real property. More recently, planners have become increasingly aware of the non-spatial aspects of public management of urban areas, such as housing and education policy. It is now realized that policies of authorities are often strongly interdependent and that advantage, in terms of community well-being, may thus result from closer co-ordination. Hence the growing awareness and acceptance of planning–programming–budgeting as a system of government management and accounting. Analyses of the outputs of government services are now beginning to command formal attention rather than just the financing and organization of the inputs to those services. This wider interest may be interpreted as a formal recognition by planners and others that improvements in the well-being of the community, and of the individuals of which it is comprised, should be the general objective of the authorities and consequently of their professional advisers.

If this interpretation of the widening interests of planners is broadly correct, it

[1] For an early statement see N. Lichfield, Cost–benefit analysis in city planning, *J. Am. Inst. Planners* **26** (1960) 273–9.

3

follows that planners should also be much concerned with identifying the welfare consequences of all types of decisions with which they are involved. All such decisions will make some individuals better off, and, usually, some others worse off in some subjective way. This is as true for the traditional land-use activities of planners as it is for the wider activities which concern government as a whole. It follows that planning decisions by authorities, to control the activities of others or to promote their own schemes, should be seen to lead to an enhancement of the welfare of members of the community.

1.2.   MEANING AND ROLE OF EVALUATION

The term "evaluation" is often used loosely in planning to refer to descriptions of planning proposals and statements of their merits. We use the term more formally to denote the process of analysing a number of plans or projects with a view to searching out their comparative advantages and disadvantages and the act of setting down the findings of such analyses in a logical framework. The essence of evaluation is the assessment of the comparative merits of different courses of action.

Evaluation involves more than a description of the possibilities under consideration. A plan or proposal may be described without reference to other plans or proposals. But a plan may be evaluated only by considering its advantages and disadvantages in relation to the characteristics of one or more other possible courses of action. (Other possibilities could include the "do nothing" case, which arises in the absence of a decision by a planning agency to take some positive course of action.)

Planning studies tend to be concerned with problems of choice between mutually exclusive plans or projects, e.g. the examination of alternative ways of locating future increases in population, employment, and ancilliary land-use activities around a region or sub-region, or alternative investment proposals to alleviate specific problems such as severe traffic congestion. Nonetheless, evaluation may be applied to the problem of choice between sets of independent plans or projects as well as mutually exclusive ones.

The activity of evaluation is distinct from the various types of analytical *tests* that are applied to each alternative separately. Tests are undertaken on particular aspects of a plan prior to evaluation, either during the course of design or as finally prepared. Their purpose is to ensure that plans put forward for evaluation are in a form which renders them capable of implementation as envisaged. Examples are the testing of plans for internal consistency (such as the consistency between predicted volumes of traffic generated by the disposition of land uses, and the capacity of the transport network to accommodate such traffic), and conformity to planning standards and principles (e.g. day-lighting and car-parking standards for buildings, and widths for certain classes of road).

Evaluation should not be confused with valuation. The former term embraces the whole process of comparing plans: the framework devised for the analysis, the principles of assessment, the measures employed in the comparison, and the marshalling of evidence. Valuation refers to one stage in the process, namely the estimation of the relative importance of items of difference in advantage or disadvantage between plans.

If, as we propose, a community welfare approach to appraisal is adopted, a comparative advantage may arise only if some individual, or some groups of individuals, would be in some way better off with one course of action rather than another. Conversely, a comparative disadvantage arises when some individual, or group of individuals, is in some way worse off as a consequence of the decision. Evaluation should be concerned with the assessment of particular consequences of planning proposals for the individuals or groups of individuals who comprise a community. In addition, this assessment should relate to some concept of their comparative well-being as between the alternative situations. *Comprehensiveness* in evaluation therefore implies that the evaluation considers and records as far as is practicable some measure of the variation in the well-being of all individuals and groups who are affected by the planning decision. A *partial* evaluation will have considered a subsection only of the community, or a subsection only of the full range of plan consequences. The relevant population for a comprehensive evaluation will normally be defined widely in two directions. First, they will encompass all groups affected by the proposals at any given point of time in the future. Second, they will encompass the effects on these groups through time. The "relevant" population could therefore embrace, as yet, unborn generations.

We employ the terms "individuals" and "groups" advisedly. The most simple unit of analysis is the individual, who may be made comparatively better or worse off by planning proposals (e.g. through variations in the level of noise from traffic, or variations in the range of job opportunities available within commuting distances). Some writers also suggest that it is relevant also to regard society as an entity or body politic which possesses objectives in a corporate capacity.[2] It is contended that such objectives are distinct from those of the individuals who make up society, and that the interests of the entity may transcend the interests of its individual members. These writers would argue that "society as an entity" may be regarded as being better or worse off in different situations. For example, we may postulate that "social mix" in residential developments rather than social homogeneity is an advantage for society, as social hostility and class conflicts might be less. There could presumably be conflict between the interests of all residents and the well-being of society as an entity, measured by the attainment of corporate objectives. It is likely to prove far more difficult, if not impossible, to obtain evidence about the nature of objectives of this entity than about the preferences of individuals.[3]

---

[2]See, for instance, the collection of essays in C. J. Friedrich (ed.), *The Public Interest*, Atherton Press, New York, 1962; and G. Schubert, *The Public Interest: A Critique of the Theory of a Political Concept*, Free Press of Glencoe, Illinois, 1960, ch. 3.

[3]Collective objectives and preferences should not be confused with the need for collective decision-taking which may be justified on the grounds of the existence of externalities (such as with control over air pollution), or public goods (such as the provision of defence), or paternalism (such as with control over the use of drugs).

Whilst recognizing such a view of society, we do not believe it to be very helpful for the evaluation of any conceivable type of urban and regional planning proposal. In this context of planning it strikes us as meaningless to talk about the welfare of society as being in some way different from the collection of the welfares of its individual members. In any event it is important to give serious attention to the implications of plans for individuals, or for groups where certain individuals are affected in broadly similar ways.

Evaluation provides information about the effects of proposals on all members of a community. There are two different users of this information: the formal decision-takers, and any members of the general public who may participate at any stage during the overall process of arriving at a decision. In this context, the latter group may be referred to as decision-makers.[4] Decision-takers require information about the social welfare consequences of proposals to help them form a soundly based choice. In debating policy they will be interested in the wider welfare effects of the options, although obviously they will also be concerned with other matters. Evaluation also generates evidence for policy-makers to use in defending their decisions as well as in the process of arriving at them. There is now considerable pressure on elected representatives to justify their decisions on planning matters publicly and to do so in terms of the differential effects of the options for the well-being of members of the community. As a result they are obliged to be formally aware of the wide-ranging interest in their decisions.

The findings of an evaluation, which precedes the selection of a preferred course of action in most types of planning decisions, should be made available to the general public, the body to whom elected representatives are normally accountable. This conforms with the widely held principle in democracies that members of the community have a right to be as fully informed about the welfare implications of the proposals and decisions of public agencies as is practicable. Urban and regional planning decisions are part of the overall responsibilities of elected representatives and should therefore conform with democratic processes. We see the importance of public availability of the information contained in evaluation exercises to be especially relevant in planning studies. If members of the public are potentially affected by a proposal, either beneficially or adversely, they should be aware of the reasons. They may then attempt to "participate" in the process of decision-making by trying to exercise some influence through debate. This will be facilitated if a comprehensive evaluation analysis is available to them. In addition, some members of the public who may not be "directly" affected by particular decisions (i.e. who do not consume any outputs of a plan) may nevertheless wish to judge the general performance of decision-takers at the time of elections. Successful operation of democratic processes requires a well-informed public. The higher the level of the discussion on planning options, and the more informed the public are about the

---

[4]This distinction between the process of decision-making and the act of decision-taking follows' that given in J. K. Friend and W. N. Jessop, *Local Government and Strategic Choice*, Tavistock, London, 1969, part I.

implications of decisions, the more likely it is that socially acceptable policies will be adopted.

Thus the primary justification for undertaking evaluation analyses is that they assist the process of decision-making. They are necessary because most urban and regional planning problems are complex, requiring solutions which have wide-reaching repercussions. A formal analysis is called for within which the various issues may be debated. Such an analysis should reduce the amount of subjective judgement which decision-takers and others have to make about the likely consequences of alternatives. A formal comparison of the alternatives should make the differences between them and the nature of the uncertainties more explicit and provide information for subsequent debate.

So far we have implicitly assumed that decision-taking precedes the implementation of a proposal. But there are other decisions; for example, a decision to *recycle* the process of plan-making, either to make some of the plans already considered more refined or detailed, or to generate superior alternatives (according to whatever criteria may be used to judge superiority). The decision-taking body, and indeed those to whom they are accountable, may be different in each type of decision. Decisions to recycle plan-making will normally be the responsibility of the planning team, with or without formal guidance from their steering committee or client. Decisions to select a particular plan will usually be the responsibility of elected representatives, although they will probably ask for a recommendation from their planning team. Evaluation in all cases is required to provide the necessary information.

We stress that formal evaluation is not decision-taking. It is only of assistance to it. Evaluation provides the factual basis of the issues for decision to the various participants in the planning process. Moreover, the findings of evaluation exercises do not lead inexorably and indisputably to particular decisions. The quality of the evidence, its reliability, and often its interpretation, will be matters for debate. In addition, the evaluation may be of only a partial nature. But even in cases of comprehensive evaluation, where all the consequences for all members of the public are taken into account, the decision-takers may wish to give special importance to some of the groups whose interests are affected by the decision. Their position affords them the privilege of acting in this way if they so choose.

Evaluation has been characterized as a learning process,[5] whereby in the endeavour to secure evidence of the advantages and disadvantages of particular plan designs, new insights are obtained which lead to the generation of superior alternatives. The evaluation of some alternatives will lead to the searching out of better ones, and the planning process becomes cyclic in form. As such, evaluation becomes an activity which occurs at a number of different points between the decision to proceed to plan and the conclusion of the planning study. Evaluation

[5]For example, D. E. Boyce, N. D. Day, and C. McDonald, *Metropolitan Plan Making*, Monograph Series, No. 4, Regional Science Research Institute, University of Pennsylvania, Philadelphia, 1970. Also D. B. Massey and M. Cordey-Hayes, The use of models in structure planning, *Town Planning Rev.* **42** (1971) 28–44.

viewed as a learning process is not inconsistent with the broad aim we have stated for evaluation, which is to assist decision-making by generating information. Evaluation may embody a substantial learning process in the case of recycling within the planning process and provide guidance on further design work that may usefully be pursued.

In practice many of the activities of a planning team, such as these design and evaluation activities, may become indistinguishable. But for our analysis it is helpful to keep the stages separate. Plan design will necessarily involve the rejection of certain possible alternatives, and hence will be concerned with the comparison of alternatives—at least implicitly. Indeed, the process of acceptance or rejection of plans at the design stage may be made according to those principles, and the measures based on them, which will be employed to compare the plans (with a view to determining their comparative advantages and disadvantages) at the evaluation stage. These are ways in which it is possible for the stages of plan design and plan evaluation to merge in the planning process. In the extreme case some kind of optimizing model may be employed to generate the preferred plan (according to specified criteria) of all plan possibilities. But to avoid confusion about the nature of the planning process the various activities of generation, evaluation, and decision-taking are best kept conceptually separate.

Normally an evaluation will be concerned either with all members of the general public likely to be affected by the planning proposals (comprehensive evaluation) or with some subset of the general public determined by decision-takers or the members of the planning team (partial evaluation). Justifications for partial analyses may be hard to find because planning decisions should be, and should be seen to be, in the interests of the public at large. Hence decisions should be based on the results of evaluation exercises which have formally considered all the wider repercussions. Usually partial evaluations will complement comprehensive evaluations in the sense of identifying particular incidence effects, presumably because they are thought likely to provide illuminating evidence in relation to some constraints on the decision. It is not uncommon, for example, for evidence to be prepared of the effects of planning proposals on the structure of local authority finances. This was attempted in both the recent Coventry–Solihull–Warwickshire Sub-regional and the West Midland Regional studies, even though each of them also included a comprehensive evaluation.

Whose Preferences in an Evaluation?

Theoretical difficulties arise with the principles to be used to assess the performance of the alternatives. How may the performances of planning proposals be determined? The expected consequences of proposals could be measured in relation to the manner in which members of the public would consider themselves to be better or worse off; the relevant coverage of the public will depend on the extent of evaluation exercise to be undertaken. Social cost–benefit analyses of the type undertaken by the Research Team of the Commission on the Third London Airport[6] purport to evaluate comprehensively according to this approach by registering the comparative well-being of all members of the public affected under alternative schemes. This method requires the collection of *independent evidence* of the differential value placed on the alternative situations by members of the public.

The manner in which the members of the planning team or their technical advisers *believe* members of the public might value the consequences of proposals could form the basis for evaluation. This approach was adopted by the planning team of the Coventry–Solihull–Warwickshire Sub-regional Study.[7] In such cases evaluation would be based on the planners' professional judgements on which particular consequences of the plans to consider and how to measure their importance. This approach may, of course, be supplemented by direct evidence of the preferences of members of the community. It may be thought that planners *ought* to be the group who decide on these matters. Alternatively, professional judgements may be substituted for evidence on community values where time and budget constraints rule out the collection of such information. Here direct evidence would be preferred but, in its absence, planners' professional judgements are used as a second-best approach to evaluation. This was the case in a study of the expansion of Peterborough.[8]

It is sometimes suggested that decision-takers should be approached to give their views about the nature and valuation of an appropriate set of objectives for proposals, and that design and evaluation should proceed on the basis of these.[9] The identification of relevant consequences then follows from a consideration of the objectives that have been formulated. It may be sensible to obtain some advance impression of how decision-takers will choose between the alternatives, which could, for example, assist the design process. But this approach does raise a number of critical issues. If the evaluation is intended to draw out the implications of alternatives for the general public it would only be valid to approach decision-takers if there are grounds for supposing that they do have knowledge of, and act in, the interests of the public at large. *A priori*, this prospect of their acting in the wider "public interest"[10] seems unlikely. Elected representatives operate under many "pressures" from sectional interests in society, and respond to those pressures. Of course, there is always the possibility of loss of public voting support. But, since that

[6]CTLA, *Report*, HMSO, London, 1971.

[7]C–S–W Sub-regional Study Team, Supplementary Report, *Evaluation*, Coventry City Council, May 1971.

[8]N. Lichfield, Cost–benefit analysis in urban expansion—a case study: Peterborough, *Regional Studies* **3** (1969) 123–55.

[9]This would seem to be the approach suggested in Friend and Jessop, 1969, *op. cit.*, and also in D. E. Boyce, C. McDonald, and A. Farhi, *An Interim Report on Procedures for Continuing Metropolitan Planning*, University of Pennsylvania, Philadelphia, January 1971, ch. 2.

[10]It may not be possible adequately to define the public interest. But, following A. Downs, we take the view that—like beauty—we can discuss it in general terms without a formal definition. See A. Downs, The public interest: its meaning in a democracy, *Social Res.* **29** (1962) 1–36.

particular pressure to act in the wider public interest occurs infrequently and is concerned with many issues, possible loss of voting support is likely to be only a minimal constraint in most cases. Even then election is based on a voting rule, such as a simple majority. Elected representatives may not wish to canvass the votes of some minority interests.

Sectional interests standing to gain or lose from political decisions on a heavy *per capita* basis will often find it worthwhile to campaign, lobby, publicise, or take other action to support their point of view. The elected representative may be influenced by the possible adverse publicity that sectional interests can generate. He may be reluctant to debate in favour of the wider public interest if there is lack of visible support. This might happen if the potential welfare gains from a decision acting against sectional interests occurred widely but in small or even insignificant *per capita* amounts. Indeed, at the local authority level many groups standing to gain from planning decisions may not be identifiable or organized. Thus decision-takers are generally likely to favour the interests of *existing* populations or ratepayers, or existing property, commercial, or other group interests. "Outsiders", such as those not associated directly with an area but who may wish to build houses there for occupation or shops there for a livelihood, are unlikely to be generally favoured by decision-takers in the quite frequent conflict between existing interests and these outside interests.

Decision-takers may rely on the goodwill of other elected representatives and officials for their own proposals, and may be induced to offer reciprocal support to their colleagues, even on issues which they would not otherwise have freely supported. In other cases outside sponsorship, campaign funds and other financial support may be withdrawn if an elected representative opposes specific issues.[11] Another possible pressure might be the prospect of militant opposition which could prove distasteful or unpleasant.

Town planning in the United Kingdom is intended in part to resolve conflicts between different groups in society. Although the elected representative is influenced by a variety of interest groups he is able in his behaviour to exercise a considerable amount of discretion. For this reason any evaluation which is based on the assumption that its contents should only reflect the decision-takers' own preferences, is obviously limited. It has not been proved that decision-takers in acting in their own interests also act in the interests of the community at large. This is because of the imperfections that exist within the political process. It is also a requirement of evaluation exercises that they should provide evidence that the public can use to debate the issues. We might be able to determine decision-takers' implied valuation of welfare effects from their past decisions, but for debate we require independent evidence of how members of the community appear to value costs and benefits arising from planning proposals.

---

[11]These points are raised in R. N. McKean, Costs and benefits from different viewpoints, in H. G. Schaller (ed.), *Public Expenditure Decisions in the Urban Community*, Resources for the Future, Washington DC, 1963, pp. 147–62.

Comprehensive evaluation of planning proposals are also likely to provide the most helpful information for the general public in their scrutiny of decisions made by elected representatives. We should also record the possibility that decision-takers may require information on every repercussion of a proposal even though they themselves may favour particular interests. This wider evidence may add weight to their own, independently determined, views on preferred alternatives, and may better enable them to justify their decisions. Alternatively, it may be that they genuinely wish to consider the social "opportunity costs" of deciding in favour of their own preferences. Decision-takers who genuinely seek proposals which are in the wider interests of the community (e.g. those concerned with proposals generated at the level of Central Government, or bodies like the Roskill Commission or Greater London Development Plan Inquiry Panel) can be expected to require evidence of the effects of proposals on all members of the public (as far as that is practicable). Examples of evaluation methods claiming (more or less) to provide such evidence have included Lichfield's planning balance sheet, as used, for instance, to compare shopping centre road proposals for Edgware,[12] the Roskill Commission Research Team's social cost–benefit analysis,[13] and Hill's goals–achievement matrix.[14] We discuss these approaches in detail below.

Between alternative plans there will be conflicts in the achievement of preferences for any one group, and also conflicts of interest between groups. If the achievements of the preferences of certain groups are in conflict (where plan A is better for item x, but plan B is better for item y), we need to know the comparative "strengths" of the interests in order to increase the information available to assist in the resolution of conflicts through decision. Indeed, a ranking of alternative plans may only be made when the criteria used for trading-off conflicting objectives are made explicit (since dominance of one plan for all objectives is rare in practice). Sometimes it is not possible to agree on these criteria.[15] Nevertheless, it is usual in undertaking evaluation exercises to try to obtain some impression of the extent of these conflicts. Measuring the strength of preference for a proposal requires two main tasks. First, we must attempt a physical representation of the effects of the plan, for example time saved as a result of improved access to workplaces, or of the views opened up by removal of an eyesore. Second, we must obtain evidence of the relative values of these phenomena represented by the physical measures, since comparisons will require the use of common units of measurement.

As with the process of deciding whose preferences to incorporate in the evaluation, the principles of assessment according to common units of value will

[12]N. Lichfield and H. Chapman, Cost–benefit analysis and road proposals for a shopping centre—a case study: Edgware, *J. Transp. Econ. Policy* **2** (1968) 280–320.

[13]CTLA, *Papers and Proceedings*, vol. 7, part 2, HMSO, London, 1970.

[14]M. Hill, A method for evaluating alternative plans: the goals–achievement matrix applied to transportation plans, PhD dissertation, University of Pennsylvania, 1966, especially pp. 215–99.

[15]For example, there are no generally agreed criteria for trading-off gains in economic efficiency, which may favour the rich, against income and wealth redistributions in favour of the poor, which may be associated with less-efficient alternatives.

depend on whose views are relevant for the trade-offs which must be made. In social cost–benefit analysis it is usual to express achievement of preferences according to the principles of what quantity of other goods and services the affected members of the public would be prepared to give up to secure particular levels of achievement. This quantity can often be expressed in the common unit of money. Accordingly, the achievement of preferences may in principle be expressed in money units. In this way the comparative strengths of preferences may be assessed, assuming the validity of the willingness-to-pay criterion. If, however, the evaluation is undertaken according to the consensus view of the planning team they may then also form their own views as to how the comparative consequences of the plans should be traded-off. This was done by the planners engaged on the Coventry–Solihull–Warwickshire Study. They established the relative values of the achievement of conflicting items by subjective judgement.[16] Both cases involve a process of transforming measures of the physical repercussions of planning proposals into some common units of relative value. Aggregation across individuals and across items of advantage or disadvantage is possible only after such a transformation procedure.

1.3. SOME LIMITATIONS OF RECENT PRACTICE

Although considerable emphasis is now generally given to plan evaluation in major planning studies, a common feature of recent practice is that evaluation is treated as an independent activity, functionally separate from the other main plan-making activities. In addition, there has often been lacking a clear notion of the nature of evaluation and the purposes it is intended to serve. These characteristics of recent practice have severely restricted the quality of evaluation exercises and their effectiveness as an aid to decision-taking.

In this section we discuss some instances of the way evaluation should be integrated with other plan-making activities, and give some illustrations of defects of contemporary practice in this regard. The illustrations are drawn partly from our own practical experience, working as evaluation consultants, and partly from a scrutiny of the work of a wide range of planning study teams (including those of our case studies). Our discussion is cursory since it is intended as a context for fuller and more detailed investigations in Chapter 3.

Evaluation and Data Collection

It is important that the data required to assess the consequences of alternative courses of action are determined at the earliest possible stage in the planning process, preferably in advance of any formal design work. This will help ensure that relevant, usable data are produced in the course of information collection, with

---

[16]C–S–W Sub-regional Study Team, *op. cit.*, pp. 64–82.

sufficient time available for the task. To help prevent a situation where the appropriate evaluation data are sought too late in a study, there must be collaboration between those responsible for preparing alternative plans, and those responsible for their comparative assessment. Therefore those who are to undertake the evaluation exercises must participate throughout the early stages of the planning process.

In this respect the work of the Research Team of the Third London Airport Commission was particularly strong.[17] Their efforts were directed, at the very earliest stages of their deliberations, to amassing evidence of passenger costs, noise effects, construction costs, and so forth used in the eventual evaluations of alternatives. With this in mind, their first statement[18] set down the main approaches to be adopted in assessing alternatives. The Research Team were able to proceed fairly quickly with the substance of their work once these initial thoughts on evaluation had been developed.

Evaluation and Design

The ability of an evaluation exercise to demonstrate the comparative merits of possible courses of action is limited, ultimately, by the quality of the plans put forward for assessment. A "good" plan cannot be chosen from a "poor" set of alternatives. By a good plan, we do not mean one that is demonstrably superior to others in any intrinsic sense. The advantages and disadvantages of plans can only be judged in relation to specific criteria, and thus a good plan is one which performs comparatively well according to the evaluation criteria laid down. It is possible to make a thorough and accurate evaluation of a set of poor plans, as well as an inadequate evaluation of a set of good plans.

Subject to any recycling that may take place, the designers should try to ensure that they do not exclude the best possibilities, either through conscious rejection or unwittingly. Hence, evaluation relates back in the planning process to the problem of generating a range of suitable plans, from which the preferred possibility may be selected. The proposed method and criteria by which the plans are to be compared should therefore be used to guide the process of design and so directly influence the nature of the plans produced. Aside from a few notable exceptions,[19] however, little attention has been given in practice to trying to achieve consistency of approach between evaluation and design activities. An illustration is provided by the West Midland Regional Study. The initial 100 or so alternatives produced were based upon different geometric concepts, themselves quite unrelated to a consideration of the likely socio-economic effects of different design possibilities. No other alternatives were investigated until virtually the end of the planning process.

[17]CTLA, 1970, *op. cit.*, vol. 7, parts 1 and 2.
[18]CTLA, *Proposed Research Methodology*, HMSO, London, 1969.
[19]Such as the C–S–W Sub-regional Study discussed in Chapter 8.

The findings of an evaluation may be used as a design tool during a cyclic planning process. By indicating the apparently good and poor features of a set of alternatives, the evaluation may help designers to produce new and superior alternatives. This was done in the West Midland Study, where the findings of the evaluation of the four short-listed options were used to produce a further alternative for evaluation which, after a subsequent evaluation exercise, led to the formulation of the preferred strategy.[20]

Evaluation and Equity Considerations

Recent suggestions have been made about the manner in which considerations of fairness and justice may be incorporated into a formal comparison of projects of plans.[21] However, whilst it is generally agreed that such considerations should be and are relevant to choice, practitioners have not been able to agree on a suitable method of incorporation into the *planning process*. Accordingly, little attention has been given in practice to the role of equity in evaluation and its implications for work on other plan-making activities.

Three general tasks are involved in an evaluation of distributional effects: the choice of criteria for grouping individuals; the tracing of the incidence of gains and losses between groups; and the "weighting" of these gains and losses to reflect the relative importance attached to the various groups. Among other things, these tasks imply the need for early collection of data concerning the criteria for distinguishing between groups of individuals (it being accepted that evaluation exercises cannot distinguish particular *individuals*), the number of persons in each particular group, and the location of those groups relative to the project(s). In this way, attention can be given at the earliest stage to methods of tracing the incidence of advantages and disadvantages.

Very few planning studies have been explicitly concerned with issues of equity. But some planning teams have used objectives relating to equity in their evaluation work and brought such considerations to bear in their recommendations. For instance, the planners engaged on the Strategic Plan for the South East gave special attention to the effects of their proposals on the well-being of the poor living in the central area of Greater London. And the planners on the Coventry–Solihull–Warwickshire Sub-regional Study had as one of their objectives for the strategy "To locate new population and employment and new investment so as to give particular assistance to those areas where existing industries are declining and where job potential generally is low". But in neither of those studies was the treatment of equity systematic or thorough. Why, in the South East Study, should the poor of central London be given special importance and no consideration be given to the poor in other parts of the region? The Coventry–Solihull–Warwickshire

[20]West Midland Regional Study, *Technical Appendix 5, Evaluation 2*, July 1972.
[21]See, for instance, M. C. McGuire and H. A. Garn, The integration of equity and efficiency criteria in public project selection, *Econ. J.* **79** (1969) 882–93.

planners may have been justified in paying special attention to the relief of
unemployment, but they can be criticized for not giving equal consideration to other
aspects of relative deprivation, such as poor accessibility to urban facilities and low
earnings levels.

Evaluation and the Testing of Alternatives

As we have noted earlier, the testing of plans (for feasibility relating to constraints,
and for internal consistency) is distinct from their evaluation. The former activity
involves the individual analysis of each plan in order to determine whether it is
practicable (i.e. capable of implementation in the form envisaged), whereas evaluation is concerned with comparative analysis. Since it is a waste of time and resources
to evaluate impracticable alternatives, the testing of plans should be undertaken
prior to evaluation. It is necessary to ensure that impracticable plans are either
rejected or suitably modified before evaluation begins.

In practice, however, these activities are often not clearly differentiated. For
instance, the land use alternatives for the Brighton Urban Structure Plan were
subjected to both testing and a preliminary evaluation as part of the same exercise.[22]
Seventeen of the twenty-one alternatives assessed were considered impracticable,
yet all were examined on a comparative basis in relation to the objectives for the
Plan. Overlap between evaluation and testing also occurred in the West Midland
Regional Study.[23] In the testing of the eight coarse options for feasibility, an
important consideration was the transportation user consequences, assessed largely
according to the total user travel costs predicted by a conventional traffic model.
This measure showed particularly large user costs for some of the plans. However,
the Study Team had no criterion for assessing infeasibility of alternatives for this
item. That is, the magnitude of the user cost items which would be sufficient to rule
out an alternative was not determined. It is difficult to think how the relevant
constraint level for user cost could be determined (except through analysis of
transport demand). The weakness of this transportation test was that the measure
adopted (user cost) was really an evaluation measure, useful for the comparison of
plans but not for assessing their feasibility.

Evaluation and Decision-taking

Even if the evaluation criteria are identical to those used by the decision-takers,
the findings of an evaluation do not determine the particular choice of alternative.
There will always be room for debate and disagreement over a number of technical
and ethical matters, such as the reasonableness of the cut-offs imposed regarding the
future time period to be considered, ignoring certain repercussions of plans due to

[22]BUSPT, *Report on the Evaluation of Alternative Strategies*, Brighton County Borough Council,
December 1971.
[23]West Midland Regional Study, *Technical Appendix 4, Evaluation 1*, July 1972.

.T.P.P.—B

high costs of information gathering, and judgements as to the equity of the incidence of costs and benefits.

Accordingly, in order to assist the process of reaching a decision, an evaluation exercise should include a clear statement of the assumptions and hypotheses employed, and an appraisal of the scope and reliability of the analysis carried out. This kind of assessment is made less frequently than it should be (probably because planners are anxious to justify their recommendations and reluctant to do anything that might cast doubts on the technical competence and thus the credibility of their work).

The Report prepared by the Notts–Derby Sub-regional Planning Unit,[24] for example, contained no comment of any substance as to the strengths and weaknesses of their work. It will have been extremely difficult for the Council members to judge the soundness of the Unit's recommendations without going through formal evaluation exercises themselves. In addition, interest groups within the community found difficulty both in understanding what had been done during the planning process and in commenting in a critical fashion on the proposals put forward.

[24]Notts–Derby Sub-regional Planning Unit, *Report*, Nottinghamshire CC, 1969.

CHAPTER 2

The Planning Process

In this chapter we develop a model of a general urban and regional planning process. This provides a framework for an investigation in Part II of the practical use of evaluation methods in the planning process, which is made through an examination of some recent studies. The model is used to facilitate analysis of the work at different stages of urban and regional plan-making.

Our general planning process was derived as follows. Firstly, a brief examination was made of about one hundred descriptive and normative studies of planning procedures, selected from the academic literature of the past decade and largely originating in England and the United States.[1] They include reference to planning procedures for a variety of public sector activities, including the overall management of public expenditures as well as urban and regional planning procedures. When we examined the literature specifically directed to urban and regional planning, we concentrated attention on procedures intended to have a general application; we considered very few relating to particular kinds of problems only or to particular organizations and institutions. Thirty-three distinct models of planning procedures, both normative and descriptive, were identified and more fully compared. From these comparisons a classification was made of planning activities from which the structure of a general model of an urban and regional planning process was constructed.

Rather than detailing the literature inspection, we shall limit ourselves here to some salient observations on the urban and regional planning process prior to a presentation of our own general model. In recent years there has been a rapidly expanding volume of literature on the urban and regional planning process. This has generated an increasing interest in many of the procedural aspects of planning activity, together with some fundamental changes in its scope and purpose. The simplified model of "survey, analysis, and plan" is no longer satisfactory. Many of the changes in the philosophy and approach to planning have stemmed from the general reorientation of planning practice from architecture and engineering towards

[1]Reference to those works found most useful are annexed to this chapter.

economic, sociological, and political considerations. Issues of a socio-economic and political nature are becoming increasingly important in the analysis and debate of planning policies. Substantial contributions to urban and regional planning theory and practice now come from a variety of social sciences.

The authors of the works we consulted are indeed drawn from a broad range of disciplines. Many of them view similar planning activities in different ways, and the variety of different approaches to urban and regional planning that are advocated is therefore to be expected. However, these differences appear to be exaggerated in the literature through the differences in terminology used throughout the range of disciplines.

For our purposes, a planning process may be defined as a course of activity that is intended to heighten understanding of the nature of problems requiring examination, of the alternative possible solutions that exist, and of the relative merits of these alternatives. Writers on the urban and regional planning process have been predominantly concerned with the *kinds* of tasks and activities that should be undertaken in arriving at a choice between alternatives, but not with *how* those tasks and activities should be undertaken. They do not intend to offer guidance on, for instance, how to forecast likely changes in the resident population or job opportunities of a study area, nor what techniques of measurement to use in evaluation.

Virtually all planning processes advocated in the literature are rational in the sense that their authors attempt to justify them by reasoned argument. Writers agree that a planning process should not be an accidental or random set of activities. They also agree that it should be continuous, having no definitive beginning and no definitive end, and enable us to proceed towards new solutions as new problems arise. Not all advocate comprehensiveness in design and evaluation. Indeed, some are far removed from this ideal, like the satisficing approach developed by Simon[2] and the strategy of disjointed incrementalism of Braybrooke and Lindblom.[3] Many writers regard any but the simplest and most immediate plans as unworkable. At the other extreme are the comprehensive planners, such as Altshuler,[4] Friedmann,[5] and Webber,[6] who argue that it is necessary to engage in the most wide-ranging and thorough form of planning design and evaluation that is possible.

Some writers who might advocate a comprehensive model confine themselves to particular aspects, such as Levin[7] who deals exclusively with the design process, and Bolan[8] who examines in detail the characteristics of decision-taking in the planning process. Moreover, there are major differences in the relative importance ascribed to

---

[2] H. A. Simon, Theories of decision-making in economics and behavioural science, *Am. Econ. Rev.* **49** (1959) 253–83.

[3] D. Braybrooke and C. E. Lindblom, *A Strategy of Decision: Policy Evaluation as a Social Process*, Free Press of Glencoe, New York, 1963.

[4] A. Altshuler, The goals of comprehensive planning, *J. Am. Inst. Planners* **31** (1965) 186–95.

[5] J. Friedmann, Comprehensive planning as a process, *ibid.*, pp. 195–7.

[6] M. M. Webber, Comprehensive planning and social responsibility, *ibid.* **29** (1963) 232–41.

[7] P. H. Levin, The design process in planning, *Town Planning Rev.* **37** (1966–7) 5–20.

[8] R. S. Bolan, Community decision behaviour: the culture of planning, *J. Am. Inst. Planners* **35** (1969) 301–10.

particular stages in the planning process. For instance the views of Batty,[9] Boyce *et al.*,[10] and Branch and Robinson[11] can each be distinguished by the way in which they specify "problem recognition" in their models. To take another example, Branch and Robinson, and also Lichfield,[12] specify some form of "review" in their models. However "review" in either case means something slightly different. Branch and Robinson emphasize the preparation "for periodic and emergency re-analysis review and revision", whereas Lichfield emphasizes "review and feedback, up-dating and reformulation in the light of time and experience".

Furthermore, there is lack of agreement on the proper sequencing of activities. For instance, although it may seem reasonable that problem recognition should precede design, this may not be so when there is some initial difficulty in defining the problem. It may then be necessary to design hypothetical solutions before a full grasp of the problem is achieved (this being an instance of a learning process), leaving the full definition to be stated later. Another difference concerns the location within the overall process of the determination of the goals for the plan. Some authors suggest that goal determination should properly follow data collection; others argue that it ought to precede it or that it should be undertaken in a tentative fashion at several stages.

2.1. A MODEL OF A GENERAL PLANNING PROCESS

From our review of the literature we concluded that there was no one generalized planning model which we could readily adopt for our purpose. But the model which we have formulated is based on the review. It is intended to provide a check-list of all main activities or operations which should characterize a planning process from the time that some "problem" is identified and a study is initiated through to implementation and review of the adopted course of action. It is also intended to represent a rational planning process in the sense noted above: capable of a reasoned defence. The model is used here only as a heuristic device, but it could also be regarded as an addition to the normative models in the literature.

We present the model at two levels of detail. In the first is shown eleven main activities, each broken down into a number of constituents in the second.

The Model in Outline

1. PRELIMINARY RECOGNITION AND DEFINITION OF PROBLEMS
2. DECISION TO ACT AND DEFINITION OF THE PLANNING TASK
3. DATA COLLECTION, ANALYSIS, AND FORECASTING

[9] M. Batty, *Systematic Design Method in Spatial Planning*, Centre for Environmental Studies, London, June 1969.

[10] D. E. Boyce, N. Day, and C. McDonald, *Metropolitan Plan Making*, Monograph Series, No. 4, Regional Science Research Institute, University of Pennsylvania, Philadelphia, 1970.

[11] M. C. Branch and I. M. Robinson, Goals and objectives in civil comprehensive planning, *Town Planning Rev.* **38** (1967–8) 261–74.

[12] N. Lichfield, Economics in town planning, *Town Planning Rev.* **39** (1968–9) 5–20.

4. DETERMINATION OF CONSTRAINTS AND OBJECTIVES
5. FORMULATION OF OPERATIONAL CRITERIA FOR DESIGN
6. PLAN DESIGN
7. TESTING OF ALTERNATIVE PLANS
8. PLAN EVALUATION
9. DECISION-TAKING
10. PLAN IMPLEMENTATION
11. REVIEW OF PLANNED DEVELOPMENTS THROUGH TIME

The Model in More Detail

1. PRELIMINARY RECOGNITION AND DEFINITION OF PROBLEMS
   1.1. Surveillance and analysis of relevant problems.
   1.2. Comparison of existing and forecast conditions, in order to identify problems requiring examination.
   1.3. Assessment of problem significance.
2. DECISION TO ACT AND DEFINITION OF THE PLANNING TASK
   2.1. Decision to investigate the problems and alternative courses of action.
   2.2. Definition of the purpose of the planning task.
   2.3. Formulation of goals for the plan.
   2.4. Formulation of approach to the study and to the design and evaluation of alternative plans.
3. DATA COLLECTION, ANALYSIS, AND FORECASTING
   3.1. Collection and analysis of data relevant to the planning problems.
   3.2. Forecasting the scope for change in urban and regional developments.
   3.3. Determination of evaluation data requirements.
4. DETERMINATION OF CONSTRAINTS AND OBJECTIVES
   4.1. Determination of constraints.
   4.2. Determination of objectives for the plan.
5. FORMULATION OF OPERATIONAL CRITERIA FOR DESIGN
   5.1. Formulation of measures for the objectives.
   5.2. Collection of evidence on the relative importance of objective achievements.
6. PLAN DESIGN
   6.1. Selection of one or more design methods.
   6.2. Use of design criteria to prepare alternative plans.
7. TESTING OF ALTERNATIVE PLANS
   7.1. Testing for internal consistency.
   7.2. Assessment of feasibility with respect to constraints.
8. PLAN EVALUATION
   8.1. Measurement of levels of achievement of objectives.
   8.2. Appraisal of the evidence produced.
   8.3. Setting down of findings in a logical framework.
   8.4. Making of recommendations to decision-takers.

9. DECISION-TAKING
   9.1. Collaboration and debate among decision-takers.
   9.2. Collective choice of the preferred plan.
10. PLAN IMPLEMENTATION
   10.1. Establishment of machinery for implementation.
   10.2. Initiation of planned developments.
11. REVIEW OF PLANNED DEVELOPMENTS THROUGH TIME
   11.1. Observation of consequences of the adopted plan.
   11.2. Comparison with predicted outcomes, and appraisal of the significance of any unanticipated consequences.
   11.3. Identification of new problems arising.

In the model, activities have been set out as a linear process. Work at each stage is seen to lead at the subsequent stage, in progression towards eventual decision-taking. Whilst this is a convenient simplification for the purpose of exposition and analysis, we recognize that in practice it will often be desirable to recycle and process at various stages, perhaps several times, in the light of what has been learned. For example, as noted in the previous chapter, recycling of plan design may be undertaken either to define alternatives in greater detail or in an attempt to produce superior alternatives.

An example of recycling for successively greater detail is afforded by the planning process of the Commission on the Third London Airport.[13] Evaluations were undertaken at each of three phases: that of reducing an initial set of seventy-eight possible airport sites to twenty-nine alternatives; then reducing those twenty-nine sites to fifteen and then to the final short-list of four sites; then the comparative assessment of these four sites leading to the decision (or, in this case, a recommendation). The decision which concluded each cycle was assisted by an evaluation which provided information on the comparative advantages and disadvantages of the alternative sites. A strategy had to be adopted to select alternatives for inclusion in the next cycle. This strategy was not the obvious one of selecting at the end of each cycle the set of alternatives apparently preferred on the basis of the evaluations. Rather, the selection procedure allowed for the possibility that some alternatives might show greater advantages in the light of subsequent refinements. In a cyclic planning process it is the final evaluation which provides all the information that available time and finance allow for the selection of a preferred alternative. We return in Chapter 3 to the problem of selecting alternatives for recycling in the absence of this "complete" information.

An example of the second kind of recycling of plan-making stages, where superior plans are identified at successive cycles, is that of the Notts–Derby Sub-regional Study.[14] The findings of the evaluation exercises at the end of each cycle were used to select a number of areas within the sub-region that appeared

[13]CTLA, *Report*, HMSO, London, 1971.
[14]Notts–Derby Sub-regional Planning Unit, *Report*, Nottinghamshire CC, 1969. For a fuller description of the design and evaluation procedures of this Study see Chapter 8.

relatively advantageous for new developments. The alternatives generated within these areas hopefully contained more desirable attributes than their predecessors.

Our linear model is not inconsistent with a cyclic approach to plan-making. Recycling may take place at numerous stages within it. We also recognize that there will always be room for differences in opinion over the appropriate sequence of some of the stages. It is also likely that many planning activities will in practice be undertaken simultaneously. It is convenient, nevertheless, to compartmentalize different kinds of activities and place them in some approximate order of execution.

2.2. GOALS, PROBLEMS, AND OBJECTIVES IN THE PLANNING PROCESS

There is now a need to amplify on certain threads within the planning process, linking the main "stages" and activities which are relevant to evaluation. A formulation is first attempted in this chapter in relation to the concepts of problems, goals, and objectives;[15] then, in Chapter 3 the role of evaluation within the planning process is discussed in some detail. The significance of problems, goals, and objectives in planning comes out most strongly in the first five stages of our generalized planning process. A clarification of these concepts is required for a proper understanding of the place of evaluation.

In stage 1 of our planning process the prime purpose is to identify that which is of concern in the planning area under discussion, the issues, and also the nature of the problems which it is hoped to tackle by the planning activity. In this sense, "issues" are matters of concern which are exercising the minds of those involved with the particular area to be studied, whether they be the public at large, the authorities, the professionals, or the decision-takers. Not all these issues are capable of being tackled by urban and regional planning: some, for example, could be simply a product of the lack of the appropriate institutions or of the presence of political conflicts. Clearly it is important to identify what issues might successfully be tackled by planning activity; these may be termed the "planning problems". We advocate that a wide view be taken of the nature of problems. A problem, we argue, stems from unsatisfied wants of the community. A problem exists if there is a "gap" between the current or expected future attainments of an individual or group within the area under study and their aims and desires.[16]

More detailed formulation of problems is unlikely to be possible until stage 3, as described below, but the presumption is that there is sufficient general background information and experience of the study area to enable a preliminary statement of problems to be made.

In stage 2 of our planning process it is visualized that a decision is made to undertake a study leading to the need to define the planning task. This involves, *inter*

---

[15]This account draws on N. Lichfield, Goals in planning, *Proceedings of the Town and Country Planning Summer School*, The Town Planning Institute, 1968, pp. 21–27.

[16]This follows the definition given in N. Lichfield and Associates and Inbucon/AIC Management Consultants Ltd., *The Oldham Study: Environmental Planning and Management*, HMSO, London, 1973.

alia, the formulation of goals and constraints. The meaning of goals in this context is the general directions in which the activity of planning is aimed. The ultimate responsibility for their formulation lies with the decision-takers; they should derive from the values of the individuals and groups who make up society. Instances of goal statements are "To achieve maximum possible opportunities for employment", "To achieve the highest possible quality residential environments", or more general still, "To use resources in the most efficient manner". By constraints are meant the limitations in relation to the possible courses of action that the planning team or decision-takers might formulate (e.g. that a city should not encroach on an existing green belt, or that certain groups in society should not incur uncompensated losses exceeding a given amount).

Having embarked on the planning task in stage 3, studies should be made of relevant past, present, and future physical and socio-economic factors. During this time the definition of the constraints and problems will become firmer in the light of new information. As a result it should be possible to be more precise about the extent of "gaps" between conditions or levels of attainment as they presently exist or as they are likely to exist in the future and the wants of individuals and groups in society.

In principle, one should consider the current and future unfulfilled wants of all populations of the study area, including prospective inmovers. But this ideal is never fully attainable, for various reasons—the sheer volume of work involved, the difficulty of consulting with people not yet in the area, and so forth. Some reliance will therefore have to be placed on various short-cut aids to design. These include, among others, ones which are conventionally referred to as planning principles and planning standards. Examples of the former are the segregation of pedestrians and vehicles in new shopping centres and hierarchical road networks. A standard is a level of performance specified in quantitative terms, such as the number of acres of open space per thousand residents, that should be attained. Both are useful to the designer, indicating fairly effective and workable solutions to planning problems. It should be noted that standards are in effect statements of what it is generally sensible and realistic to try to achieve in practice. But when these principles and standards are formulated they should be done so with reserve and scrutiny as to their appropriateness to the local area.

The planning team may find that other instruments are useful in their design tasks as well. Measures of the extent to which problems are solved or objectives are achieved may be found which can be easily adapted to provide information to help them; the development potential technique would fall into this category. Collectively these various design tools become the operational criteria for design.

Having defined the planning problems in a comprehensive manner and subjected them to public discussion and scrutiny as necessary, their solution become the "planning objectives" for the particular study area. This is clearly a "problem-solving" approach to planning. The task is to find the best method of tackling those shortfalls between attainments and desires or wants, which are viewed to present a set of problems.

Now we should outline the relationship between goals and objectives in our schema. Goals are very general and abstract statements as to the aims of planning activity, and are intended to be applicable to virtually all planning studies. They relate to the main considerations of planning activity: residential environments, accessibility, employment opportunities, and so forth. Objectives relate to particular problems within the study area in question, and are thus specific to any one study. They are derived from empirical studies of problems, unlike the goals–achievement approaches advocated in the literature where they are derived from a consideration of the initial goals. Further, the achievement of the objectives is valued for themselves rather than for their contribution to achieving the goals.

While there is widespread acceptance of this approach to planning, there do exist differences of opinion about the nature of the problems which should be solved. Compared with our usage there are many who take a more restricted view, where planning problems are seen as existing or potential circumstances considered to be *strongly* undesirable or unacceptable. To illustrate this distinction we cite Needham, who is representative of the latter approach. In his view "problems are real inadequacies, such as bad housing, traffic congestion, poor environment or over-crowded countryside".[17] To solve a problem, he says, is to make an unacceptable situation acceptable. He does not believe that problem-solving should be more wide-ranging. The distinction here is the level at which the gap between attainments and wants is viewed as relevant; in our view any gap is relevant in principle no matter how small it is. The popularity of Needham's view is easy to understand. Its appeal stems from the fact that there are relatively large benefits to be secured from eliminating or reducing the severity of serious problems. But it ignores the possibility that there can be social pay-offs in tackling the "less severe" problems, and where the resulting *net benefits* may be greater.[18] It is thus important when setting objectives not to overlook the opportunities for improving conditions that are already satisfactory or acceptable; in practice severe problems tend to be obvious, whilst it requires enterprise to seek out opportunities for improvement.[19]

It is now possible in stage 4 to determine the constraints and objectives which are to be the basis for plan generation. These are then used at stage 5 to formulate operational criteria for design. Plan generation takes place at stage 6. During this design process some further conclusions will be reached as to alternative policies and projects to be investigated.

It is at the evaluation stage that the contents of the alternative plans in terms of the

---

[17]B. Needham, Concrete problems, not abstract goals: planning as problem solving, *J. R. Town Planning Inst.* **57** (1971) 319–19.

[18]There is no *a priori* reason for thinking that the costs of solution will be similar for both minor and severe problems. It is to be expected that in many cases the costs of solving the minor ones will be relatively small.

[19]As with any problem-solving approach, the solution of some initial problems may result in the creation of further problems unless the initial set of problems is comprehensive. Although it is necessary to be prepared for unintended consequences, they cannot always be easily anticipated. We should not count ourselves successful in overcoming existing problems if we merely end up with a new set.

extent to which they will meet the "planning objectives" are seen. The actual content of the plans will not necessarily completely eliminate any of the gaps between attainments and wants identified earlier at stage 3. Typically, there will remain a certain shortfall. The content of a plan may for convenience be termed a "planning programme", since it consists of a package of projects and policies for implementation over a certain period of time.

The standards used in design and the planning programmes may be adjusted if the plans as initially formulated do not pass the tests in stage 7, and so need to be modified or rejected. They may also be adjusted if there are major deficiencies between the programmes arrived at in design and the statement of objectives. In each case a recycling of plan generation activities will be required. The set of plans emerging from these plan generation stages still have to pass various tests of feasibility and internal consistency. But having done so, the plan programmes of this "best set" of plans may still, on scrutiny, be found to be quite different from the achievement of the initial objectives. However, the issue now becomes one of identifying as far as possible what are the comparative advantages and disadvantages of these options as eventually arrived at for submission for evaluation. For this exercise we need the plan programmes. The initial objectives, which were helpful as aids to design, are not appropriate for this evaluation exercise. Nor are any standards used in design; their only valid role is as plan generation tools. In evaluation we assess the options against the full range of objectives of all sectors of the community.

2.3. THE USE OF OBJECTIVES IN PLANNING AND EVALUATION

Quite clearly objectives constitute a central part in the process of plan generation and evaluation and have an operational significance which is of a more substantial nature than any of the other concepts discussed here. We therefore discuss them more fully in this section.

The broad aim of planning activity should be generally to improve community well-being (or welfare). Accordingly, planning should be concerned with achieving objectives which thereby lead to some improvement in the well-being of persons within the community. It is possible to employ objectives whose achievement contributes to the general well-being of the community, without reference to the groups who happen to gain or lose. These objectives can be stated in general policy terms: raising the level of aggregate consumption of goods and services; reducing cyclical fluctuations in national prosperity; increasing the range of choice in the provision of urban facilities. But there are two main drawbacks to using such objectives in planning. Firstly, the issue of who will gain or lose will often be of critical importance to the decision. Secondly, by their very general nature they are too difficult to use in the form in which they are stated. For operational purposes it is necessary to define them in greater detail by specifying their constituent elements. In the case of the consumption objective mentioned above we would wish to know which particular goods and services are relevant and to investigate the consequences of proposals for each.

In order to estimate the extent to which individuals or groups may be better or worse off as a result of the implementation of proposals, it is necessary to have some conception of their preferences. We must identify those items of consequence that will affect people's well-being and then determine their directions of preference for those items. That is, we must determine whether (other things being equal) they will prefer a greater amount of each item to less of it, or vice versa. The particular preferences of individuals or groups may be expressed as their objectives for evaluation purposes. For example, individuals may be considered to have objectives related to traffic noise (to minimize such noise, other things equal), and to job opportunities (to have the greatest range of job opportunities possible, other things equal). In each case, greater achievement of the objective leads to an improvement in well-being inasmuch as persons individually or collectively consider themselves better off. In the process of achieving an objective to some measurable extent, and at no loss elsewhere, a contribution is thereby made towards the well-being of an individual or group of individuals. Objective achievement is an input to the welfare level of members of society.

Although they are closely related, the concepts of objectives and preferences are different and therefore should not be used interchangeably. Objectives have behavioural overtones; they reflect the purpose, or intention, of action. Preferences are passive in nature and express likes or dislikes. People have attitudes or preferences concerning the consequences of plans that will affect their well-being, but, aside from holding these preferences, they do not necessarily set themselves objectives to be achieved by plans (e.g. to reduce their travelling time or to enjoy more pleasant physical environments); they would only do so if they are called upon to influence the attributes of plans in the making, and thereby their consequences. Thus the objectives to be formulated and adopted for planning and for evaluation should express community preferences; they should state an intention to fulfil particular items of preference.

Normally it is impracticable to undertake evaluation exercises for particular individuals *per se*. Accordingly, it is usual to aggregate individuals into reasonably homogeneous groups, who have common preferences. The nature of the groups will vary with the requirements of the particular evaluation. The groupings might be based, for example, on income levels, or on some functional classification of land users such as residents or travellers, or related, when appropriate, to some product of the plan such as people who are sensitive to traffic noise or who particularly value outdoor recreation facilities. We use the term "sectors" to refer to these convenient classifications of individuals and the term "sectoral objectives" to refer to their preferences regarding the consequences of planning proposals. The objectives express intentions to attain goods and services or to avoid reductions in the amount of goods and services which are currently enjoyed, and are either acquisitive or retentive in nature. They form criteria for choosing between situations which offer different benefits or costs to individuals or groups, other things being equal.

Evaluation exercises should be directed towards the assessment of the comparative performance of plans in terms of the achieved levels of sectoral objectives. For example, in the case of the evaluation of alternative forms of rail link for London's Heathrow Airport to the centre of the city, one consideration was the preferences of passengers who would use the alternative facilities if they were provided.[20] It is possible to envisage passengers as a group, with preferences related to the comfort, reliability, speed, safety, fares, and other variable elements of the travel facilities. In order to try to determine which alternative facility was likely to make any passenger, and *ipso facto* all passengers, better off, the respective achievements of the alternative facilities in catering for the passengers' sectoral objectives had to be estimated.

The criteria for comparing plans cannot always be expressed simply. We need to identify objectives that come as close as possible in their meaning to people's well-being. For example, residents would prefer, other things being equal, the "best" housing environment. But such environments are composed of a number of physical or social elements, such as the number of trees in the street or the rate of crime in the district. The resident's preference may, in its turn, be subdivided giving a vast number of distinct items all relevant to the analysis of alternative plans giving different environments.

In certain cases it is useful to combine or amalgamate particular items of preference into a more manageable form. The concept of accessibility is a case in point; travel costs and trip-end benefits may be combined into one measure, an index, which takes account of both these elements. By amalgamating several objectives into composite "bundles" we do not, however, move any further away from our aim of measuring welfare gains and losses.

We have already encountered in this chapter another term, which frequently appears in the literature, that of "planning objectives". Since evaluation has meaning only in terms of improving the well-being of members of society, and hence in the achievement of what we term sectoral objectives, it is important that the distinctions between sectoral and planning objectives should be understood. We have said that the objectives which are used to guide the process of plan-making we refer to generally as planning objectives. Sectoral objectives may be viewed as particular types of planning objectives. As we have seen, they relate to particular preferences or categories of preferences of individuals (or groups) for different situations. They are derived, for example, from evidence obtained from attitude surveys or analysis of behaviour. People generally feel they are better off with less rather than more noise pollution or greater rather than fewer job opportunities. In consequence, we may observe people attempting to secure more of these (and other) items of preferences in, for example, their choice of residential locations. But planning objectives are not necessarily derived from observation or investigation of individuals' preferences; they are not necessarily sectoral in nature. Typically, planning objectives are derived from the analysis of planning situations and certain "prob-

[20]Ministry of Transport, *Report of a Study of Rail Links with Heathrow Airport*, HMSO, London, 1970.

lems" that have been identified. In setting themselves the task of overcoming these problems, planners are able to formulate objectives for their plan. The degree to which these objectives have been achieved are measured by the extent to which the stated problems have been overcome. Although the formulation of particular planning objectives clearly depends on the way planning problems have been formulated, the process of plan-making would take the following form. Some planning "problem" is identified. The planning team set themselves the task of overcoming the problem, the planning objective being the solution to that problem. The team then devise alternative solutions, and each solution is compared in the evaluation by reference to the resulting welfare gains and the costs of implementing the solutions.

In practice some planning objectives are formulated in terms of specific policies. These "policy objectives" may often be interpreted as means or instruments by which problems may be solved and by which sectoral objectives may thus be achieved. As an example, the South East Joint Planning Team, when considering the future development of their region, decided to include as an objective, "to encourage or promote decentralization from Inner London . . .".[21] This objective did not overtly refer to components of the welfare level of particular individuals or groups. But it is clear that the Planning Team did have in mind the welfare of society and groups within it when they formulated this particular objective. The justification for including it as an objective of the regional strategy proposals was: "so that redevelopment of obsolescent housing, modernization of community facilities and improvement of the environment generally in Inner London may be undertaken."

All of these *latter* considerations may be given interpretations in terms of sectoral objectives for residents and others remaining in the city centres. Such planning objectives may be viewed as the means or instruments by which a number of sectoral objectives may be achieved. Policy objectives are therefore further removed from our concern for improvements in welfare than are sectoral objectives. Other examples of policy objectives might be: "to control the growth of the city" or "to encourage industrial development in depressed areas".

Clearly such policy objectives are of use insofar as they facilitate the planning process, especially at the stage of plan design. The designer may be able to interpret and carry out his task more easily if he is asked to attempt to "promote decentralization from Inner London" rather than to "redevelop obsolete housing, modernize community facilities and improve the environment generally", although clearly these sectoral objectives may be achieved even in the absence of population decentralization.

The instances of policy objectives given above may be said to represent broad aims for the plan. They therefore permit a range of different design solutions. In the case of controlling the growth of a city, that aim may be achieved by offering financial incentives to industrialists to locate in other areas, by making other areas

[21]SEJPT, *Strategic Plan for the South East*, Studies, vol. 4, *Strategies and Evaluation*, HMSO, London, 1971, p. 169.

more attractive by investing in improvements, by land use zoning, or by a number of other methods. But it is also possible that some of these solutions to planning problems might themselves become policy objectives. An example would be the objective "to preserve, as far as possible, the Green Belt".

In cases where planning objectives are expressed as sectoral objectives, their comparative achievement in alternative plan designs will be assessed in relation to how people perceive the stated cost or benefit and how they would value the differentials in the degrees of achievement of those items. But where planning objectives are expressed as policies, assessment of their achievements between plans presents special difficulties. It is impossible to obtain direct substantial evidence of benefits resulting from an increase in the achievement of the objective and of how much they would value that increase.

Specific policies often have consequences for a large number of items of preference, affecting different groups of individuals in different ways. Decentralization of activity from a city, for example, will tend to confer various benefits on those who remain, including lower costs of access to, say, shopping and entertainment facilities and the surrounding countryside and lower costs of residential accommodation. However, these people will lose by reduction in the scale of provision of general urban facilities, and whether they will experience a net gain or loss is problematical. Those who move out of the city "involuntarily" will experience considerable reductions in accessibility benefits, though these may be offset by gains in amenity. Hence, to know how many people and jobs will decentralize if one plan is adopted instead of some other is not of much help in deciding on the desirability of a plan. It is not possible to say overall whether welfare is likely to be improved or reduced, and certainly not by how much. It is necessary to measure the achievement of the various sectoral objectives involved in order to obtain indications concerning these issues.

There are a number of implications for the working of the planning process stemming from the use of planning objectives when these are not expressed as sectoral objectives. Firstly, unthinking adherence to the literal statement of a planning objective could lead to absurd results if plans are designed which in no way serve the interests of the community in terms of furthering their well-being. This could arise if the original rationale of the planning objective, in terms of the sectoral objectives which it represents is forgotten. The growth of the city should not be limited, and the Green Belt preserved, at any cost of foregone opportunities to improve people's well-being. When a planning objective such as these is adopted its likely adverse effects on the achievement of other sectoral objectives must also be taken into account, as well as the positive effects.

Secondly, planning objectives should be justified before they are adopted by the planning team as aids to design. There is little comfort in adopting a broad objective such as "controlling the growth of the city" in order to achieve the sectoral objectives of preserving of open countryside amenities, reducing congestion and so on, if, in controlling city size, one or other of these objectives will not actually be achieved.

Thirdly, whatever use is made of planning objectives during the plan-making process, at the evaluation stage differences between alternative plans are likely to be of meaning only if expressed in terms of the achievement of sectoral objectives, since these are closest to our main concern of identifying and measuring increases and decreases in people's levels of welfare. Ideally, the statement of the evaluation results should make clear which individuals (or groups of individuals) have been considered, what objectives of those affected have been taken into account, and by what principles the performance of the alternatives for the level of attainment of those objectives has been assessed.

To summarize, "policy" objectives may have a role to play in plan design, but they are not helpful for plan evaluation in terms of welfare. Plan evaluation must be undertaken according to an analysis of the fulfilment of people's preferences, translated into sectoral objectives for convenience. In our view sectoral objectives should also be used in plan design procedures wherever practicable, which is one of the topics we pursue in the next chapter.

SELECT BIBLIOGRAPHY

ALEXANDER, C., *Notes on the Synthesis of Form*, Harvard UP, Cambridge, Massachusetts, 1964.

ALTSHULER, A., *The City Planning Process*, Cornell UP, Ithaca, New York, 1965.

ALTSHULER, A., The goals of comprehensive planning, *J. Am. Inst. Planners* 31 (1965) 186–95.

BATTY, M., *Systematic Design Method in Spatial Planning*, Centre for Environmental Studies, London, June 1969.

BOLAN, R. S., Emerging views of planning, *J. Am. Inst. Planners* 33 (1967) 233–45.

BOLAN, R. S., Community decision behaviour: the culture of planning, *J. Am. Inst. Planners* 35 (1969) 301–10.

BOR, W., Milton Keynes—the first stage of the planning process, *J. Town Planning Inst.* 54 (1968) 203–8.

BOYCE, D., DAY, N. and McDONALD, C., *Metropolitan Plan Making*, Monograph Series, No. 4, Regional Science Research Institute, University of Pennsylvania, Philadelphia, 1970.

BRANCH, M. C., *Planning: Aspects and Applications*, John Wiley, New York, 1966.

BRANCH, M. C. and ROBINSON, I. M., Goals and objectives in civil comprehensive planning, *Town Planning Rev.* 38 (1967–8) 261–74.

BRAYBROOKE, D. and LINDBLOM, C. E., *A Strategy of Decision: Policy Evaluation as a Social Process*, Free Press of Glencoe, New York, 1963.

CATANESE, A. J. and STEISS, A. W., Systemic planning—the challenge of the new generation of planners, *J. Town Planning Inst.* 54 (1968) 172–6.

CHADWICK, G. F., *A Systems View of Planning: Towards a Theory of the Urban and Regional Planning Process*, Pergamon, Oxford, 1971.

DAKIN, J., An evaluation of the "choice" theory of planning, *J. Am. Inst. Planners* 29 (1963) 19–28.

DAVIDOFF, P. and REINER, T. A., A choice theory of planning, *J. Am. Inst. Planners* 28 (1962) 103–15.

DROR, Y., The planning process: a facet design, *Int. Rev. Adm. Sci.* 29 (1963) 46–58.

DROR, Y., *Public Policymaking Re-examined*, Chandler, Scranton, Pennsylvania, 1968.

DYCKMAN, J. W., Planning and decision theory, *J. Am. Inst. Planners* 27 (1961) 335–45.

EDISON, T., *Local Government: Management and Corporate Planning*, Leonard Hill, Aylesbury, 1973.

EMERY, J., *Organizational Planning and Control Systems*, Macmillan, London, 1969.

ESHERICK, J., Problems and the design of a design system, in Jones, J. C. and Thornley, D. G. (eds.), *Conference on Design Methods*, Pergamon, Oxford, 1963.

FRIEDMANN, J., Comprehensive planning as a process, *J. Am. Inst. Planners* 31 (1965) 195–7.

FRIEND, J. K. and JESSOP, W. N., *Local Government and Strategic Choice*, Tavistock, London, 1969.

HANSEN, W. B., Metropolitan planning and the new comprehensiveness, *J. Am. Inst. Planners* **34** (1968) 295–311.

HARRIS, B., New tools for planning, *J. Am. Inst. Planners* **31** (1965) 90–94.

HARRIS, B., The limits of science and humanism in planning, *J. Am. Inst. Planners* **33** (1967) 324–35.

HAYEK, F. A., *The Road to Serfdom*, Routledge, London, 1944.

HINRICHS, H. H. and TAYLOR, G. M., *Program Budgeting and Benefit–Cost Analysis*, Goodyear, Pacific Palisades, California, 1969.

HOVEY, H. A., *The Planning–Programming–Budgeting Approach to Government Decision-making*, Praeger, New York, 1968.

HUFSCHMIDT, M. M. *et al.*, *The Metropolitan Planning Process: An Exploratory Study*, Department of City and Regional Planning, University of North Carolina at Chapel Hill, 1970.

JONES, J. C., Design methods compared, *Design*, Nos. 212 and 213 (1966).

KOZLOWSKI, J. and HUGHES, J. T., *Threshold Analysis: A Quantitative Planning Method*, Architectural Press, London, 1972.

LEVIN, P. H., The design process in planning, *Town Planning Rev.* **37** (1966–7) 5–20.

LICHFIELD, N., Economics in town planning, *Town Planning Rev.* **39** (1968–9) 5–20.

LINDBLOM, C. E., The science of muddling through, *Public Adm. Rev.* **19** (1959) 79–88.

LOWRY, I. S., A short course in model design, *J. Am. Inst. Planners* **31** (1965) 158–66.

LUCKMAN, J. *et al.*, An approach to the management of design, *Operational Res. Quart.* **18** (1967) 345–58.

LYDEN, F. J. and MILLER, E.D. (eds.), *Planning Programming Budgeting: A Systems Approach to Management*, Markham, Chicago, 1968.

MCLOUGHLIN, J. B., *Urban and Regional Planning: A Systems Approach*, Faber & Faber, London, 1969.

MANHEIM, M. L., *Problem-solving Processes in Planning and Design*, Department of Civil Engineering, Massachusetts Institute of Technology, 1967.

MEYERSON, M. and BANFIELD, E. C., *Politics, Planning and the Public Interest*, Free Press of Glencoe, New York, 1955.

MORSE, P. M. (ed.), *Operations Research for Public Systems*, MIT Press, Cambridge, Massachusetts, 1967.

ONTARIO COMMUNITY PLANNING BRANCH, *Network Diagrams and the Official Plan*, Department of Municipal Affairs, Ontario, 1968.

SCHULTZE, C. L., *The Politics and Economics of Public Spending*, the Brookings Institution, Washington DC, 1968.

SIMON, H. A., Theories of decision-making in economics and behavioural science, *Am. Econ. Rev.* **49** (1959) 253–83.

STEWART, J. D., *Management in Local Government*, Charles Knight, London, 1971.

WATERSTON, A., *Development Planning, Lessons of Experience*, John Hopkins, Baltimore, 1965.

WEBBER, M. M., Comprehensive planning and social responsibility, *J. Am. Inst. Planners* **29** (1963) 232–41.

WILSON, A. G., Forecasting "planning", *Urban Studies* **6** (1969) 347–67.

CHAPTER 3

Evaluation in the Planning Process

WE NOW intend to trace the interrelationships between evaluation and other planning activities. More specifically, we shall be concerned with identifying the ways in which the adopted approach to evaluation should influence work connected with other activities of the plan-making process. Given the information requirements of evaluation, this involves identifying which other planning activities should be linked in a functional manner with evaluation and investigating the content of these linkages. Since the views that emerge will be used in appraising the case studies in Part II, we shall structure the discussion around the general planning process presented in the previous chapter.

In that planning process stages 1 and 2 are preliminaries to the main activities of the planning team, and stages 10 and 11, which follow the decision, will not involve the planning team unless they are also the agency for implementation and review. Thus it is stages 3–9 (which cover the activities of planning analysis, plan design and assessment, and lead to the stage of decision-taking) which concern us here.

Our aims in investigating the way evaluation should influence work at other stages are twofold. We wish as far as possible to improve the quality of decision-making by improving both the quality of plan designs and the information generated about their various welfare consequences. A greater understanding of evaluation principles and methods will benefit the process of decision-making. Also, improvements to plan-making are likely if the principles of plan assessment and the nature of the measures to be used in the evaluation are known in advance to those whose task is to design. They will thereby have information available which can be used directly to assist their work, and will be better able to produce designs which consciously reflect the advantages and disadvantages of plans likely to arise during evaluation.

Accordingly, consistency of effort will be achieved by identifying those stages where a knowledge of the principles to be used at evaluation and the measures to be employed should influence the nature of work which is to be undertaken. We require to know at which stages these principles and measures (when known) are to be used, and in what ways, and hence how best to ensure consistency and increased effectiveness of the evaluation as an aid to choice.

We wish also to improve the *efficiency* of the processes of plan-making and evaluation; that is, we wish to ensure that the time and other resources available for a study are used in the most productive, or least wasteful, way, and (other things being equal) to minimize the time and resources devoted to plan-making activities. There are a number of dimensions to the efficient use of study resources. They include the elimination of duplication of effort in collecting data which could be used for both planning and evaluation, and ensuring that data collected specifically for evaluation is relevant and usable. Improvements in efficiency may be effected by investigating the nature of the dependence of the evaluation stage on work undertaken at prior stages in the planning process.

3.1. LINKAGES BETWEEN EVALUATION AND OTHER PLANNING ACTIVITIES

We have already considered the relationship between evaluation and decision-taking and have seen that evaluation facilitates decision-taking by providing evidence of the welfare consequences of alternative courses of action. We now focus attention on the stages that precede decision-taking. We shall consider two planning processes. In one of them the design of plans is undertaken without prior information about the evaluation efforts to follow. In this case the designers have to prepare a set of plans according to criteria which do not necessarily reflect the way the resulting plans will be assessed. By way of contrast, we then consider the case of a fully integrated planning process where the principles used in design consciously reflect the principles to be used in assessment. Our view, which we shall attempt to justify, is that the closer we move towards the latter case, the better are the prospects of integrating and thereby improving both design and evaluation procedures, and decision-taking. Most planning processes, for reasons which we discuss below, will lie somewhere between these two extremes, many being too far removed from the close integration of design and evaluation criteria.

The first planning process which we consider is the one which results from the activities of two independent groups of professionals, one responsible for the generation of plans and the other for their evaluation. This situation is very common in practice and is exemplified by evaluation exercises undertaken independently by specialists and by partial evaluations which attempt to trace particular effects of proposals, such as effects on the structure of local authority rates. In such cases there would be no consistency between the two groups (except coincidentally) in, for example, the range of objectives which are adopted or the approaches to their measurement.

But it is possible to envisage inconsistent approaches to design and evaluation arising even within one planning team. For instance, the designers may not have considered all the likely consequences of their proposals: later, at the evaluation stage, they realize the importance of some of these omitted effects. The Panel of the Greater London Development Plan Inquiry, who were responsible for making recommendations to Central Government on the Greater London Council's planning proposals (thereby effectively assuming a decision-taking function), at several stages of the Inquiry requested additional evidence on various consequences of the GLC's proposals for members of the public. One such request produced a document which demonstrated by example the environmental consequences of urban motorways.[1] The request was made in order to establish how new motorways might affect the nature of the environment. It was clear that the designers of the motorway proposals did not explicitly take all these effects fully into account in their design or assessment of the plans generated. A related case would be the generation of plans undertaken according to a set of conventional problem-solving objectives which, on subsequent evaluation of the alternatives by reference to sectoral objectives, were seen to be only partial in their scope.

The main consequence of this approach is that alternatives are generated which do not necessarily appear advantaged in the evaluation by comparison with alternatives which *could* have been generated. Either the range of alternatives is inadequate (according to the assessment criteria) because the plans do not include relatively good possibilities, or the evaluation is inadequate because considerations taken into account in the design are not reflected in the assessments of the alternatives. Either way the planning process is deficient and wasteful of the resources of the planning team.

Normally it will be hard to justify planning processes in which the range of objectives and the adopted approach to their measurement are inconsistent in plan generation and evaluation. Nevertheless, there would still be an advantage in presenting the alternatives which are generated at the design stage in a *form* which facilitates the estimation of their welfare consequences. For example, in the evaluation it may be intended to undertake measures of accessibility between land uses, such as the accessibility of work-place locations for residents. The design forms should allow for easy estimation of such measures by specifying the locations and nature of the land uses with sufficient precision. Liaison between those undertaking the design work and those carrying out the evaluation (where they are different groups) is likely to be valuable if it helps to ascertain the general nature of the designs in advance and the range of likely differences between them. Those undertaking the evaluation will not wish to spend effort on the estimation of traffic congestion costs, for example, if none of the alternative proposals are likely to lead to significant traffic congestion, or if the differentials in congestion levels are likely to be slight.

Time will be saved by starting work on evaluation prior to data collection (stage 3 of our general planning process) in order to influence the kind of data collected. Here evaluation will need preliminary work to identify the nature of the preferences of the groups to be considered. This could sometimes involve original research through attitude surveys and other investigations into individual wants and values. Data on the physical and institutional conditions within the study area, such as qualities of agricultural land which might be lost, recreation areas which might be more

[1] GLC, GLDP Inquiry Background Paper No. 383, *Environmental Effects of the Construction of Primary Roads—Illustrative Examples*, October 1970.

intensively utilized, or areas with special tax concessions, will also need to be gathered. They may have a bearing on the extent to which the wants of various members of the public are satisfied and hence are relevant to the evaluation. Obviously this kind of preliminary input can be undertaken before the designs have been fully prepared.

These efficiency considerations (early data collection and the design of plans in a form suitable for evaluation) perhaps exhaust the potential for improvements to planning processes where planning objectives used for plan design are not derived from the objectives which are used in evaluation.

We turn now to the contrasting type of planning process. Here the evaluation consists of assessing alternative plans according to sectoral objectives which are also used in the design—directly or in summary form. An example will illustrate this case. In the Notts–Derby Sub-regional Study procedures were used for estimating the accessibility of residents to job opportunities.[2] The results of the modelling exercise were used to measure this objective. However, the model was also used at the design stage to identify those local areas where residents had high accessibility to job opportunities. It was employed in plan generation to identify areas of favourable potential for new development, in terms of the objective. In this way residential accessibility to job opportunities, and its measure of achievement, were used in generating alternative projects as well as in evaluating them.

Some of the methods of measurement used in the evaluation work of the Stevenage Public Transport,[3] Third London Airport, and Coventry–Solihull–Warwickshire studies in each case provided information to assist in the plan designs. In these studies the approach to evaluation, which was to be carried out at the penultimate stage of the planning process, had to some considerable extent to be determined in advance, and information on some approaches to measurement was gathered before design work was begun.

In addition, in each of these studies two general issues of fundamental significance at all stages in the planning process were settled early on. They were decisions to include or exclude particular sectoral objectives at the evaluation stage, and decisions about the methods of measuring the performance of plans in terms of the sectoral objectives. In practice the extent to which all objectives and all approaches to measurement can be determined in advance is normally constrained by time and financial resources available for gathering information at preliminary stages of plan-making. Nevertheless, if we are to integrate design with evaluation principles we must set down those principles at the earliest possible stage in the planning process, since information which is subsequently generated will inevitably lead to revisions or modifications to the initial approach to design.

Consider the example of the decision of whether or not to include maximizing the

[2]Notts–Derby Sub-regional Planning Unit, *The Potential Surface Technique*, Record Report 38, undated.

[3]N. Lichfield and Associates, *Stevenage Public Transport Cost Benefit Analysis*, vols. 1 and 2, Stevenage Development Corporation, Stevenage, May 1969. The two other studies referred to are discussed as case studies in Part II.

accessibility of residents to shopping facilities as a sectoral objective. It would be assumed that, other things being equal, residents would benefit by increases in levels of accessibility. Clearly the designs of a set of alternative land use plans will be partly determined by whether or not the objective of maximizing residents' accessibility to shopping facilities is included as a design consideration. But, if this objective is included, the designs will depend on how, out of the wide range of possibilities, this accessibility is to be measured. It might be by travel costs of residents to the nearest shopping centres in each of a number of "hierarchical" groups, or by means of a simple accessibility index, or by a more complicated intervening opportunities index, or in still other ways. Each must give different assessments and thereby different designs.

When the most appropriate measure is selected there still remains the problem of the units of assessment. As we have seen, these may have to be chosen to ensure comparability with units of assessment of other objectives in the generation and evaluation process. Transforming the index or measurement units into units comparable with measures to assess other objectives may also be undertaken in many different ways.[4]

These substantive decisions about the approach to evaluation are needed chronologically in the early stages of the planning process. We want to be sure that in the design of plans, alternatives are generated which consciously reflect, where possible, the treatment of the objectives in the comparative evaluation which will attempt to identify the "best" and "worst" features of plans; other things equal, we want to incorporate as many of the best features as possible.

These preliminary activities may be categorized as part of stages 4 and 5 of our general planning process, i.e.

Stage 4: Determination of constraints and objectives.
Stage 5: Formulation of operational criteria for design.

The first part of stage 4 involves the setting of constraints on the areas of search for alternative designs with a view to limiting the area, and hence the costs, of search for alternatives. A constraint will imply that either some groups are excluded from consideration at the design and evaluation stages or, of the groups which are included, boundaries are set on the relevance or importance of their objectives for design and evaluation, e.g. maximum distance from car parks to shopping centres. Absolute constraints on planning solutions hardly ever exist in reality since it will generally be possible to breach any apparent technological or institutional limitations—at a cost. In the frequently used example of excluding building on marshy ground liable to flooding, the constraint is justified only if there is a strong *a priori* expectation that in the overall assessment of alternative plans the disadvantage associated with alternatives located in this way will always be sufficient to eliminate them from the final choice; that is, that the costs of foundations and flood control will be prohibitive.

[4]M. Hill and Y. Tzamir, Multidimensional evaluation of regional plans serving multiple objectives, *Papers of the Regional Science Association* **29** (1972) 139–65.

We recognize that in practice it will generally be helpful to impose certain limits on the activities of the study team by specifying some constraints, either from within the team or without. But as soon as it is decided to proceed by the imposition of constraints in this way, comparative assessments will thereby have been made, if only implicitly. Therefore a constraint should always be regarded as "provisional", to be tested through the generation of some plans which deliberately breach them. If all alternatives are generated within the constraints, the "opportunity costs" of having to meet those constraints will never be revealed.

Stage 4 of our general planning process is also concerned with the choice of objectives. A great number may be considered, some of which may be consciously rejected. The processes of rejection of objectives and of arriving at a final set are clearly critical for both design and evaluation. Whereas the constraints are introduced as guidelines to facilitate the design process, the conscious rejection of possible objectives constitutes a decision by the planning team that some groups, or some groups' objectives, are to be deliberately excluded from consideration. The only justification for this is that these objectives are likely to be considerations which neither the decision-takers nor the general public will wish to take into account in appraising the alternatives.

For example, at the Inquiry into the siting of the Third London Airport the relevance of time-saving for foreigners travelling to and from airports in the United Kingdom was debated at length. If one airport site imposed greater travel burdens on foreigners than another then the decision-takers might legitimately wish to disregard the impact on the grounds that the appropriate population to consider for a UK project using UK funds would be UK citizens. They might not wish to consider foreigners unless there was a likelihood of retaliatory action, for instance by decisions which involve UK citizens travelling to less convenient airports in other countries. Similarly, local authorities, when contemplating developments, may legitimately doubt from their own standpoints the relevance of benefits to ratepayers and others located in adjacent authorities and which cannot be recouped (although they should recognize that Central Government might think otherwise when reviewing these decisions).

In both of these cases a decision which would result from excluding considerations of the costs and benefits of particular groups should nevertheless be based on an evaluation which was comprehensive in scope for all those objectives of groups which were used during the design process. Following this, the rationale for exclusion (or inclusion) of objectives in reaching decisions ought to be stated in terms of some conception of the community who are considered relevant, involving the delimitation of the geographic boundaries of that community.

Stage 5 of our general planning process is concerned with the transformation of the set of objectives for the plan (established at the previous stage) into some operational form, useful for design. If these have not previously been expressed in terms of some groups' objectives, they should if possible now be translated into sectoral objectives.

This stage will involve decisions by the planning team regarding the nature of the eventual assessments of objectives during the evaluation at stage 8 (specifically, decisions regarding the measurement of advantages and disadvantages of the plans). The previous example of shopping accessibility illustrates the relationships between design and evaluation which are desirable. It may not always be possible or practicable to adapt the evaluation measurement techniques to assist design by demonstrating how design solutions may lead to the greater benefits or lower costs for some. But, undoubtedly, the more that this kind of adaptation can be undertaken the better will be the range of generated alternatives.

Complete measurement implies that it is possible, in principle, to produce *optimal plans*, in the sense of the fullest achievement of the specified objectives. We may do this by systematically using manual design techniques to identify all possible plans (assuming sufficient time and budget, and ignoring problems of knowing when the totality of alternatives was exhausted), or by using mathematical programming techniques to help generate the optimal plan.

The latter would be the limiting case of the merging of design, evaluation, and decision-taking stages. However, in most situations three difficulties at least (apart from practical modelling difficulties) are likely to preclude the application of programming and optimizing techniques: first, expense; second, the uncertainties surrounding much of the evidence as to the measurement of achievement of objectives, although we may test the sensitivity of findings to changes in measurement assumptions; third, the comparatively rare occurrence in practice of the complete merging of the evaluation and decision-taking functions. Although the decision-takers are responsible for formulating optimality criteria, they may not be prepared to state them. Hence planners may not know them in advance of the selection of the preferred alternative. Moreover, differences of opinion may always exist over the reliability of the evaluation work.

It is generally considered helpful in the design process to develop various simulation models of real world phenomenon. Such models may directly aid design, as did the residential location model used in the Notts–Derby Sub-regional Study.[5] Alternatively, they may be used to help identify physical or behavioural consequences of designs which might not be immediately apparent. For example, in design exercises for the associated urban development (AUD) for the Third London Airport, a journey-to-work model predicted that only a percentage of AUD workers would actually work at the airport. Airport jobs would be filled partly by workers in existing settlements and some of the AUD workers would find jobs elsewhere, thus obscuring the resultant commuting patterns. A possible implication of this for design would be that urbanization associated with the airport need not be so large as to accommodate all airport workers and their dependants.[6]

Models used in this way should be based on behavioural assumptions consistent with those to be used for measurement in the evaluation. Further, they should be constructed, wherever possible, for use in evaluation measurement. An example

[5]Notts–Derby Sub-regional Planning Unit, *The Garin–Lowry Model*, Record Report 39, undated.
[6]E. L. Cripps and D. H. S. Foot, Urbanization effects of a third London airport, *Environment and Planning*, **2** (1970) 153–92.

may demonstrate these requirements. Increasing general accessibility for residents of the study area may be an objective of the planning work. If so, it may be possible to adapt a transport model which could in the design process predict traffic flows for a given alternative land use and infrastructure provisions, or assist in computing general accessibility benefits at evaluation. Accessibility benefits may more readily be derived if a "behavioural cost" travel deterrence function is used in the model rather than a deterrence function based only on travel time or distances. It could prove worthwhile to spend extra resources on computing the more detailed behavioural costs, bearing evaluation in mind, even though these may not be necessary for the use of the model in traffic-flow forecasting as an aid to plan design.[7]

Stages 4 and 5 in effect lead to a design brief. The sectoral objectives which the planning team consider relevant to the problem will have been stated and the approach to measurement to be used in their assessment worked out. The objectives can thus be used directly by the designers at stage 6 to find a range of alternatives likely to promote the interests of the various sectors of the community. This is a difficult task. We would accept the validity of many intuitive, or imaginative, approaches to design problems. Nevertheless, in urban and regional planning the greater the degree of quantification of advantages and disadvantages, the more it will be possible to employ mechanical aids to provide information to assist design. In a land-use planning exercise, designers will welcome any information of the potential variations in the magnitude of cost or benefit items across space which would result from proposed developments, and hence those locations where costs are likely to be comparatively low and benefits comparatively high. The greater the quantification of likely effects, the greater the information consistent with the approach to the evaluation which will aid the designers. The relative emphasis placed in practice on intuitive and formal methods of design will depend on a number of factors, including the complexity of the problem and the cost of gathering data. Sometimes, therefore, the formal approach may only supplement the intuitive.

Stage 7, Testing Alternative Plans, is concerned with checking various aspects of internal consistency and with ensuring feasibility in the sense that any constraints on design are met. This is necessary for the following reasons. If internal inconsistencies exist the plan will not be capable of realization as envisaged, and, if evaluation were then to proceed, items of advantage or disadvantage would be incorrectly estimated. All alternatives ought also to be feasible in the legal, administrative, financial, and technological sense. Checking these matters is best considered as a quite separate preparatory function from the evaluation.

We have now considered the consequences of work at the evaluation stage of the planning process for each of the other main stages of the planning process prior to that of evaluation. In discussing these interrelationships we have introduced the term

---

[7]H. Neuburger, User benefit in the evaluation of transport and land use plans, *J. Transp. Econ. Policy* **5** (1971) 52–75. The author points out the relevance of this particular issue in relation to the massive London Transportation Study which used travel times, and the consequential difficulty in interpreting the measures of benefits for evaluation purposes in that instance.

"evaluation-associated linkages" to identify where the principles and methods which are adopted for evaluation should determine the kind of planning input at other stages. Figure 3.1 attempts to summarize the discussion of this section.

We see these linkages, where evaluation is conditioned by the inputs at other stages, as essentially resulting from practical considerations. Our thesis is that it is desirable *in principle* to adopt throughout the planning process common objectives and common approaches to the measurement of advantages and disadvantages. These objectives and approaches should derive from the way plans or proposals are to be compared; they should derive from the requirements of the evaluation.

In this discussion we have ignored the possibility of difficulties arising at various stages which can cause modifications to the preferred approach at evaluation. The linkages between stages need not, as we have suggested here, all emanate from the requirements of the evaluation. An obvious example would be the case of data availability. Some kinds of evaluation work may not be feasible because of limitations of data and "second-best" approaches will then have to be adopted.

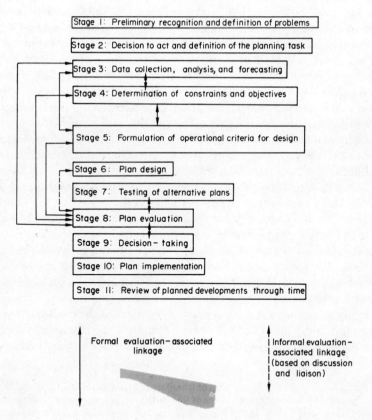

FIG. 3.1. Linkages between stages in the planning process.

3.2. GENERATION OF ALTERNATIVES

Only by investigating the merits of every possible alternative may we be confident of not having overlooked the preferred of all plans. However, we are never able to assess all the possibilities formally and comprehensively, nor to design all of them in the detail required for implementation within the limitations of time and other resources made available (given, as we have already noted, that optimization procedures are unlikely to be generally useful for this purpose in planning studies). Moreover, in addition to the practicability factor the efficiency of using the study's resources must still be considered. Attention should be focused more on likely "winners" than on alternatives generally. Accordingly, most studies must adopt methods which allow for short-cuts in the selection of a set of solutions which, hopefully, will approximate to the "best" set of alternatives. We now consider how that might be achieved.

It has been suggested that the decision-takers' criteria for choosing between alternative plans will not normally be fully known in advance of evaluation, and the basis for choice not made explicit. Moreover, in practice decision-takers generally reserve the right to interpret proffered evidence on advantages and disadvantages of alternatives in their own way. It may well be that principles and measures adopted by the planners for demonstrating differences between alternatives are not accepted by decision-takers as the basis for eventual choice. In these circumstances the planners responsible for generating solutions cannot always assume that the particular set of alternatives submitted for decision will contain one which is satisfactory, still less optimal, to the decision-takers. This dilemma is only likely to be resolved in practice by the submission of a number of alternatives, with significant differences in magnitude of comparative advantage and disadvantage and differences in incidence effects for the groups which will gain and lose. In principle, some alternatives ought to be prepared to the necessary degree of detail even though they do not appear to be at all favoured by the results of the evaluation. By contrast, when the team has a reasonable idea of the likely choice criteria of decision-takers, some alternatives can be produced with the conscious intention of serving their particular interests. But in addition they should produce others in order to make known what society is being asked to forego in opting for the alternatives which decision-takers prefer, particularly since the general public can rarely be excluded from the debate on planning decisions and are unlikely wholly to agree with the decision-takers' views. Whatever the circumstances the practical problem still remains, however, of deciding on *which* alternatives to include in those put forward to decision-takers for their serious consideration.

For most studies the efficient solution to the problem of eliminating alternatives will be by means of a cyclic planning process. This may involve eliminating alternatives from a large number by successive refinement of the designs, or by the generation of modified or new alternatives in the light of improved understanding of the problems at hand, or by some mixture of these two. Consider the first case of successive elimination down to a manageable short-list. At each phase refinements may occur in the detailing of the designs. This should lead to greater knowledge of their respective merits as the search for differences is widened in scope. But, in addition, the evaluation techniques which are employed may become more refined as, through time, an increasing amount of evidence is collected and thought given to the issues raised.

In this process the possibility exists that alternatives rejected at earlier stages might appear advantageous after greater detailing of designs and more extensive and sophisticated evaluations; early synthesis of alternatives may be made in comparatively large vacuums of information. Either continuous re-checking of rejected alternatives is needed, or some procedure must be adopted which tends to minimize the likelihood of overlooking the truly preferred alternative.

One approach that meets the requirement that alternatives of a wide-ranging nature should be generated for final consideration is to select one or more at each phase in a cyclic plan-making process from each of a number of different ranges of plans. Thus at each phase an alternative is selected which appears to be "best" (according to the evaluation findings) of the "worst" set of plans, along with the "best" alternative from the "next worst" set, and so on for all ranges of plans up to that set appearing to be "optimal". A reasonable selection of alternatives to be detailed is thus available for the next phase. (Greater emphasis may, of course, be given to selecting more of the apparently better alternatives.) In this way a wide range of alternatives may be generated which, whilst not necessarily including the overall preferred possibility at the ultimate phase, should nevertheless include an alternative fairly close to it. In passing it should be said that alternatives which are not best according to the evaluation criteria adopted by the analysts should only be retained according to stated principles. There is no justification for capricious or unthinking retention of proposals, and we do not wish to encourage that.

In the light of the foregoing remarks, the decision by the Roskill Commission to include the apparently disadvantaged alternative of Foulness in their short-list may have been sensible. The Commission may have had good grounds for eliminating Foulness, but they could not have determined the Government's criteria for choice, which were obviously different. Thus, even where planners have complete control over the content of the design and evaluation stages of the planning process, it may prove worthwhile to include *some* designs which appear to perform poorly according to the principles and methods used in the evaluation.

The planning team of a study may often be requested, in their terms of reference, to recommend an alternative to the decision-takers.[8] In these cases the principles and methods used to evaluate plans may then lead the team directly to a choice. Complete integration of the work undertaken at each of the stages in the planning process is then possible, and it becomes valid and sensible only to design plans for the evaluation to follow, and only to evaluate so as to select a preferred alternative. Nevertheless, it may still prove useful to design a wide range of alternatives and to

---

[8]It should be realized that a recommendation is not implied by an evaluation unless specific choice criteria have been employed.

include one or two "poor" alternatives in the detailed evaluation. In that way we may judge the extent of the desirability of the preferred alternatives, and also minimize the risk of overlooking good schemes.

Clearly the precise nature of the linkages that should exist between decision-taking and evaluation, and evaluation and plan design will vary from situation to situation. Mostly, it is likely to prove efficient in the use of time and other resources if there are some formal connections in the work undertaken between evaluation and the generation stages. For the additional aspects of consistency of effort, these links will be those based on common objectives and common methods for measuring the achievement of objectives in the plan.

Finally, we should mention the rather obvious factor that considerable time may elapse between the design stage and the implementation of one of the plans or proposals. Many planning proposals, of course, require considerable time for implementation. The nature of the problem, its physical and institutional context, and the most appropriate methods of securing increased benefits or reduced costs, may change during this time. Accordingly, alternatives should be specified only as frameworks for detailed decision-taking as events command. It follows that techniques for evaluating such plans should match the precision or "robustness" of the designs; in some cases differences indicated by the use of very sophisticated techniques will not be capable of useful interpretation.

3.3. AN EXAMPLE OF EVALUATION-ASSOCIATED LINKAGES: ACCESSIBILITY BENEFITS

In order to demonstrate the evaluation-associated linkages that ought to exist between stages in the planning process we can use an example of a frequently encountered sectoral objective in planning studies—that of accessibility, or, more specifically, residents' accessibility to jobs and job opportunities. Details of various measures of accessibility are discussed in Chapter 6. Here we focus on the main components and limit our discussions to the interrelationships of stages in the planning process, assuming a consistency of approach between plan generation and evaluation.

Our problem will be to submit to a client body of decision-takers a set of land-use plans which have been comprehensively evaluated. We are thus interested in all residents in the study area. The planning proposals offer differentials in the levels of accessibility to job opportunities, and the greater the accessibility the better off are residents (other things being equal). For evaluation we want to assess comparatively how well off residents in the aggregate will be in each of the plans.

The concept of accessibility between land users of the kind considered here has two components. Some travel costs must necessarily be incurred by one set of land users to secure benefits (in this case employment opportunities) elsewhere. Other things equal, the lower the travel costs the better for the residents. The second component of accessibility relates to the level of benefit obtained at the end of the journey. Other things equal, the greater the level of trip-end benefits the better for the resident. He will be better off with a plan which gives the greatest differential between trip-end benefits and the travel costs which are necessary to secure those benefits. The differences between trip-end benefits (total benefit) and travel costs (total costs) is referred to as the residents' net accessibility benefits.

No entirely satisfactory measure of net accessibility benefits has been found; we can fairly readily estimate travel costs, but comparable measures of trip-end benefits have tended to be elusive. Several indices of accessibility have been suggested, usually derived from spatial interactance models of travel behaviour. But in general the measures are difficult to interpret because the indices are amalgams of independent estimates of trip-end benefits, such as the size of the destination activity, and complex functions of travel costs. The units of the indices have no intrinsic meaning. Other attempts have recently been made to estimate net accessibility benefits directly (i.e. without reference to either travel costs or travel benefits).[9] They have been based on land rents and "careful" manipulation of travel-cost data (such as generalized travel costs) holding travel benefits constant.

For one such possibility, to use an example, accessibility is defined in terms of access (i.e. travel costs) to a specified number of job opportunities. We must endeavour to compute the necessary travel costs for all residents in each of two alternative plans under consideration to secure common levels of job opportunities, and hence benefits. With benefits constant, we can compare plans for travel costs, taking least cost as preferred. This requires a procedure for specifying that level of benefits which seems to be most appropriate to use, and then a procedure for estimating the costs. We achieve this by plotting, for any residents at location (i) in the two plans, a cumulative distribution of the numbers of jobs against travel costs. Figure 3.2 illustrates the procedure. We then define some "grand average" of travel

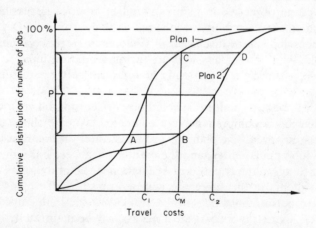

FIG. 3.2. Cumulative distribution of jobs against costs for a resident at (i).

[9]See, for instance, Neuburger, 1971 *op. cit.*; J. F. Smith, The design of a transportation study with particular regard to the evaluation of its output, *Regional Studies* **4** (1970) 193–204; West Midland Regional Study, *Technical Appendix 5, Evaluation 2*, July 1972, pp. 67–81 and 189–204.

cost for the journey to work, obtained from general experience in the study area, or from running a journey-to-work traffic model for the two plans if one is available. This "grand average" might be equivalent to a travel time of 40 or 50 minutes. There will be as many pairs of curves as residents in the study area, although many residents will have similar curves.[10]

The "better" plan is that represented by the upper curve, plan 1, except for low values of travel costs at the lower extremity of the distribution. At the grand average travel cost C_m the resident has (CB) more job opportunities in plan 1 than plan 2. But we may take the mean value of this difference and define a "grand average" of job opportunities, at the Pth percentile in Fig. 3.2. At P it is possible to read back to the distributions and find the corresponding differences between plans in terms of travel costs (C_2-C_1). Multiplying (C_2-C_1) by the expected number of trips each year gives us a measure of the resident's annual level of accessibility benefits of plan 1 over plan 2. The exercise may be repeated for all residents to yield estimates of total costs for both strategies at comparable levels of accessibility benefit, which would then be used in the evaluation as the main source of evidence for the comparison.

This approach requires data on population and employment distributions for each of a number of future years for each plan, and also a matrix of generalized travel costs between population and employment locations. The future travel-cost matrix could present some practical as well as conceptual difficulties in estimation. It will be partly dependent on investments into the communications infrastructure and partly on the degree of "congestion" (affecting time spent travelling and user costs) in the infrastructure. The former cannot logically be determined without some project appraisals, which are outside the terms of reference of many planning studies; and the latter (congestion) cannot be obtained without estimating in advance the extent of the infrastructure and without some modelling of travel behaviour. But these problems are too sophisticated for the measure which we wish to employ. In general it will be possible to make reasonable guesses at future travel cost matrices without traffic modelling and appraisals of individual communication projects. Future travel-cost matrices are unlikely to differ substantially from existing ones, and where major differences are expected they can be independently determined.

The data requirements are therefore comparatively straightforward. None are required for the existing land-use situation except possibly some evidence on existing commuting behaviour in the study area (to establish "grand average" travel costs). Analysis of existing situations is unnecessary, and the method does not depend on a transport model for the estimates.

Having decided to include jobs accessibility benefits in the evaluation, and having decided on the method of assessment, the consideration is how best to incorporate the approach to measurement into the process of designing alternative plans. The design process may be "intuitive", in that whilst the designers have in mind the achievement of various objectives and the measurement of achievement, such as

---

[10]A similar view of accessibility is presented in R. Thomas, A method for the evaluation of alternative forms of urban growth by means of a comparison of accessibility, paper given at the Urban Studies Conference, Oxford, September 1967.

accessibility benefits, when formulating proposals, their designs are not explicitly based on these measures. Alternatively the design process may be more "mechanized" (based on notions of what constitutes relatively high and low levels of accessibility benefits and the relative importance of those levels of "achievement"). In the latter case areas of high development potential may be pinpointed with computer aids using the measurements to be employed in the evaluation. But in either case the approach to measurement can be of assistance to the designers.

In the case of "intuitive" designs, some evidence may be generated as to the potential range of variation of accessibility benefits in the study area by an analysis of existing conditions. When compared with the potential range of variations of other objectives a rough order of relative importance in the achievement of objectives may be determined. Thus, in the generation of alternatives, greater stress can be given to the more important objectives.

With more mechanized aids to design, the problems of identifying accessibility benefits are that both population and employment are to some extent locationally mobile. Yet accessibility measures depend on the juxtaposition of both populations and employments. Accordingly, in order to define areas of high accessibility benefits and identify locations which, other things equal, would be advantageous for workers, one must first define areas of high accessibility for residents holding the locations of job opportunities constant and then (or alternatively) hold population locations constant and identify those locations of job opportunities which give residents high accessibility benefits. Clearly there are likely to be severe computational difficulties, especially as similar problems will arise with the measurements of other objectives. Indeed, the achievement of other objectives may in part be dependent on the level of achievement of accessibility benefits (e.g., the amount of traffic congestion may be highest when accessibility benefits are greatest).

This suggests that it is doubtful whether it is worthwhile establishing complex relationships between objective achievements in order to help the design process. Where studies have employed concepts of locational development potential, some attempts have been made to tackle computational difficulties. A limited but clearly useful approach was employed in the Coventry–Solihull–Warwickshire Sub-regional Study where the planners based their designs on defined areas of high potential for development according to the existing land-use pattern and then investigated likely changes to their development potential surfaces resulting from implementation of those designs.

The method that we have discussed enables a statistic of accessibility benefit (the travel cost necessary to secure P job opportunities) to be estimated for each residential location (i). By plotting cartographically the accessibility benefit estimates over the range of population zones, it is possible to observe those areas for residential or employment development which seem to give the greatest level of net accessibility benefit. Furthermore, the results will quantify superiority for this item over the other areas which might appear more favourable for the achievement of other objectives. Designers thus have information which is broadly consistent with that to be generated at the evaluation stage on the comparative advantages and disadvantages of alternative plans. But because of the likely complexities of interaction between objectives, this information will probably no more than indicate design solutions. This is one reason why there is a need to generate a number of independent design alternatives for submission to a comprehensive evaluation.

This example permits demonstration of another instance of evaluation-associated linkages. Stage 7 of our planning process is concerned with tests of feasibility of the design alternatives. Some alternatives could be infeasible if the rent (or its accessibility component) or related location costs exceed the level of general accessibility benefits. Residents will choose not to occupy those developments.

We have used this example to show the interrelationships between the evaluation effort and work in the preceding stages of the planning process. Whilst appreciating that generalization from this particular case should not be made, a summary of our findings may be of some relevance.

First, it is possible to find simple yet satisfactory measures of costs or benefits, or the achievements of sectoral objectives, *once some thought has been given to the nature of evaluation requirements*. Thus the preliminary stages of the planning process should be used to think through the principles to be used in the eventual evaluation of alternatives. The measures follow on from the principles. Too often planning studies have generated a range of indicators of plan performance for "accessibility" which are either misleading or impossible to interpret.[11] This probably happens because inadequate attention is given to the purpose of the evaluation early in the planning process and insufficient thought given to the usefulness of the measures which are to be employed in comparing plans.

Second, just as measures follow on from principles, so do data requirements for evaluation follow from the measures. They need be fairly limited and easy to collect, and in a form which makes computation a simple process. Certainly, measures of net accessibility benefit may be obtained from much less-sophisticated data than are often used in transport studies. The analysis of this data also need be much quicker and less expensive than through the traffic models that are employed in those studies. By giving early thought to data collection, more time can be devoted to other, more intractable, elements of the evaluation.

Third, it is unlikely, even with objectives such as accessibility, the achievement of which can readily be quantified, that design and evaluation can be fully and successfully integrated. However, it is normally possible to make information available to the designers to facilitate their work which is broadly consistent with eventual evaluation. In the example given this information would be based on the results of measures used to determine magnitudes of costs and benefits suitably adapted to indicate geographic areas having "development potential", at least in relation to the particular items under consideration.

In brief, given that *full* integration is not necessarily to be achieved, integrating evaluation criteria with plan generation criteria generally need not be a difficult process. But the necessary requirement is that consideration be given at the earliest possible stage to the nature and measurement of objectives for inclusion in the evaluation.

[11]Many of these indicators are catalogued, without critical comment, in D. E. Boyce, N. D. Day, and C. McDonald, *Metropolitan Plan Making*, Monograph Series, No. 4, Regional Science Research Institute, University of Pennsylvania, Philadelphia, 1970.

CHAPTER 4

Current Methods of Plan Evaluation

AT THE outset of this book we considered the essential characteristics of evaluation as a planning activity and its role within the decision-making process. This served as a basis for exploring in the previous chapter the linkages between evaluation and other planning activities. We now consider a variety of different methods which are available for evaluating planning proposals and, in the second section of this chapter, present a justification for using the social cost–benefit approach and the planning balance sheet method in particular.

4.1. A REVIEW OF CURRENT METHODS

This review comprises a largely descriptive survey of a number of methods for evaluating planning proposals which either are in current use or have been recently advocated. Its purpose is to outline the more prominent contemporary methods that are available to the practitioner. Similar reviews have appeared elsewhere,[1] and it is not our intention either to update what has appeared before or to provide a more thorough-going coverage. Rather, we offer a broad appreciation of current methods as a background to following discussions in which we, firstly, try to justify the use of a social cost–benefit approach to plan evaluation in preference to other approaches. Then in the next chapter we attempt a critical comparison of planning balance sheet analysis, which is a particular application of the social cost–benefit approach, with the goals–achievement matrix method, which are widely discussed at present in the United Kingdom.

---

[1]For instance: N. Lichfield, Evaluation methodology of urban and regional plans: a review, *Regional Studies* **4** (1970) 151–65; Department of the Environment, *Evaluation in structure plan making*, final report of the Forecasting and Evaluation Working Group, September 1971, unpublished; H. B. Fisher, Evaluation of alternative plans for new communities: towards application of the competition-for-benefits model, PhD dissertation, University of North Carolina, Chapel Hill, 1971, ch. II; and West Midland Regional Study, *Technical Appendix 4, Evaluation 1*, July 1972, ch. 3. D. Boyce *et al.* discuss the methods of evaluation used during many of the recent land-use transportation studies undertaken in the United States; see D. E. Boyce, N. D. Day, and C. McDonald, *Metropolitan Plan Making*, Monograph Series, No. 4, Regional Science Research Institute, University of Pennsylvania, Philadelphia, 1970.

Although we have not undertaken a fully comprehensive coverage of methods, our aim, in deciding which to consider, is to deal with those generally regarded as of major importance. We shall discuss the methods under a number of headings descriptive of different general approaches, each governed by a common set of principles or a common philosophy stemming from a particular kind of academic or professional discipline. The general approaches to be reviewed are headed as follows:[2]

Financial investment appraisal.
Check-list of criteria.
Goals–achievement analysis.
Assessment of resource costs.
Social cost–benefit analysis.
Planning balance sheet analysis.
Optimization techniques.

We shall discuss briefly the characteristics of each approach and give examples of practical applications.

Financial Investment Appraisal

Methods in this category have been developed separately from economics, accountancy, and real estate valuation. The common purpose is to estimate the future streams of capital and operating costs and revenues which will result from the implementation of investment projects.[3] It must be realized that no matter how comprehensive a financial appraisal is in relation to those groups in the community financially affected, the analysis is by its very nature restricted to items which are subject to market transaction. Furthermore, the value of those items is measured according to prevailing market prices, and these may not always be a reliable indication of their worth to society (for instance, the true cost of using labour that would otherwise be unemployed is zero, not that indicated by wage payments; also the price of many outputs are "distorted" by the presence of taxes and subsidies).

The main aim of such appraisals in the public sector is to determine the financial implications of alternative investments to the decision body. The analysis is usually confined to those financial costs and returns which are of direct interest to the particular agency sponsoring the project. An example is an analysis of the financial experience and expectations of six English new towns in the process of construction.[4] After introducing the cost elements for the towns as a whole, including all agencies, the analysis concentrated on the interests of the New Town Development Corporations, relating both to the financial costs incurred by them and to the

[2]This classification is a somewhat modified version of that employed in Lichfield, 1970, *op. cit.*

[3]A discussion of the role of financial appraisal in assisting choice between alternative planning schemes, and of some of the main practical and conceptual problems that arise, is presented in N. Stocks and G. Gleave, Financial analysis and town centre development, *Urban Studies* **8** (1971) 255–69.

[4]N. Lichfield and P. F. Wendt, Six English new towns: a financial analysis, *Town Planning Rev.* **40** (1969) 283–314.

prospective financial returns. Their experience was reviewed up to 1961 and forecasts made on a comparable basis up to expected completion dates. On the costs side all investments were included and on the revenue side all rents, after deducting real estate operating expenditures. The focus of this study lay in costs and returns at the dates mentioned, relating to partial and total completion and not in providing the basis for a set of decisions.

Investment appraisal *per se* involves the discounting of expected streams of costs and returns to the date of decision. An instance is provided by an appraisal of alternative town centre development schemes for the new town of Skelmersdale.[5] An estimate was made of the financial consequences (using discounted cash flow techniques) of three illustrative alternatives for the town centre, on the assumption that the New Town Corporation would be responsible for undertaking the developments.

With the growing number of large-scale urban development and renewal schemes there have been some recent attempts at more comprehensive assessments where those repercussions external to the decision body are taken into account. An example is an analysis of the financial implications of alternative urban renewal projects in Skelmersdale, which had regard to all sectors of the community affected as either producers or consumers.[6]

The examples so far have related to project *construction*. Appraisals of costs and revenues to public agencies responsible for *running* projects are most notably made by local authorities concerned with developments affecting their municipality. These are undertaken in the everyday exercises of municipal treasurers in short or long-term budgeting. But, in addition to aiding the preparation of budgets so that the appropriate amount of finance is available when required, these appraisals are also made to help test the feasibility of proposals. This was the intention of the planners engaged on the Notts–Derby Sub-regional Study, for instance. They had discussions with the county treasurers to try to determine whether the capital likely to be made available was sufficient for implementation of their development proposals.[7]

Check-list of Criteria

In its simplest form, this approach ranks alternative proposals on an ordinal basis in relation to a number of specified criteria (representing the desired attributes of the plan), with a subjective judgement on the alternative preferred according to the criteria employed. It has been developed by professional land-use planners, and until recently was the approach to evaluation most commonly used in practice.

Kitching has demonstrated the approach in relation to regional planning considerations affecting the four short-listed sites selected by the Roskill Commission for the

[5]Drivers Jonas, *Skelmersdale New Town: Investment Appraisal for Three Alternative Forms of Town Centre*, April 1968.

[6]Civic Trust for the North West, *Environmental Recovery, Skelmersdale*, Manchester, 1969, Appendix V.

[7]Notts–Derby Sub-regional Planning Unit, *The Investment Project*, Record Report 25, December 1969.

Third London Airport.[8] He first enumerated seven characteristics ideally sought in siting a major international airport in the South East Region: communications, airport noise, growth potential of population and industry, labour costs, amenity and agriculture, and services. He then examined the four sites in relation to each of these criteria in turn, using such data as were available, and formed a view as to the order of choice of sites in each case. The findings were set out in a summary table with the sites ranked 1–4 for each criterion (1 being the best, 4 the worst). The rank scores were then aggregated, leading directly to conclusions. This implied the dubious assumption that the differences between plans for all criteria were equally important.

An earlier case of some interest is provided by the Central Lancashire Study.[9] The task of the planning team was to propose areas for major urban growth and to define the spatial arrangement of land-use activities within those areas. They selected ten areas which they considered to be feasible. These were then assessed on nine criteria representing various goals that the plan should achieve. A two-stage evaluation procedure was adopted. First, those options which performed very poorly on one or more of the criteria were eliminated. The surviving three options were then developed in greater detail and reexamined against each criterion in turn. That analysis enabled the team to form a clear preference for one of the options, it being stated that the preferred option had the least number of *items* of disadvantage as well as the greatest overall benefit.

An improvement on this application of the check-list approach was developed by the consultants appointed by the Roskill Commission to find suitable locations for the associated urban development of each of the four short-listed alternative airport sites.[10] The process of comparison and selection was agreed with the Commission, and was basically the same for all four sites. Firstly, certain elements of the urban developments were costed (construction of site development, engineering, transportation, provision of major services and shopping centres, land acquisition, losses in agricultural output, user transportation costs) and a large number of additional criteria listed on which schemes were also to be assessed. These criteria were then applied to the alternative strategies in three stages. At the first stage all strategies were roughly ranked on a five-point scale in respect of each criterion without any quantification of cost elements. Pairs of strategies were then compared, and when one strategy was found to be dominated by another it was rejected, thus reducing the number of alternatives. At the second stage the costed items were introduced, the alternative with the lowest total cost being provisionally selected. Finally, the uncosted criteria were examined to try to establish whether there were any factors which might outweigh cost advantages. This led to the selection of the preferred strategy. Subjective judgement played a major part in the final comparisons.

[8]L. C. Kitching, Regional planning considerations, in Cambridgeshire *et al.*, *Evidence Submitted at Stage III to the Commission on the Third London Airport*, 1969 ch. 2.
[9]R. Matthew, Johnson-Marshall, and Partners, *Central Lancashire, Study for a City*, HMSO, London, 1967.
[10]Llewelyn-Davies, Weeks, Forestier-Walker and Bor, and Shankland, Cox, and Associates, *Airport City: Urbanisation Studies for the Third London Airport*, HMSO, London, 1970.

Goals–Achievement Analysis

Goals–achievement methods have in common a basic approach of attempting to determine the extent to which alternative plans will achieve a predetermined set of "goals" or "objectives". The terms "goals" and "objectives" are used somewhat differently by those advocating this approach, but they are both used to denote the aims which it is thought the plan should achieve. The progress towards and retrogression from the specified goals or objectives represent respectively the advantages and disadvantages associated with alternative plans.

The division between this category of methods and the previous one of check-list of criteria is far from sharp, however. The methods we included under check-list of criteria could be regarded as crude applications of goals–achievement analysis. The criteria form an explicit statement of general aims towards which the plan should be directed and in relation to which alternatives are to be compared. The distinction between the two categories is largely one of emphasis. With check-list applications there is a notable lack of attention given to quantifying the extent of fulfilment of the criteria and in particular to establishing their relative importance.

In the main, goals–achievement methods have originated in the United States in the field of transport engineering and land-use–transportation studies. Transport proposals form a very important element of nearly all studies on which such methods have been developed. In the main, those who have used the approach in this country have been land-use planners.

There appear to be four main characteristics of this approach. First, goals or objectives are always formulated (in a preliminary fashion at least) in advance of both the design of alternative plans and the analysis of their consequences. Although the goals or objectives are established at the outset of the planning process, there is no *inherent* reason why they should not be modified in the light of experience during a study.

Second, the objectives are said to be "multi-dimensional", that is, to include those of an "aesthetic", "environmental", and "political" nature, as well as those which the advocates of the approach characterize as "economic". An instance of objectives which advocates often consider to lie outside the scope of social cost–benefit analysis are those concerned with the quality of the physical environment, health, and safety. Goals–achievement advocates claim greater scope for their own method of analysis than social cost–benefit practitioners for theirs.

Third, all goals–achievement methods have been designed to compare mutually exclusive plans only; that is, the considered plans represent alternative ways of tackling a particular problem (e.g. producing a particular output, locating given amounts of population and employment within an area, relieving traffic congestion).

Finally, the objectives used for the evaluation are generally either assigned a "weight" to reflect their relative importance, or are ranked in order of presumed importance, *prior* to the comparative analysis of plan consequences. It must be borne in mind that it is meaningless to assign relative importance to objectives *a priori* without reference to either differences in levels of objective achievements (which cannot be specified in advance of design) or to the units in which those achievements are to be measured.

Whilst it is possible to make these observations about the general nature of goals–achievement methods, it is extremely difficult to discern the *principles* governing their application. The authors devote very little attention to the crucial issues of evaluation from whose viewpoint and according to what principles of assessment. Those responsible for developing the methods have almost entirely been concerned with general *procedures* for arriving at a choice of plan rather than with governing principles. This has meant that the approach can be readily utilized by different groups of planners, who are free to choose the principles by which the data in the cells of the matrix may be derived.

We now consider a variety of these goals–achievement methods. They may be divided into two groups according to their degree of sophistication: those involving a simple ranking of plans with respect to the various objectives, and those that use performance measures to assess the extent to which plans are likely to achieve the objectives. Methods in the former group vary in their treatment of the relative importance of objective achievements. Kreditor's policy evaluation matrix,[11] for instance, is confined to a statement of objectives, with no indication of their relative importance. In his schema the effectiveness of the alternatives in achieving stated policy objectives is expressed in the following terms: a significant positive effect; a partial or marginal effect; a significant negative effect; or no apparent relationship. The preferred option is chosen on the basis of this classification, but Kreditor does not suggest the rule to be used in making the choice. With the methods developed by Schlager[12] and Holmes,[13] however, the objectives themselves are ranked in order of the considered importance of their achievement, with the objectives being ranked in advance of analysing the repercussions of proposals.

Three methods employing quantitative assessments of objective achievement should be mentioned. Those engaged on the Eastern Massachusetts Regional Planning Project used a procedure that applied numerical weights to reflect the differential importance of the objectives.[14] Four of the twelve objectives were treated as twice as important as all others, and various performance measures used to indicate the extent of objective achievements. The plans were then ranked on an ordinal basis according to their particular performance scores. The preferred plan was selected by a simple summation of rank scores multiplied by the objective weights, which gave an overall weighted score to each alternative. As a result of this

[11]A. Kreditor, The provisional plan, in *Industrial Development and the Development Plan*, An Foras Forbartha, Dublin, 1967, ch. 8.

[12]K. Schlager, The rank-based expected value method of plan evaluation, *Highway Res. Record*, No. 238 (1968) 153–6.

[13]J. C. Holmes, An ordinal method of evaluation, *Urban Studies* 4 (1972) 179–91. It should be noted that Holmes makes a distinction between the goals to be achieved or "purchased" and the resources that have to be expended in order to achieve them. In his schema, the comparison of plans in terms of goal–achievements is undertaken separately from their comparison in terms of resource costs.

[14]This procedure is discussed in Boyce et al., 1970, *op. cit.*, pp. 197–221.

procedure the quantitative information obtained from the performance scores for objectives were discarded.

The two other methods in this group do make use of such information. One of these is an "effectiveness matrix" approach put forward by Schimpeler and Grecco[15] for evaluating alternative transportation proposals. In their procedure the objectives are each given a numerical "utility" value to represent their relative importance. Effectiveness values are then assigned to the alternatives in relation to each of the objectives in turn; again this is done with little discussion of the principles of measurement. A value of 1·0 signifies the fullest possible level of achievement of a particular objective, and a value of 0·0 signifies zero achievement. In this way a matrix of plan effectiveness is drawn up, and the total utility expected from implementing a particular plan is given by the sum of its achievement scores times the utilities attached to the various objectives.

A procedure which is essentially the same as the above has recently been applied by R. Travers Morgan and Partners working as principal consultants on the London Docklands Study.[16] This particular application is of interest for two main reasons. The procedure is discussed in unusual detail and the principles governing the procedure are given explicit consideration. In addition, it demonstrates the problem-solving approach to evaluation, where the objectives for evaluation are formulated in terms of solving various problems identified by the planning team. The Team were asked to consider alternative land-use proposals and to assess their consequences in social cost–benefit terms as far as practicable. In their design and evaluation work, the Team addressed themselves to the task of trying to remedy the problems of the Study area, which were thought of as deficiencies in the provision of facilities, such as a lack of uncrowded housing and of job opportunities. Forty problems were identified, and their solution became the objectives for the plan. Eighteen plans were prepared; these were evaluated by the extent to which they would solve the specified problems and the level of associated resource costs. A plan was considered to "solve" a given problem if it resulted in a defined level of provision of the facility in question. No value at all was placed on increments of provision above that level.

Finally, the most sophisticated and well-known method in this category is that which has been developed by Hill under the title of the goals–achievement matrix.[17] We discuss this method in detail later, but outline it here. A set of ideals and objectives for the plan are formulated at the outset, in advance of the design of

[15]C. C. Schimpeler and W. L. Grecco, Systems evaluation: an approach based on community structure and values, *Highway Res. Record*, No. 238 (1968) 123–52. A conceptually similar decision procedure is presented in Jessiman et al., A rational decision-making technique for transportation planning, *Highway Res. Record*, No. 180 (1967) 71–80.

[16]London Docklands Study Team, *Docklands: Redevelopment Proposals for East London*, Vol. One—*Main Report*, GLC, London, 1973.

[17]M. Hill, A method for evaluating alternative plans: the goals–achievement matrix applied to transportation plans, PhD dissertation, University of Pennsylvania, 1966. For summary accounts see M. Hill, A method for the evaluation of transportation plans, *Highway Res. Record*, No. 180 (1967) 21–34; and A goals–achievement matrix for evaluating alternative plans, *J. Am. Inst. Planners* 34 (1968) 19–29.

alternatives. The objectives are then defined in operational terms in order that measurements of the extent of their achievement by the plans may be obtained. The relative importance of the objectives is then established, this usually being denoted by a set of numerical values. The plans' levels of achievement are estimated for each objective in turn, and then weighted by the respective values of the objectives (the results being presented in a matrix). If practicable, the incidence of objective achievements for different groups in society should be traced. The weighted achievement levels of the objectives are then summed to give an overall index of objective achievement for each plan. This index value would then be adjusted to take account of the equity of the resulting distribution of gains and losses. This completes the comparison of the plans.

There are two main distinguishing features of this method—the attention given to equity considerations and the use of a hierarchy of goals. We comment on these in turn. In the evaluation matrix, individuals in the community are grouped according to some criterion viewed relevant to an assessment of the justice and fairness of the proposals, such as income levels. A set of "incidence weights" are assigned to these groups in order to represent the preference "of the community" with respect to alternative distribution of gains and losses which are to be applied to the totals of net gain. Accordingly the analyst has to trace the incidence of the gains and losses in relation to specified groups. The formulation of the incidence weights is considered to be the responsibility of the decision-takers. But planners must obtain evidence as to these weights from whatever sources they can if decision-takers cannot or will not state their own preferences on issues of equity.

The other distinguishing feature is that the objectives employed in Hill's matrix are not valued in themselves but for their achievement of certain higher level goals ("ideals") which denote very general policy aims, concerned with areas such as "social justice" and "choice and opportunity". Conceptually, the objectives are said to be derived from a consideration of the postulated ideals.

With the exception of Hill's method, all the goals–achievement methods discussed here have been developed in response to difficulties encountered in studies on which the authors were engaged, and all have been applied in practical situations. Schlager's method, for instance, was developed for use by the South Eastern Wisconsin Regional Planning Commission in evaluating land-use–transportation plans, while Schimpeler's and Grecco's was developed for use on the Louisville Metropolitan Transportation Program.

Assessment of Resource Costs

This category comprises those methods which have been developed to estimate the value to the community of the resources used up in undertaking urban and regional developments, particularly industry and housing. Attention is confined to an examination of the inputs associated with alternatives where these include the resources required in both establishing and operating projects. There is clearly some overlap between this category of evaluation and that of social cost–benefit analysis

(SCBA), since the estimates of resource costs that are obtained would form part of the evidence of a SCBA.

Methods in this category have been developed from two sources—economists interested in the resource implications of planning policies, and physical planners who recognize the need to introduce a consideration of resource costs into their design and evaluation procedures. We discuss, firstly, a contribution from economists and then a method developed by physical planners.

Costs-in-use

Stone has developed and applied procedures for estimating both private and public capital and operating costs involved in urban developments. He terms these "costs-in-use", which may be expressed as average *per capita* costs for various phases in the implementation of projects or plans. The procedures have recently been applied to estimating costs of construction and land required for maintenance, improvement, and additions to the housing stock of Britain over the period from the mid 1960s to the end of the century.[18] A range of costs are presented to reflect alternative possible rates of growth and change in the spatial distribution of population, and alternative standards of quality that could be adopted for housing provision. Analyses on similar lines have been made in relation to other types of urban facilities, such as roads and public utilities, to assist in the long-term formulation of urban development policies.[19] Work of a local nature has been undertaken by the Greater London Council for the inquiry into their Development Plan.[20] Investigations were made of (*inter alia*) the resource implications of various possibilities for the future rate and scale of urban developments in the London area.

Threshold Analysis

The theory and method of threshold analysis originated in Poland from the work of Malisz.[21] It developed initially in the early 1960s and was introduced into the United Kingdom by Kozlowski who has since done much to elaborate and refine its theoretical aspects.[22] The first application of the method in the United Kingdom was

[18]National Institute of Economic and Social Research, *Urban Development in Britain: Standards, Costs and Resources 1964–2004*, Vol. 1, *Population Trends and Housing*, by P. A. Stone, Cambridge University Press, Cambridge, 1970.

[19]P. A. Stone, *The Structure, Size and Costs of Urban Settlements*, Cambridge University Press, Cambridge, 1973.

[20]GLDP Inquiry Proof E111/1, *Subject Evidence at Stage 1, General Strategy and Implementation*, GLC, May 1971; GLDP Inquiry Support Document S11/120, *The Implications of Alternative Population and Employment Levels for London and the Region*, GLC, undated.

[21]B. Malisz, Urban planning theory: methods and results, in J. C. Fisher (ed.), *City and Regional Planning in Poland*, Cornell University Press, Ithaca, New York, 1966, pp. 57–84.

[22]The theory and practical applications of the analysis are discussed at length in J. Kozlowski and J. T. Hughes, *Threshold Analysis: A Quantitative Planning Method*, Architectural Press, London, 1972. This work contains recent refinements to theoretical aspects of the method and some discussion of its use within the planning process.

in 1966 on the Grangemouth/Falkirk Study,[23] and it was subsequently applied to the Central Borders Study.[24] In both cases it was used to demarcate areas considered most suitable for new residential development.

Threshold analysis concerns those physical characteristics of an area which would cause significant fluctuations in the unit cost of future urban development. It thus deals only with costs which vary with location. The main subject of investigation is those costs of location (both capital and operating) associated with residential development, although in principle the analysis may be applied to other land-users such as industry and commerce.

A threshold is said to occur when new units of development (e.g. dwellings) cannot be constructed and serviced at their previous unit cost levels and substantial additional outlays are required. The presence of a threshold is indicated either by a rise in the gradient or a discontinuity in the marginal cost curve of urban development. Changes in the unit cost of additional development may be caused by a variety of physical characteristics, e.g. the topography of an area or the physical capacity of public utility networks. Thresholds cost items could, therefore, include the cost of extending electricity supply, building new roads, or draining marshy areas for new dwellings.

The analysis is designed to help decisions on the following types of issue: In which direction should a town expand? In what sequence should future growth areas be developed? Is it better to intensify development within existing urban areas or locate in new areas and incur additional fixed costs? The analysis provides information about the magnitude of changes in unit development costs for alternative locations. These prospective outlays are related to the number of new inhabitants and are presented as an average threshold cost per new inhabitant.

Obviously the significance of the analysis depends on the extent to which different categories of threshold costs tend to reinforce each other instead of occurring in different time periods. Lean[25] has pointed out that the troughs in the cost curves of one category may coincide with the crests in another category, thus reducing or annihilating the total significance of the thresholds. There has not yet been sufficient empirical work carried out to establish whether or not this occurs frequently.

Whilst threshold analysis may be used to help search out solutions to accommodate future urban growth, its principal advocates do not claim that choices should be based on evidence only of costs. They recognize that benefits will generally vary a great deal among urban development possibilities, and perhaps by more than variations in costs. Benefit variations might result, for example, from difference in levels of accessibility to jobs and shops and in the quality of residential environments. The main use of threshold analysis is considered to be in the initial narrowing down of the range of possibilities, which helps in selecting a manageable number for

[23]*Grangemouth/Falkirk Regional Survey and Plan*, HMSO, Edinburgh, 1968.
[24]*The Central Borders: A Plan for Expansion*, HMSO, Edinburgh, 1968.
[25]W. Lean, An economist's note on the validity of urban threshold theory, *J. Town Planning Inst.* **55** (1969) 311.

detailed investigation. Its advocates suggest that the analysis could be used to provide some of the information required by other methods of evaluation, such as the goals–achievement matrix or social cost–benefit analysis. But they admit that its relatively low level of sophistication does not make it suitable for finely detailed comparisons.

Social Cost–Benefit Analysis (SCBA)

This approach has been developed by economists for appraising the social worth of public sector projects, particularly those involving the commitment of resources. It draws on a variety of traditional aspects of economic study. To quote Williams,[26] SCBA

"is essentially a means of adapting the rules for profit-maximizing investment behaviour by private firms to fit the different circumstances under which governments operate, which in turn means trying to take account on the one hand of externalities and the peculiarities of 'public goods' compared with 'private goods', and on the other recognising that the budgeting processes of government may require further reformulation of the rules if they are to be appropriate in a setting which is far removed from the classical one of a small firm operating in a large and perfect capital market."

SCBA has usually been applied to the comparison of alternatives within single sectors, such as transport or health, although intersector comparisons are sometimes practicable. It may be used to aid choice not only between alternative ways of carrying out a particular project (such as catering for a certain volume of passenger traffic), but also among a number of independent projects competing for a limited amount of investment funds. The use of SCBA in planning studies is now well established, although much confusion over its principles and scope exists within the planning profession and with the public at large. This has led to some reservations to accepting the approach which are, in our view, unjustified.

Items of cost and benefit for inclusion in the analysis are all the gains and losses of every member of society whose well-being would be affected by the projects or plans if implemented. Concern is with the welfare of a defined society and not with any smaller part of it. The benefits and costs are measured on the basis of the preferences of the individuals who are affected (or in our terminology on the basis of sectoral objectives), rather than those of, say, decision-takers. The analysis seeks as far as possible to establish the value of individuals' costs and benefits on the basis of evidence derived from observing people's behaviour, rather than from their stated preferences.

A distinctive feature of the SCBA approach is that assessments of advantages and disadvantages are undertaken according to a clearly defined set of theoretical

[26]A. Williams, *Output Budgeting and the Contribution of Microeconomics to Efficiency in Government*, CAS Occasional Paper, No. 4, HMSO, London, 1967, p. 8.

principles, which most practitioners now agree are appropriate. There is now an extensive and easily accessible literature on the principles of the analysis.[27] Because it is comprehensive, the social worth of a project is judged by its net contribution to raising the level of aggregate consumption of items of value, regardless of whether or not they are bought or sold. Nevertheless, many goods and services do enter into a market situation, and this is particularly true of the outputs of planning activities. Their value to members of society can fairly easily be estimated.

Costs and benefits are defined in terms of the quantity of other goods and services which are equivalent in value to the disadvantages or advantages of the plans being investigated. We try to measure a benefit by the quantity of alternative goods and services which would give the same amount of satisfaction to the beneficiaries. Conversely, a cost is measured by the goods and services which would provide sufficient compensation to the losers or which, in other words, would restore them to their initial level of well-being. These analyses of items of consumption are normally referred to as efficiency analyses. Considerations of equity, relating to the fairness and justice of the incidence of costs and benefits on different groups in society, are also relevant to SCBA. However, the treatment of equity does not match the general acceptance of principles of assessment of efficiency gains. The literature contains much debate as to whether and how it is appropriate to include distributional equity in the analysis.[28] Those who consider distribution important usually argue that we should have regard to the preferences of decision-takers in specifying the weights to be applied to particular groups. This is the position adopted by the proponents of goals–achievement analysis, although, in those methods, the weighting is done prior to the tracing of incidence. But, like goals–achievement analysis, there are difficulties in discovering how decision-takers wish to "trade-off" equity considerations against efficiency considerations.

Applications of SCBA in the public sector have been well reviewed by Prest and Turvey.[29] They discuss the use made of the approach up to 1965 in a variety of fields—water supply, transport, land use (embracing urban renewal, recreation, and land reclamation), health, education, research and development, and defence. Subsequent applications in various sectors up to 1973 are reviewed by Peters,[30] and the same writer has also undertaken an extensive review of applications in British studies of land-use allocation.[31] One of the most striking features of the

[27]See, for instance, R. N. McKean, *Efficiency in Government Through Systems Analysis*, John Wiley, New York, 1958; E. J. Mishan, *Cost–Benefit Analysis: An Informal Introduction*, Allen & Unwin, London, 1971; A. K. Dasgupta and D. W. Pearce, *Cost–Benefit Analysis: Theory and Practice*, Macmillan, London, 1972.
[28]For a discussion of the controversy over the inclusion of distributional effects, see P. D. Henderson, Some unsettled issues in cost–benefit analysis, in P. Streeten (ed.), *Unfashionable Economics: Essays in Honor of Lord Balogh*, Weidenfeld & Nicolson, London, 1970, pp. 275–301.
[29]A. R. Prest and R. Turvey, Cost–benefit analysis: a survey, *Econ. J.* 75 (1965) 155–207, Part III.
[30]G. H. Peters, *Cost–Benefit Analysis and Public Expenditure*, 3rd edn., Eaton Paper 8, Institute of Economic Affairs, London, 1973.
[31]G. H. Peters, Land use studies in Britain: a review of the literature with special reference to applications of cost–benefit analysis, *J. Agric. Econ.* 21 (1970) 171–214.

Relate my case studies to
usual method
used eg SCBA for roads

application of the analysis within the public domain is the great variety of sectors in which it has been used, and the considerable broadening of its use in recent years.

As one would expect, the procedures adopted in applying SCBA has differed somewhat between problems and with those carrying out the analysis. However, in the main they have been essentially similar; there are thus few variants of the approach. Cost-effectiveness and cost-minimization are often thought of as being significantly different from conventional SCBA. But both of these may be interpreted as the application of SCBA in special circumstances. Cost-effectiveness analysis is appropriate when a fixed amount of investment funds has been allocated to an agency or project and the best way of using the total budget allocation is to be determined. Cost-minimization analysis is appropriate in finding the least cost way of undertaking a particular project (such as different ways of producing a given output of electricity, or catering for a given volume of airport traffic), where the same benefits are assumed to result in each case. It is implicit in the former approach that no alternative use for the funds is practicable, and in the latter that the minimum cost alternative will be worth undertaking compared with using the resources on some other project(s) elsewhere.

Planning Balance Sheet Analysis (PBSA)

This method is a particular application of the social cost–benefit approach to evaluation, being an adaptation of the general approach of SCBA for use on urban and regional planning studies. Since it is the principal exception to conventional applications of SCBA and intended specifically for evaluation in planning, we discuss it here separately. The PBS was developed by Lichfield.

We consider the conceptual development of the PBS in the following chapter (where we compare it with Hill's goals–achievement matrix method). But it is pertinent here to mention why Lichfield thought it necessary to adapt SCBA as then generally practised. He has suggested two main reasons. First, SCBA has typically been applied to investment projects in a single sector, such as that of water resources and highways. As a result, the cost and benefit items have related largely to the particular "system" of which the project forms a part. The analysis has therefore focused mainly on the costs and benefits falling directly on those who produce and operate the project and on those who consume the goods and services it generates. In contrast, urban and regional planning proposals typically involve concurrent investments in a range of different sectors or activity systems. Consequently, evaluation is made more difficult than in single-sector project appraisals. A greater number of groups will be affected, the repercussions of proposals being far more wide-ranging, and the number of imponderable factors present will tend to be much greater. This means that at the infancy of applying SCBA to planning problems, numerous important non-quantifiable and incommensurable items are likely to exist. Thus, *because of the multi-sectoral nature of proposals*, greater regard will have to be paid than in conventional applications of SCBA to those items which cannot be quantified or measured in common units. Therefore instead of the usual practice of representing intangibles and incommensurables to the decision-takers in the prose

why
PBSA
developed
from
trad
SCBA

accompanying the cost–benefit arithmetic, PBSA includes a statement of such items in the same table as those for which valuations can be established. Those responsible for decision-taking will have a convenient summary of all the information which has been produced. We suggest that they will therefore be more likely to give intangibles and incommensurables due consideration in forming their judgement as to the preferred options, and subsequently in justifying their choice. However, the decision itself may be made more difficult because such a presentation of results tends to force the decision-taker to make explicit the subjective judgements about the value of the intangibles and incommensurables.

The second reason for wishing to adapt conventional SCBA is the importance of equity considerations in urban and regional planning. As normally practised, SCBA does not conveniently bring out the incidence of costs and benefits on the various groups affected. The PBS allows the analyst to set down the items of cost and benefit against each group who will experience the consequences of the option, and to trace the ultimate incidence of gains and losses. In the analysis an attempt is therefore made, if practicable, to determine the incidence of gains and losses on groups within the community.[32]

In brief, the procedure of PBSA is as as follows. The first task is to enumerate the various groups who play a role in establishing and running the various projects. These groups are collectively termed "producers/operators" and are listed vertically in balance sheet form. Each producer/operator is, as far as possible, paired with the appropriate groups of individuals who will be consuming the goods and services generated by the projects. Each linked, or associated, pair of producers and consumers is considered to be engaged in either a notional or a real "transaction", whereby the former produces services "for sale" to the latter. These transactions are obviously not confined to goods and services exchanged in the market. They would extend, for example, to include visual intrusion imposed upon residential occupiers by the builders of an urban motorway. Thus the balance sheet aims at presenting a comprehensive set of social accounts. In addition to the "transactions", which embrace all outputs, estimates are made of the resource costs involved in generating the goods and services.

The generality of many planning studies, especially at the sub-regional or regional scale, and their inevitable complexity, has meant that in practice PBSAs have not achieved full documentation of all transactions among all groups affected. But the framework exists for extending the analysis if study resources permit. The analyst aims at complete social accounting, but takes short-cuts where necessary. In addition, if quantification of costs and benefits proves to be impossible, as was the case in many early studies,[33] the method allows symbols to be inserted into the accounts to represent the costs and benefits in their appropriate position in the balance sheet so that they do not get overlooked. Thus the balance sheet contains a

[32]For an attempt, see N. Lichfield, Cost–benefit analysis in planning: a critique of the Roskill Commission, *Regional Studies* **5** (1971) 157–83.

[33]For instance, the Swanley and Worthing Studies. See N. Lichfield, Cost–benefit analysis in town planning—a case study: Swanley, *Urban Studies* **3** (1966) 215–49; N. Lichfield and Associates, *Worthing: Cost–Benefit Analysis of Alternative Road Proposals*, Borough of Worthing, 1966.

statement of the proposals considered; the various "sectors" within the community who are potentially affected, either adversely or beneficially; the various items of plan consequence and the sectoral objective for each of those items; the nature of the units of measurement employed; and the results of the analysis in relation to the preferences of each sector considered.

The PBS has proved a convenient aid to *tackling* plan evaluation, particularly in the categorization of effects. Instead of proceeding item by item, in conventional fashion, the analysis is organized around the affected groups of individuals. An evaluation cannot, of course, be undertaken without explicit consideration of both the items of cost and benefit and the persons who will experience those items. But, given the complexity of typical planning proposals, it is generally easier to think initially about *who* is likely to be affected and then *in what way* they are likely to be affected. Unlike the case of most single-sector projects, the nature of many of the potential items of cost and benefit of planning is not at all obvious. Individuals affected may be more easily identified than are items. Furthermore, a comprehensive coverage of objectives is more likely to be achieved than in the abstractions about the purpose of the planning proposals that characterize some plan evaluation methods.

Optimization Techniques

Developments in linear and non-linear programming have led to techniques which, in certain problem situations, can rapidly and efficiently search out preferred solutions from all the existing possibilities. For this purpose preference criteria (i.e. an objective function and any constraints that apply) have to be specified in advance of their use, and since the techniques are quantitative they can only be employed when the problem is formulated in mathematical terms.

Although possibilities exist for applying these searching procedures to choice situations in urban and regional planning, there are several obvious difficulties associated with their use. The foremost of these is the specification of the criteria of preference. It has generally proved difficult to find specifications that are sufficiently wide in scope. In our view it is not possible to know how decision-takers will weigh up the various advantages and disadvantages of plans, nor in what way the influence of the various interested parties will be felt. Furthermore, even if we could elicit the views of decision-takers, there are those of other groups in society to be considered. For these reasons, universally acceptable objective functions for urban and regional planning are not likely to exist. Other difficulties relate to the constraints to be applied to solutions; these cannot always be specified quantitatively. Also, data collection problems are often enormous, since all possible design solutions have to be allowed for. Uncertainties surrounding much of the evidence as to the measurement of the achievement of objectives create further difficulties, although we may test the sensitivity of the model results to changes in measurement assumptions. Nevertheless, there is something appealing about the efficiency of a process which allows for design and evaluation to be merged into one mechanized step; accordingly we shall briefly discuss some of the optimizing procedures which have been advocated in the literature.

Ben-Shahar *et al.* have developed a model for allocating residential and employment land uses and determining transport investments in urban development planning.[34] The model has been applied in Israel and to a number of projects in other countries, including (using a modified form) an examination of alternative plans for Irvine New Town in Scotland.[35] The model has a linear programming formulation where the objective function is to maximize the total demand prices for all buildings, less construction and demolition costs for new ones, and also less all costs associated with the provision and use of communications infrastructure and capital. Although the authors point out (correctly) that only decision-takers can determine optimality criteria, they nevertheless claim that this function is generally valid for public planning activity.

Another linear programming model of interest is that of Schlager for land-use plan design.[36] This model generates a complete land-use plan which minimizes total public and private investment costs subject to a number of design constraints. It was applied to metropolitan areas in South East Wisconsin by the Regional Planning Commission. Given forecasts of population and employment, aggregate demand for each land use is determined by applying a conversion coefficient (or standard) to each population and employment group. Land use is allocated by type, location, and density, subject to constraints regarding zoning (e.g. flood plain zoning, density controls) and design requirements (e.g. desired proximity of land uses, schools, shopping). These constraints, which express conditions for the acceptability of alternatives, can be regarded as minimum, fixed levels of achievement of planning objectives. By shifting constraint levels for service land ratios, zoning criteria, or land use proximity requirements, choice of the optimal plan will be affected. The costs of the levels of the constraints can be tested by determining the sensitivity of the outcome to the constraints. The effects of such shifts can be measured in monetary terms in the model by determining the changes in overall costs of the plan.

This model was subsequently modified by the South Eastern Wisconsin Regional Planning Commission because the discrete nature of the location of activities was not considered to be well reflected in the linear form of the model; nor was the true cost of development thought to be adequately reflected since it considers only locational costs, not linkage costs. Appropriate changes have been incorporated in a dynamic programming formulation of the model,[37] in which relationships can be non-linear. This also includes facility for multiple stage decision processes. The model leads to a minimum cost combination of land uses constrained by design

[34]H. Ben-Shahar, A. Mazor, and D. Pines, Town planning and welfare maximization: a methodological approach, *Regional Studies* **3** (1969) 105–13.

[35]PA Management Consultants and the Israel Institute of Urban Studies, *Irvine New Town Planning Study*, 1969. For a discussion of its use on this study, see Chapter 10.

[36]K. J. Schlager, A land use plan design model, *J. Am. Inst. Planners* **31** (1965) 103–10.

[37]South Eastern Wisconsin Regional Planning Commission, *A Mathematical Approach to Urban Design*, South Eastern Wisconsin Technical Report No. 3, 1965.

standards. Accordingly, whilst this formulation is more realistic than Schlager's in its ability to incorporate non-linear and dynamic elements, its essential innovation is in the design of alternatives and not their evaluation. The objective function is still essentially concerned with cost minimization.

More recently, Scott has provided another demonstration of the use of dynamic programming to locational issues in urban and regional planning.[38]

Finally, we should mention the work carried out by Polish planners since the early 1960s under the name of the Warsaw optimization method.[39] Although this method is still in the early stages of development, it has to date been applied to problems of locating new residential developments and industrial employments. Examples of studies on which it has been used are the Master Plan for Skopje in Yugoslavia (1965) and the Master Plan for the Warsaw Urban Region (1968).

The method is essentially an extension of threshold analysis to the task of choosing optimal locations for and intensities of urban land activities. Its aim is to maximize the benefits resulting from a given amount of new urban development as well as to minimize the associated capital and operating costs. The measurement of benefits, however, has proved very difficult. As a compromise, the approach adopted in practice is based on minimizing investment costs subject to meeting certain standards of provision that it is considered the plan should attain. These standards relate to matters such as the quality of residential accommodation and access to central urban facilities. During the initial stages of the method, threshold analysis is used to narrow down the area of search for preferred locations. This delimitation of broad areas for further investigation is based largely on the criterion of minimizing investment costs; but some consideration is given to gains and losses of benefits by constraining out areas such as those which are highly inaccessible or have outstanding scenic quality. Where conflicts occur between increases in items of benefit and minimum investment costs, the analyst makes a subjective judgement as to the relative importance of the benefits. The search is then directed to minimum cost locations which will safeguard the set of performance standards laid down for the plan.

Concluding Remarks

Despite the wide array of methods described above, in the past few years there has been a crystallization of attitudes in this country to evaluation procedures in urban and regional planning. In addition, there has been a strong tendency for views to polarize around the social cost–benefit and goals–achievement approaches; in particular, there has been a considerable increase of interest in the use of the

[38]A. J. Scott, Dynamic location–allocation systems: some basic planning strategies, *Environment and Planning* **3** (1971) 73–82.

[39]For a brief account of the method see J. M. Kozlowski, Optimization method—a case for research, *J. Town Planning Inst.* **56** (1970) 134–7. A fuller discussion, containing a description of some practical applications of the method, is given in S. Broniewski and B. Jastrzebski, Optimization method, in *Analytical Techniques in the Urban and Regional Planning Process: Threshold Analysis, Optimization Method*, Planning Research Unit, University of Edinburgh, 1970.

planning balance sheet (PBS) and the goals–achievement matrix (GAM) methods.

The PBS has been applied in practice in the United Kingdom since the early 1960s, very largely by or in close association with its originator, Lichfield. A wide range of studies have been carried out. Recent applications include the analysis of proposals for different mixes of investment in public and private transport,[40] the analysis of regional development proposals,[41] and as assessment of the social costs of blight resulting from motorway proposals.[42] In addition, following the successful application of the method in connection with the Third London Airport,[43] it has been used to aid choice between alternative airport locations in the vicinity of Oslo.[44]

The originator of the GAM has in contrast applied his method in an illustrative fashion only,[45] its use in practice being by others. In the United Kingdom it has been used extensively in recent studies at the sub-regional and urban scales.[46] In each case the method has been adopted by the planning team to accord with their own views on the principles of assessment, as well as to suit the particular problem at hand.

4.2. THE RATIONALE FOR PLANNING BALANCE SHEET ANALYSIS

Because of the polarization of views on evaluation methodology, it is useful to examine each of these two methods, PBSA and GAM, in greater detail. Our preference is for the former, and we shall now present our main justifications for using the social cost–benefit approach for evaluation as adopted in its PBS form. We then shall compare and contrast the characteristics of the PBSA and GAM methods in Chapter 5. Since the PBSA is adapted from SCBA, much of its rationale will be similar to a rationale for CBA. There are, however, good reasons for the particular adaptation used which we draw out towards the end of this section.

At the outset we suggested the need for some kind of "formal welfare test" of planning proposals. A more closely reasoned justification is now called for, which

[40]N. Lichfield and Associates, *Stevenage: Cost Benefit Analysis of Alternative Public/Private Transport Modal Split*, 2 vols., Stevenage Development Corporation, Stevenage, May 1969.

[41]West Midland Regional Study, *Technical Appendix 5, Evaluation 2*, July 1972.

[42]N. Lichfield and Associates, GLDP Inquiry Support Document S27/222, *Planning Blight in Social Cost Benefit Analysis: The North Cross Route in Camden*, London Borough of Camden, 1971.

[43]Cambridgeshire CC *et al.*, *Evidence Submitted at Stage III to the Commission on the Third London Airport*, July 1969, ch. 14, Cost-benefit analysis: N. Lichfield and Associates.

[44]Norwegian Institute of Urban and Regional Research, *Innstilling Del I om Flyplasser i Oslo-omradet*, Oslo, 1970 (in Norwegian).

[45]Hill, 1966, *op. cit.*, pp. 215–99. The method was illustrated with reference to the transport aspects of alternative plans for the City of Cambridge in England. For the purpose he used the data and material employed by Lichfield in his PBS evaluation of the city plans, to be found in N. Lichfield, *Cost–Benefit Analysis in Town Planning, A Case Study of Cambridge*, Cambridgeshire and Isle of Ely CC, 1966.

[46]Major applications include the following: C-S-W Sub-regional Study Team, Supplementary Report 4, *Evaluation*, Coventry City Council, May 1971. BUSPT, *Report on the Evaluation of Alternative Strategies*, Brighton County Borough Council, December 1971. South Hampshire Plan Technical Unit, *Evaluation of Alternative Strategies*, Working Paper No. 18, August 1972. Those recently engaged on the Strategic Plan for the North West Region of England also used the GAM approach in their evaluation work; see North West Joint Planning Team, *Physical Pattern of Development*, Technical Paper 9, 1973.

will lead to a discussion of the requirements of an effective evaluation methodology for decision-making.

Some planning activities and proposals are almost entirely of an investment nature: to redevelop a central area, to build a motorway, or construct a new housing estate. At the opposite extreme, planning activities involve control over the *use* of land and existing facilities; here there need be no sanctioning or commitment of resources. Conservation areas and areas of outstanding natural beauty are designated in order to control activities within them, often without knowing what kinds of development would have taken place without preservation or, indeed, whether there would have been activity at all. Many planning activities fall between these two extremes. Policies under the general improvement area provisions of the 1969 Housing Act may be cited as involving both investment-related and controlling functions in attempts to improve and "tidy-up" residential areas.

Formal welfare tests may be easier to justify for investment activities. If the money is not spent (and hence resources used) on the schemes(s) in question, it can be spent elsewhere. A test is required to indicate the best use of the resources. However, for controlling activities of planning authorities, such a test may, on consideration, seem less feasible and necessary.

Yet the result of control over the use of facilities, preservation, and conservation policies and non-investment-related planning activities is to make some individuals in society better off than they would otherwise have been and some individuals worse off. These advantages and disadvantages may be "subjective" in nature but they are no less real for that. Indeed, it is possible to argue that no real distinction is possible between subjective costs and resource costs. Frustrating the change of use of a building will impose a cost on the potential user no less real than an imposed tax to finance the provision of a new building for someone else's benefit. Of course subjective costs, like benefits, are often difficult to measure. But because planning activity involves the lives of people and their well-being, a welfare test is legitimate for all types of planning decisions. Problems in measurement should not cloud the principle that a welfare test is valid wherever some groups are made better off and others worse off as a result of planning activity.

A fairly substantial literature exists (given the current immaturity of practice) on the application of SCBA in planning to demonstrate this point. Not all of the studies have investment costs as major items for consideration, for example:

(a) The closing of a main shopping street to traffic, where some alternatives required the provision of a replacement road, the cost of which was only one of a large number of factors for consideration.[47]
(b) The maintenance of public services for residents and others in a rural area, as opposed to alternatives given by degrees of population migration to towns.[48]

[47]N. Lichfield and H. Chapman, Cost–benefit analysis and road proposals for a shopping centre—a case study: Edgware, *J. Trans. Econ. Policy* **2** (1968) 280–320.
[48]J. J. Warford, *The South Atcham Scheme: An Economic Appraisal*, HMSO, London, 1969.

(c) Alternative regional development strategies, where the resource cost differentials between strategies were insignificant compared with considerations of accessibility, amenity and congestion in the city.[49]

SCBA has been developed in order to assess the significance of all these various costs and benefits. In principle, it is as applicable to decisions in urban and regional planning as to any other area of decision-making. In our view attention to the details of the methodology is rewarding for the insights it gives to planning analysis. Indeed, of all the evaluation methodologies currently developed, we believe SCBA, in its adaption as the PBS, to be the most rigorous and useful. Here we attempt to justify that view in relation to the general approach.

Perhaps we should try first to clear up some popular misconceptions. The most obvious is that SCBA is confined to "economic" applications. It is therefore not thought to be planning analysis, since planning is reckoned to be a wider-ranging activity than one which is purely economic. This error might be less prevalent if the full title of the analysis were always stated when it is discussed, which is SCBA. The costs and benefits should include *all* of the *social* advantages and disadvantages of planning proposals, that is, all which are of interest in society. *Any* decision which makes individuals feel better or worse off is legitimately the subject-matter of CBA irrespective of the label which may be conveniently attached to it. Kinship ties, aesthetics, and community action are all susceptible to this kind of analysis. They may, of course, be susceptible to other kinds of analysis also. But sociological or aesthetic appraisals are not precluded by or incompatible with the undertaking of CBA.

Another frequent misconception is that CBA is limited to items for which monetary values are readily obtainable. As much as possible measurement in money values is sought, and it is conventional practice to present a summary table of results for those factors for which quantitative estimates of their value in money terms is possible. Yet no respectable CBA will omit discussion of the alternatives in terms of unquantified costs and benefits in the written material accompanying the table of results. In those cases where the analysts do make judgements as to the preferred alternative, the unquantified items ought in general to be carefully considered in relation to those for which a valuation has been made. A recent example is the work of the Roskill Commission on the siting of the Third London Airport.[50] In presenting the summary analysis the Commission was fully aware that it contained only partial evidence; some of the other relevant evidence related to non-measurable items. In arriving at their recommended choice of site the members were at great pains to take account of all relevant evidence that had been produced, not just the quantified cost–benefit estimates appearing in the table summarizing the analysis based upon their Research Team's studies. The assessment of alternative proposed rail links

[49]West Midland Regional Study, *Technical Appendix 5, Evaluation 2*, July 1972.
[50]CTLA, *Report*, HMSO, London, 1971, chs. 12 and 13.

between Heathrow Airport and Central London is another example of a CBA containing a convenient summary of qualitative factors affecting choice but not capable of quantitative assessment.[51]

The principles by which incommensurable and intangible items should be handled are no different from those where items can be quantified in common units. Indeed, it is helpful to see unquantified costs and benefits in perspective by referring to the way they might be assessed were sufficient evidence available. Because in the past some advantages and disadvantages of planning proposals have not been capable of quantification in common units the possibility of obtaining sufficient evidence is not ruled out. "Critics frequently confuse (a) the logical possibility of valuing an intangible outcome, (b) the empirical possibility of evaluation, and (c) the morality of the value if one is derived."[52] The fact that items exist which cannot be expressed in units common to other items does not invalidate the approach but only limits its usefulness, given the current state of the art.

Another misconception is that all items in a CBA must necessarily be aggregated to give an overall result. Of course, one of the purposes of the exercise is to try to derive evidence of advantages and disadvantages in a rough order of magnitude. But each item needs to be interpreted and the validity of the results appraised. Nor is it correct to assume that a "rate of return" or a figure of "net present value" must be derived from the analysis. It is true that in cases of possible heavy investments, such as in transport planning, it may be practicable and desirable to try to determine whether the investment of a given amount of resources in one sector is justified at the expense of other sectors, such as housing or education. We might also wish to know the rates of return for society that would result from particular plans compared with a decision not to undertake them. Yet without estimating these the analysis may nevertheless indicate which of alternative courses of action will make members of society potentially better off.

Some planners might object to the idea that CBA can and should become part of the tools of planning. In the past planning has developed intuitively, with issues being much debated but not necessarily formally analysed. In contrast economics has developed through formalised deductive analysis. Yet in the matter of the analysis of choice, economists do not automatically secure "property rights" over the tools they have developed, to be purchased at the price of three years' study. Some economists have the technical know-how to undertake CBAs reasonably well, but simply because in the past they have carried out CBAs, "This does not mean that the economist's skills are the only ones needed in making such analyses or, indeed, that economists are very good at making them".[53] What matters is whether this analysis can illuminate planning choice.

Successful analysis required a willingness to think in terms of all the community interests in particular decisions (rather than selective sectional interests) and an

[51]Ministry of Transport, *Report of a Study of Rail Links with Heathrow Airport*, HMSO, London, 1970.
[52]D. W. Pearce, *Cost–Benefit Analysis*, Macmillan, London, 1971, p. 12.
[53]R. N. McKean, *Public Spending*, McGraw-Hill, New York, 1968, pp. 135–6.

ability to appraise the available evidence of the strengths of those interests. The former prerequisite is obviously not limited to particular disciplines. The latter, an ability to appraise evidence on community preferences, may be aided by economic analysis. Yet the evidence itself is probably generated from a number of sources, some within the activity of the planning team, through model building exercises and surveys of various kinds, and are likely to result from multi-disciplinary efforts. As long as the approach to the measurement of relative values is consistent and acceptable (and economists clearly have a contribution to make here) and measurement exercises will benefit from a wide application of skills.

The Approach to Advantages and Disadvantages

The measurement of advantages and disadvantages is central to evaluation. We discuss measurement issues more generally in Chapter 6. But a concentration on some of the main aspects of the CBA approach is necessary here since, if alternative methodologies to SCB *are* comprehensive in that they try to discover the relative importance of all the social consequences of proposals, as some claim, then they may differ only in their approach to the measurement of those advantages and disadvantages. Measurement principles and practice must form a central part of the rationale of any evaluation method.

Our purpose is to find out how much planning proposals contribute to the well-being of beneficiaries or decrease the well-being of losers. The term "utility" or "satisfaction" is used to represent this abstract notion of welfare. Ideally, we wish to obtain measures for the contribution to the utility of individuals in society, measured in units of utility.

However, no satisfactory way exists for direct measurement of these contributions. In order to proceed we must compromise by adopting an inferior, but practicable, approach to the measurement of relative values. Although it is fraught with conceptual difficulties, the approach currently employed as part of conventional CBA is worthy of consideration. The approach most frequently used is one which considers the quantity of alternative goods and services which are *equivalent* in magnitude to the gains or losses resulting from the planning scheme. This usually takes the form of willingness by the beneficiaries to sacrifice goods and services in order to receive the benefits and, in the case of losers, the goods and services they would consider adequate compensation.[54] These goods and services need not, of course, be restricted to those available by purchase in the private sector.

Now, these quantities of diverse goods and services have also to be measured in common units of relative value. Little information is gained from knowing that an increase in traffic noise resulting from a planning proposal is worth so many bags of flour (or whatever) to a sufferer, whilst savings in travel time are worth so many hot meals (or whatever) to a beneficiary. We must convert units of noise into the same

---

[54]There are a number of variations on these generalized concepts, but these approaches to benefits and costs are generally accepted and used in cost–benefit studies. See Mishan, 1971, *op. cit.*, part II.

units of value as units of time. We could use bags of flour for both, or hot meals for both (or units of noise or time if that were possible). But since the medium of money provides a rate of exchange between bags of flour and hot meals and between a large number of other valued goods and services, it seems *convenient* to use that medium as the basis for conversion into common units.

It is seldom clear whether the widespread objection which undoubtedly exists to the use of money as a unit of common relative value is to the use of money as such (rather than some other unit of accounting like bags of flour or hot meals) or whether it concerns the approach to measurement. On the first, there can be no rational objection to the use of money as a *unit* of account: if we do not admit its use then we cannot legitimately admit the use of any unit (and hence that of any formal or quantified evaluation study). Moreover, the problems associated with inventing some *other* appropriate unit of measurement, and familiarizing people with it sufficiently to be able to express relative values seem unnecessarily difficult, if not impossible, in practice. On the second, objections to money values arise because of doubts about the legitimacy of measuring individuals' relative values of items of advantage or disadvantage by reference to equivalent alternative goods and services; or because of objections to the attempts to measure (i.e. to describe precisely) at all.

These latter objections were amongst those raised by Self and Buchanan in considering the Third London Airport investigations.[55] They did not necessarily object to some of the measures of the "physical" differences of one airport location rather than another. The facts, as best they could be determined, were that eight Norman churches would probably be seriously affected by noise or displaced if one site were chosen rather than another; that air travellers would generally spend more time reaching the more inaccessible site and on average this might amount to anything from 5 to 35 minutes; that flying activities would be adversely affected at ten defence airports for one site and at fourteen for another; and so on. Such estimates are necessarily speculative. Some are more uncertain than others. This uncertainty obviously constitutes an element of the debate. Yet the physical repercussions of the alternatives are some of the subjects for debate. Both Self and Buchanan, who expressed serious doubts about the CBA, agreed that this kind of information was useful. But they objected to the CBA of that study partly because they thought that the appropriate relative values to employ should those which emerged from the debate between interested parties and experts. They also objected because of the supposedly tremendous uncertainties and conceptual problems surrounding the estimation of values of members of the community.

Let us consider their objection to measuring relative values by reference to quantities of alternative goods and services. To measure this way seems reasonable for items of "pure" taste; that is, if A is willing to pay more for hot meals compared with travel time savings than B because he prefers eating as a pleasure more than B dislikes inconvenience of travel. Where the willingness to give up, or to pay,

[55]P. Self, Nonsense on stilts: cost–benefit analysis and the Roskill Commission, *Political Quart.* **41** (1970) 249–60; C. Buchanan, Note of Dissent, in CTLA, 1971, *op. cit.*, para. 34.

criterion as a measure of benefits is likely to meet serious objection (and this is well recognized by cost–benefit practitioners), is that willingness is clearly both influenced and constrained by ability. The rich, with more income, may be willing to pay more for given items of benefit of particular schemes. Yet the satisfaction derived may be no more, indeed may be much less, than that derived from a comparable item of benefit by the poor. The rich may assume "weight" in the analysis by virtue of the existing distribution of income. This objection loses some of its force for the compensation principle for involuntary losses; that is, what is the minimum losers would willingly accept for that loss—an amount which is clearly unconstrained by income level (although again clearly influenced by it).

Some may comment that the analysis simply reflects reality. The rich demand more than the poor because they are better off. Others may think that CBAs are inevitably biased towards the affluent. We would argue that the findings of CBAs of planning proposals do not *necessarily* favour the better off, although they may do so. For example, the poor outnumber the rich, and may be able to secure their objectives by "out-bidding" the rich by virtue of weight of numbers, if not of *per capita* income. The poor may demand high accessibility in residential locations. They may out-bid the rich for some highly accessible sites in cities because they are prepared to accept lower space standards *per capita*.

In a CBA there are two kinds of adjustments that can be made to the findings obtained by using the willingness to pay criterion which overcome any objections of bias in favour of those who are presently better off. The first adjustment is to weight the sums of gain and loss by the presumed marginal utilities of income of their recipients so as to arrive at magnitudes which truly reflect prospective changes in utilities. In this way an item of benefit giving the same amount of utility to both rich and poor would have the same value attached to it in the analysis no matter to which income group it accrued. However, whilst in principle it may be possible to make comparisons of utility changes as between different individuals, no one has yet put forward an acceptable method for doing so.[56] The best we can do at present is to guess at people's marginal utilities, which is not very helpful. Since we have not yet solved this measurement problem we use the willingness to pay (or be compensated) criterion as a second-best approach in determining relative values.

Secondly, we may adjust the figures of gain and loss assessed on the willingness to pay criterion by factors which reflect considerations of fairness and justice in the distribution of those gains and losses between different community groups. These factors are usually referred to as equity weights. It should be noted that we may wish to weight either the distribution of changes in utilities (assuming we could measure utilities on an interpersonal basis), *or* the distribution of changes in well-being derived from the willingness to pay criterion. The first case would be based on the view that it is the distribution of the total amount of utility within society that is relevant in discussing matters of equity; the second would rest on the alternative

---

[56] See, for instance, J. Rothenberg, *The Measurement of Social Welfare*, Prentice-Hall, New Jersey, 1961.

view that it is the distribution of income and wealth (or, in other words, the means of obtaining utility).[57] In the latter case there is no need to measure utilities as such before applying the equity weights; we only need to know the alternative goods and services that individuals are prepared to forego for benefits or accept in compensation for losses. This latter view is the popular one, but in either case the crucial problem, of course, is what weights to apply? Although the literature contains some suggestions on making suitable allowance for equity considerations, none is without difficulty and none has found universal acceptance.[58]

We favour the conventional view that the analysis should attempt to measure costs and benefits of planning schemes according to the principles outlined earlier. But, in addition, the analyst should, wherever practicable, present the resulting distributions of costs and benefits in terms of useful incidence groups. Participants in the decision-making process may *then* debate the relevance or otherwise of particular considerations of fairness and justice in the light of the information available.[59]

Two practical problems of some importance exist before this analysis and presentation of results may be achieved. Firstly, the definition of relevant incidence groups has to be decided upon in advance of the analysis. Preferably these groups should be defined by the decision-takers, so that the presentation can be made accordingly, as they are responsible for deciding the desirable distribution of gains and losses. It may not, however, for a number of different reasons always be possible to obtain their requirements. Decision-takers may possibly be inaccessible to the study team; or they may be diverse groups of individuals and hence not readily available for contact; or they may not be able to agree amongst themselves; or they may simply be unable or unwilling to say in advance which groups they are most interested in. In these cases the responsibility for defining incidence groups will reside in practice with the analysts undertaking the evaluation, who will try to assess which classification of groups will be most useful.

In PBSA the incidence of costs and benefits is stressed. The convention used is that incidence groups should be based on a functional classification, which is adapted from problem to problem as appropriate. The classification has been based on those groups who produce and operate the new developments, on the one hand, and those who consume the goods and services arising from those developments, on the other

[57]These two views are discussed in S. K. Nath, Are formal welfare criteria required?, *Econ. J.* **74** (1964) 548–77.

[58]See, for example, the following. O. Eckstein, A survey of the theory of public expenditure criteria, in J. M. Buchanan (ed.), *Public Finances: Needs, Sources and Utilization*, Princeton University Press, Princeton, 1961. C. D. Foster, Social welfare functions in cost–benefit analysis, in J. R. Lawrence (ed.), *Operational Research and the Social Sciences*, Tavistock, London, 1966, pp. 305–18. B. A. Weisbrod, Income redistribution effects and benefit–cost analysis, in S. B. Chase (ed.), *Problems in Public Expenditure Analysis*, the Brookings Institution, Washington DC, 1968, pp. 177–208. J. Wise *et al.*, *Evidence Submitted at Stage V to the Commission on the Third London Airport on behalf of Buckingham CC*, March 1970.

[59]N. Lichfield, Cost–benefit analysis in planning: a critique of the Roskill Commission, *Regional Studies* **5** (1971) 157–83.

hand. Some examples of groups might be residential occupiers of new developments, displaced industrialists, travellers on the road network, and so on. The main reason for adopting a functionalist approach is that it helps the analyst in preparing the balance sheet by offering a systematic procedure where no relevant groups are likely to be omitted, and the decision-taker when he poses the question, Which groups in society are likely to be affected by the proposals? But there is no need to be restricted to this approach to sectors if it is known in advance that such a classification will not really help those taking the decision. Groups based on income or other aspects of comparative social deprivation, or on geographic location, kind of gain or loss experienced, taxpaying category, or whatever, could well be used in the PBS.

The second practical difficulty is that of measuring the true impact of costs and benefits according to these groups. At present our techniques of measurement are so insufficiently developed that many, including cost–benefit practitioners, seriously doubt whether some important effects of proposals can be measured at all. But difficult though problems of obtaining measures of "average" values may be, in order to trace incidence we require additional data and still more sophisticated modelling techniques. This is because the ultimate incidence of costs and benefits depends not only on the nature of the planning proposals but also on the system of taxation and subsidies, the status of legal compensation for losses, the way individuals may choose to pass on their gains to other groups, and the structure and ownership of real property. Thus the search for information relevant to equity considerations makes our current measurement capabilities even more inadequate.

There are many problems of choice where CBA cannot, as yet, be particularly helpful in providing evidence as to people's values, either because no evidence exists or because prediction of the consequences of schemes is too difficult. But here the framework of the analysis can still be helpful.[60] The approach to itemizing costs and benefits and also to the measuring of costs or benefits can be used by decision-takers in helping to remove some of the obscurities, fallacies, and obfuscations which surround complex issues. Further, when formal analysis of the consequences of proposals is impossible, it may prove useful to place the inevitable guesses about them (by decision-makers, experts, and others) in the framework of the analysis. That is, some participants in the decision process could attempt to guess at the likely values that members of the community would hold about the consequences of the proposals. The approach imposes a discipline on guesswork which might otherwise tend to degenerate, and was adopted in the Peterborough Study,[61] although it was not there suggested that judgements by members of the planning team was a substitute for full analysis of preferences, but a necessary second-best in the absence of information.

[60]N. Lichfield, Cost–benefit analysis in city planning, *J. Am. Inst. Planners* **26** (1960) 273–9; and Cost–benefit analysis in plan evaluation, *Town Planning Rev.* **35** (1964) 160–9.
[61]N. Lichfield, Cost–benefit analysis in urban expansion—a case study: Peterborough, *Regional Studies* **3** (1969) 123–55.

But the guesswork itself can be further disciplined by providing partial evidence on values in the cost–benefit framework. Where items cannot be reliably measured in units of common relative value such as money (the incommensurables), it is possible to measure in physical terms. Then there are items which cannot be measured to indicate the extent of the difference between alternative schemes, but for which some ranking of schemes is possible by using proxy indicators. Both kinds of item should be included in the analysis to extend the measurement of effects as far as practicable. There can be no good reason to exclude them from the evaluation, for they provide some information for decision-takers, although it is less than that provided by commensurable items. This was undertaken in the Swanley Study.[62]

Clearly the usefulness of any cost–benefit study depends, *inter alia*, on the quality of the evidence on values. For many planning studies the community costs and benefits are "internal" in the sense that proposals have a direct consequence for the planning agency's costs of operation, and thus suitable evidence may be comparatively easy to obtain. But evidence on externalities, especially of pollution and environment, is far more difficult to obtain. It must be admitted that insufficient research has been undertaken to inspire confidence in many of the estimates of these kinds of consequences. The estimates generated by elegant modelling exercises for aircraft noise nuisance in the debate on the Third London Airport were, in the final reckoning, only informed "guesses" (although this was a classic case of how the cost–benefit approach could be used to guess at community values in a constructive manner, using whatever limited information was available). Yet the difficulties surrounding the problems of obtaining useful evidence of values for many public goods or "bads" do not seem to be completely insurmountable. We do not agree with the view that research into these topics is unlikely to prove fruitful.[63] But it is true that present CBAs are likely to be of more limited help to decision-takers in planning studies where pollution effects are dominant than in other areas of planning concern. This point also applies to other evaluation methodologies.

We have tried both to show the potential usefulness of the cost–benefit approach as a planning tool and to meet some of the objections to its use in urban and regional planning. The approach has its problems, both conceptual and practical, which limit its usefulness. But we agree with Prest and Turvey[64] that, "The case for using cost–benefit analysis is strengthened, not weakened, if its limitations are openly recognized and indeed emphasized". Limitations of a technique are relative. We believe the approach to evaluation afforded by CBA to be more rigorous and enlightening than other methodologies. This is not, in itself, a justification, even if the view is accepted. It would have to be shown that CBA (and any evaluation exercise) is also worth undertaking. That must remain a matter of judgement. However, we believe there is sufficient evidence from published case studies to suggest that the

[62]N. Lichfield, Cost–benefit analysis in urban redevelopment—a case study: Swanley, *Urban Studies* 3 (1966) 215–49.

[63]As implied in M. E. Paul, Can aircraft noise nuisance be measured in money? *Oxford Economic Papers* 23 (1971) 297–322.

[64]A. R. Prest and R. Turvey, Cost–benefit analysis: a survey, *Econ. J.* 75 (1965) 203.

approach can in practice lead to the asking of the right questions and can provide some, at least, of the broadly correct answers.

A Rational Decision-making Model

A very obvious feature of urban and regional planning procedures is that there are many diverse participants in the decision-making process. First, there are often many decision-takers, as ultimate responsibility may reside with a committee. Then the debate is widespread: many of the participants have different sectoral interests to foster. Clearly, information upon which the debate is based should not cater for the requirements of any one particular individual or group. But why should it be desirable to construct a fully comprehensive set of social accounts in the manner we have advocated?

If the debate is wide there are obvious advantages in presenting as much information and evidence as possible to all involved groups. This makes all participants more fully aware of the likely implications of particular alternative courses of action and of the evidence which was used in the evaluation, the quality of which may then be discussed. Planners may also be under pressure through public opinion to make known the "full consequences" of proposals when these are revealed. Particular groups may, of course, have an interest in suppressing some of the information. Some may argue the case for not publishing evaluation results on the grounds that typically the exercises are too complex and difficult for the non-practitioner and could mislead, or be used in order to mislead. This problem is accepted, but appears to us to be less important than the risks involved in not disseminating information widely.

The decision-making process will vary from planning issue to planning issue. Political decisions characteristically do not conform to a particular and consistent rule. Accordingly, it is not legitimate to suppose that the eventual information on which judgements are formed will be of any particular variety. Before it is known how particular decisions will eventually be made, the scope of information requirements needs to be wide.

Different individuals will probably form different views of the relative merits of alternative courses of action. (Indeed, the same individuals when acting in different roles, are likely to assess choice situations differently.) Any information made available should therefore be capable of interpretation. Its reliability and scope should be assessed, and ethical judgements should be pinpointed. Such judgements will mainly relate to matters of justice and fairness, and whether decision-takers *should* base their decisions on community preferences. The quality of the evidence collected would clearly be a subject of debate, as would equity issues associated with the incidence effects that had been identified. The evaluation would thus provide a starting point for debate. We concur with McKean[65] in believing that the evaluation should be the decision-takers' "consumer" research—the information base upon

[65]R. McKean, 1968, *op. cit.*, p. 138.

which to form judgements. A method of evaluation must therefore be adopted which allows for this. Just as in day-to-day life the decisions of individuals are considered poorly founded if some of the resulting costs and benefits are ignored, or are inadequately perceived or measured, so does this apply in urban and regional planning.

Decision-takers will often not know what kind of information can be made available, or even what information would be useful. Certainly they will not be aware of the technical know-how available for estimating various consequences of proposals. Subject to reasonable limits on the costs of information collection it would seem foolish for planning decisions, like any other decision, to be made without reasonably complete information of the full consequences. Thus, information should be obtained and evidence assembled on the wide implications of planning decisions.

Within the context of existing institutions and practice, our preferred mode of decision-making is as follows. In the course of the planning process the planning team will generate a set of alternatives to be submitted to the process of decision-making. (During this process all of these may be rejected, in which case the process must start again, but one or other of the alternatives could be selected for implementation.) As well as generating the alternatives, the planning team also produce information on their relative advantages and disadvantages, i.e. the evaluation. This evaluation, if it is to provide for all decision-making contingencies, must be comprehensive. That is, it must attempt to assess advantages and disadvantages to all individuals or groups of individuals who will be affected, and it must do so for all effects which may contribute to or reduce their well-being. This evaluation must be impartial in the sense that no particular group is given either special attention or is left out. It is the decision-takers' function to decide the importance, in their view, of making some groups better off and some worse off. Professional officers should not, in our opinion, contribute as professionals to the debate on equity matters unless asked to do so by the decision-takers.

Evaluation by CBA principles aims to provide evidence of the effects of proposals as perceived by each affected group. It attempts to identify who would be affected, in what way, and by how much. We believe that from this comprehensive information "better" decisions will emerge from the debate. We do not have in mind any particular choice criterion; selection of these is left to the participants in decision-making. But we would like to be able to identify all the welfare effects, their relative valuations, and—as far as practicable—their ultimate incidence. We would hope that the evidence marshalled about physical effects and the strengths of interests could be debated along with the fairness and justice of the distributions of gains and losses. True, this high aim is rarely achievable in practice, but the PBS adaptation of CBA does try to overcome some of the practical problems. It provides a systematic framework within which consequences and their incidence can be traced, which helps to reduce the possibility of oversight, and which places costs and benefits against the groups affected.

We accept that we still have a long way to go before costs and benefits are reasonably well measured. We accept that we have even further to go in modelling the incidence of welfare effects. But whilst accepting its present limitations, the PBS insists that the best information currently available should be used, even when (reluctantly) this information is based on only "informed guesswork" and therefore to be treated with caution. We can always debate our best efforts, even if they are known not to be as satisfactory as we should like. As modelling and measurement techniques improve so too will PBS evaluations, and CBAs generally.

More importantly, however, we believe it is possible to achieve far better insights than otherwise by utilizing the cost–benefit *approach*, preferably as adapted for the complex problems of choice in urban and regional planning in the PBSA. That is, we should always think in terms of comprehensiveness, of groups affected, the nature of their preferences, and the likely magnitude of costs and benefits to be incurred or enjoyed. Given existing decision-making procedures, we believe the rational approach is to provide decision-takers and the community with the best possible information for debate and choice. If the decisions may not always appear to be rational we should still not rule out the rational approach.[66] For this we must collect independent and comprehensive information not only on the physical effects of proposals but also on the relative values of members of the community, and set that evidence down in a logical frame of reference. There is a *prima facie* case for publication of this independent evaluation exercise (undertaken by the planning team), at least for major issues, in order that its significance and findings can be debated prior to the decision. This type of procedure appears to us as rational and defensible.

[66]N. Lichfield, Cost–benefit analysis in town planning, in Lawrence (ed.), 1966, *op. cit.*, pp. 337–45.

CHAPTER 5

A Comparison of the Planning Balance Sheet with the Goals–Achievement Matrix Method of Evaluation

HAVING expressed our preference for the social cost–benefit approach to evaluation, in the planning balance sheet (PBS) form, and having tried to justify our views by drawing out the main advantages of the approach, we shall now make a critical comparison of the PBS with the goals–achievement matrix (GAM), currently in the United Kingdom the most widely used of the other methods. The purpose of this comparison is to clarify the *relative* strengths and weaknesses of the two methods as a guide to their use by urban and regional planners.

The methods are compared first by showing their origins and development in the writings of their respective authors, Lichfield and Hill, and then by contrasting the way they deal with four central issues that must be faced in undertaking any evaluation exercise. The comparison ends with a brief summary and some concluding observations.

5.1. ORIGINS AND DEVELOPMENT OF THE METHODS

The conceptual development of the PBS method took place during the 1950s and early 1960s.[1] It was devised as a generally applicable aid to reaching decisions on urban and regional planning proposals. In essence, Lichfield proposed a particular *framework* within which the methodology of social cost–benefit analysis (SCBA) could successfully be applied. At that time the practice of SCBA within the public sector was in its infancy, and he argued that the application of such an approach would introduce some much-needed rigour into the urban and regional planning process. Planning agencies, it was argued, may properly be regarded as supra-invest-

---

[1] The method's characteristics were explained in N. Lichfield, *Economics of Planned Development*, Estates Gazette, London, 1956, part IV; and 1960, *op. cit.*, pp. 273–9. The method was first demonstrated in three case studies prepared in 1960: N. Lichfield, *Cost–Benefit Analysis in Urban Redevelopment*, Research Report 20, Real Estate Research Program, University of California, Berkeley, 1962.

ment agencies, since through their policies they provide a framework for the investment decisions of many others (various private organizations and also other public
bodies), in addition to undertaking projects themselves. Since economists had developed SCBA for the specific purpose of assisting decisions on investment
opportunities in the public sector, and given the nature of urban and regional
planning proposals requiring decisions, it was considered appropriate to utilize that
kind of analysis in the planning field. It was for this reason that the PBS was founded
on the principles and techniques of SCBA.

The matter has been put as follows:[2]

"Planning analysis . . . starts with this wide-ranging concept of needing to take
account of all the costs and benefits that are likely to flow from the decision at
hand (subject to the necessary cut-offs from the viewpoint of the decision maker
and the problem at hand) and also the need to consider the incidence of repercussions. But planning analysis unhappily has lacked the rigorous tools which would
enable it to pursue this complex path and come up with a decision which was
demonstrably the best in the public interest, that is having the maximum net
advantage to the community as a whole. It was in the recognition that cost-benefit
analysis techniques could be adapted for this purpose, without any loss to the
objectives of the planners, that led to the formulation of the planning balance
sheet analysis technique."

Over the years PBSA itself has been developed largely through practical
application to a range of studies. Although advances have been made in techniques
of quantifying costs and benefits, it has not been found necessary to change the basic
framework and approach of the analysis since the initial studies in 1960. In particular
the "Table A" has remained the centre piece of the analysis (though presented in
varying forms). This table has been devised to present in easily understood form the
differential impacts of proposals on various groups within the community who are
affected.

Hill first discussed the GAM method in his doctoral thesis of 1966 where he
presented it in detail, with summary accounts following soon after.[3] He developed
the method as an attempt to overcome what he viewed to be weaknesses in existing
evaluation methods, particularly with regard to conventional SCBA and to the PBS.
Hill argued that neither of these satisfied the requirements of "rational" planning
which, with respect to resource allocation, he defined as "a process for determining
appropriate future action by utilizing scarce resources in such a way as to maximize
the attainment of ends held by the system". This definition implies that an evaluation
of alternative plans should consist of a comparative assessment with respect to their

---

[2]N. Lichfield, Cost–benefit analysis in planning: a critique of the Roskill Commission, *Regional Studies*
5 (1971) p. 174.

[3]M. Hill, A method for evaluating alternative plans: the goals–achievement matrix applied to
transportation plans, PhD dissertation, University of Pennsylvania, 1966. For summary accounts see M.
Hill, A method for the evaluation of transportation plans, *Highway Res. Record*, No. 180 (1967) 21–34; and
A goals–achievement matrix for evaluating alternative plans, *J. Am. Inst. Planners* **34** (1968) 19–29.

extent of achievement of specified ends (or objectives) of the "system" under consideration.

Hill recognized that the PBS aimed at overcoming his objections to conventional SCBA. What is of interest here, therefore, is his view of the weakness of PBSA in fulfilling the requirements of rational planning. In his thesis Hill criticized PBSA primarily for its lack of attention to objectives as such. The costs and benefits contained in the balance sheet did relate to a range of community objectives. But in omitting an *explicit* statement of those objectives, Hill argued that the method did not appear to recognize that items of benefit and cost have meaning only in relation to particular objectives. The criticism was that costs and benefits were treated as if they did not depend for their "existence" and validity upon the achievement of particular objectives; that is, as if they possessed independent value. Accordingly, it was argued that Lichfield's criterion for choice, of maximizing net benefits to the community, was meaningless if specified in the abstract. The point that objectives should be made *explicit* in evaluation was accepted by Lichfield as a valid criticism in relation to early applications of his method. Indeed, he had begun to remedy this before Hill had completed his thesis. Objectives of various sectors of the community were explicitly introduced into his Cambridge Study[4] in 1962–4, and the role of objectives in his method was stressed further in a study immediately following of planning proposals for Swanley, in Kent.[5] The stating of objectives has made PBSA clearer and helped to focus attention on the preferences of those groups affected. The treatment of objectives has been a matter for continuing development.

In his thesis Hill also made a critique of a specific PBS case study (mentioned above), that of redevelopment proposals for the City of Cambridge, and then demonstrated the GAM method by using the same case in an attempt to show how it could be applied with better advantage. For this he adapted Table A of the PBSA, introducing certain changes in the format. The revised version then became the matrix used in his own approach. Hill does not explain specifically the differences between the displays contained in a typical PBS Table A and his matrix. However, this would seem to amount simply to the introduction of weights as between different groups within the community and the weighting of objectives (in addition to that of groups) in advance of the comparative analysis of plans. The matter of *a priori* weighting is one of the significant differences between the methods, as discussed below. Despite the wish to take equity matters into account, the PBS has not recorded any weighting between groups (except in two illustrative cases) because of the difficulty of ascertaining a relevant set of ethical judgements from the decision-takers.

The methods have been developed differently in practice. As indicated, PBSA has been matured through application to a wide range of planning problems and in

[4]N. Lichfield, *Cost Benefit Analysis in Town Planning: A Case Study of Cambridge*, Cambridgeshire and Isle of Ely CC, Cambridge, 1966 (see table A, pp. 58–61).

[5]N. Lichfield, Cost–benefit analysis in town planning—a case study: Swanley, *Urban Studies* **3** (1966) 215–49.

writings by the originator and his colleagues. Although it has rarely been attempted by others under that name, it has influenced the nature of a number of evaluation exercises using SCBA principles. In contrast, Hill has carried out no substantial applications of the GAM, although he has developed selected aspects in the literature, notably indices of measurement and the application of scaling techniques. Concurrently, various planning teams in Britain have over recent years carried out plan evaluation using approaches based on the GAM. In this they have introduced certain interpretations of Hill's work and adaptation of what he has proposed. This situation makes it difficult to decide on the relevant literature for the following comparison. We have chosen here to compare the methods by drawing for the GAM almost entirely on the writings of Hill himself and referring to the PBS in general terms, calling on evidence from particular studies where appropriate. Our discussions in Part II contain a detailed consideration of two applications of the GAM approach and one application of the PBS.

5.2. THE METHODS AND CENTRAL ISSUES IN EVALUATION

As indicated above, the GAM was introduced by Hill as a departure from SCBA and PBSA. It might therefore be thought simple to trace the nature of the departure. But this proved not to be so. A more operational approach is therefore used here, which is to contrast the methods in relation to central issues that have to be faced in evaluation. These are:

(a) scope of the analysis and its relationship to decision-taking;
(b) formulation of the relevant set of objectives by which to compare alternatives;
(c) measurement of the achievement of objectives;
(d) incorporation of equity considerations.

Scope of Analysis and Its Relationship to Decision-taking

Both methods claim to be comprehensive in scope in that they each purport to provide a framework for analysing all factors that should be taken into account in making decisions on urban and regional planning proposals. Neither is intended as a substitute for the decisions themselves; both aim to provide information to assist those responsible for decision-taking and to facilitate general debate on alternatives. Whilst they provide the basis for the decision, it should be noted that neither is designed to take explicit account of political repercussions; that is, the effects on the elected representatives which stem from action by those members of the community who will be directly affected by the decisions made.

The authors of the methods also agree that the taking and justification of decisions on urban and regional planning proposals should be based on some conception of the "public interest". That is, they argue that such decisions should take account of the interests of the community at large, and not of some particular interests at the disregard and expense of others.

This leads us to two critical questions: Who is to constitute the relevant community?, and (having defined that community) What precisely is meant by the "public interest"?

Establishing the relevant community revolves around a "boundary" problem. When repercussions of proposals extend beyond the geographic area of political jurisdiction by the decision-taking body, should the analysis take account of the effects on those living outside its territory? Hill does not discuss this issue directly, but he implies that it should be determined by the decision-taking body. It is probable that decision-takers will take account of the well-being of individuals outside their area of jurisdiction only insofar as those individuals or their governments may bring influence to bear, directly or indirectly, on their personal preferences or objectives. Whether any "outsiders" whose well-being is potentially affected will be deemed to have any such significance is any empirical matter.

PBS analysis proceeds according to the view that any extraterritorial welfare effect is in principle relevant for investigation. This reflects the tenet that decision-takers should always be confronted, if possible, with all the welfare effects of proposals, regardless of to whom they apply. There are a number of reasons why information on extraterritorial effects may be useful. In a national planning issue, for instance, the citizens of that country, and thereby its government, may wish to act altruistically. But even if the decision will be made in relation only to the welfare of the domestic community, there may, nonetheless, be advantages in analysing and stating the effects on foreign communities. In particular, there may be a danger of foreign retaliation. If the British Government in making its decisions excludes costs and benefits to foreigners, other countries may retaliate by excluding welfare effects on British citizens in arriving at their own government decisions. On balance, the British community might become worse off in choosing to ignore foreigners.

Given the existence of a defined community, there are a variety of different conceptions of the nature of the public interest; that is, as to its constituent elements.[6] What is to be regarded as "good" for society (or an "improvement") is ultimately a matter of ethical judgement. Hill *deliberately* leaves open the question of which particular conception of the public interest is to be employed. He treats the goals which are relevant for evaluation as "givens" and simply notes the different approaches to identifying the relevant goals implicit in certain conceptions of the public interest. He is concerned hardly at all with the process of formulating the goals themselves:

"It is assumed that the choice of the mechanism for identifying community goals has been made—this being a major value judgement—and that by means of this mechanism the array of goals held by the community and groups with the community has been established. It is also assumed that the relative valuation of these goals has been determined. ..."[7]

[6]See, for instance, the classification given in M. Meyerson and E. C. Banfield, *Politics, Planning and the Public Interest: The Case of Public Housing in Chicago*, Free Press of Glencoe, New York, 1965, pp. 322–9.

[7]Hill, 1966, *op. cit.*, p. 37.

The analyst thus has no guidance on principles to govern the approach to be adopted.[8] By admitting the whole variety of views, Hill's method acquires maximum generality, and therefore offers the widest possible potential use.

As it has been practised, PBSA takes a markedly different view. It is based on the notion that the public interest consists of some aggregation of all the interests or preferences of everyone who comprises society: it is based on an individualistic conception. In addition, the view is taken that the public interest is not necessarily a simple summation of individuals' gains and losses. The significance of a given amount of gain or loss for the welfare of society as a whole may differ with the recipient. However, the desirability of alternative distributions of gains and losses, being a matter of ethical judgement, is left for political decision. In addition it is recognized that private valuations may not be a suitable basis for social evaluation; for instance, decision-takers may consider that they give insufficient regard to future generations.

There are two further aspects of the scope of the methods which require brief consideration. The first concerns the nature of choice; the second relates to the comparison of projects within different sectors of planning activity such as transport, recreation, and housing.

On the first, the methods are similar in that they have both been designed to deal with problems involving mutually exclusive alternatives, the projects constituting alternative ways of tackling particular problems. Although the PBS may be used to assess whether a project is worth undertaking as opposed to some other use for the resources, in practice it is normally used to assess the relative merits of a set of defined alternatives, one of which it is assumed will be implemented. The GAM treats the desirability of the projects in question as given. But, since it is also possible to compare the levels of goals–achievement in a "do-nothing" situation with changes in those levels which are likely to result from a particular project, there seems little difference here between the two methods.

The GAM was developed for assessing alternatives within single-functional sectors (such as water resources or transport), where the activities and associated land uses are planned and managed as distinct operations. Hill suggested that his procedure could not be used for comparing alternatives involving multi-sectoral projects, because it does not register the interaction and interdependence of objectives relevant to different sectors. However, it would seem that unless the analyst is faced with having to identify the optimal alternative, application of the GAM does not require an understanding of the way in which the achievement of one objective affects the level of achievement of others. Planning teams have applied the method to proposals embracing a variety of types of urban developments. The experience now gained from its use on the Coventry–Solihull–Warwickshire Sub-regional Study and the Brighton Urban Structure Plan Study has shown that in practice this particular difficulty feared by Hill is not a real one.

The PBS was specifically developed to deal with the multi-sector characteristic of

---

[8]He may either adopt his own personal view or seek guidance from the elected representatives of the community or adopt a view in the hope that it will be relevant to decision-takers.

planning proposals. It takes a system-wide view of the consequences of proposals. Although the interaction between objectives of different sectors of planning activity is not regarded as a source of conceptual difficulty in evaluation, it may present practical problems of prediction.

Formulation of Objectives

We shall consider three main aspects of formulating objectives for evaluation:

(1) Whose interests or preferences are to be taken into account—i.e. evaluation from whose viewpoint?
(2) To which kinds of consequences do the objectives relate? (e.g. do they embrace variables other than those conventionally thought of in planning practice as strictly "economic"?).
(3) Who should formulate objectives and by what procedures?

In any evaluation it is necessary to determine whose interests are to be taken into account. Having done this, one must then determine what those interests are and how they are likely to be affected by planning proposals; that is, what influence the planning activity in question will bring to bear on them.

In his first exposition of the GAM, Hill stressed the necessity to establish the objectives of the planners' "clients". The clients were described ambiguously as those persons affected by the planning proposals.[9] It was not made clear, for instance, whether all those affected in any way were to be considered, nor whether all the interests of those deemed relevant were to count. However, Hill has recently clarified his position in a personal communication. In his view it is the responsibility of the analyst to identify *all* people whose well-being will be affected in some way by the planning proposals, and to determine how they will be affected. The elected representatives should then decide whose interests ought to count in choosing between the alternatives. This view follows PBS practice.

Hill has also drawn a distinction between objectives held by various groups of individuals within the community and other objectives relating to the community as a whole, the latter being identified by decision-takers. He writes:

"The objectives of the community, as perceived by its formal decision-making body as well as the objectives of the various sectors of the community that are affected by the plans are identified.... The implications of plans for both community objectives and sectoral objectives are (then) determined...."[10]

Although Hill states that both kinds of objectives are to be taken into account, he does not define what is meant by "community objectives" beyond saying that they are perceived by those elected representatives who are responsible for taking the decision. The possibility must be discounted that Hill is interested in including, for

[9]Hill, 1966, *op. cit.*, p. 12.
[10]M. Hill, The fallacy of "The cost–benefit fallacy", *Official Architect. Planning* 35 (1972) 103–4.

evaluation purposes, the objectives of individuals in their capacity as decision-takers. Another possibility is that they are intended to represent objectives pertaining to the community as a corporate entity or body politic, having an existence in some sense distinct from its individual members. Whether such objectives exist is a metaphysical matter, and how they would be measured and assessed is therefore open to question. Again Hill has recently clarified this matter in a personal communication. The nature of his community objectives, and the persons responsible for their formulation, will depend on the way the public interest is defined in any particular community. Hence, as with the concept of the public interest, Hill deliberately leaves the definition open, to be resolved afresh in each planning study.

In contrast, PBSA proceeds according to the principle of estimating the effects of proposals in terms of the interests of all members of the community likely to be directly affected, either beneficially or adversely. The objectives specified are meant to express the preferences of individuals, or groups of individuals with broadly homogeneous preferences, relating to the consequences of proposals which will affect their particular interests. Besides being termed "sectoral", these objectives are also described as "instrumental", since they are valued for their effects on individual welfare rather than for themselves. Thus, time savings, or a wide range of choice in retail provision, for instance, would be included in a PBS assessment because they contribute to an individual's level of well-being. It is recognized that items of consumption are alternative means of increasing a person's well-being, and are therefore substitutable.

The notion of community objectives clearly represents an area of significant difference between the methods. With the GAM it is argued that there exists objectives over and above gains and losses to members of society. The PBS always treats proposals in terms of welfare gains and losses for all those who comprise society. It is true that "society", through its government, may have stated objectives, but in PBSA these are treated as no more than representative of categories of sectoral objectives, which need to be clarified as such in order to avoid confusion resulting from the use of generalized statements.

An illustration of the PBS view is provided by an evaluation of some recent national new town development proposals for Israel.[11] Dispersal of population was thought a desirable aim for the proposals: but why was this so? Israel has several "national objectives", some of which are likely to be affected by decisions on population and employment dispersals to its new towns. These objectives related to defence, settlement of the land, spreading Jewish influence, and so on. They could in turn be divided into more detailed categories of objectives, and further questions asked: Which groups would be defended? In what way? What other ways of defending them could be found? The PBS could then begin to break down the general policy objective of population and employment dispersal into its sectoral objective components. However, in practice this procedure was not followed.

---

[11]N. Lichfield and M. Whitbread, Evaluation of the hypotheses, in *Israel's New Towns: A Development Strategy*, Institute for Planning and Development, Tel Aviv, 1971, ch. 11.

Instead, alternative designs were generated that were each assumed to meet the dispersal objective to at least an acceptable minimum extent. The alternatives were then evaluated according to objectives specified by the planning team for the sectors affected: these objectives related to benefits for new town residents, the outputs of the manufacturing sector, the costs of construction and provision of infrastructure, and so forth. No firm conclusion could be reached about the desirability of dispersal as such, but the relative advantages and disadvantages of alternative forms of population dispersal were thereby expressed. Since a "natural trends" alternative was also included in the designs, some opportunity cost estimates of dispersal were derived.

We have stressed that in PBSA the scope of costs and benefits ranges wider than those popularly thought of as "economic". As well as those entering directly into the production and consumption process by virtue of market transaction, it includes all associated external costs and benefits. The evaluation attempts to take account of all consequences of proposals (both positive and negative) to those whose well-being will be affected. Thus, the disruptive effects of a motorway on existing networks of social relationships would be a matter for inclusion in the evaluation.

Hill also contends that many objectives other than "economic" ones are relevant to decisions on planning proposals. In his schema the objectives are said to be derived explicitly from a consideration of ideals, and so their scope is conditioned by the nature of the ideals deemed relevant. In considering transport proposals in his initial formulation, Hill put forward the following ideals: health, happiness, peace of mind, choice and opportunity, economic welfare, and social justice. Later, in a paper with Mordechai Shechter on the planning of recreation facilities,[12] he suggested another group (some of which overlap with those just listed)—physical and mental health, enjoyment, equity, economic welfare, social stability, and ecological balance.

Efficiency and equity are included within the many ideals that Hill postulates. However, in SCBA most economists would subsume under these two heads all or virtually all of the other ideals listed. The reasons why Hill postulates ideals separate from considerations of efficiency and equity are twofold. Firstly, he contends that whilst SCBA practitioners generally pay lip-service to intangibles, they do not really enter the analysis, and that as a result efficiency has in practice been equated with the maximization of the value of *market* goods and services. Secondly, and more important, Hill views the *economist's concept* of efficiency (i.e. aggregate consumption of all goods and bads) as too narrow for evaluation purposes, even if distributional matters are taken into account, contending that there are a number of dimensions of welfare other than the aggregate amount and distribution of consumption. He cites economists such as Marglin[13] to support this view. This is an interesting and controversial area of debate (as well as one fraught with difficulties), but it need not detain us here. Since in PBSA the attempt is made to identify and

[12]M. Hill and M. Shechter, Optimal goal achievement in the development of outdoor recreation facilities, in A. G. Wilson (ed.), *Urban and Regional Planning*, Pion, London, 1971, pp. 110–20.
[13]See S. A. Marglin, *Public Investment Criteria*, Allen & Unwin, London, 1967, pp. 37–8.

measure changes in the total well-being of all those affected in the community, such an evaluation must be as comprehensive as a GAM analysis that incorporates ideals relating to individual welfare. The difference is that the PBS does not seek to distinguish between different dimensions of welfare. Rather, the sectoral objectives used relate to those plan consequences which affect people's welfare; it seeks to be comprehensive through the identification of welfare effects.

We turn now to consider procedures for formulating objectives and who has responsibility for the objectives that are adopted. Unfortunately, Hill nowhere indicates how objectives might be derived from a set of specified ideals. Instead, he addresses himself directly to the problem of establishing objectives. Apparently his description of the relationship between ideals and objectives is intended largely for conceptual purposes rather than for practical guidance. He argues that in setting objectives the analyst should seek guidance from the elected representatives, since in constitutional democracies it is generally agreed that ultimate responsibility for the objectives pursued by public agencies should reside with them. "In general, the problem of setting objectives . . . ought to be approached from a particular theory of government. In a constitutional democratic state, for instance, there is general agreement that elected representatives should have ultimate responsibility."[14] But he rightly suggests that it will probably prove very difficult in practice to get elected officials to state these objectives, and points out that the problem of determining them in planning situations is much too complex and varied to assume the existence of a single universally applicable approach. A number of approaches which planners might adopt are suggested. Direct approaches include consultations with elected officials, consultations with members of community interest groups, sampling of various "publics" in the community, and public hearings. Among the indirect approaches which might be employed are the analysis of patterns of behaviour of community groups and of previous allocations of public investments in order to determine the implicit goal priorities. "In any event", Hill concludes, "it is desirable to approach the determination and valuation of community objectives from different points of view, simultaneously."[15]

Although Hill suggests those whom the planners might "consult" and various ways in which this might be done, he does not discuss what constitutes satisfactory *evidence* in support of postulated objectives nor what must be done to obtain it. To say, for instance, that the planner might obtain evidence from analysing the behaviour of groups in the community is not by itself very helpful. It is necessary for us to know what principles and techniques of analysis should be used and what inferences we may hope to draw from the information obtained. Hill avoids discussion of these substantial issues.

In marked contrast, the procedure adopted in PBSA relies to a substantial degree on a well-debated set of principles. These principles are not unique to the PBS, but

---

[14]Hill, 1968, *op. cit.*, p. 27. Although he does not say so, the presumption must be that planners should attempt to ascertain the ideals from the elected representatives also.

[15]*Ibid.*

are based on the methodology of SCBA. Thus as far as practicable in PBSA, empirical evidence is obtained as to the direction of preferences of individuals or groups in the community (i.e. Will they prefer to experience greater or lesser amounts of each item of consequence?). If revealed preference analysis cannot be employed, the analyst might attempt as a second-best approach some experimental gaming (in which the individual's behaviour is observed under simulated conditions). This is thought to be generally superior to any form of survey of public opinions and attitudes concerning postulated objectives and far superior to the use of intuition from experience. However, resort to intuition has been made in some PBS studies when there was very limited evidence available about the nature of individuals' preferences.[16] In these cases the guesses were treated as hypotheses about the actual preferences of affected groups, and were offered for comment and possible testing at a later date.

Measurement of Objective Achievements

Once the objectives for evaluation have been specified it is necessary to attempt to measure the extent to which the alternatives put forward will achieve those objectives if adopted, so producing evidence of their advantages and disadvantages (or their benefits and costs). In the previous chapter we gave some attention to the approach adopted in PBSA, which is based on SCBA principles. Despite continuing debates, including those on intangibles and equity considerations, the methodological base of the conventional SCBA approach to measurement has a soundness and consistency which is founded in theory. As we have already suggested, Hill's schema is thin on matters of measurement. Indeed, in our view this is the weakest part of the GAM. To avoid unnecessary repetition of the SCBA discussion, we focus here on the measurement possibilities in the GAM and show where we believe the weaknesses lie. It should be stressed, however, that both Lichfield and Hill are of the view that quantification of the impacts of planning proposals is desirable.

There are two essential measurement problems in assessing the performance of plans. First is the measurement of the "physical" impacts of the proposals; for example, acres of recreational open space lost through new urban development, and the time spent travelling and agricultural output lost when rural motorways are constructed. Second is the conversion of these impacts measured in physical or index units into common units of value, requiring measurement of their relative importance. (These concepts are discussed more fully in the next chapter.)

Hill has proposed a variety of index measures for specific items of impact, but has not adequately debated the principles he would regard as suitable for empirical testing of their validity. Nor has he adequately discussed the principles he would propose for the relative valuation of these impacts.

[16]See, for instance, N. Lichfield, Cost benefit analysis in urban expansion—a case study: Peterborough, *Regional Studies* **3** (1969) 123–55.

Consider, first, the subject of indices. In his paper with Shechter[17] on the provision of outdoor recreation facilities, indices were constructed by which to assess the achievement of objectives relating to distributional equity, the preservation of natural areas, choice and public participation in the use of the proposed facilities. For none of the objectives were alternative indices described or debated. The indices actually put forward were not examined against any evidence of their suitability for the purpose at hand. Yet by using different values for the parameters within the indices, or by adding to or changing their dimensions, it would be possible to alter the index values obtained, and thereby the findings of the evaluation. Without substantiation therefore the indices proposed are arbitrary. This is perhaps recognized in the paper which states that it was not addressed to the vital problem of empirical estimation of the indices proposed. It was argued that "the effectiveness of the suggested indices could be enhanced by additional theoretical and empirical research". But we do not know what kind of evidence the authors would regard as suitable for purposes of empirical testing, since no information is given on the principles of measurement of objectives. We are concerned at Hill's reluctance to debate these principles.

By contrast, the physical measures selected for use in PBSA are, as far as practicable in the circumstances, ones which have been checked by a "calibration" procedure against people's perceptions, derived wherever possible by obtaining direct evidence of their behaviour with respect to the phenomena under consideration. In the practical circumstances of a study, it has often proved impossible to fulfil this requirement of behavioural validation, due to lack of established evidence and of study time and resources available for independent investigations. But, however inadequate the measures for these reasons, there is no doubt as to the *principles* of measurement. The measures should be those which correlate most closely with people's perceptions of the items. There is doubt over principles with the GAM.

Turning now to measures of the relative value of objective achievements, Hill has several observations to make but leaves unanswered the essential question of *how* the relative values are to be derived. For example, he and Tzamir have discussed the problems of transforming measures of items made in disparate units into some common unit.[18] They indicate three types of solutions to this "aggregation problem" by unification of the measurement scales: CBA, where money is used as the common unit of relative value; transformation functions, where x units of achievement of objective A are assumed equivalent to y units of achievement of objective B, and so on throughout the range of differences between plans in scores of achievement; and weighted indices, where the scores for objectives are presented in the form of indices which themselves are expressed in common units. This tripartite

[17]Hill and Shechter, in Wilson (ed.), 1971, *op. cit.*
[18]M. Hill and Y. Tzamir, Multidimensional evaluation of regional plans serving multiple objectives, *Papers of the Regional Science Ass.* 29 (1972) 139–65.

identification of approaches is misleading, since all three are equivalent with regard to the *process* of deriving relative values. The parameters derived from evidence of willingness to pay in SCBA are no more than "weights" to be applied to the appropriate physical measures. "Weights", appropriately specified, themselves perform the same role as transformation functions. They are not alternative concepts, but formally equivalent. This attempt at classifying the approaches to aggregation seems only to lead away from the central aspect of aggregation, namely the *principles* by which the weights or the transformation functions (i.e. the relative values) are to be derived. Willingness to pay, as a concept, is one approach to the way in which the weights or transformations may be derived. Hill and Tzamir avoid discussing other approaches.

The relative values which are employed in Hill's schema are said by him to reflect the community's valuation of the objective achievements. When the objectives are those held by individual members of the community whose well-being would be affected, the meaning of this is clear: the weights would be intended to reflect their own valuations of the consequences of the alternatives, although—as we have indicated—it is not clear whether Hill would support the SCBA *approach* to measurement here. We suspect that he would not, but are not clear as to the reasons. However, it is not at all clear what Hill has in mind when objectives are held by the "state" or "society" as an entity. Are the values of objective achievements to be assigned by elected representatives, since they are ultimately responsible for the decision and for making collective choices generally? This would accord with Hill's approach to setting objectives, but in this case how could the values ever be determined? There is also the problem of somehow comparing the achievement of objectives held by individuals with those held by the "state" or "society", even if weights for the latter could be derived. Hill also leaves this conceptual problem unresolved.

Despite some confusion on the principles of relative valuation, Hill has made his position clear on the less substantial issue of which units of assessment to use, or rather not to use, in evaluation. It will be recalled from the previous chapter that, following SCBA, the aim in PBSA is to use money units wherever practicable, these being the most *convenient* units available. Not only is money familiar to people, but many items for inclusion in the evaluation of any set of urban and regional planning proposals are already expressed in money terms by virtue of market prices. There are difficulties with a number of items (especially those affecting the quality of the physical environment),[19] but the PBS pursues the research path of trying to extend the use of money wherever possible.

---

[19]Generally, a PBS analysis is likely to contain a number of incommensurable and intangible items, and others may have to be treated as uncertain for lack of evidence on impacts. Whilst it is not possible to draw a firm conclusion in such cases (unless one plan is dominant), PBSA is based on the view that it is often possible, and legitimate, to form an intelligent view about the range of values which apply to the contentious items. A process of reasoning and subjective judgement may often result in a worthwhile opinion on the overall merits of alternatives. It should be noted that forming a view in the absence of evidence about the preferences of those affected by proposals does not involve judgements of an ethical nature, but rather subjective judgements of fact (i.e. as to what preferences they actually hold).

By contrast, Hill prefers to use notional units of relative value, proposing numerical "points" for the purpose. This is especially so whenever it is considered that market prices are an inadequate measure of real costs and benefits and shadow prices cannot reliably be determined; in these circumstances he says that money units are not credible. This reflects Hill's concern that "the assignment of monetary values to the consequences of certain courses of action is often arbitrary and may serve to confuse rather than clarify".[20] But, as we have pointed out, the units serve only to *express* relative values. The use of points as the unit of relative value is no different in this respect from the use of money. The units, in this sense, are unimportant. If relative values cannot reliably be determined using money, then the use of notional units cannot overcome the problem of credibility. Nonetheless, Hill generally prefers the use of numerical points by which to express the relative values.

In the GAM objectives are valued for their contributions to the attainment of higher level goals (the "ideals") rather than for themselves. The relative values placed on objective achievements should reflect the relative values of the achievement of their associated ideals. As Hill points out,[21] the relative values applied to the objectives can in principle only be determined if one can also determine the relative values of the ideals. He suggests that this presents a logical difficulty: the ideals describe desired states which "by their very nature" are not subject to precise and unambiguous description. The abstract and general nature of ideals also fosters many different interpretations of their meaning, thereby compounding the difficulty.

Some of those who have applied Hill's method have sought to overcome these difficulties by regarding the ideals as composite statements of objectives. The ideals are thus regarded as specific statements of higher level goals, which then have to be broken down into their component elements. For instance, the Coventry–Solihull–Warwickshire Sub-regional Planning Team had a high-level goal to achieve "the greatest choice of opportunities". They decomposed this into statements about choice of sites for those people seeking new homes, choice of job opportunities for workers, choice of labour supply for firms, the opportunity for all residents to obtain employment, the range of shopping facilities available and ease of travel to those facilities, and choice of transport routes and modes. These objectives may be identified with the sectoral objectives used in PBSA. Once the various elements of choice with which the strategy was concerned had been defined fairly precisely, measures could be devised for each in order to assess the relative performance of alternatives. Hill has confirmed in a personal communication that this treatment accords with his own view of the relationship between ideals and objectives.

The problem still remains of identifying the *principles* of measurement, a point on which the Coventry–Solihull–Warwickshire (C–S–W) Planning Team are as vague as Hill. The reader of the C–S–W Study is left on his own in considering the adequacy of the measures used. This lack of precision in the GAM approach is a reflection of Hill's position. It seems to be his intention that the matrix should be all things to all

---

[20]Hill, 1966, *op. cit.*, p. 60.
[21]*Ibid.*, appendix C: Determining the relative weights of objectives from the relative weights of ideals.

men. The critic cannot judge the merits of attempts at measurement in GAM evaluations if the principles of those undertaking the evaluation are not stated, nor, of course, can he debate the correctness of those principles.

To sum up briefly on the approaches to measurement of the two methods, it would appear that for the PBS a clear set of principles exists and is followed as far as practicable. Particular approaches to the measurement of items will vary from item to item and from study to study depending on the nature of the problem and the resources available. To date the principles underlying the evaluation measures have remained essentially unaltered, although new techniques of measurement are being developed. In contrast, there are no GAM principles of measurement; they are whatever the particular study team want them to be. Not only does a team have discretion over principles, they have to construct their own rationale for evaluation. This seems to us to constitute a critical weakness in the GAM approach, given that the measurement of advantages and disadvantages (or of objective achievements) is central to the whole evaluation exercise.

Equity Considerations

The term "equity" is normally used to refer to the ethical desirability of redistributing real income and wealth between groups of individuals, and to the injustice caused to individuals by substantial uncompensated losses. Authors of both methods argue that matters of equity are rightly of considerable importance in choosing between planning proposals. Accordingly, both methods are designed to incorporate equity considerations.

Since we are primarily interested in principles and methodology, we assume here that the enormous practical difficulties of tracing through the incidence effects of proposals have been overcome. There are two additional tasks that have to be accomplished in order to take full account of equity, and which concern us here. It is necessary both to decide on the criterion for grouping individuals and to determine what adjustments should be made to the estimates of gains and losses to the various groups so as to reflect their relative significance for the welfare of society as a whole. It is assumed here that the measures made of gain and loss are judged to be reasonably accurate indications of prospective changes in individuals' well-being.

The basis for grouping individuals should be conditioned by the scope and nature of the factors to be taken into account. Hill restricts the notion of equity to the community's view of what constitutes the best distribution of costs and benefits resulting from the proposals. However, like other principles used in his method, he deliberately leaves the criterion open. He writes: "It is necessary to identify those sections of the public, considered by income group, occupation, location, *or any other preferred criterion*, who are affected by the consequences of a course of action since inevitably the consequences are unlikely to affect all sections of the public served uniformly" (emphasis added).[22] Whilst it is nowhere stated, we presume that

[22]Hill, 1968, *op. cit.*, p. 22.

the criteria Hill has in mind would all be related to notions of relative deprivation, be they direct expressions of deprivation, such as low wage payments or poor accessibility to urban facilities, or proxies such as residence in a particular geographic area or membership of a certain racial group. The analyst should consult the decision-takers about the nature of the criterion to be used.

In applying the PBS, Lichfield has advocated that the analyst should try to assist the decision-takers by bringing out the equity implications of the alternatives, on lines of interest to the decision if practicable. In one case, where decision-takers could not indicate their interest, the analysis incorporated two main factors:[23]

(a) the degree to which the prospective redistribution of income and wealth is regarded as equitable;

(b) costs which are involuntarily incurred by individuals who remain uncompensated for their losses.

Hence the magnitudes of the various items of cost and benefit should be adjusted up or down to reflect these two factors. The weighting of uncompensated losses in PBSA is intended to reflect the injustice caused by infringing individual liberty. In this case individuals are regarded as possessing rights of amenity, and decision-takers to be responsible for protecting the various amenities they enjoy from spoilation or destruction by others without agreed compensation for their loss. The enforced imposition of an amenity loss is therefore viewed as unjust and must be counted as a disadvantage of a proposal. The groupings of individuals which are used in the PBS to organize the efficiency analysis are usually based on a functional classification of activities: residents, travellers, shoppers, industrialists, and so on. These groups are also helpful in determining which individuals will incur uncompensated costs, since these costs are related to particular kinds of activities people perform. However, we recognize that the use of such groups creates difficulties for equity purposes. Firstly, there is the problem of determining whether people will actually receive compensation to offset losses they incur.[24] Secondly, there is the complication that an individual may be represented in more than one activity group, e.g. a residential occupier who lives alongside a new road and incurs amenity losses and who will also use that road for travel. It is therefore not always possible to determine by the use of functional groups the extent of people's net losses or gains.

When consequences are examined for the prevailing distribution of income and wealth (or some other measure of relative deprivation, such as poor accessibility to jobs and other opportunities), the functional groupings would only be relevant if those performing a particular activity all have similar incomes and wealth (or

[23]N. Lichfield, *Supplementary Proof of Evidence on Weighting of Sectors and Objectives*, submitted to the CTLA on behalf of Cambridgeshire CC *et al.*, July 1970, Ref. 5021/31.

[24]The existence of other forms of compensation besides direct money payments, such as increases in property values resulting from various aspects of proposals, makes it enormously difficult to predict whether on balance individuals will receive sufficient compensation to fully offset any losses incurred.

whatever). Since this will not be the case in practice, individuals must be regrouped. Data difficulties have prevented such an exercise being undertaken so far, except for a crude attempt in relation to the siting of the Third London Airport.[25] Nevertheless, there is, in principle, no objection to using alternative incidence groupings in the PBS if desired.

An appropriate set of equity weights has to be established by which to adjust, upwards or downwards, the magnitudes of gain and loss. It is only after such weights have been applied that a summation of all items provides a true indication of the social worth of a project. If unadjusted magnitudes are summed, the total figure only indicates whether the gainers from a proposal could profitably compensate those who would suffer to the extent of their loss (assuming that the cost of administering transfer payments are smaller than the sum of aggregate net benefit).

The view taken by both authors is that determining equity weights is a matter of ethical judgement, and that whilst the analyst can point out the distributional effects of a proposal he can offer no help as an analyst on the weights to be used. Both agree that the elected representatives should be held responsible for deciding on the weights.

However, with the GAM it is suggested that the weights be specified by the decision-takers prior to the comparison of plans. With the PBS the analyst should first attempt to trace the incidence of costs and benefits without such prior weighting, and then invite the decision-takers to form conclusions on the overall merits of plans in the light of the estimated incidence. To aid decision-taking further, the PBS analyst may use one or more hypothetical sets of equity weights and go through the arithmetical exercise in order formally to demonstrate the concept of equity weighting, and to draw out the implications of using different weightings.[26]

5.3. SUMMARY AND CONCLUDING OBSERVATIONS

We now briefly summarize what emerges as the most important similarities and differences between the PBS and GAM methods, and draw some final observations.

Both methods claim to embrace all those prospective consequences of proposals which should be taken into account in making decisions in urban and regional planning. They are intended to provide information to assist those responsible for decision-taking and to aid the general debate on alternatives. Neither method is intended as a substitute for decisions themselves.

Whilst both methods try to help determine which proposals are in the "public interest", they differ in their approach to its definition. The PBS has taken an individualistic approach, following modern welfare economics, leaving the decision-takers to determine the manner in which individual welfares should be

[25]Lichfield, 1971, *op. cit.*
[26]This was undertaken in submitting PBSA evidence to the Roskill Commission. See Lichfield, July 1970, *op. cit.*

aggregated. Hill deliberately leaves the nature of the public interest unspecified; it will therefore vary as between applications.

The PBS objectives represent the preferences of those within the relevant community whose well-being is potentially affected by the consequences of proposals. Where possible, evidence is collected through observation and analysis of choice behaviour. Reliance is placed wherever possible on revealed rather than stated preferences of individuals or groups. The objectives are dictated by the preferences that have been identified. In contrast, in Hill's schema the objectives are said to be derived from an explicit consideration of higher level goals or "ideals" which are specified in advance of the analysis of plans. These ideals are formulated by planners, elected representatives, and other participants in the planning process. Hill suggests some which might be applicable to a planning study, although he does not attempt to define a complete set. Likewise in formulating objectives the planning team should, in Hill's view, seek guidance from elected representatives. He does not discuss what he considers would constitute good evidence in support of any particular objective which might be suggested, nor how to verify any evidence which might be produced. The attempt is made to specify these objectives before the analysis of plans is begun. In addition, Hill distinguishes both community objectives and sectoral objectives; the PBS identifies only sectoral objectives.

Both Lichfield and the proponents of the GAM advocate that objectives be measured according to the way the effects of plans are likely to be perceived. There is agreement that one should use the highest-order measurement scales practicable. But Hill has not cited evidence to support the particular measures which he has suggested should be employed.

Valuations in PBSA are made according to precise principles—of opportunity cost, and of willingness to forego alternative goods and services (for benefits) or to receive goods and services in compensation (for losses). Only in cases where it has been proved difficult to obtain this kind of evidence have "points" (i.e. a notional unit of value) been used in PBS studies. Even here the principles of valuation still apply. Hill makes no alternative suggestions for principles by which the achievements of objectives are to be valued. With his method the relative values should if possible be established at the outset of the evaluation.

The PBS and the GAM are both designed to enable considerations of the fairness and justice of proposals to be incorporated into the evaluation. On the issue of who should formulate equity weights, both authors agree that this is properly the responsibility of decision-takers, since the weights reflect ethical judgements. In PBSA emphasis is placed on presenting decision-takers with a display of plans' distributional effects, leaving them to form judgements as to their equity. In contrast, in GAM analysis emphasis is placed on determining a relevant set of equity weights in advance of an estimate of distributional effects.

It will be noticed that Hill advocates that if possible objectives should be set, and the relative values of achieving different objectives be established, in advance of any analysis of plan consequences; and that equity weights are introduced before the incidence of gains and losses for different groups has been indicated. With the PBS this is not so. Hill recognizes that in practice the prior identification of objectives, their relative values, and equity weights may present severe difficulties. In personal communications he has stressed that they may all be modified as a result of subsequent analysis of plan consequences and liaison with decision-takers. However, his stance does point up an essential difference of philosophy.

GAM analysis proceeds from the identification of goals, the focus throughout being on levels of goal–achievement for the community as a whole and for groups within it. Objectives are derived from a set of higher level goals (or "ideals") whose formulation is the ultimate responsibility of the decision-takers. The objectives provide the basis for determining the relevant items of advantage and disadvantage. In contrast, the PBS starts from the identification of welfare effects and the preferences of those groups who are affected, the objectives being formulated on the basis of *their* preferences. Thus the GAM seems to be directed at examining whether the plans have achieved certain aims which the planners and decision-takers consciously set out to achieve. The PBS is directed at something different: what will be the consequences of the plans in question for the welfare of all those who are affected.

Our views here are also supported by Hill in certain statements he has made. The following is taken from his conclusions after reviewing a range of PBS studies.[27]

"(1) Goals–achievement analysis emphasizes goals–identification as the point of departure and the entire focus of this method is on level of goals–achievement for the community as a whole and for sectors within it. The Planning Balance Sheet emphasizes the identification of sectoral effects as the point of departure. . . .

"(2) In GA analysis, community goals and sectoral goals are assumed, identified *a priori*, and provide the basis for both plan formulation and the determination of costs and benefits for purposes of plan evaluation. The Planning Balance Sheet emphasizes the identification of sectoral objectives in the course of the analysis of costs and benefits.

"(3) GA analysis emphasizes the explicit derivation of objectives from higher level goals. The PBS by contrast has focused its attention on the instrumental objectives."

(We have on some previous occasions used the term "instrumental" to refer to objectives used in PBSA, on grounds that their achievement led to improvements in well-being. We now use one term only, referring to them as sectoral objectives.)
Finally, Hill has stated that:

"By determining how various objectives will be affected by proposed plans, the goals–achievement matrix can determine the extent to which certain specified standards are being met. Is the transportation plan likely to meet minimum accessibility requirements and minimum standards of comfort and convenience?

[27]Reproduced from an unpublished Working Note prepared during our research project in 1971.

Are levels of air pollution and noise likely to exceed specified standards? Is the fatal accident rate within prescribed acceptable limits? These are the types of questions that the goals–achievement matrix is designed to answer."[28]

Aside from these differences of viewpoint, the most striking feature of the GAM method is the lack of stated principles of plan assessment; Hill sets down very little in the way of guiding rules and propositions to help the practitioner. In the literature he is notably unforthcoming on the basic questions of evaluation from whose viewpoint and according to what principles of measurement. Decisions on these matters have to be made for each separate application by those who use the method.

An examination of planning studies reveals that there are many similarities between the GAM *as applied in practice* and the PBS. Those who have applied the GAM appear to have been attempting evaluations which come quite close, in their *intentions*, to the SCBA approach, despite the fact that the formal intellectual processes are not those of the welfare economist. We wait to see to what extent, in their search for principles, practitioners of the GAM will consciously lean on the literature of SCBA and welfare economics.

[28]Hill, 1968, *op. cit.*, p. 27.

CHAPTER 6

Measurement in Plan Evaluation

IN THIS chapter we shall discuss two main aspects of contemporary planning practice in relation to evaluation. Firstly, we justify the activity of quantifying effects of planning proposals. Not all advantages and disadvantages of schemes can be quantified; this we accept. But this does not rule out the use of quantitative measures wherever possible or, indeed, attempts to extend analysis into new areas of search for quantitative evidence. We should, in our view, be moving away from qualitative description into potentially more accurate types of investigation.

Since the urban development model is aimed at measurement of urban phenomena, it is appropriate to consider the use of such models in the context of measurement in evaluation. These models are an integral part of the conventional planning wisdom and are now extensively used in practice, such as for residential location, traffic, and shopping. The "systems" view of planning has done much to promote the use of modelling techniques in recent years, but their protagonists have done little to show how they can assist decision-taking, although some good work has been undertaken in adapting traffic models for evaluation purposes. We take a fairly sceptical view of the theoretical validity of these spatial interaction models, but try to show how they may be adapted to give useful outputs for evaluation, assuming that the models are reasonable predictors of behaviour.

The discussion in this chapter is concerned with general measurement issues and is not specifically related to any one type of evaluation.

6.1. THE ROLE OF MEASUREMENT[1]

"Measurement is concerned with finding an expression for the degree of difference in distinguishable qualities or characteristics."[2] We might ask the question, Why measure? The answer is that more information can be obtained than would

[1] Some earlier discussions are in N. Lichfield, The evaluation of amenity in relation to transport costs and benefits, *Transportation Engineering*, 1972, 103–7; and Valuation in cost–benefit analysis: the contribution of the surveyor, *Chartered Surveyor* **105** (1972) 48–54.

[2] R. Stone, *The Role of Measurement in Economics*, Cambridge University Press, 1951, p. 5.

otherwise have been the case. We measure the consequences of planning proposals in the evaluation to increase the information about the choice facing decision-makers. More formally, we measure in order to:

(a) assist in acquiring knowledge about certain phenomena, and hence;
(b) facilitate comparative descriptions through the indication of differences; and
(c) formally test propositions and theories.

All of these considerations are of relevance to planning. The main justification for measurement in evaluation is that it reduces the extent of subjective judgement, although this can never be eliminated because uncertainty inevitably surrounds the quantification of forward-looking estimates. The issue of differences is obviously more critical here. To say that scheme A costs more to construct than scheme B is interesting information, as is that scheme A provides better facilities than scheme B. But it is even more interesting to know in what way and for whom they were better and by how much. That information may be used to determine whether, in the decision-taker's view, the additional expenditure for A would be justified.

There are a number of distinct measurement scales varying in their information contents.[3] To illustrate them, consider the case of identifying which of a pair of alternative plans would minimize the loss of agricultural land. To do this we could estimate the area of countryside displaced for urbanization in each plan and classify them according to the area. Each plan would be placed in one of a number of categories which would each denote a certain range of displacement, and would be named or numbered, involving the use of a *nominal* scale. It might then be reasonable to assume that the smallest number would be preferred. So we may *order* (or rank) the plans according to a scale of preference, in this case the "least acreages the better". If all farmland acres are identical, then we may go further and say that one plan is better by the extent of the difference in acreage lost. This introduces the concept of an *interval* scale. Alternatively, we may express advantage as a *ratio* of the acreages of farmland which are lost, where one plan is, say, twice as good as the other for this item. Of these four scales—nominal, ordinal, interval, and ratio— clearly the latter two are likely to be the most useful, since they convey the most information. In evaluation in urban and regional planning we normally seek to measure *differences* between plans; that is, using an interval scale.

We have already discussed in passing the two distinct components of measurement used in evaluation. Firstly, it is necessary to derive appropriate physical measures of phenomena. For fuller information these must then be transformed from their disparate units into measures in common units representing relative values. Attention is normally focused on this latter issue, but the appropriate physical measure is not always obvious. In the above example, acres were helpful because this unit directly relates to the nature of the losses incurred; namely, farm produce. But consider the case of nuisance resulting from traffic noise. This is

[3] R. L. Ackoff, *Scientific Method: Optimizing Applied Research Decisions*, John Wiley, New York, 1962, p. 179.

probably some function of the frequency of noise, the distribution of intensity of the noises from different vehicles, the amount of background noise in the area, duration of particular noises, and so on. Here we want to be sure that the measure we adopt is an adequate measure of the phenomenon we are investigating, otherwise our plans will be inadequately specified and evaluated. What index based on these various components is correct? Because of the subjective nature of noise nuisances, the principle we should adopt is that of finding that index based on the components of noise which appears to correlate most closely with some independent measure of people's reactions. For example, we could observe the rate of heartbeats at different nuisance levels if this is thought to be appropriate; or we could ask people to score the nuisance on an interval scale with a range from "quiet" (at 0) to "unbearable" (at 10). The measure to use in the analysis would then be that which correlates closest with such independently observed measures of reactions. Perception studies attempt to derive these measures for subjective phenomena such as noise.

Having, then, obtained our suitable measure in physical (index) units, evidence should then be found for the transformation of these physical units into appropriate units of relative values. This is necessary if the performance of plans is to be compared for different items of advantage and disadvantage; how important is, say, the difference in traffic noise in relation to accessibility differences, construction cost differences, landscape loss differences, and so forth?

The precise measures used in assessing items and their relative values are clearly significant, and changes to them may affect the nature of designs which are generated if information derived from them is used to assist design. It could also alter the ranking of the plans produced by the evaluation.

Finding the "correct" measure of a consequence of a plan must be based on clearly stated principles about *whose* advantage or disadvantage is being measured and *how* a gain or loss is to be treated. Our previous example of the loss of agricultural land through urban development is a frequently encountered issue in planning studies, and demonstrates much of the confusion which exists about measurement.

Taking agricultural land for urban development may involve other losses besides that of agricultural output (such as amenity), but we shall ignore them here for simplicity and focus on the agriculture. Who are the losers in this case? There may be "immediate losers" the farmers and farm workers. Almost certainly the existing owners will lose if the land is acquired for urban development compulsorily and full compensation is not paid. Farm workers will lose by having to find alternative employment. Nearby farmers who remain may lose if the encroachment of urbanization brings problems of severance and splitting up of farm units, trespass, and vandalism. A final group of losers might be members of the general public who may, following development, have less food than before or find that the same quantity of food costs more to produce.

There are strong agricultural lobbies for these kinds of interests in planning decisions made by government, and some elected representatives may derive the bulk of their political support from their attitudes to planning decisions. If we assess the loss to elected representatives who support planning decisions which cause confiscation of agricultural land, we might measure their loss (if any) in relation to withdrawal of sponsorship and campaign funds by agricultural pressure groups, resignations from the party because of the decision, or loss of votes at the next election. There would be obvious practical difficulties here, but in addition estimates may not reasonably reflect the differences in the losses as between alternative proposals. The agricultural lobby may be as vociferous if 1000 acres of agricultural land are lost than it would be for 1200 acres, and may not, moreover, grade its opposition in relation to the quality of the land. Indeed, in some circumstances there may be incentives to preserve less good quality farmland in preference to the better quality. This might be so if the better quality land were used less intensively in terms of the labour force, or if alternative job opportunities in areas of poor agricultural land were lower than job opportunities for the displaced labour force elsewhere.

These interests fail to reflect one obviously important aspect of the agricultural loss: the reduction in agricultural produce caused by turning land over to urban development. The acreage lost will be a poor or misleading measure if the assumption that one acre is much the same as another is not valid. In the absence of other information we might weight the acreages by some factor reflecting the Ministry of Agriculture classification of quality, e.g. weight class I land by, say, a factor of four, class II land by a factor of three and so on. The differences in the scores of plans, derived from the sum of the products of the weights and acreages, could then be used for the evaluation. But this weighted index may still be an inadequate measure. It assumes that an acre of class I land would have a relative value 4/3 times an acre of class II land and twice that of an acre of class III land, and so on. This may not be the case. Clearly we need to investigate more fully the nature of value, or relative value, in order to test the proposition that such a weighted index of farmland loss is suitable. That is, we need to investigate the relative values of different types of farmland. We also need to derive some indication of the relative value of these farmland acres against other cost and benefit items relevant to the planning study.

We could measure the losses of the agricultural produce to the general public directly by estimating how much foodstuff—gallons of milk, tons of wheat, thousands of eggs—would be foregone and the value of the contribution of the land to their production. Estimates of the labour and farm machinery used in production would not be relevant if these could be used elsewhere, albeit at some differences in disruption costs as between plans.

There are at least three alternative possible lines of approach to estimating the value of the loss.[4] First comes the agricultural value of the land which may be easily obtained by using the expertise of the surveying departments of the authorities involved. In general this will represent the amount of alternative goods and services that some farmers are prepared to forego in order to acquire the land for productive purposes, and this amount will in turn represent the value of the contribution of the

[4]G. Wibberly, *Agriculture and Urban Growth*, Michael Joseph, London, 1959.

land to agricultural output. However, despite the ease of obtaining it, the agricultural value may be an inappropriate measure, since it tends to be inflated because agricultural production is heavily supported by the authorities in the United Kingdom and certain tax advantages accrue to owners of farmland. Some speculative component may also exist whereby landowners hope that their agricultural land will have urban uses permitted at some time in the future.

Alternatively, it is possible to estimate the value of gross agricultural outputs of the area in question and subtract the costs of all inputs except land. This is termed the "value-added approach" and puts heavy reliance on the likelihood that errors of measurement in the non-land aspects of production process will cancel out. It obviously involves more calculations than the previous approach.

Perhaps even more complex is the approach called the food-replacement method. In this method an attempt is made to determine which would be the least costly alternative method of producing the same amount of agricultural production as in the area under consideration. The costs of production at the current location and its next best alternative are compared, the difference in cost is the measure of the loss of agricultural output. Estimation problems are clearly very difficult here. But estimation errors aside, the analysts can never be entirely sure that the assumed next-best alternative production method is, in fact, the correct one. All three approaches require estimation of losses as they will occur in future. By building on agricultural land now we lose a stream of products, year by year, until such time as the land would otherwise have gone out of agricultural production. Inputs to the production of foodstuffs may be valued more highly in the future than now, especially if war is a possibility. Alternatively, technological developments may lead to opposite effects. Obviously we do not know what will happen, but allowance for expectations must still be made. These expectations must be reflected to some degree in current market prices.

We have dwelt on the measurement issues surrounding agricultural losses because this example seems to identify fairly well a number of fundamental principles. The first of these is to establish which groups in society are the losers or beneficiaries. In the agricultural example there are several groups. The second principle is to identify the nature of the losses or gains. In this instance the general public lose agricultural output, for they consume less of it, or, if they so choose, less of alternative goods and services when more resources are devoted to agricultural production to maintain the level of output. The third principle is to establish an appropriate measure of the item and an appropriate parameter expressing its relative value. Here the measure used was the contribution of land to total agricultural output. The general public express preferences for agricultural produce in obvious ways. These may be used to derive evidence and estimates of their valuation of the contribution of the land to agricultural production relative to other costs and benefits of the planning proposals.

Ackoff, in a discussion on comparing items measured in different units, has succinctly summarized the issue of relative values in expressing different items of advantage or disadvantage in common terms. He says:[5]

---

[5]Ackoff, 1962, *op. cit.*, pp. 42 and 43.

"Since addition is necessary if we are to evaluate the courses of action relative to all the relevant outcomes, we must find some way of either transforming one scale into another or transforming both into some other scale . . . . We do not yet have scales of absolute value [so] it is necessary first to transform the outcome scales into each other and then to find the *relative value* of units among one of these scales."

Ackoff points out: "Successive units on one scale may not be equally valuable relative to units on the other . . . . Such transformation functions are seldom linear."

In this last point he is suggesting that the value of, say, landscape loss resulting from a planning proposal would depend upon the amount of landscape amenity which is already available to the potential losers. This accords with the well-known postulate of economic theory: the personal valuation of any item (landscape amenities, in this case) will be lower, other things equal, the more of that item which is available. Thus, in the case of the Third London Airport, the amenity loss of certain historic churches through construction of an airport in the countryside would have to be considered in relation to the total number of similar historic churches which are still available (as well as their accessibility). The greater the number of comparable churches, the less valuable is any particular church.

Objections are raised from time to time of evaluations with a commitment to quantification, and especially of cost–benefit analysis, that point estimates of items give a spurious appearance of accuracy. This may be countered if the sensitivity of the findings to changes in critical assumptions is emphasized. Alternatively, a "probability distribution" approach may be used which explicitly allows for the potential variation of the true value of an item about the estimated mean.[6] Here probabilities would be applied to, say, the various possible values of time spent travelling, and all other items in the analysis, in order to give best estimate of overall values and the dispersion of likely values about the best estimate. The additional costs of computation and the problems of deciding on what probability distributions to use, will mean that the point estimates with sensitivity analysis will generally prove the more popular approach. But either method answers this weak criticism of quantification.

Some Observations on Ranking

It has been suggested that it is possible to evaluate schemes without measurement by using ratio or interval scales. This suggests that a ranking of alternatives for specified cost or benefit items is all that is necessary for informed decision-making. In an approach suggested by Schlager,[7] the essential feature is that meaningful comparisons of plans may be obtained by comparing overall score values for plans

[6]As suggested in J. Parry Lewis, *Misused Techniques in Planning—Cost Benefit Analysis*, Occasional Paper No. 2, Centre for Urban and Regional Research, University of Manchester, undated.
[7]K. Schlager, The rank-based expected value method of plan evaluation, *Highway Res. Record*, No. 238 (1963) 153–6.

V_j, where

$$V_j = \sum_i n_i m_{ij}$$

where n_i is the rank order of importance of the ith item of advantage or disadvantage, and m_{ij} the rank order of plan j for the ith item.

Thus the items of cost or benefit are first listed in order of their importance, and the plans are then ranked for each of the cost and benefit criteria. The V_j scores are then easily computed.

Holmes has suggested that a procedure of ranking items and ranking plans for items as in Schlager's method can be used in conjunction with a simple decision rule.[8] He suggests that the plan which is ranked first for the most important criterion, or which obtains most firsts when a number of criteria are viewed to be equally important, is to be preferred over all others. If two or more plans are then found equivalent, that with the greatest number of "second positions" is considered preferred, and so on.[9] This procedure is thus based on a lexicographic ordering of criteria or objectives.

There are in our view a number of serious objections to this kind of approach.[10] As a matter of procedure it is not logically possible to rank items of advantage and disadvantage in correct order of importance *before* estimates have been made of differences between alternatives. Importance must relate to the magnitude of the differences between alternatives, which cannot be determined until after the schemes have been designed and the differences between them subsequently identified. This mistake also occurs in other approaches which incorporate measurement on interval scales.[11] For the same reasons it is not possible to weight criteria in advance of design and in advance of the specification of the physical measurement units.

There may be some confusion in Holmes's mind between importance of criteria and relative value. He may, for example, really be saying that one unit of environmental quality (say 10 square miles of outstanding natural beauty) is of greater value (i.e. more important) relative to one unit of damage to agriculture (say 10 square miles of farmland). But since the items are ranked independently of measurement it is meaningless to say that environmental quality is more important than damage to agriculture. Relative values cannot be stated until the units of measurement are specified. Alternatively, importance may refer to the magnitude of the "most likely" or probable differentials between schemes, if only those magnitudes could be determined. But this implies pre-judging the significance of the

[8]J. C. Holmes, An ordinal method of evaluation, *Urban Studies*, **9** (1971) 179–91.

[9]A "second position" refers either to a ranking of second place on the most important criterion or to a ranking of first place on a criterion of second importance.

[10]For a fuller discussion of these objections see P. Kettle and M. Whitbread, An ordinal method of evaluation: a comment, *Urban Studies* **10** (1973) 95–99.

[11]For example, in C. C. Schimpeler and W. L. Grecco, Systems evaluation: an approach based on community structure and values, *Highway Res. Record*, No. 238 (1968) 123–52. It is also to be found in the C–S–W Sub-regional Planning Study.

differences between the alternative designs and rules out any prospect of "interesting" (i.e. unexpectedly superior) alternatives. If important items are those where differentials between alternatives are likely to be large, relative to other—less important—items, we must ask the question How do we know that?; and hence we return to the question of measurement. This, surely, is not Holmes's intention since if we *can* measure, then why restrict the analysis to rankings?

Thus there exist logical impossibilities in the procedures suggested by Schlager and Holmes. But in any event, ranking of items is an unsatisfactory approach to evaluation. With ranking information before us and no other, it is impossible to form a view as to the preferred alternative plan except in the trivial case where dominance exists. It may allow us to focus on critical areas for debate, and possibly on items for which some measurement of differences should be attempted. But with ranking the problem remains that for any one item the design differentials between a pair of alternatives might well, if quantified, completely obliterate the differentials on all other items. For this same reason it is inadmissible to sum rank scores for plans, which has been done on a previous occasion as a "last resort" in the absence of measured items.[12] The solution to this approach will depend on the number of criteria in the evaluation matrix. Whether or not, say, residential accessibility is measured under one heading of general accessibility, or under a hundred headings of accessibility to different land uses, will depend on the problem under study, the approach adopted to evaluation, the form of the plans, the requirements of the clients, and many other fairly "arbitrary" factors. But the result of summing rankings will clearly depend on the extent of disaggregation of criteria into constituent items. Conversely, it is always possible to derive composite criteria, and hence alter the sum of the rank scores. Thus this approach is essentially arbitrary, as are all of the ordinal ranking approaches to evaluation for this reason. One alternative is no more likely to be preferred than any other. In this context any decision procedure or "rule" is no more superior than random selection. More sophisticated techniques of analysis of ranked data are possible, but they are no more helpful in identifying the preferred alternative. One recently suggested is that of multi-dimensional scalogram analysis.[13] We are aware that in certain circumstances metric estimates can be obtained from non-metric experimental data, but the necessary conditions do not apply to an evaluation matrix that only contains ordinal data.

A further point of some importance for the proper understanding of the role of measurement in evaluation must be made about ranking. The function of evaluation is to provide the best information possible to those whose responsibility it is to make and justify decisions. It is for planners to provide this information, and for others to use it as they see fit. The planners' role in evaluation is not that of decision-takers,

[12]For example, N. Lichfield and H. Chapman, Cost–benefit analysis in urban expansion—a case study: Ipswich, *Urban Studies* **7** (1970) 153–88, table B.

[13]M. Hill and Y. Tzamir, Multidimensional evaluation of regional plans serving multiple objectives, *Papers of the Regional Science Ass.* **29** (1972) 139–65.

whether or not the planners have a decision-taking role delegated to them, for example when asked to recommend a course of action. But that role, which involves using evaluation evidence, should not be confused with the evaluation itself. Evaluation evidence does not indicate which alternative should be selected as preferred. Accordingly, the methods of Holmes and Schlager must be interpreted as *their* decision-taking models in situations of limited information rather than as evaluation methodologies.

Sources of Evidence

Conceptually, any perceived advantage or disadvantage is relevant, but in some cases decision-takers may elect to limit the boundaries of relevance; that is, to take into account fewer groups than those affected by the proposals. The decision-taker may not wish to take into account all the affected sectors in the community (e.g. those who are not highway users in a highway appraisal); or those who are living outside the area of jurisdiction (e.g. the impact of a new shopping centre in one shire county on established shopping centres in the adjacent authority); or of future generations (when a limit of, say, twenty years is put on the project for the purpose of the evaluation). While such delimitations by sector, geographical area, or time are perfectly legitimate constraints on choice by the decision-taker, choice indicated by an analysis which is constrained in this way could clearly give different results from one not so constrained.

Of course, not only *existing* populations are relevant; the evaluation must also take account of future populations, such as migrants into the study area or as yet unborn generations. In addition the evaluation, to be comprehensive, must also consider gains or losses to non-participants in the decision. They may never directly use any of the facilities under consideration but may value the prospect that others will derive benefit from them.

We have used the term sectoral objectives to represent particular preferences of individuals (or groups of individuals) classified according to some concept of homogeneity. We may derive measures of sectoral objectives and their relative values from the evidence of attitudes or behaviour. What kinds of evidence should we seek when we assess plans in terms of these sectoral objectives? There are a number of possible approaches. In some cases we may observe how people spend their income when faced with a range of goods and services with prices attached. It may, for example, be possible to infer how various aspects of housing services are valued by analysing house purchase activities. In general this kind of behavioural evidence is the best if only because such situations produce real choice. But this is not sufficient, since people's values are not necessarily reflected in market prices but also in consumers' surplus, namely the difference between what people actually give up for goods and services and the maximum that they would be prepared to give up. Independent research into consumers' surplus values, say for housing, where the quality of housing services is to be affected by some proposals, would also be necessary. Evidence on preferences may also be obtained by observing behaviour.

For example, evidence for people's apparent valuation of time saved by improvements in communications infrastructure has been derived by analysis of modal
choices, route choices, use of toll bridges, and so on. A third source of evidence
comes from getting individuals to participate in hypothetical games in which
simulated choice situations exist relating, for example, to improvements in their
residential environment. In the game participants must trade-off one improvement
against another. The "priority evaluator" falls into this category of evidence, and
also the REAL experiment at the Transport and Road Research Laboratory.[14]

A further category of evidence is based on questionnaires which survey attitudes
or values. Attitude surveys are probably the least reliable sources of information of
the four main lines of inquiry, since respondents are not asked to *make* choices and
do not receive rewards for thoughtful or "correct" choices. Problems immediately
arise over the interpretation of questions and the motivations of respondents. Yet,
somewhat surprisingly in view of these limitations, many recent planning studies
have evaluated on evidence about community preferences obtained from attitude
surveys.[15] The reasons for the popularity of the survey approach are difficult to
discern, but are probably associated with the comparative ease of collecting and
programming information on complex and diverse subjects and to the virtual
certainty that information will be available, as respondents can nearly always be
induced to answer questions. (Other methods of investigation are more risky.) Thus,
the survey method is often the "easy" solution if we disregard the reliability of the
findings. Yet there may be other reasons for its popularity. Members of the planning
team may be unaware or inadequately informed, of the growing volume of more
substantially based and relevant evidence on preferences or may think that such
evidence derived from elsewhere is inappropriate for the area or problem under
investigation. But some planning teams may genuinely think survey evidence is
superior to other evidence. This could well be so, for example, where individuals'
range of experience is insufficient to provide substantive behavioural evidence, and
in such cases attitude surveys may be an acceptable approach. But for very many
sectoral objectives relevant to planning studies such a reason for not trying to obtain
evidence by revealed preferences is unacceptable.

Obtaining evidence about externalities, especially pollution and general environmental externalities, is more difficult. It must be admitted that insufficient research
has been undertaken to be confident about their consequences. The difficulties
surrounding obtaining of useful evidence of values for many public goods or "bads"
do not seem, on the face of it, to be completely insurmountable. But it is true that at

---

[14]G. Hoinville, Evaluating community preferences, *Environment and Planning* 3 (1971) 33–50. Also, R.
F. Dawson, Assessments of the environmental effects of traffic, paper presented at CES Seminar on the
economic evaluation of residential relocation and environmental quality, at the London School of
Economics, March 1974 (unpublished).

[15]For example South Hampshire Plan Technical Unit, *Evaluation of Alternative Strategies*, Working
Paper No. 18, August 1972. C–S–W Sub-regional Study Team, Supplementary Report 4, *Evaluation*,
Coventry City Council, May 1971. BUSPT, *Report on the Evaluation of Alternative Strategies*, Brighton
County Borough Council, December 1971.

the present time all evaluation methodologies are likely to be of limited help to decision-takers in planning studies where pollution effects are dominant.

Confusion sometimes arises over the distinction between "real" (or technological) and "pecuniary" effects of proposals. The distinction is important for using appropriate measures. Pecuniary effects of proposals, which are changes in the money income or wealth of individuals, are significant in making some of those individuals better or worse off, but do not always measure adequately the *total* gains or losses. Those gains or losses may be better measured directly; to include pecuniary effects as well would be to double-count some items. Alternatively, some pecuniary effects are alterations in the distribution of wealth by groups in society rather than additions to it. Unless distributional considerations are important, these pecuniary gains and losses will cancel out and may be ignored. The case is frequently cited of possible reductions in travel costs with the construction of a new motorway. Savings in time, fuel, and wear and tear of vehicles are real effects of the motorway, and will lead to some properties becoming relatively more desirable than before as residential and commercial locations. As a result, the prices of those properties may rise. This rise in price is a pecuniary effect of the motorway development, and may measure some of the advantages to residents and others of the real effects of the proposals (although it is debatable whether land-value changes are appropriate measures of benefits). But the price changes are not in themselves part of the real services afforded by the proposals.

As an example of transfers of wealth between groups in society, a distinction is frequently encountered in transport planning between perceived costs and resource costs. Resource costs are the value to society of the resources which would be used as a result of a planning proposal. In the case of the motorway example, amongst the cost savings mentioned were those of vehicle users' costs, including fuel. The price of fuel to the motorist contains a substantial element of tax which is channelled into the National Exchequer and used for schemes elsewhere. That money would have been used by the motorist on the purchase of goods or services for his own benefit had it not been paid in tax. It therefore represents a transfer of resources. Thus the value of the resources saved on fuel when the motorway opens would be given net of fuel tax. Clearly costs perceived by the motorist when purchasing fuel and resource costs in fuel consumption are not identical. We would want to use perceived costs when modelling motorists' behaviour but resource costs when trying to estimate the cost savings of the scheme. Either way we would have to find the best measures possible (which would be relatively easy in this case) and then use each in its appropriate context.

Finally, we should mention the difficulties of measurement in relation to policy objectives rather than sectoral objectives. In Chapter 2 these were interpreted as the instruments by which planning "problems" may be overcome; for example, to control the growth of the city or to decentralize employment activities, the intention being to restrict the growth of congestion, limit amenity losses at the periphery brought about by growth there, and so on. These are procedures by which a number of sectoral objectives may be achieved. Whilst physical measures of the achievement of objectives of this kind are possible, two difficulties stand out. First, we have no way of knowing whether any particular measure is the "correct" one. This difficulty arises because it is impossible to correlate the achievement of the objective with the responses of particular members of the community. To do this we must analyse the several component sectoral objectives which flow from the provisions of plans. The second difficulty stems from the first in that it is impossible to derive directly relative values of members of the community for the achievement of policy objectives. It is again necessary to disaggregate them before we can obtain the requisite relative values.

6.2. THE USE OF URBAN DEVELOPMENT MODELS FOR EVALUATION

In this section we consider urban development models, the main ones falling into the categories of shopping, residential location, and traffic. During the past decade considerable efforts have been made to develop these mathematical models in order to assist the prediction of the effects of alternative planning strategies. Although the relationships expressed in them are, by and large, derived from empirical observations rather than from accepted theory, several models are operational and have been applied with success.

In spite of the profusion of mathematical model-building in urban and regional planning, little attention has been paid to the incorporation of their outputs into the plan evaluation process. The exception is the optimization model, which is generally based on linear programming, in which the generation and the evaluation of the feasible plans are part of one and the same process. But optimization models are less extensively used and, for various reasons, largely related to their complexity and the difficulties of identifying satisfactory objective functions, they are less likely to become accepted as part of the planners' everyday technique, at least in the foreseeable future. This is not so for spatial interaction models, which we consider here and which are now extensively used. We have considered a number of these models and, despite the claims of their authors, we have found them not to be of great value for evaluation, at least as currently used.

Spatial interaction models are descriptive. They describe future states of existence of parts of the total urban and regional system, given assumptions about other parts of that system. By changing these assumptions so also do we change the resultant descriptions which are given as the model outputs. But to describe two states of affairs is in no way to compare their comparative desirability. A further step has to be taken before comparative assessment, which is to proceed to convert the model outputs into expressions of relative advantage and disadvantage. This step has been consistently ignored by promotors of urban development models, at least within the planning profession, although some promising work has been undertaken by transport economists with traffic models.

We shall assume here that urban development models can describe future states of the urban and regional system well, i.e. that they are good predictors. Their lack of theoretical content makes that assumption questionable, it is true. But few attempts have been made to forecast traffic flows between population locations and employment locations, or shopping trips between residential areas and shopping centres, or new residential locations resulting from employment increases, other than by means of gravity-type formulations of behaviour. As the models are now extensively used we shall proceed on the basis that they predict accurately.

What, then, are the main kinds of "impacts" of planning decisions which urban development models can help us to assess? Since they are based on concepts of behaviour of individuals, albeit in some kind of zonal or aggregated form, the impacts will be in terms of individuals' costs and benefits. The results of any evaluation exercises using such models are likely to be in terms of the achievements of sectoral objectives, of which we can identify two main groups—those relating to direct and those relating to indirect costs and benefits. The former will concern the individuals or groups of individuals who are the subject-matter of the models—the residents, shoppers, and travellers. The latter, the indirect costs, and benefits, will be those which result from the behaviour of the persons being modelled but which are not formally part of the modelling exercise itself. To illustrate, it is conceivable that in a traffic model travellers' costs or benefits, or both, in different planned situations may be estimated from outputs of predicted behaviour. But travellers may create certain differences in externalities as between plans in the form of traffic noise and other nuisances which would be felt by persons living or working adjacent to their routes. From forecasts of traffic flows, and from other data such as housing or employment densities and the disposition of buildings and spaces adjacent to the routes, these nuisance costs may be estimated. Estimating the externalities is better left to techniques which are specific to the "impact", whether it be traffic nuisance, destruction of the viability of shopping centres, or amenity losses from residential development. Urban development models may help in estimating these external effects by providing one input of the many which are required, but they cannot of themselves provide the estimates.

If the use of urban development models for evaluation is to be successful, the main improvements are likely to come from producing cost and benefit estimates of the participants in the model, i.e. the direct costs and benefits. The main direct costs and benefits, which we consider below for two types of model, are essentially travel benefits (and disbenefits), which we refer to as accessibility benefits. The models are of spatial interaction between land users where the principal interaction modes are vehicles. We have already seen (in section 3.3) that accessibility measurements can be found without the use of spatial interaction models. Nevertheless, if these models are to provide estimates of direct costs and benefits, they will be within the field of accessibility.

Accessibility Benefits and the Shopping Model

Several forms of shopping model exist,[16] but the one developed and tried by Lakshmanan and Hansen in the Baltimore metropolitan region is becoming increasingly popular.[17] We shall discuss it here. Our notation follows the convention form.

[16]National Economic Development Office, *Urban Models in Shopping Studies*, NEDO, London, 1970.
[17]T. R. Lakshmanan and W. G. Hansen, A retail market potential model, *J. Am. Inst. Planners* **31** (1965) 134–43.

The model can be expressed as follows:

$$S_j = \sum_{i=1}^{m} R_i \frac{\dfrac{F_j^{\alpha}}{C_{ij}^{\beta}}}{\sum_{k=1}^{n} \dfrac{F_k^{\alpha}}{C_{ik}^{\beta}}},$$

where S_j is the sales in the jth centre of a series of n centres; R_i the consumer retail expenditure available in the ith residential zone of m zones; F_j the attractive power of the jth shopping centre; C_{ij} the travel costs between residential zone i and shopping centre j; α the exponent applied to F; n the total number of competing shopping centres in study area; m the total number of residential zones in the study area; β an exponent applied to C; k a competing shopping centre in the series n; and i a residential zone in the series m.

The model distributes the retail expenditure of residents on durable goods amongst all the shopping centres in the study area. It is hypothesized that the distribution of expenditure amongst these centres is a function of: (i) their relative attraction power; (ii) their relative travel costs from each residence zone.

Measures may be found for both of these items. We shall assume that the model has been adequately calibrated in that an appropriate pair of (α, β) values have been determined and the model is ready for use in forecasting.

The model is origin constrained; that is, a certain amount of expenditure must be allocated over the shopping centres no matter which plan we consider. That amount is given by the total population of the study area (assumed constant between plans) and the appropriate factors applied to population to give expenditure on goods. That money may be spent in any centre; there is no constraint on destination. Let us hypothesize two alternative mutually exclusive plans representing a not uncommon situation in current practice. In one a new and large out-of-town centre is to be provided; we shall call this the "with-centre" case. In the other there is no new centre and the expenditure is allocated exclusively to existing centres in the region; this we call the "without-centre" case. The *only* difference between plans is that the sizes of centres are different. Which of the two plans will shoppers, in the aggregate, prefer?

Many planning studies have recognized the essential issues of accessibility of the kind considered here. The usual approach adopted for its measurement in evaluation is the use of a simple index incorporating the concepts of quantity of opportunities and travel costs. The total accessibility A of all residents to all shopping facilities in a plan might therefore be assessed as

$$A = \sum_i \sum_j R_i F_j^{\alpha} C_{ij}^{-\beta},$$

where α, β are constants derived on calibration.

For an ordinal indication of the preferred plan (for shoppers) such an index may not be too misleading, but there are two main problems associated with its use. First, it can *only* give a ranking of plans since the units of the index have no meaning in themselves; they cannot readily be transformed into other units of common relative values. Second, the index is obviously not a true measure of shoppers' accessibility benefits. The index has not been calibrated by a correlation analysis against shoppers' *preferences*, but against *behaviour*. There are quite distinct differences between these concepts. Since, by altering the parameters of the index, we can alter the plan scores and their ranking, it is important to find the correct measure.

Another approach may be tried which uses the model's ability to predict behaviour in order to deduce preferences. If we are comparing one alternative with another, when the size of a particular centre increases all those shoppers who use that centre in both plans are better off. If the size of the centre diminishes, the converse is true. We need to know how much in the aggregate shoppers would be prepared to sacrifice for the increased attractiveness of one alternative over the other. We do not know this amount. But we may identify travel cost changes (which are easy to measure) equivalent, in terms of their effect on shoppers' behaviour, to changes in the attractiveness of centres. The basic idea is to hold shopping benefits themselves constant between the alternatives (the F_j^α values) and then to measure the travel cost differences between the alternatives at that given level of shopping benefits.[18]

Consider one of the alternatives, e.g. the "without-centre" case. The model forecasts how shoppers will allocate expenditure between the shopping centres available to them in the study area. That is, it forecasts the values for the S_{ij}'s, where S is the flow of expenditure. We now introduce the new centre. All the F_j values change, and a new pattern of expenditure flows is forecast by the model. But, we may ask, What are the changes in the C_{ij}'s which, when used with the *initial* set of F_j values in the model, will produce a forecast pattern of expenditure flows which is the same as those of the "with-centre" alternative? Once the new C_{ij}'s have been determined, it will then be possible to estimate travel cost changes between the alternatives, and hence to compare accessibility benefits. The procedure is as follows. We have plan 1 ("without-centre") and plan 2 ("with-centre"):

> For plan 1, the size of centre $j = F_j$.
> For plan 2, the size of centre $j = F_j + f_j$.
> All other centres are identical between the two plans.
> In plan 1, the model calculates S_{ij}^1.
> In plan 2, the model calculates S_{ij}^2.

It is assumed that we can easily convert S_{ij} into the number of trips between i and j by using an expenditure per trip constant.

We observe that $S_{ij}^2 > S_{ij}^1$ because in plan 2 the centre is larger and so more expenditure is attracted. We then set the attraction factor of j at F_j again. We then calculate new values for C_{ij} (call it C_{ij}^*) such that the flow of expenditure from i to j is S_{ij}^2. The travel costs will have decreased by $(C_{ij} - C_{ij}^*)$. Now, all shoppers

---

[18]Methods discussed in this section were presented as evidence in the public inquiries into the Cribbs Causeway out-of-town shopping proposal near Bristol in 1972, and the Stonebridge proposal near Birmingham in 1973.

represented by the expenditure in plan 2 are better off (or at least no worse off) than in plan 1. All those represented by the S_{ij}^2 expenditure are better off by the decrease in travel costs, since they now travel to the same centre but at reduced cost. The extra expenditure attracted to the centre when it is larger $(S_{ij}^2 - S_{ij}^1)$ means that additional shoppers are better off on average by roughly half the fall in travel cost. Thus the benefit B_{ij} is given by

$$B_{ij} = S_{ij}^1(C_{ij} - C_{ij}^*) + \tfrac{1}{2}(S_{ij}^2 - S_{ij}^1)(C_{ij} - C_{ij}^*)$$
$$= \tfrac{1}{2}(S_{ij}^1 + S_{ij}^2)(C_{ij} - C_{ij}^*).$$

Hence overall benefit of plan 2 compared with plan 1 in year 1 (assuming we can easily convert the S_{ij}'s to numbers of trips) becomes

$$B = \sum_i \sum_j \tfrac{1}{2}(S_{ij}^1 + S_{ij}^2)(C_{ij} - C_{ij}^*).$$

This formula for benefits was first used in the London Transportation Study.[19] It should be pointed out that when the C_{ij} values are converted to "behavioural" travel costs (e.g. fares and out-of-pocket expenses, plus time costs) between i and j pairs, some of the travel cost savings between plans are simply savings in taxation, such as petrol tax, and are not real resource savings. Accordingly, a "non-resource correction" must be included to obtain the total travel resource cost and disbenefit estimate. That non-resource correction is given by

$$R = \sum_{ij} S_{ij}^2(C_{ij} - r_{ij}) - \sum_{ij} S_{ij}^1(C_{ij}^* - r_{ij}^*),$$

where C_{ij} are the behavioural costs for plan 1; r_{ij} the resource costs of plan 1 (the behavioural costs less tax); and C_{ij}^* as before.

B less R measures the differences in travel costs and disbenefits between the alternatives on the assumption that the shopping benefits given by the attractiveness of centres are assumed to be common.

The next problem is to estimate the values for C_{ij}^*, i.e. the changed cost penalties which are identical to the attraction factor changes. These C_{ij}^* values may be obtained as follows. For alternative plans 1 and 2 we have

$$S_{ij}^1 = \frac{R_i F_j^{\alpha 1} C_{ij}^{-\beta}}{\sum_j F_j^{\alpha 1} C_{ij}^{-\beta}}, \qquad S_{ij}^2 = \frac{R_i F_j^{\alpha 2} C_{ij}^{-\beta}}{\sum_j F_j^{\alpha 2} C_{ij}^{-\beta}}.$$

But

$$S_{ij}^2 = \frac{R_i F_j^{\alpha 1} C_{ij}^{*-\beta}}{\sum_j F_j^{\alpha 1} C_{ij}^{*-\beta}}.$$

[19]It is more extensively discussed in H. Neuburger, User benefit in the evaluation of transport and land use plans, *J. Transp. Econ. Policy* **5** (1971) 57–75.

The equations are equivalent, so

$$\frac{R_i F_j^{\alpha 2} C_{ij}^{-\beta}}{\sum_j F_j^{\alpha 2} C_{ij}^{-\beta}} = \frac{R_i F_j^{\alpha 1} C_{ij}*^{-\beta}}{\sum_j F_j^{\alpha 1} C_{ij}*^{-\beta}}.$$

Since the denominators are in practice virtually equal, we can cancel and obtain

$$C_{ij}*^{\beta} = \frac{F_j^{\alpha 1}}{F_j^{\alpha 2}} C_{ij}^{\beta};$$

therefore

$$C_{ij}* = \left(\frac{F_j^1}{F_j^2}\right)^{\alpha/\beta} C_{ij}.$$

Hence values for $C_{ij}*$ may be computed quite easily from the values of C_{ij} once the ratios of the attraction factors of the shopping centres in the two plans are known from the forecasting runs of the shopping model.

In this way we have obtained a money measure of the benefits of the new centre (which may be negative) across all shoppers in the study area. This measure is *net* of any travel costs they may incur. Suitable capitalization factors may be applied to make it comparable with other measures which might be used in the evaluation, e.g. of the construction costs involved or displacements of land uses.

More sophisticated methods of computing some aspects of the shopping benefits measure can be tried. Wherever the two plans involve markedly different retail patterns, the assumption that we can represent net benefit changes to people who switch centres by the average of their "cost" differences may be unsatisfactory. Various numerical integration possibilities are available if use of computer time in the study is not a major limitation.

However, for new centres, where the attraction factor is zero in the "without-centre" alternative, it is not possible to compute benefit measures directly. Absurd results would be given as $C_{ij}*$ becomes infinite, implying a social cost of not building the new centre that is infinitely great. Various ways around this difficulty exist, some of which are suggested here.

We may set the size of the new centre in the "without-centre" case at a low value, but not zero. Several different low values may be tried for examining the sensitivity of the results. Alternatively, we might assume that the size of the new centre remains unchanged at its level in the "with-centre" plan, but we assume that in the "without-centre" case it is located in a very inaccessible place for all shoppers. Several notional C_{ij} values may again be tried for sensitivity testing. Either way an approximation to the true measures of benefits is obtained. (These two procedures are not required for comparisons which do not involve the provision of new retail facilities at completely new locations.)

The shopping model can be used to generate additional information of use in the planning process. It may help in design, indicating the rough order of likely turnovers at new and existing centres, thus assisting in assessing floorspace. At evaluation it may help with the assessment of the physical and social consequences resulting from reductions or increases in retail activity at the centres that are modelled, although the full social costs and benefits of "viable" centres in urban areas have yet to be adequately examined. The model may help in the assessment of traffic effects although these are likely only to be locally important in the provision of access facilities and for local congestion. The differential external effects of traffic from retail trips are likely to be insignificant as between most plans, as are differences for traffic accidents. The model might conceivably be of help in forecasting beneficiaries and losers in the alternatives. This is most likely for the division of trade between existing and new retailers, developers, and landowners. It may also be possible to identify which groups of shoppers will benefit and lose as a result of the schemes, although the extent to which such gains and losses are compensated for by property value changes (and hence accrue to landowners) has never, as far as we are aware, really been examined.

Accessibility Benefits and the Traffic Model

Journey-to-work gravity models with population locations as the origins and employment locations as the destinations, are a familiar and much-abused feature of most large-scale planning studies. The accepted approach of most of the recent regional and subregional planning studies in the United Kingdom has been to run such a model for future alternative distributions of populations and employments.[20] The model predicts traffic flows between zones, i.e. the T_{ij}'s. Following this each flow can be multiplied by the corresponding travel costs, the C_{ij}'s, to obtain the aggregate travel costs. Such information, in the absence of corresponding travel benefits, is quite useless for evaluation purposes. Even when models are doubly constrained to give the same number of trips for each plan, it does *not* follow that "least cost is best".

A similar kind of procedure to that outlined for the shoppers' accessibility benefits can be used for traffic models, where attempts are made to hold travel benefits constant and to compute travel-cost differentials between plans. A different variation of this general idea was tried by the South East Joint Planning Team (SEJPT).[21] They were conscious of the problems associated with variations in trip-end benefits, and their effects on travel behaviour, rather than changes in trip costs and *their* effects on travel behaviour. In the latter case one can compute net benefit differentials, but in the former there is no obvious way of doing so.

The SEJPT employed the formula suggested in the London Transportation Study (and utilized above in our assessment of shoppers' benefits) of the net benefit difference between plans. That formula is

$$B = \sum_i \sum_j \tfrac{1}{2}(T_{ij}^1 + T_{ij}^2)(C_{ij}^1 - C_{ij}^2),$$

[20] As documented in J. N. Jackson, *The Urban Future*, Allen & Unwin, London, 1972, ch. 8.

[21] SEJPT, *Strategic Plan for the South East, Studies Volume III, Transportation*, HMSO, London, 1971.

where T_{ij}^{1} is the forecast number of trips between i and j for plan 1 and C_{ij}^{1} the cost of travel between i and j for plan 1.

The C_{ij} values were assumed to vary between plans according to the investments to be made in communications infrastructure. But the SEJPT applied the formula to differences in both land use patterns *and* communications infrastructure. In order to do so they specified a "do-nothing" base (in terms of infrastructure) for each plan, and worked out the net benefit improvement of each plan over its do-nothing base. In order, then, to compare differences between plans for these travel benefits, it was necessary to make the critical assumption that "the do-nothing points within each hypothesis give an equal satisfaction level". The justification given for that assumption was "principally because of the small differences between hypotheses".

That is, the approach adopted by the SEJPT was to *assume* that for the same communications infrastructure different land-use plans would give the same level of net accessibility benefits, and differential accessibility benefits would arise only through differential provisions of infrastructure. Whereas that assumption may have been tenable (for the reason given) for the SEJPT's exercise, it cannot be considered generally reasonable or acceptable. Land-use planning decisions can substantially affect the well-being of some members (at least) of society. If in doubt we ought to start from the *a priori* assumption that alternative land-use plans give substantially different levels of satisfaction. Accordingly, whilst the SEJPT approach was interesting in its attempts to come to grips with making evaluation sense out of the traffic model, its limiting basic assumption makes it of doubtful value for general use in planning situations.

More recent thinking on the use of gravity-model formula as a demand equation has led to some significant findings. In particular, Neuburger has obtained a measure of net accessibility benefits directly from the calibrated gravity model.[22] This important development might be considered a more sophisticated version of the benefits measure outlined above for the shopping model. It also accepts the proposition that in land-use planning there is little difference (in accessibility terms) between the location of two settlements close together with conventional access between them and those settlements being located further apart but with motorway or some other low user-cost access between them.

The calibrated gravity model function is viewed as a demand function for travel to specific destinations. Demand is a function of price (i.e. costs of travel), the nature of trip benefits, the availability of substitute destinations, and possibly other factors. Neuburger claims that this function may be treated in an analogous way to the demand curve of traditional analysis in that the level of benefit (or surplus) which is to be derived from changing, say, the costs of travel, may be obtained by integrating the function with respect to costs over the range of cost change. In addition, it is also claimed that the differential in benefit between plans from changing the level of trip end benefits may be derived by integrating the demand function with respect to travel cost over the range of attraction factor variation. By expressing the rate of

[22]Neuburger, 1971, *op.cit.*

change of travel costs in terms of the rate of change of attraction factors it is possible to integrate the demand function with respect to the attraction factor measure over the range of attraction factor variation, and so obtain the surplus measure associated with a change in trip-end benefit. That is, for the resident at location i and level of net benefit or surplus S between plans 1 and 2 is given by

$$S = \sum_j \int_{C_{ij}^1}^{C_{ij}^2} T_{ij} dC_{ij}$$

$$= \sum_j \int_{W_j^1}^{W_j^2} T_{ij} \frac{\partial C_{ij}}{\partial W_j} dW_j.$$

The nature of the W_j value has to be investigated. The precise form of the benefits measure S depends upon the constraints which are being imposed by the planning team on the number of trips originating in particular zones and those finding their destinations in particular zones. Normally,

$$W_j = b_j D_j$$

in a model where

$$T_{ij} = O_i D_j a_i b_j e^{-\lambda C_{ij}},$$

$$a_i = \left(\sum_j D_j\right) \bigg/ \sum_j b_j D_j e^{-\lambda C_{ij}},$$

$$b_j = \left(\sum_i O_i\right) \bigg/ \sum_i a_i O_i e^{-\lambda C_{ij}}.$$

In many cases $\partial C_{ij}/\partial W_j$ can be derived from the travel demand function (this is not possible with the "power" form of deterrence function as used in the shopping model discussed above). So the surplus equation may then be solved. Neuburger generalizes the results for land-use plans where both land uses and communications infrastructure may vary. When the gravity model takes the exponential form, the resultant level of surplus differences for the resident at i is given by the difference of two comparatively simple accessibility indices. His derivation is

$$S = \frac{1}{\lambda} \left[\log \left(\sum_j W_j^2 e^{-\lambda C_{ij}^2} \right) - \log \left(\sum_j W_j^1 e^{-\lambda C_{ij}^1} \right) \right].$$

This measure can be easily obtained once the gravity traffic model has been calibrated and once the distributions of populations and employments in the future alternative planning situations are generated by the planning team.

Neuburger's analysis lends support to the view, expressed above for the shopping benefits calculation, that the frequently used simple index of accessibility is an inadequate measure of accessibility benefits. Neuburger's measure obviates the need to run the traffic model for future planned situations to evaluate travel costs and benefits. This is somewhat surprising in view of the importance usually given to the running of such models in planning studies. Of course, traffic models would have to be run for the calculation of external costs and benefits such as traffic nuisances and environmental costs. Also it is often impossible to gauge the extent of congestion on the infrastructure without using such a model. In the West Midland Regional Study it was considered impossible within constraints of budget and time to attempt to estimate "optimal" infrastructure investments for given population and employment distributions. However, the traffic model had the facility of estimating the costs (of property and construction) of providing infrastructure to allow traffic to run to at least minimum speed assumptions in urban areas. Thus these costs could be determined for any given speed assumption. They would not necessarily be estimates of actual infrastructure costs since the roads may never, in the event, be built. If they were not, there would be additional congestion. Accordingly, the infrastructure provision costs resulting from the model output might be taken as a *combined* measure of infrastructure and congestion costs, where congestion costs are measured by the outlays necessary to *overcome* congestion, or to reduce it to a common (speed) standard as between alternative plans. The problem remains of deciding on an appropriate speed standard, but the approach provides an interesting use of the traffic model.

Concluding Remarks

It is clear that urban development models have some potential in plan evaluation, although it has not yet been realized. Some simple concepts have been used here to show how the models may usefully be adapted and some general principles can be identified. Firstly, it is often possible to find fairly simple yet satisfactory measures of costs or benefits (or the achievements of sectoral objectives) once some thought has been given to the nature of the requirements. But entering into the evaluation "blind" is likely to lead not only to errors of assessment but also to waste of study resources. Certainly urban development models are not cheap to construct and run; they should be employed only with a full understanding of the value of their outputs to the decision-making process. The preliminary stages of the planning process should be used to think through the principles to be used in the eventual evaluation of alternatives. The measures follow on from the principles, and the data requirements follow on from the measures. In contrast only too often planning studies have generated a range of indicators of plan performance for "accessibility" which are either misleading or impossible to interpret. This is probably due to inadequate attention being paid to the purpose of the evaluation in the early stages and to insufficient thought being given to the value of the measures to be used to compare plans. To some extent this is revealed in our analysis of planning studies in Part II. This was also a finding of the study by Boyce, Day, and McDonald of US land-use transportation studies,[23] although they failed to show ways in which the modelling exercises could be used to provide information for evaluation, as we have tried to do here.

[23]D. E. Boyce, N. D. Day, and C. McDonald, *Metropolitan Plan Making*, Monograph Series, No. 4, Regional Science Research Institute, University of Pennsylvania, Philadelphia, 1970.

Secondly, data requirements for evaluation can be fairly limited and easy to collect. By giving very early thought to the data collection problem, more time can be devoted to other, more intractable, elements of the evaluation. Obviously the data should be collected in a form which makes computation a simple process.

Turning to the activity of design, we consider that it is unlikely, even with objectives such as accessibility, whose achievement can be easily quantified, that design and evaluation can be fully and successfully integrated. But we would suggest that it is normally possible for information to be made available to the designers which facilitates their work, and which is broadly consistent with eventual evaluation. This information would be based on the results of measures to be used to determine magnitudes of costs and benefits, suitably adapted to indicate those geographic areas having "development potential", at least in relation to the particular items under consideration. Certainly the measures we have obtained from the urban development models could be adapted to provide plan designers with useful information. But again, integration of evaluation criteria (objectives and their measures) with plan design criteria does require that consideration be given at the earliest possible stage in the planning process to the approach to measurement. Any future elaborating and refining of urban development models should involve taking evaluation requirements more fully into account.

PART II

An Exploration and Critique of Recent Evaluation Practice

Introduction

WE HAVE selected seven planning studies for review. The reviews are presented as a critical examination of recent UK experience in the application of evaluation methods to urban and regional planning problems. Our general intention is to examine the extent to which the planning process adopted by each study team facilitated the most effective use of their evaluation method.

We shall focus attention on two principal issues. Firstly, whether the time and resources available to the study teams were used to best advantage; secondly, the degree of consistency between the approach adopted to the evaluation of alternative plans and the work undertaken at other stages of the planning process on which evaluation relies for inputs, with particular attention to the range of objectives and the approach to their measurement. In addition, we also discuss the nature and quality of the evidence produced for use in evaluation and the ease with which those formally responsible for decision-taking could form a view as to the "best" plan in terms of the interests of the community at large. We attempt to identify the strengths and weaknesses of the studies in relation to these matters and to suggest ways in which some of the weaknesses could have been overcome so as to increase the effectiveness of evaluation as an aid to choice.

These investigations will be made in the light of Chapter 3, which considered the implications of the information requirements of a "comprehensive" evaluation for other activities in the plan-making process. The term "evaluation-associated linkage" was introduced to refer to those cases in which the principles and methods adopted for evaluation should determine the kind of work to be input at other stages of the planning process.

In investigating the relationships between evaluation and other planning activities we have two aims. We are first of all concerned with improving the quality of proposals put forward for evaluation and the scope and reliability of evidence made available about their comparative advantages and disadvantages. Achieving this aim should lead to greater awareness, both on the part of those members of the community who will be directly affected and the decision-takers, of the consequences of opting for alternative possible courses of action. In this way the level of

123

debate about the relative merits of alternatives should be raised, thereby producing more soundly based decisions.

Our second aim is to help ensure the most efficient use of the time and resources devoted to planning studies. In this context there are two aspects to consider. It is obviously desirable that studies should not be unnecessarily lengthy and expensive. The intention here is to cut down the amount of effort required for a study without lowering the quality of what may be achieved, so that additional resources can be used elsewhere on other planning problems. The other aspect is the requirement of allocating the resources for a particular study in the best way between different stages of the planning process. Efficiency in this case has a number of dimensions. One is ensuring that data collected specifically for evaluation is both relevant and usable; another is the avoidance of duplication of effort at different stages of the planning process in producing information that may be useful for evaluation. Probably the most interesting aspect of efficiency concerns the appropriate allocation of effort between design and evaluation activities. It is rarely, if ever, possible to identify and assess all possible courses of action in a formal and thorough-going manner. Some method is therefore required for narrowing down the whole range of possibilities fairly quickly so as to concentrate on assessing the comparative merits of a few relatively good ones.

The case studies have been selected with a number of considerations in mind. We required examples of what we view to be advanced studies; in particular, ones that give serious attention to the conscious searching out of alternative courses of action and a formal, systematic evaluation procedure. Secondly, we wanted to investigate studies that dealt with "standard" planning problems, such as the location of urban developments within a sub-region and the formulation of an urban structure plan, so that suggested improvements to planning procedures can have a general application. Thirdly, we have chosen studies which illustrate a variety of evaluation methods. Although we favour the use of social cost-benefit analysis, it is not the predominant method used at present, and other methods will continue to be used in the future. Fourthly, since we want to examine all stages of the planning process, the studies had to be completed, or virtually so. Finally, it was necessary that the studies should be well documented and the reports be fairly easily accessible. This is important should the reader wish to check our interpretation of the study teams' work, or to examine certain aspects further. We have not been able to review all the studies we should have liked, owing to lack of time. Those we have had to omit include the Study for the Strategic Plan for the South East, the South Hampshire Plan Study, and the SELNEC Transportation Study.

The discussions of the case studies are structured around the model of a general urban and regional planning process presented in Chapter 2. That model is only an aid to these discussions and has been used in a flexible manner. Each review begins with some comments on the purpose of the study and the general approach that the planners adopted. The discussion of the adopted approach includes an outline of the evaluation method (or methods) used and the procedure that the team followed in

arriving at their conclusions and recommendations. This then leads to a consideration in some detail of the nature of the linkages between evaluation and other
activities carried out during the course of the planning process.

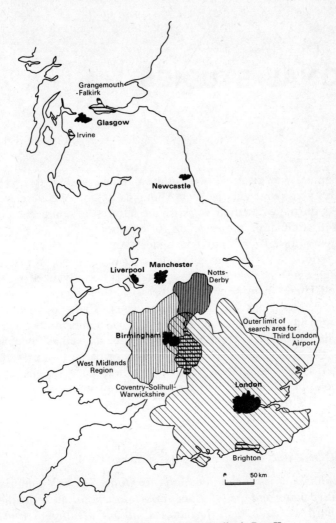

FIG. I.1. Geographic areas of case studies in Part II.

CHAPTER 7

REGIONAL STUDIES

IN THIS chapter we discuss two studies, concerned respectively with the Grangemouth/Falkirk area and the West Midlands Region. We were, in fact, engaged as consultants on the evaluation work of the latter study, and the experience was instrumental in stimulating the research for this book.

The Grangemouth/Falkirk Study was undertaken at a much earlier date than that of the West Midlands. It is convenient to consider these two instances of plan-making through time since planning theory and practice advanced a good deal in the interim period.There have been a number of other regional studies since the Grangemouth/Falkirk Study was undertaken, probably most of which would now be considered more advanced in technique. Nevertheless, this Study serves to illustrate a number of limitations of current planning practice as well as, by comparison with some of the other case studies, the development of certain aspects of technique in recent years. It is also of interest because threshold analysis was used as a major evaluation tool, the potential of which for physical planning has recently been dealt with at length by Kozlowski and Hughes.[1] Threshold analysis has been employed on only one other major study in Britain.[2]

GRANGEMOUTH/FALKIRK (October 1964–December 1966)

Two main phases of work characterized this Study. The first comprised the design of six alternative plans and the selection of one of them for more detailed considera-tion. These plans were deliberately formulated without attention to transport implica-tions. They were introduced at the second main phase, where three "idealized" networks were designed with respect to the chosen land-use plan and then evaluated. Following the choice of a preferred transport network, the plan was developed to the level of detail required for implementation and modified in the light of criticism prior to recommendation.

[1] J. Kozlowski and J. T. Hughes, *Threshold Analysis*, Architectural Press, London, 1972.
[2] Scottish Development Department (SDD), *The Central Borders: A Plan for Expansion*, vols. 1 and 2, HMSO, Edinburgh, 1968a.

7.1. BACKGROUND

The study was undertaken for the Stirlingshire, West Lothian, and Falkirk Growth Area Planning Advisory Committee in association with the Scottish Development Department (SDD). The initiative came from the SDD who, in their White Paper on development in Central Scotland,[3] had identified the Grangemouth/Falkirk area as a major growth area capable of accommodating a population increase of about 50,000.

This White Paper presented the Government's proposals for stimulating economic growth in the region of Central Scotland, and claimed to represent "a more positive approach to regional economic development than any Government in this country has yet attempted".[4] The proposals were intended partly to alleviate a number of major problems, including high unemployment caused by new industries creating insufficient job opportunities, net out-migration of young people, and urban decay resulting from run-down industries. But they were also intended to exploit some of the region's opportunities in order "to achieve a reasonable level of prosperity in the region as a whole". These opportunities related to the presence of factors favourable to economic growth. For instance, Central Scotland was found to have "a highly concentrated industrial society with a long tradition of engineering and other industrial skills"; interregional distances were short and communications were being rapidly improved; and "excellent export facilities" were available through major sea and air ports, facilities all capable of expansion.

The main policy recommendation of the White Paper was for the creation of growth areas in locations thought to exhibit the best potential for industrial expansion. Growth was to be stimulated by financial incentives to induce modern industries to locate there; by increasing public investment in "main roads, docks and airports; regional water schemes; the repair and renewal of the older industrial areas; and [by] a substantial programme of new housing and essential development". It was also stated that "in these growth areas, there must be some assurance that the wide range of financial inducements available to industry in development districts will be maintained until there is strong evidence of a general and sustained improvement in Central Scotland as a whole".[5] This was the first attempt to establish growth areas in Britain, and one of the first steps towards solving the problems of depressed areas through regional development policies rather than concentrating assistance in localities with high unemployment rates.

The petrochemical industry was seen as the cause of the recent "economic vitality" of the Grangemouth/Falkirk district. There had lately been considerable expansion and, "at the request of the firms concerned, further land adjacent to the existing oil refinery and its associated plants [had] been scheduled in the local authorities' development plans for industrial development".[6] The choice of this district as a growth area was also influenced by the fact that there was sufficient land

---

[3]SDD, *Central Scotland: A Programme for Development*, Cmnd. 2188, HMSO, Edinburgh, November 1963, para. 26(d).

[4]*Ibid.*, para. 3.

[5]*Ibid.*, para. 12.

[6]*Ibid.*, para. 51.

to allow further industrial and housing development on "a considerable scale" and that the district fell within the spheres of the economic and cultural influence of both Edinburgh and Glasgow.

The Grangemouth/Falkirk district was deemed to present a physical planning task of great complexity. It was decided that a special study should be made in order to prepare a comprehensive Growth Area Plan. One of the main planning problems of the Grangemouth/Falkirk area appeared to stem from control by four different local authorities; the interests of individual authorities were in conflict, and they would not co-operate without the prior preparation of an agreed plan for the area as a whole. This division of control was only mentioned in passing in the White Paper, but in the report of the Study it is repeatedly stated that the area should be planned as a single unit, which suggests that there were strong forces acting against such unitary planning. This diversity of interests was a major reason for the Study.[7]

Subject to discussion with the local authorities concerned, the Government decided to invite the teams from the universities of Glasgow and Edinburgh who had carried out the Lothians Study to conduct a similar study of the Grangemouth/Falkirk area. The joint directors of the Study were Professors Sir Robert Matthew and Percy Johnson-Marshall in Edinburgh and the late Professor Donald Robertson in Glasgow. It was started in the autumn of 1964 and took two years to complete, although the resulting report was not published for a further two years.

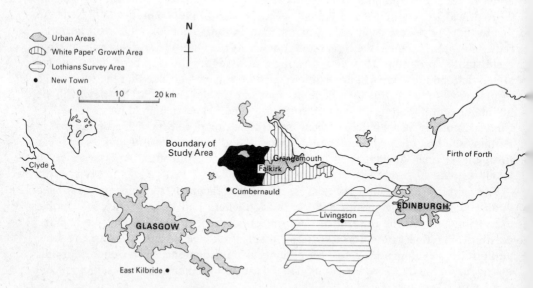

FIG. 7.1. Grangemouth/Falkirk study area and its location. (Source: *Grangemouth/Falkirk Regional Survey and Plan*, vol. 1, p. xvi, location diagram.)

[7]R. Bigwood and J. T. Hughes, in personal discussions.

Terms of Reference[8] *and the Organization of the Study*

The terms of reference stated that the planning teams should "carry out a survey and prepare a scheme of development for the area defined in the White Paper . . . and for this purpose consider and report on the economic, social and physical planning problems presently existing and likely to arise in the course of the development of the Area along the lines indicated in the White Paper". The results of the work had to be reported to the Joint Planning Advisory Committee by the end of 1966, giving two years for the completion of the Study.

Little attention was paid in the terms of reference to the manner in which the Grangemouth/Falkirk area should be developed; it was only stated that "a comprehensive economic and physical expansion scheme [should be] designed to increase [the] population in the area by about 50,000".[9] The White Paper of 1963 did contain general guidelines for development in Central Scotland, but these were concerned primarily either with physical planning issues at the regional level (such as designing the provision of major infrastructure) or with aspatial economic and physical planning issues (such as recommending the mix of public and private enterprise in house building activities.)[10]

The date by which the population increase should take place was not stated in the terms of reference, nor was it specified whether the increase of 50,000 residents was to consist of a net inward migration of 50,000 persons *plus* their natural increase or a total population increase combining both net inward migration and the natural increase of in-migrants. The teams chose to interpret the population target as net inward migration *exclusive* of natural increase and decided that 1986 should be the year by which the target was to be achieved. This implied a total population for the area of about 230,000 by 1986 and about 300,000 by 2001; but Robertson emphasized that the year 1986 should be regarded more as a guideline than a target.[11] The important point, he said, was not to worry about target dates but rather to ensure that the increases in population and employment in the area would not become imbalanced, since without employment opportunities population increases would cause unemployment problems, and without population increases the incentive to industrialists to locate in the area would be much reduced.

The study teams were asked to make specific recommendations and not just to examine the nature and merits of possible alternatives. So whilst the formal decision still lay with the SDD, the task of arriving at a choice of the course of action to be adopted had been delegated to the planners.

A further stipulation was that the teams should carry out the Grangemouth/Falkirk Study in a manner similar to that for the Lothians, which they had recently undertaken.[12] This was not explicitly mentioned in the terms of reference, but it had

[8]SDD, *Grangemouth/Falkirk Regional Survey and Plan*, HMSO, Edinburgh, 1968, vol. 1, page 1, and vol. 2, p. 5.

[9]SDD, Cmnd. 2188, *op. cit.*, para. 26(d).

[10]*Ibid.*, para. 89.

[11]SDD, 1968, *op. cit.*, vol. 1, para. 1.5.

[12]SDD, *The Lothians Regional Survey and Plan*, vols. 1 and 2, HMSO, Edinburgh, 1966.

been indicated in the White Paper. Consequently the Glasgow Team were given particular responsibility, as in the Lothians Study, for social and economic aspects, while the Edinburgh Team were responsible for physical aspects. Similarly, the report of the Study was produced in two volumes, each volume reporting the work of one team. There are very few explicit references in either volume to co-operation between the two teams. However, former members of the teams have indicated that co-operation was quite close in a number of respects, whilst agreeing that it could have been better if they had not been working in different cities.

7.2. SELECTION OF THE PREFERRED URBAN DEVELOPMENT STRATEGY

Outline of Methodology

The process of selecting the preferred urban development strategy was divided into two main phases. In the first a preferred land-use strategy was selected from a number of alternatives at a coarse level of design; in the second main phase the selected strategy was modified a little and designed in greater detail to meet the requirements of implementation. Following this the recommendations of the preferred development strategy were spelt out in detail.

The principal reason for this twofold division of design work was that the planning authorities wished to have an early general outline of the proposals to guide their decisions on current applications for development, so that these decisions could be consistent with long-term proposals. Accordingly, the Study was organized so that after a year (at the end of the first phase of the planning process) it was possible to give a rough outline of the nature of the final development proposals.

The adopted planning process may be summarized as follows.

Phase I

(1) A hundred or so idealized land-use distributions were produced on the basis of theoretical studies of urban form, six of which were represented as alternatives for initial evaluation.

(2) Check-list of criteria used to evaluate these six alternatives, three of them being selected to form a short-list.

(3) The three short-listed alternatives were "bent onto" the Study area and evaluated against a set of objectives (which differed from the check-list of criteria employed earlier). One of these alternatives (model 7) was selected for detailed investigation during the second phase, following consultation with the clients.

Phase II

(4) Three idealized transport networks were designed and "bent onto" model 7. The resulting networks were evaluated and one chosen as preferred.

(5) Model 7 was then modified a little and developed in greater detail following the application of threshold analysis and a consideration of small-scale design features. The revised plan was known as model 8.

(6) Model 8 was altered in the light of the clients' criticisms to become the recommended plan.

During the first phase of the planning process two lines of investigation were pursued simultaneously. On the one hand, growth potential analysis (concerned mainly with existing physical features) was used to assess the suitability of all parts of the Study area for industry, housing, agriculture, forestry, and recreation. On the other hand, various "idealized" patterns of land use were generated and evaluated. A large number of such patterns were considered initially, although it appears that only six of them were formally represented as design possibilities for comparative assessment. These were referred to as "hypothetical development models". We know little about how they were produced. The Study documents simply state that they resulted from certain theoretical studies of urban form. After a comparison of their advantages and disadvantages against a check-list of criteria, three of the six designs were selected for more detailed consideration. This check-list of criteria was said to include "a large number of critical factors", but unfortunately these factors are nowhere set down.

Each of the three development patterns was then roughly "bent onto" the Study area in such a way that it would accommodate about a quarter of a million residents. In this bending-on process, regard was paid to the area's physical characteristics. The three alternatives were then evaluated by examining the extent to which they each achieved a set of objectives for the plan. These objectives had been specified in advance of plan design and were distinct from the check-list of criteria employed earlier. A preferred development strategy was selected after consideration of the results of that evaluation exercise, and this strategy was then bent "more accurately" onto the Study area using the information provided by the growth potential analysis. The resulting development pattern was named model 7. At the end of phase I this development pattern was presented to a technical committee, working parties, specialist consultants, and representatives of central and local governments for comment. Although a few criticisms were made, the general outline of development proposed by model 7 was accepted and became the basis for the more detailed design work of phase II of the planning process.

In phase II threshold analysis was used to investigate in more detail the suitability of land throughout the Study area for new urban development, with particular emphasis on its suitability for residential development. But, unlike the earlier analysis of residential growth potential, this analysis considered not only existing physical characteristics of potential locations, but also the level of investment needed to make land suitable for development. Also, three idealized transportation networks were designed, these being roughly "bent onto" the land-use distribution of model 7 and then evaluated. However, the evaluation method used here was sketchy, being based primarily on simple indicators, such as the use which would be made of existing roads. There were also lengthy discussions in this phase about detailed aspects of urban design.

The results of these studies were then used to adapt and detail the design of model 7. The refined land-use strategy (referred to as model 8) was also presented to the various committees, working parties, and government officials for consideration. Their criticisms were taken into account in producing the recommended strategy, which was presented to the Joint Planning Advisory Committee.

Criteria for Plan-making

The Team stated that the function of a plan at the scale they were considering should be "to act as an effective medium for communication between the levels of Urban and Regional Planning; as a guide in areas under development where there is no comprehensive Regional Plan; and as an agent for the formulation of principles and the general framework of development as a whole". The Team were of the opinion that in order to produce such a plan the planning process should aim to develop a strategy which would lead to the realization of "the best environment based on a functionally interdependent settlement pattern".

This explicitness about what the Team wanted to achieve is welcome, but they did not go on to make their concept operational. There is no statement as to what they viewed to be the requirements of the "best" environment, or how they would attempt to make operational the evaluation of alternative plans according to a list of such requirements. This seems to us a serious omission since consistency of plan generation and evaluation requires an early statement of these principles.

Later in the Study, after the selection of the preferred idealized development pattern, the aims for the plan were reformulated more formally, as follows:[13]

(1) To promote the development of the urban region into a physical structure consistent with the "growth area" concept.
(2) To unify the development structure into an identifiable whole, either under one authority or as a distinctive sub-regional unit.
(3) To create a proper balance of functions within the physical structure, i.e. a considerable degree of self-containment.
(4) To provide the most satisfactory environment for meeting specific urban goals.

Aims (1) and (2) were derived directly from the terms of reference and from prior observations that the physical characteristics of the Study area favoured it being treated as a single unit. Aims (3) and (4), however, were formulated in equally vague terms to the earlier "best environment" statement. It was stated that in the optimum plan for the area, urban developments would exhibit some degree of self-containment, but no definition of self-containment was offered. Nor was there any indication of what benefits would be derived (and by whom) from achieving that aim. Further, there was no statement of what would constitute the "most satisfactory

[13]Reproduced from the SDD, 1968, *op. cit.* vol. 2, p. 103.

environment". Here, the criteria of assessment were the "specific urban goals". These referred to various aspects of an ideal environment, but they were nowhere defined in the report. Hence there was still, at this stage, no clear statement of the principles on which to select a preferred plan.

The Edinburgh Team were sceptical of the proposition that the quality of an environment should be assessed in welfare terms, and no welfare-based measures of environmental quality were used to guide them in their work. It was their view that the assessment of environmental quality should be based on intuition gained from experience, and it was with respect to an intuitive understanding of what constituted good environment that the strategy was eventually selected.

7.3. EVALUATION IN THE PLANNING PROCESS OF THE GRANGEMOUTH/FALKIRK STUDY

As we have noted, the plan-making process had two main phases: the generation and evaluation of a number of alternatives at a coarse level of design—leading to the selection of one of these for further investigation, and the detailed design of the selected plan together with recommending the preferred course of action. We shall now discuss the role of evaluation in relation to these two phases.

Generation and Evaluation of Coarse Alternatives

The study teams were at liberty to examine all possible locations for the development of the housing, industry, and sub-regional infrastructure required for a population increase of 50,000 and to consider any particular phasing programme for those developments. Nevertheless, team members indicated that they felt constrained in at least two ways. Firstly, they were not fully convinced that the Grangemouth/Falkirk area was the most suitable location to establish this population increase. Robertson,[14] for instance, remarked that even though the Grangemouth complex was growing rapidly, the sub-region did not have the buoyant employment structure usually associated with a potential growth area. The Grangemouth complex was highly capital-intensive, whilst other more labour-intensive industries in the area had been much less successful. Robertson was therefore led to consider whether it would not be better to improve the decaying urban areas of Grangemouth/Falkirk rather than to try to inject substantial new population and employment into the sub-region. But he finally concluded that the introduction of such growth was probably one of the best ways to encourage redevelopment. Other members of the teams indicated that they thought it would be in the interests of the region as a whole to extend the boundary of the Study area to include the Lothians area; the Study would then have been concerned with the best way to accommodate a given population growth in that extended area.[15]

[14]SDD, 1968, *op. cit.*, vol. 1, paras. 1.16 and 1.17.
[15]This point, and the one following concerning physical constraints on development, were made by R. Bigwood and J. T. Hughes in personal discussion.

The second factor which made the teams feel somewhat constrained was the physical nature of the Study area. They considered that only a very limited amount of land was suitable for urban development. Land on northward facing slopes or above the 600 ft (183 metres) contour was deemed to be too exposed for new urban development. This applied to much of the area and meant that the amount of land available for urban development was little more than that which would be required to accommodate a population growth of 50,000 plus their natural increase. Hence, alternative locations for housing, industry, and so forth were severely limited. We shall consider further the way in which physical features were treated later in this section, in our discussion of growth potential analysis.

The design of coarse alternatives began with the examination of a range of idealized development patterns exhibiting simple geometrical shapes, three of which were chosen for more detailed consideration. These were monocentric, polynucleated, and linear developments. Although the Study report states that these three were chosen from six development patterns, initially about a hundred possible patterns were briefly examined. Our interest lies in finding out the extent to which attempts were made (a) to ensure that all possible development alternatives were "considered", and (b) to ensure that the early selection of the three coarse development patterns did not preclude the "best" alternative from being revealed in the later (more detailed) design stages of the planning process.

By examining many initial development patterns rather than a few there was, of course, a greater chance of considering the whole range of possibilities. Nevertheless, no attempt seems to have been made to ensure that those development patterns which were examined exhausted all, or most, of the basically different possibilities.

The Study report does not discuss the way in which the three chosen development patterns were selected. We are not told either whether they were deemed to represent the best ones for the area, to represent extreme possibilities, or whether they were otherwise representative of development possibilities. Obviously they were chosen to represent the most *promising* possibilities. We understand that selection was made partly against a check-list of criteria (left unspecified in the report), but largely on an intuitive basis.

The three idealized development patterns were then evaluated in relation to their achievement of a number of objectives. As was appreciated, attempts to evaluate "ideal" development patterns in isolation from empirical considerations can be of very limited value. Consequently these ideal patterns were "bent onto" the existing settlement pattern in order to take account of "authentic physical features, limitations and potential for expansion of the Growth Area". Each alternative was designed to accommodate a total resident population of 250,000 by 1986.

During this process of bending the "ideal" plans onto the Study area, some adjustments were necessary in order to make plans compatible with existing site characteristics. For this reason it was better to evaluate them after they had been bent onto the site rather than beforehand. But, since the nature of their advantages and disadvantages will have changed somewhat during this bending-on process, in practice a relatively poor "ideal" plan might have emerged as preferred. One or two sub-optimal "ideal" plans, at least, should therefore also have been bent onto the site in order to reduce the risk of overlooking the truly preferred alternative.

Before discussing the objectives used in the formal comparison of the three selected development plans and the evaluation procedure adopted, we shall consider the use made of survey and analysis work to aid the bending-on process. The main body of this work comprised an analysis of "growth potential" of different parts of the Study area. These growth potential studies provided the prime link between the survey and analysis work and the coarse design process. Their purpose was to examine the potential for growth in the five major land uses—industry, housing, agriculture, forestry, and recreation. At the time it appeared intuitively obvious that natural features would be of overriding importance to the location of these activities. This view was taken because much of the land in the area was very exposed, being either above the 600 ft. contour or on a north-facing slope, whilst other land was waterlogged, had low load-bearing capacity, or some other physical disadvantage.

In order to assess the growth potential for a particular activity, the suitability of each zone of land was considered against a number of factors and the results aggregated in order to rank the overall suitability of the various zones. Although not explicitly stated, it may be presumed that the Team intended the factors chosen for inclusion in the analysis of a particular activity to be representative of all major factors which would influence the choice of a potential locator.

Factors for each activity were assigned to three categories according to whether they were deemed to be "negative factors", "modifiable limitations", or "positive factors". This classification was clearly based on the scale of resource costs involved in establishing new developments. Negative factors were those which would prevent development or seriously restrict it and make it undesirable. Modifiable limitations were factors which would make land less suitable or less desirable for development than normally because prior capital expenditure or negotiations would be required. Positive factors were those conducive to development.

Presumably, the Team intended the assignment of factors to these three categories to represent the comparative costs and benefits which would be perceived by the locators of each activity. However, no evidence was provided to show that the associated costs or benefits represented the preferences of locators. Indeed, an examination of the different growth potential surfaces suggests that preferences other than those of the locator were permitted to enter into the analysis. For example, in the surface of industrial potential, public open space was deemed to be a negative factor. In this case the preferences of those using public open space were taken account of rather than the preferences of those locating industry (who might actually prefer the proximity of open space, other things being equal).

The Study area had already been examined during the survey and analysis work to find which land zones were influenced by each factor, the results being recorded cartographically. Therefore, in the growth potential analysis it was only necessary to bring together information which was already available. Consistency between stages of the planning process led to obvious efficiency advantages in reaching the preferred option.

The results of the growth potential studies, we are told, were systematically compared and "an allocation of priorities and further assessments of land suitability led to a series of possible solutions culminating in what was called model 7". However, it appears that these results were not used in a direct manner in plan generation. Yet, since the growth potential studies dealt with the suitability of all parts of the Study area for all major land uses, they could have formed the basis for a systematic examination of a wide range of development possibilities. Consequently, much information which could have been used to select coarse alternatives in a systematic manner was discarded. Instead, the Edinburgh Team favoured a more consciously "imaginative" or "creative" approach to plan design. This approach was chosen mainly because it was felt that a deductive progression from survey and analysis to the design of alternatives could easily result in overlooking the best possibilities.

We appreciate that designing coarse alternatives on the basis of the output from the growth potential analyses may have led to the generation of rather conservative plans, particularly since the treatment of accessibility benefits in those analyses was scant. However, to have ignored the opportunity to investigate systematically the design implications of integrating the various analyses of growth potential seems wasteful of resources.

The choice of objectives for the formal evaluation of the three selected development options was said to result from "a general analysis of development priorities, coupled with the selection of suitable physical planning principles". It would appear that "development priorities" referred to the objectives to solve planning problems such as accommodating the growing population or improving depressed areas. In contrast, physical planning principles were said, in general, to take the form of

"propositions, establishing a desirable scale of urbanisation, conditioning the size of settlements within the urban region; and stressing the relationship of residential to industrial and recreational areas and community facilities. Detailed considerations of environmental qualities at the scale of the residential district, the location and size of industrial sites, and the distribution of services, are set within a regional framework. Other principles stress a desirable pattern of linkages, establishing priorities for certain types of mobility and accessibility for specific functions".[16]

It appears that "planning principles" were traditional physical design guidelines or standards.

The planning principles were derived from the planners' professional views as to what should "guide development and ultimately define the physical environment". The development priorities presumably stemmed from the findings of the survey and analysis but no basis, other than professional judgement, was given for the inclusion of certain objectives and the rejection of others. Also, there was no suggestion that the items of advantage and disadvantage considered did exhaust all the items of

[16]SDD, 1968, *op. cit.*, vol. 2, p. 93.

significant difference which would result from implementing the three alternatives. Further, no rationale was offered for the choice of the five groups (demographic and social factors, economic development, infrastructure, environment, and programming and implementation) into which the objectives were classified, yet this classification system affected the output from the evaluation.

The approach adopted for the evaluation was to assess each alternative against the objectives to determine whether or not they were achieved; an alternative was said to either achieve or not to achieve a given objective. No indications are given as to what constituted achievement. Whether an objective was achieved or not was a matter for subjective judgement.

After achievement of the objectives had been assessed, the results were aggregated in order to find the alternative which best fulfilled the objectives in each of the five groups. For any particular group of objectives, the alternative was selected which achieved the greatest number of objectives in that group. This is most unsatisfactory, since it ignores the varying importance placed on the achievement of different objectives.

The results of this analysis were not used directly to choose between the three alternatives. A discussion of the performance of each alternative in relation to the objectives concluded this second section of phase I of the planning process; the selection of the preferred alternative was left until the beginning of the next section (the First Synthesis). This selection was made not on the basis of the results of the objective achievement analysis but on an intuitive assessment of the extent to which the three alternatives fulfilled the "overall planning objectives" for the area; that is, the objectives listed on page 132. This seems an admission that the objectives employed in evaluating the coarse alternatives did not adequately represent these overall objectives.

Whilst the objectives used for evaluating the coarse alternatives were collectively termed "policy objectives", quite a number of them were, in fact, sectoral objectives. That is, they represented the preferences of groups whose well-being would be affected by planning activities. It is fairly easy to identify the sectors and their preferences which the Edinburgh Team had in mind when they formulated these objectives. However, most of the objectives were not specified as intentions to maximize or minimize the item in question. In some cases it is easy to deduce the associated intention, but in others the statement of the objective is too vague for this to be done. For instance, one objective was "shopping (consumer goods)"; the associated intention might have been "to maximize the scale of provision of shopping centres" or "to maximize the ease of access to given shopping centres" or some combination of these two. It is not clear what the Team had in mind.

Detailed Design and the Selection of the Preferred Alternative

As we have noted, towards the end of phase I of the planning process the decision-takers accepted the land-use plan which had been recommended by the teams as the basis for detailed work. In phase II, three alternative transport networks were designed and evaluated, and the chosen network fitted to the selected land-use plan—model 7.[17] In addition, model 7 was modified a little and developed to the level of detail required for implementation, resulting in model 8. The refinements of model 7 resulted mainly from threshold analysis.

When all the detailed design work was completed, no further evaluation was made in order to check that model 8 was in some sense better than model 7 or any of the alternatives initially considered. In order to do this it would have been necessary to design other alternatives in more detail and subject them to the same evaluation. This would have entailed extra work, but might have been worthwhile. For example, the alternatives which fared badly before the preferred transport network was designed could have fared better than model 8 after that network had been incorporated.

The criterion which was in fact used to decide whether model 8 would be satisfactory was to put it to the steering committee and the various working parties for criticism. This was referred to as "testing"; provided the strategy was found acceptable, the planning teams did not believe it was necessary to consider whether or not model 8 was in some sense the "best" alternative. That is to say, it was not, in its turn, formally assessed against any of the previously considered alternatives.

The Use of Threshold Analysis

We shall now consider how the results of the survey and analysis work were incorporated more fully into the detailed design process through the use of threshold analysis. The areas for such analysis were selected on the basis of the results of the growth-potential studies. This implied that the latter studies would enable attention to be focused on essentially good or interesting alternatives.

The use in the Grangemouth/Falkirk Study of threshold analysis was its earliest application in the United Kingdom. Whilst some effort had already been made to establish firm principles to guide the application of threshold analysis and the interpretation of the information which it provides, essentially the method was still at a crude stage of development.[18] Moreover, the method was applied under great pressure of time and resources. As a result, the analysis which was made may be described as extremely rudimentary.

Threshold costs indicate the magnitude of those resource costs of urban developments which are associated with differences in physical characteristics as between alternative areas of location. For residential development, threshold costs are defined as the resource costs (arising from physical characteristics) incurred in locating a new inhabitant (or dwelling unit) in a given place, over and above those which would be incurred in locating that inhabitant (or dwelling unit) in a place with no adverse physical characteristics (i.e. an area of firm, flat land, already served by

---

[17]Unfortunately the transport study was not written up in the published reports.

[18]Since that time, further research has attempted to refine the principles of the analysis and establish more clearly the advantages and limitations of its use. See Kozlowski and Hughes, 1972, *op. cit.*, part III.

public utilities and with reasonable access to main roads). The analysis tries to take account of all physical characteristics which differ with location. In the Grangemouth/Falkirk Study this was effected by basing the analysis upon all three types of characteristics which were studied in the earlier survey and analysis work and which were thought to exhaust all aspects of the physical environment: namely, natural features, land uses, and infrastructure.

In the Study, threshold analysis was used to assess the suitability of land for a particular activity on the basis of the costs of developing an area and providing it with certain "essential" amenities (which were taken as the provision of public utilities and reasonable access to good roads). It was used to examine the suitability of land for housing and industry, although the emphasis was very much on housing. Initially, suitability for these two types of development was considered jointly under the heading of urban development. Only later was there a differentiation between land suitable for housing and land suitable for industry. The Team chose this approach since the locations for industry chosen during phase I were regarded to be largely fixed—there were only a limited number of sites in the Study area which were considered suitable for industry. Suitability for urban development was classified as follows:

"(a) land unsuitable for urban development, i.e. areas for which preparation for new networks, etc., would be disproportionately costly;
"(b) land needing improvements before becoming suitable for urban development, i.e., requiring additional capital expenditure to open up given areas for urban development;
"(c) land immediately suitable for urban development, i.e., areas where the cost of location of new inhabitants is relatively normal."

The land was examined in relation to each of the three types of characteristics (natural features, infrastructure, and land uses), and three overlay maps were produced indicating the suitability of land for urban development with respect to each set of characteristics. The information from the three partial analyses was then synthesized. Land which was unsuitable for development in relation to any set of characteristics was eliminated from further consideration, and land which was immediately suitable for development with respect to all three sets was defined. Successive threshold lines were then drawn, which were said to delimit areas which were fairly homogeneous in that "the additional per capita (threshold) costs of the location of new inhabitants were for the most part similar".[19]

"1st, 2nd, 3rd and Ultimate Thresholds were shown". The first threshold contained existing urban areas and land immediately suitable for urban development. The second contained land requiring essential improvements, involving substantial capital investments, to be made suitable for urban development. The third contained land of the type defined for the second threshold, but which was in isolated locations; and the ultimate threshold contained land which was unsuitable for

[19]SDD, 1968, *op. cit.*, vol. 2, p. 117.

development. (The ultimate threshold was also referred to as an area in which development was highly undesirable.) In the case of the Grangemouth/Falkirk area, most of the land contained in the ultimate threshold was very exposed. The concept of an ultimate threshold has recently been abandoned by the advocates of threshold analysis, since in many areas it may be worth incurring very high development costs if by so doing one can obtain a high level of benefits. It has been replaced by the concept of a regional threshold to indicate those areas unlikely to be developed in the foreseeable future.

Each threshold was composed of a number of unconnected sub-areas whose capacity was assessed using average density standards, and, finally, the threshold costs associated with each area were assessed.

The definition of threshold areas was the result of an attempt to divide up the Grangemouth/Falkirk area into units of land which were few enough to be handled manually yet not too large for the purpose of identifying the approximate margins of development cost.

There are a number of inherent features of threshold analysis which limited its scope. Firstly, while the differential costs of providing "essential" amenities in different areas were computed, no account was taken of the differential benefits which would accrue from developing different areas, arising from such factors as accessibility to employment opportunities. Secondly, only the resource costs from physical characteristics of location were considered. No account was taken of other resource costs which vary with location, such as the costs of building materials and labour. Thirdly, no investigation was made into the variations in threshold costs arising from economies of scale dependent upon the size of area to be developed.

Since the analysis took no account of differential benefits, it was only justifiable to use it for assessing development costs and not in defining those areas which would offer the greatest net benefits. It is suggested in the Study report that the analysis was used to give a comprehensive assessment of the development potential of different areas. However, the results obtained were used in a more modest way to make marginal adjustments to the development proposals of model 7. In that context, the assumption that the benefits offered by a slight variation on model 7 would not differ significantly was fairly reasonable.

The results of the analysis were also used to phase the development proposals. Here two other shortcomings of the criteria of the analysis emerge. Firstly, no distinction was made between stepped and graded thresholds. Many of the thresholds were, in fact, graded (for instance, steeply sloping land), but they were all taken to be stepped.[20] With stepped thresholds the costs associated with locating a new inhabitant are very high when a threshold line has just been crossed, but they immediately fall to zero as the land is developed. In contrast, with graded thresholds the costs associated with locating each new inhabitant in the threshold area remain roughly constant. Therefore, in the case of a stepped threshold it is significant

[20]SDD, 1968, *op. cit.*, vol. 2, p. 121.

whether or not the land is fully developed soon after the threshold line has been crossed. No account was taken of this difference in the Study.[21]

Secondly, the criterion which was used for sequencing the development of areas was broadly that the cheapest areas in terms of threshold costs should be developed first. For this criterion to be consistent with economic efficiency there must be no significant variation in the level of benefits derived from developing different areas and no significant variation in costs other than threshold costs. In general, these assumptions would not be valid.

7.4. CONCLUSIONS ON THE GRANGEMOUTH/FALKIRK STUDY

In appraising the Grangemouth/Falkirk Study it is necessary to bear in mind that it was one of the earliest studies of its type in Britain. At that time planning was regarded primarily as an intuitive process, based largely upon subjective judgement. The teams were aware of the necessity to use some kind of systematic planning framework: "it need not be argued [they said] that logic and consistency in the planning process are vital to the construction of optimal regional or sub-regional plans".[22] To this end they attempted to improve the conventional approach to sub-regional planning through the development of a "model" planning process. For this they deserve much credit; it did facilitate a more systematic approach based upon empirical evidence.

Despite the reluctance to state the principles governing the evaluation work, there was a considerable move away from conventional intuitive assessments with the introduction of growth-potential analysis, threshold analysis, and the assessment of the fulfilment of objectives. In addition, some formal attention was given to the welfare effects of proposals. This reflected the influence of economists on the Study, and is clearly brought out in Hughes's discussion on efficiency in the use of resources (in his Public Investment chapter) and in Robertson's introduction.

The socio-economic work that was carried out made the Study much wider in scope than was normal at the time. The initiative here came from the Scottish Development Department, where there was a close liaison between those responsible for economic development and for physical planning.

We shall conclude by drawing attention to what appear to us to be the major weaknesses from our particular standpoint. The main weaknesses of the evaluation and assessment procedures were in our view as follows. There were no statements made as to whose preferences were to be taken into account in the decision-making process and, probably as a result of this omission, no empirical evidence was produced in support of the identification and measurement of preferences concerning the consequences of alternative plans.

[21]Threshold analysis was refined to take account of this difference soon after the Grangemouth/Falkirk Study. See Kozlowski and Hughes, 1972, *op. cit.*, part III.
[22]SDD, 1968, *op. cit.*, vol. 2, p. 6.

Although it was probably intended that the objectives should be "comprehensive", in general no attempt was made to justify that they were so.[23]

The planners developed a methodology which they believed would enable them to converge on the preferred plan, but they failed to define in clear operational terms the criteria by which to identify that plan. The search techniques for finding the preferred alternative according to one set of criteria may differ radically from those which would be required for another set. But there was no clear specification of what was meant by the "best environment" and other terms which were intended to specify the preferred alternative. Consequently, some of the decisions which were made in the planning process seem rather arbitrary.

In measuring the extent to which objectives were achieved, alternatives were in general deemed either to fulfil or fail to fulfil a given objective; no intermediate levels of achievement were employed. Also, in many cases, there was no clear specification of measures by which to judge whether or not a plan achieved an objective.

Finally, it was generally assumed, and without justification, that the achievement of each objective had the same relative value.

Having noted these points about the assessments of alternative plans, we now summarize what we consider to be important weaknesses in the linkages between evaluation and other stages of the planning process. Much of the information which was generated by the growth-potential analyses was not fully utilized in the design of coarse alternatives; and information which was provided by both the growth-potential analyses and the threshold analysis was not fully utilized in the detailed design process since it was not integrated in a systematic fashion. In addition, the results of the analysis of objective achievement were not used in any systematic manner, so that one could not conclude that the development alternative selected for detailed design was in some sense the best of all possibilities.

Finally, a few observations are in order on the planning process itself. A major requirement was that a preferred outline plan be produced early on to form the basis of the final proposals and to provide the planning authorities with a basis for determining development application decisions. As we have seen, this resulted in two main phases of work. If the results of the phase II analyses had conflicted seriously with those of phase I, much more work would have been required to detail an alternative development proposal. This would have been expensive and caused delays in commencing the development of the area. Fortunately for the Study, serious conflicts were unlikely to arise since those locations where new developments could be established were very limited in number and extent.

Separate teams worked on the physical and the socio-economic aspects of the Study. A division of labour in this way may have been desirable, but its effectiveness must have been hindered by working some distance from each other.

A reading of the Study documents gives the impression that the process of arriving at the preferred option was confused at times; it was certainly difficult to follow. An

---

[23]The only exception was when physical factors were divided into natural features, land uses, and infrastructure. It was argued that this subdivision was exhaustive.

instance is the use made of aims to guide the planning process. During the examination of the plan designs, use was made initially of a "check-list" of criteria and later use was made of two sets of "objectives" which had been established before the start of design work. The relationships between these sets of aims is far from clear, and they may well have contained inconsistencies. If so, this would have had serious implications for the sieving procedure which was employed during the evaluations. Alternatives which showed up poorly on the early check-list might have appeared advantaged in the light of later assessments during phase II. The reintroduction of some previously rejected designs could have reduced the likelihood of error in selecting the preferred alternative, but this was not done.

WEST MIDLAND REGIONAL STUDY (February 1968–October 1972)

In this discussion of the West Midland Regional Study our main concern will be with the planning process adopted by the Team. The Study has special significance for us because many of the preliminary ideas behind our researches were developed whilst contributing to it as consultants. The integration of evaluation with other activities in the planning process seemed increasingly important to us when we reflected on studies that both we ourselves and others had undertaken. But at the time of the West Midland Study we thought that the particular lessons to be learned from it were of general interest and worthy of more detailed investigation. To the extent that we are now critical of parts of the Study, the criticism necessarily reflects on us.

There were eight cycles to the Study which may be identified by reference to the alternatives which were generated and evaluated. The first four cycles involved the successive elimination and greater detailing of alternatives from over a hundred diagrammatic possibilities down to a short-list of four. The subsequent four cycles were concerned with the search by a process of iteration for the preferred alternative by generation of hopefully superior alternatives at each successive cycle. Not all of these final cycles were envisaged at the outset. Work on the main evaluation exercise was not started until the fourth cycle of this planning process, that is, until the short-listing stage. As a result there were no linkages between the main evaluation activities and the initial phases of plan generation and elimination of early designs. This led to certain inefficiencies in the use of the Team's resources and to a protraction of the planning exercise; for only by extending the Study was the evidence produced at the evaluation capable of being used to generate superior alternatives in the latter four cycles of the planning process.

7.5. BACKGROUND

The *West Midland Regional Study Report 1972* was published in October 1972. It had been preceded by the *Report of the West Midland Study: 1971*, published in September 1971, a discussion document containing much detail not included in the *Report 1972*. These documents were the result of the work of a Study Team set up by the West Midland Planning Authorities Conference. The Conference is composed of representatives of all the (then) county and county borough councils who are planning authorities in the Region.These authorities, after consultation with Central Government, decided to resolve their conflicting interests in the development of the Region by joint commissioning of a development strategy which, after debate and modifications, they all could accept. The Study Team was composed of technical officers from the Region's local authorities but acted as an independent organization. They were, however, "guided" by working parties staffed also by technical officers of the member authorities, Central Government, and consultants under a technical officer's panel. The purpose of the Study, and the result of the Team's work, was the preparation of a plan or development strategy covering the whole of the West Midland Region. Although they contained other proposals, the main differences between alternative strategies produced by the Team were of the future spatial allocations of populations and employments to parts of the Region, together with indications of the nature of concomitant developments. Obviously these strategies, being on a regional scale and looking as far forward as the turn of the century, could only make outline proposals for development in terms of location, scale, and nature.

Attention was focused in particular on the growth of the West Midland Conurbation. Although a number of other problem areas were identified, the Team concentrated much of its work on the relationships between activities in the new population and employment growth areas and the existing dominance geographically of activities within the Conurbation. This issue was largely concerned with mobility, particularly employment mobility, from the Conurbation. In this sense the possibilities of actual achievement of the plans seemed to dominate the Team's deliberations just as much as the desirability of the planning solutions.

The Team employed various consultants to assist them. The report of the evaluation consultants (Nathaniel Lichfield & Associates) was published in July 1972 in the form of *Technical Appendix V, Evaluation 2*, to the Study. Also of interest to us here is the report of the evaluation exercises undertaken by the members of the Team themselves, which was published as *Technical Appendix IV, Evaluation 1*. The communication consultants (Freeman, Fox Wilbur Smith & Partners) provided various pieces of evidence for use in the evaluations of alternatives. Their contributions to the Study were published in *Technical Appendix VI, Communications*. The Team also requested treasurers from various local authorities in the Study area to prepare a report on those aspects of local authority finance which would be affected by proposals in the alternative plans. We refer to the work of all these consultants to the Study.

We are primarily concerned with the efficiency of the planning process and whether the best use was made of the time and resources at the Team's disposal. Secondly, we shall investigate the consistency of approach (if any) as in the stages of plan generation and the evaluation of the alternatives. We are particularly concerned with the range of objectives, how they were derived, their validation and the approach to their measurement in the planning process. In addition, however, we discuss the nature and quality of the evidence used in the evaluation, and also whether it is possible to consider the preferred alternative strategy, in the light of the design and evaluation exercises, as defensible in terms of some recognizable concept of the general public interest.

The *Report 1972* contained the proposals constituting the recommended regional development strategy submitted by the Conference to the Secretary of State for the Department of the Environment. The Conference were not acting, strictly speaking, as ultimate decision-takers; that authority resides with the Secretary of State. But for practical purposes here we can consider the Conference to have such a decision-taking role since it was their task to put forward the strategy. The Team were working as a planning team for the Conference.

It should be also pointed out that the Team were themselves asked by the Conference to recommend a strategy. That is, they themselves were asked to take on the role of decision-makers and to suggest which of the alternatives they had generated was, in their view, to be preferred. This they did in the *Report 1971*. Thus we can analyse the planning process which was adopted by the Team for consistency between objectives used in plan design, those used in evaluation, and the decision-making criteria of the Team. Most of our discussion focuses on these activities of the Team.

7.6. THE ADOPTED PLANNING PROCESS IN OUTLINE

The planning process of the Study was cyclical. There were eight clearly identifiable cycles. Each contained a number of stages of plan preparation, as follows:

(1) The generation and investigation of a large number, possibly over a *hundred*, diagrammatic variants of spatial developments in the Region.

(2) The coarse options cycle, when the first alternatives were reduced to *eight* more formalized alternatives embracing the wider solutions initially considered.

(3) *Four* fine options were then selected for more detailed investigation.

(4) The *four* fine options were reworked in the light of refined forecasts, founded on common assumptions, and growing appreciation of the planning issues involved.

(5) From the evaluation of the four fine options by cost–benefit analysis and other exercises, the Team generated a further alternative known as the *fifth strategy* which, it was hoped, would exhibit superiority over the best of the fine options, at least according to the principles and measures used in the CBA. This was evaluated against the four fine options.

(6) From the fifth strategy the Team generated a further alternative, the *sixth strategy*, bearing in mind all the evidence they had collected.

(7) Minor modifications were made to the sixth strategy for it to become the Team's *preferred alternative* of the *Report 1971*.

(8) The *Report 1971* was published and circulated to various interested agencies and organizations for critical comment on the preferred alternative; a sum-

mary was also made available to the general public. Over a hundred separate observations were received, and these, along with further work by the Team and others, were considered. The *preferred strategy* was presented in the *Report 1972*. It was essentially similar in the long term to the preferred alternative of the *Report 1971*, although several modifications were made for the period up to 1981.

The initial four cycles involved reducing a wide variety of possibilities to a manageable number of four for intensive investigation. Alternatives were prepared in successively greater detail in terms of precise locations and the nature and scale of development envisaged. The latter four cycles involved the successive "improvement" of particular alternatives partly to obtain greater understanding of their relative merits, but mainly in order to move towards the preferred option. Improvements in certain basic assumptions and forecasts in the light of on-going work by the Team led to some minor variations in the form of subsequent sets of alternatives. They were not, however, specified in any greater design detail in moving from one cycle to the next.

Accordingly, the cycles fall conveniently into two groups: that group where, in moving from one cycle to the next, the number of alternatives is reduced and the alternatives are given in greater detail; and, that group where a superior strategy is hopefully produced by marginal adjustment to a basic design.

However, the Team did not always consciously pass through the same stages of plan generation and evaluation in each cycle. These stages may be identified in a network of activities given in the *Report 1971* of the Study. From that network it is clear that the stage of definition and measurement of objectives was of obvious importance to the Team. Other steps in their planning process included the undertaking of forecasts and other planning studies covering a large range of matters, the design process, and the evaluation and testing of the alternatives. The Team themselves undertook decisions, both to recycle the planning process and also in their recommendation of a preferred alternative, and they identified two aspects of decision-making, the appraisal of the evaluation excercises, and the selection of the strategies.

7.7. THE PLANNING PROCESS IN MORE DETAIL

The Initial Cycle

We have very limited information about the nature of the wide range of initial diagrammatic variants of the development strategies or the way in which they were reduced to eight coarse options. Nevertheless, two main intentions are apparent. The first was for the Team to obtain some idea of the relative importance of the problems of the Region, and the second to derive some impressions of the plausible development strategy possibilities open to them. The idealized strategies were generated largely in the absence of formal background information. Nevertheless, the composition of the Team guaranteed that it possessed certain ideas, possibly strongly formulated ideas, about those problems and possible strategy solutions. The first cycle was an attempt to set all of them down to represent a "universe" of solutions based on intuition.

They were then studied so that essential differences in form between possible designs could be identified. These plan possibilities were crudely assessed, not to derive differences in advantages and disadvantages as between plans, but rather to identify essentially common design features among the various groups of plans. The idealized strategies were "intuitively developed strategies" and "professional judgement" was employed to analyse them in order to shed greater light on feasible design forms for the cycles of the planning process to follow.[24]

This approach is of some interest for us. Rather than thinking initially about desirable consequences of developments (i.e., Study objectives) and then trying to design in such a way that objectives would be achieved as far as possible, the Team started by trying to envisage *all* possible kinds of design solution. This approach has certain advantages as a first step and has been used in other studies.[25] It gives maximum freedom to intuitive design; it focuses the mind rapidly and explicitly on the task at hand, and it allows for some design activity whilst the usually protracted stages of objectives formulation and approaches to measurement are being worked through.

The Team also claim similar advantages for this approach, largely relating to the speed with which it was possible to focus on realistic alternatives. Certainly there seems no objection to the investigation of possible design solutions without having first thought through the rationale for design, so long as the resources devoted to such an exercise are comparatively limited, as seems to have been the case here. But it is not possible, by the process of design, to identify desirable design solutions. Formal evaluation is required. "Professional judgement" was therefore an informal evaluation exercise applied to the hundred or so alternatives. From that judgement (rather than from formal evidence) the importance of the Conurbation in the design process began to emerge at this time. "Early studies [had] thrown into relief the relationships that exist between the extent of mobility within the population and within employment. . . . We therefore thought it advisable that the wide range of possible strategies which were available to be tested should reflect differing levels of dispersal of population and employment."

Clearly of some concern to the Team, and presumably to the local authorities in the Region when they set up the Study, was the extent of desirable (and feasible) decentralization of population, and activities from the Conurbation, and, presumably, of the location of any new urbanization in areas adjacent to the Conurbation in the Green Belt. These seem to be the major issues coming to the forefront at an early

[24]J. Stevenson, Evaluation of structure plans: lessons from the West Midland Regional Study, a paper given by the Director of the West Midland Regional Study to the TPI/CES Conference, University of Birmingham, April 1971, paras. 2 and 3.
[25]For example, by the Commission on the Third London Airport, as discussed in Chapter 11.

stage. Accordingly, the Team considered three types of strategy to be worthy of more detailed study. These were:

> "(i) the maximum dispersal of development, with the minimum amount of commuting, applied to the expansion of the major existing towns of the Region;
>
> "(ii) the maximum concentration of development, with the maximum amount of commuting, applied to the peripheral expansion of the Conurbation;
>
> "(iii) the attainment of a level of dispersal (from the Conurbation) and commuting that lay between these two extremes, applied to the stimulation of development in 'directions of growth'."[26]

At the conclusion of the first cycle the Team were clearly convinced of the importance of focusing attention on the advantages and disadvantages of developments close to and further away from the Conurbation. This conviction seemed to be justified by subsequent evaluation work. It arose from the Team's first-hand acquaintance with the history of the development of the Region and the conflicts arising from the various possibilities.

Amongst the eight coarse options were a wide variety of development strategies ranging from two alternatives of building close to the Conurbation, within the area now considered as Green Belt (which to some extent might have been interpreted as the "do-nothing" alternative, although the precise location of developments would be planned), to a fairly dispersed strategy which involved the expansion of many of the existing out-lying towns in the Region. The population and employment locations were specified for the year 2001. Between these two extremes were various alternatives lying within the stated concept of a sector growth, which was that the populations within any one strategy would be predominantly located in one direction away from the Conurbation; to the north, to the north-east, to the north-west, to the south-west, and to the south-east. It is not made clear why the Team concentrated, in their intermediately dispersed strategies, on the sector of growth concept; like the importance of mobility from the Conurbation, this development in the Team's preliminary thinking is not fully explained. But, like the mobility issue, the sector of growth idea has been part of the Region's planning debate for many years. It was part of the thinking of the Economic Planning Council. One of the justifications was that developments can thereby be "strung out" along lines of communication. In any event it was clearly felt by the Team that there were advantages and disadvantages associated with both concentrated alternatives and dispersed alternatives, and possibilities between.

At this junction we should discuss whether any interesting alternatives which fit the Team's requirements fail to be represented in the eight coarse options. They had, by the time of the course options cycle, fixed on the complete range of options to be investigated, and were unlikely to embark upon a search for new ones. Certainly each of the coarse options may be categorized into one or other of the three types of

[26]*Report 1971*, p. 55.

strategies mentioned. In terms of the differentials between strategies it appears that these eight were restricted to allocations of population growths to *new sites* for development in the Region, outside existing built-up areas, although in many instances contiguous with them. At the coarse option phase, then, the Team had ruled out the possibility of differential population and employment quantities *with-in* existing urban areas, particularly the existing built-up area of the Conurbation. Extra density was considered "unacceptable and impracticable", and required extra costs.[27] The extra accessibility advantage that might outweigh this cost was not tested nor the inacceptability of higher densities to those living in them. Such an alternative did appear, in one form or another, in the initial hundred or so alternatives since the terms of reference imposed no constraints on permitted population and employment growths within the Conurbation, and the initial range of alternatives was meant to be comprehensive. It was then rejected for these reasons of costs, acceptability, and practicability.

The Coarse Options Cycle

The eight coarse options were subjected to a more formal evaluation which was used to help select four fine options. Of this evaluation it is stated that alternatives were the subject of an appraisal of their performance against criteria developed from the initial objectives of the Study. These objectives, "which we came to adopt", formed a hierarchy ranging from a general statement of intent down to very precise aims. The general statements, or primary objectives, were too general to be measured. For example, under the heading of "population and housing", a primary objective was given as "To provide within a satisfactory total environment a range of housing in accordance with future assumed population characteristics". So, in order to make the analysis more manageable, they were subdivided into "secondary and tertiary" objectives, which were to be precise enough for measurement. By way of example, two tertiary objectives stemming from this primary objective were given as "To combat housing obsolesence and make provision for the continued alleviation of sub-standard housing conditions", and, "To provide reasonable range of choice in the housing market".[28]

In fact no details are provided of how the eight coarse options were evaluated in terms of the plans' achievements of these objectives. No measures are stated for the secondary and tertiary objectives. Indeed, in spite of the claims made, it is difficult to see how many of them could have been measured.

Some quantitative evidence was forthcoming and was provided on the transportation consequences of the options. The communications consultants were employed at this and subsequent cycles of the planning process. They operated a standard gravity-type transportation model using as main inputs to the model the spatial allocation of population and employment provided by the Team. The traffic model

[27] *Ibid.*, para. 26.
[28] *Technical Appendix 4, Evaluation 1,* appendix C.

gave valuable insights into the alternatives in terms of their operational assessments on traffic grounds. But one of the main statistics used by the Team from the model was the comparison between plans of total user travel costs. In brief, this figure is arrived at by multiplying the predicted quantity of traffic between each pair of places (zones) in the transportation study area and the costs of travel between those places, and then summing the result over all pairs of zones. We have indicated elsewhere[29] the problems of interpretating the travel costs which are often calculated from the forecast traffic flows of traffic models in land-use planning exercises. In the absence of information on *travel benefits*, which vary with alternative land-use dispositions, travel-cost information is of no value at all in evaluation because travel costs are an ambiguous measure of overall performance (i.e. the least-cost plan of two possibilities might be best or worst on traffic grounds).

As one would expect, travel costs were found to be least for the option having greater dispersal of activities and population (expanded towns), since this was intended to be a low commuting plan. The most centralized alternatives had highest user travel costs. But largely on this basis the Team described the expanded towns option as having emerged from the communications consultants' tests "particularly well".[30] For the one item which does appear to have been quantified, the Team seem to have given it an unacceptable interpretation.

That the centralized alternatives were not without merits on travel grounds was acknowledged when alternatives were discussed. The Team did consider accessibility as an *advantage* when expressed in terms of location of population and employment in proximity to or within the Conurbation.[30] Nevertheless, accessibility, as an advantage, does *not* appear in the list of objectives. Yet it influenced the selection of one of the centralized alternatives for inclusion in the short-list, since this is the main and possibly the *only* advantage of centralization. If there were these advantages of centralization, why, then, were they not reflected formally in the list of objectives?

Clearly the actual process of evaluation and selection of options at this coarse-options stage needs to be interpreted in the light of the statements which have been made and the range of options actually chosen. The Team's description is an inadequate guide to their actual procedure. In our view it would appear that they did *not* use any formal process involving the measurement of objective achievement (i.e. evaluation) at the coarse-option stage, and their objectives appear to have played no formal role in the design and evaluation of alternatives; it is as if they were added as an afterthought. The impression given is that the Team were, at this point, uncertain as to the magnitude of the various differential advantages and disadvantages of the alternatives which they had generated. This is perfectly comprehensible; the Study was in its early phases and information about the advantages and disadvantages of particular courses of action was not yet forthcoming, and no complete view of alternatives likely to show most promise was possible at this early stage. Indeed, it was necessary that they should opt for a selection strategy which

[29]In the discussions of accessibility in Chapter 6.
[30]*Technical Appendix 4, Evaluation 1,* para. 44.

was "risk-averting" in the sense of including in the short-list a *wide range* of options. This is just what the Team did. In their short-list they kept two extreme alternatives: developments within the Green Belt and expansions of existing towns (giving maximum feasible dispersal). They eliminated from the coarse options some of the sector of growth alternatives between those two extremes. The *range* of the four fine options was as wide in terms of their spatial form as the eight coarse options from which they were obtained. A diagrammatic representation of the four options selected from the eight coarse option possibilities (for the population component) is given by Fig. 7.2. The range of the options suggests that the Team did not know, at the time, likely differences between alternatives for the well-being of members of the community. The spatial differences were not then identifiable, even in a broad way, with welfare differences.

In this situation the approach adopted by the Team was, in our view, commendable. They used their experience to identify the range of the Region's planning issues and opted for a procedure which led to a wide variety of design solutions for detailed evaluation. What seemed less commendable was the attempt to justify the selection of the four fine options in terms that would be used to justify the selection of a preferred alternative. As there was no formal evaluation of the coarse options, in our view the extensive discussion in the documents[31] about objectives and measures at this stage seems irrelevant to the selection procedure, even though it may have been helpful in other ways.

One final point may be made about an aspect of the planning process of some importance at this coarse-options stage. Ideally, the Team ought to have satisfied themselves that the alternatives selected for the fine-options stage were feasible or practicable, as there is little point in considering in detail alternatives which will never be implemented in the form envisaged. In fact the Team expressed doubts about the feasibility of the dispersed (expanded towns) alternative. They were clearly worried about the mobility issue, and whether (given likely incentives and controls) population and jobs could be expected to decentralize to the extent indicated. They included the strategy only because "it was considered nevertheless that this concept should be further studied".[32]

Clearly the Team were hoping to undertake most of their analysis of alternatives at the short-listing stage. This would necessitate further stages involving the successive iteration of alternatives if a satisfactory solution was to be found. It was inevitable that the fine-options stage would be protracted, since all the analytical work was to be concentrated there.

The Fine-options and Subsequent Cycles

It was at the start of the fine-options cycle that the evaluation consultants were commissioned. Their terms of reference were agreed in March 1969, and although they expected to complete their study in that year they did not, in fact, submit their

[31]*Ibid.*, para. 38, and *Report 1971*, para. 140, following.
[32]*Technical Appendix 4, Evaluation 1*, p. 24, para. 43.

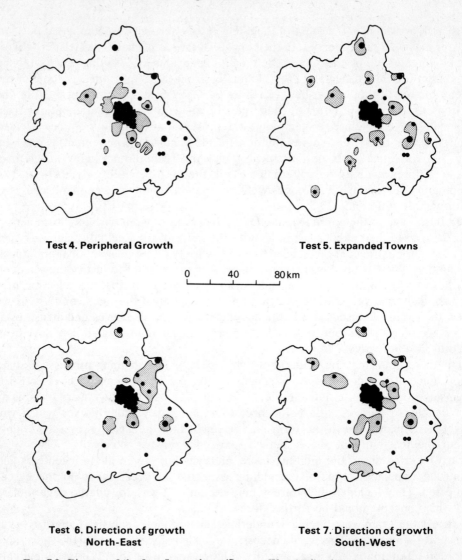

FIG. 7.2. Diagram of the four fine options. (Source: *West Midland Regional Study Report 1971*, fig. 11, sub-diagrams 1, 2, 5, and 7.)

report on the four fine options until December 1970. The evaluation consultants were commissioned by the Team to undertake a social cost–benefit analysis in the form of the planning balance sheet. The Team preferred this approach to other evaluation methodologies because they disliked "subjective and arbitrary weighting systems" in evaluation.[33] It was pointed out that this would be the first attempt to apply

[33]*Ibid.*, p. 39, para. 80.

conventional social cost–benefit techniques to a planning evaluation of this scale and degree of generality of proposals. The Team, however, had assumed that the evidence produced by the evaluation consultants would not be comprehensive, and regarded it as only one of a number of pieces of evidence which they would take into account in deciding on their preferred strategy. Indeed, it was intended that the results of the cost–benefit analysis (CBA) would be fed into the Team's own evaluation matrix,[34] and would become part of the evidence that the Team would themselves use in suggesting to the Conference a preferred alternative. Subsequently, after the submission of the evaluation consultants cost–benefit study and as the published documents show, it was decided that the CBA would form the central means of evaluation to which the other technical studies would lend support.

As we have seen, four further cycles were adopted before the preferred alternative was generated but do not appear to have been fully envisaged at the outset. It would seem that the Team had some difficulty in comprehending the implications of certain aspects of the CBA (which is hardly surprising given that it is over a hundred pages long). The fifth strategy in particular was not generated as a feasible alternative in itself, but as the Team's attempt to find the best design according to the evaluation consultants' criteria and measures.[35]

Possibly the findings of the CBA did shed new light on the design possibilities open to the Team; the sixth strategy and the preferred alternative may have reflected these possibilities as well as the work of the communications consultants, the treasurers, and the results of the Team's own investigations into various matters. We shall consider some of these analyses of the four fine options and the role they were expected to play, and that they could play, in the final selection.

The treasurers were asked to estimate the effects of the proposed options on the finances of the local authorities within the Region, and were also asked to rank the alternatives in order of financial preference. Their task was a daunting one. In fact they were unable to distinguish between alternatives—perhaps not surprisingly in view of the extensive time horizon and the already impending changes to local government organization and finance. This perhaps allowed the Team to avoid indicating how they would have used the treasurer's results in arriving at their overall conclusion.

It appears that in their own evaluation exercises the Team focused on landscape quality, environmental impacts of possible motorways in the Conurbation, physical constraints on new development and on microclimatic issues. They clearly thought either that these issues warranted detailed investigation because of their importance, or that they were not being adequately taken into account by others, such as the evaluation consultants. They are all items which, in principle at least, should be embraced by a comprehensive CBA.

The communication consultants undertook a series of essentially similar exercises at the fine-options cycle and subsequent iterations to the preferred alternative as

[34]Stevenson, 1971, *op. cit.* paras. 33 and 35.
[35]*Ibid.*, para. 7.

they had already undertaken at the coarse-options stage. Parts of the results of their work were included in the evaluation consultants CBA. These related to the capital costs of providing road space to meet speed/flow requirements specified by the Team. The user costs item as an output of the traffic model was not, however, included in the CBA for the reasons we have discussed previously.

Indeed, understanding the issue of travel costs and benefits was clearly difficult for all concerned. The appendix of the evaluation consultants' report contains two separate items discussing the nature of travel costs and travel benefits and the reasons why the communications consultants estimates of travel costs were not included in the CBA. The documents show much debate on this issue but no clear indication of how it was resolved.

Finally, the evaluation consultants undertook their cost–benefit exercises at this cycle of the planning process. We discuss this input to the Team's work more extensively in the next section. In brief the exercise was meant to be a comprehensive analysis of all the wider social effects of the proposals. As such it was bound to play some role in the determination of a preferred alternative strategy. An issue of some importance was how the evidence of the evaluation consultants fitted in with other evidence on the alternatives produced by the Team and their other consultants. Was there an agreed framework for evaluation evidence? There is no clear answer to this question. We do know that after the cost–benefit evaluation of the four fine options the Team seemed to consider the evidence of some use in helping them improve upon the designs of the fine options in generating further superior alternatives. They used it to generate their fifth strategy. They then went to generate the sixth and preferred strategies using wider evidence. But there is only a partial indication of the process by which integration of this mixture of evidence was achieved in the generation of the alternatives after the fifth strategy.

7.8. EVALUATION IN THE PLANNING PROCESS OF THE WEST MIDLAND REGIONAL STUDY

The issues on which we shall now focus are the efficiency of the planning process and the consistency in the use of objectives in plan generation and evaluation. In short, could the time and resources taken to reach the preferred alternative have been reduced by an alternative structure to the planning process? Was the preferred alternative, as far as we can tell, amongst the best of all possible alternatives? In section 3.1 we have identified linkages associated with evaluation and the other stages in the generalized planning process. We indicated the efficiency advantages of incorporating a set of objectives and the approach to their measurement in all of the stages of our generalized planning process from the decision to plan through to the evaluation and where appropriate, as here, to the decision on the preferred alternative. We consider these linkages in relation to the generalized planning process applied to the West Midland Regional Study.

Evaluation and Constraints and Objectives

In the *Report 1971* of the Study (pp. 50–52) the Team set down their constraints on the design process. They were identified in relation to the main elements of the design form—population and housing, economic growth considerations, communications, and so on. These constraints do not seem to be limits imposed by institutional factors, or limits which the planning team themselves wished to impose in order to concentrate on most likely areas of good alternatives. Rather, they were observations on advantages and disadvantages of alternative plans. For example, one of the constraints was that "The strategy must be directed to the selection of locations for development that are likely to prove attractive to employers and economic activity in general, by virtue of their locational advantages, their accessibility to the central urban complex, particularly the Conurbation, the presence of an extensive pool of labour, and inherent economic growth potential and an efficient infrastructure".[36] In this form a constraint is more like a guidline for design. It is not a constraint in the sense that it limits the design procedure in any way. As far as it is possible to tell there were no formal constraints except those that would arise as a result of the analysis of advantages, or, more particularly in this case, disadvantages of alternative possibilities.

Following the discussion of constraints, the Team go on to discuss their counterpart—opportunities. These were statements of intent in the design process. They tended to be rather vague. For example: "The definition of a regional strategy offers a salient opportunity to ensure that social, economic and physical values are seen as an integral part of the wider concepts, rather than as distinct areas of concern. The opportunities here relate to the achievement of standards and the satisfaction of needs that will grow more exacting as people move towards a greater measure of prosperity, education and leisure".[37] This statement does not allow the design team to focus on the location of future developments.

Nevertheless, the Team must have gone through the process of identifying likely areas of advantage and disadvantages at the coarse-options stage, despite their over-general statements about opportunities and constraints. They did, for example, analyse the physical attributes of various parts of the Region, and produced a sieve map of the traditional kind to identify areas for development which were physically suitable.[38] They then identified areas of "sensitivity", such as the National Parks, or where there would be local restrictions such as areas of outstanding natural beauty of first-class agricultural land, or where there were very localized difficulties for development such as landscape value, water-safeguarding, and so on. However, there is no indication that such a survey in itself led to suggested design solutions for accommodating the future urban growth. Areas having no constraints on development according to the sieve map would clearly help the design team to focus their

[36]*Report 1971*, para. 154.
[37]*Ibid.*, para. 169.
[38]*Ibid.*, fig. 7.

minds on likely areas for development. But obviously the design solutions could not be constrained to conform only with such areas. Such a negative approach ignores the opportunities which may be realized from developments which are contrary to those crude constraints. In fact the Team chose to locate development on some top-grade agricultural land which would then be lost to urbanization in one of the strategies. In the minds of the designers there must have been some compensating advantages for this loss. It would appear that the attitude to constraints and opportunities adopted by the Team, whilst being rather vague in intent, was sensible, for it did not rule out interesting possibilities from their design solutions. But full identification of disadvantages and advantages of alternative design solutions was to be the task of the evaluation.

The *Report 1971* contains considerable discussion on the matter of objectives. They are also discussed in the *Technical Appendix 4, Evaluation 1* of the Team. We have already noted that the Team's objectives formed a hierarchy descending from very general statements of intent to a series of more precise aims. These primary objectives could be defined largely as "efficiency objectives" in the cost–benefit sense. That is to say, they are related more to the achievement of benefits and reduction in cost items than to matters of the *incidence* of costs and benefits. In the *Report 1971* (p. 48) it is stated that objectives, if they were to have meaning, must be capable of measurement either directly or through certain indicators. Hence the primary objectives which were too general for this purpose were resolved into the more specific secondary or tertiary ones. We have seen that the documents give no indication how those tertiary objectives were measured. Hence we do not know how they contributed to the design of alternatives. Although the objectives were reported to have been used in the evaluation of the eight coarse options, when these were reduced to four in the fine-option cycle, no *details* are given in the *Report 1971* of how they were used.

The evaluation consultants also listed objectives, which were postulates of the objectives of members of the community concerning the way that various strategies would affect them, measured according to independent evidence of how members of the public perceive and value them. However, the Team's objectives and the objectives of the evaluation consultants were not the same. As we have shown, in practice this did not matter since the Team's objectives did not appear to be used in either the generation of alternatives or in their formal evaluation. Had they been used, there would have been inherent inconsistencies in the approach of consultants and Team. For example, it is possible to identify important objectives appearing in the evaluation consultants' work which are not in the list from the Team. One objective was of residential accessibility to job opportunities; others relate to the treatment of the timing of developments by the Team and to the social costs of congestion.

In the evaluation of the four fine options, the objective of accessibility was of some significance. This was predictable, since the alternatives ranged between very concentrated developments close to the Conurbation, where clearly alternative job opportunities and other "interaction" possibilities are highest, and developments further away in the various towns of the Region, where these opportunities are lower. Of course, it is not *a priori* evident that the item accessibility would be important in comparison with other items; that would depend on how members of the public valued it against other items, as well as on the extent of difference between the plan designs for the item. But it might have been anticipated that accessibility differences would have appeared important. We have seen that the Team, by virtue of including a concentrated alternative in their short-list, must have thought so. Yet they did not have accessibility in their list of objectives at the coarse-options cycles.[39]

The evaluation and communications consultants demonstrated that the congestion cost disadvantage of locating additional populations and activities in or around the Conurbation would be large. This was also to be expected. The new residents travelling to work and to other destinations within the Conurbation would obviously impede existing residents and others journeying to work, and thus add to existing congestion. But the Team had no objective of minimizing the social costs of congestion. Their primary, secondary, and tertiary communications objectives make no mention of congestion at all.

In another important way, the treatment of the timing of events, the approach of the evaluation consultants led the Team to make changes in the design of alternatives. This aspect of planning is generally referred to as discounting. The Team's terms of reference specifically requested them to give particular attention to developments in the period up to 1981. However, the four fine options were based on the assumption that prior to that time development proposals were "committed" and presumably could only be changed at considerable cost. Accordingly, the fine options were generated as strategies for developments after 1981, to the turn of the century. The evaluation consultants' report stressed the likely significance to members of the community of the phasing of advantages and disadvantages over time. At conventional discount rates the pre-1981 developments would loom much larger in importance for the decision now (possibly six or more times as large) compared to developments taking place after that date. The Team did modify their attitude to the committed developments. The sixth strategy differed from the four fine options at 1981 as well as at 2001. The preferred strategy of the *Report 1972* also gave greater emphasis to developments prior to 1981 than those in the longer term. With greater consistency of approach as between design and evaluation, explorations of design variations of this nature could have been undertaken much earlier and more effectively within the planning process.

To a certain extent the objectives, the costs and benefits, and the approach to their measurement, which were used by the evaluation consultants, were utilized by the Team as information imputs in the design of the fifth and sixth strategies. They used

---

[39]They had as one of their tertiary objectives: "To make provision within acceptable journey times for *adequate* job choice" (our emphasis) *Technical Appendix 4, Evaluation 1*, appendix C. This is not the same concept as accessibility. In addition it is stated that "attractions to residents in terms of environment and job opportunities" was considered (*ibid.*, para. 38). Again this is not necessarily synonymous with accessibility, and as we are not told *how* this criterion was considered we have no way of judging.

also the evidence on measured costs and benefits from the evaluation consultants' work in their selection of the preferred alternative. But the Team appeared to accept some of the evaluation consultants' evidence at a late stage in their planning process after their preliminary analysis and designs of alternatives were completed. It surely would have been more efficient to have commissioned the evaluation consultants to liaise and work with the Team at the outset rather than to have waited until the fine-options stage.

Evaluation and Data Collection, Analysis, and Forecasting

Collecting information to be used in the comparison of alternative plans at a very early stage in the planning process is necessary, firstly, so that evaluation work can proceed rapidly to its conclusion, and, secondly, so that the best possible evidence on advantages and disadvantages can be generated. If too little thought is given to the approach to measurement of advantages and disadvantages at early stages in planning studies, the evaluation suffers in consequence. In the West Midland Regional Study over nine months elapsed between the agreement of the terms of reference and the time when the evaluation consultants submitted their request for data. From then to the appearance of the report of the evaluation consultants was nearly a year. It is evident that the consultants and the members of the Team were conscious of the need to collect data for evaluation at an early stage; and documentation clearly shows that the evaluation consultants and Team discussed together the form of presentation of the regional development strategies so that the type of evaluation and the measures used could be compatible with the generality of the plan statements. Again, the Study appears to have been efficient on this aspect.

Evaluation and Design and Testing

We have indicated how the selection procedures adopted by the Team at the coarse-options cycle may be interpreted as attempts to minimize the risk of omitting advantageous alternatives through inadequate information on the comparative advantages and disadvantages of alternatives. The four fine options include a fairly wide range of alternatives in term of spatial variations. The preliminary cycles were attempts to reduce the alternatives to manageable numbers, whilst still maintaining a variation in design form.

However, as indicated previously, at least one possible alternative was eliminated at the earliest stage of the planning process, that of differentially greater populations in the city centres which might be brought about through rehabilitation or renewal. The findings of the cost-benefit evaluation of the four fine options suggested that such an alternative might have been a comparatively advantageous one had it been considered in more detail than at the initial screening of a hundred or so diagramatic variants; it would certainly have been interesting to consider it in some detail. It was found that accessibility to jobs and service facilities seemed to be highly valued by residents in the Region, and accessibility benefits are highest in the central areas of the Conurbation. By locating larger populations in and around the city centres (rather than peripherally to the Conurbation), journey to work costs and possibly congestion costs could have been reduced because shorter movements are likely within the built-up areas as journey-to-work distances are reduced. Of course, increased densities in the city centres have disadvantages on other counts; for example, the longer distance to rural recreation areas and the rising costs of accommodation. Nevertheless, the Team did not submit a completely full range of alternatives for evaluation in spite of their focus on the Conurbation, although the range of alternatives submitted was clearly quite wide in scope. Perhaps had they utilized measures of objectives in the design process the full advantages and disadvantages of such a solution might have been more apparent.

It should also be stated that the Team did not formally test the assumption reached at an early stage, that the Conurbation should be the focal point of the strategy. Perhaps it was too obvious an issue? But the Team could, by the way of example, have considered an "equity" alternative, one which consciously tried to aid disadvantaged residents. The spatial form of such an alternative is unknown and not at all easy to attempt to specify in developmental terms. But as the disadvantaged in society are distributed across the Region, in city centres, rural areas, and areas of economic decline and high unemployment, the spatial form of such a strategy might not have focused on the Conurbation in the manner of the four fine options. So a critical initial assumption about spatial form was never completely tested for its welfare implications.

With the delay in appointing the evaluation consultants, the Team could not have incorporated systematic modelling procedures to help with their design process if they were also to use the objectives and measures used in the consultants' evaluation. Again this is a case where, in order to incorporate the measures used in evaluation into the design process to help identify areas of potential advantages for urban development, attention must be given to the problems of objective identification and measurements at the very earliest stage.[40] Had the Team themselves found suitable measures for their own objectives at the coarse options-cycle and had confidence in using them, then it would not have been necessary to employ outside consultants.

In the event of going on to generate the improved fifth strategy and then the sixth, the Team were able to use the evidence of the cost–benefit evaluation to assist in the design of further and superior alternatives. They did not directly employ the measures used by the consultants to identify areas of urban development potential. By that time it was too late to "mechanize" the design process. But the consultants did suggest a way in which the design might be altered to achieve a better overall result in terms of community well-being according to the objectives and measures used by the consultants. For example, by decentralizing some of the central area employment activities and yet still locating populations and employment peripherally to the Conurbation, it would be possible to reduce congestion whilst leaving accessibility

---

[40]The Coventry–Solihull–Warwickshire Sub-regional Study offers a good example of how such procedures may be carried out.

advantages more or less unchanged.[41] In this way the advantages of concentration would be maintained and some of the disadvantages removed. This feature and others, where evidence from the evaluation was used in design, was probably, to some extent at least, eventually incorporated into the design of the preferred strategy.

Once the preferred strategy had been identified, the Team *then* asked the questions (*Report 1971*, p. 93): "Is the strategy practicable in terms of the deployment resources and viable in terms of local government finance? Will legislation be required?" Clearly the Team must have made some attempt to test for feasibility prior to this, for what would have happened had the answers been negative and the preferred strategy found impracticable or non-viable?[42] If that had been truly the case, the preferred strategy would have had to have been rejected and presumably the process of evaluation and selection repeated. Indeed, the possibility exists that all of the options considered at the post fine-options cycles would have been impracticable or non-viable in the sense suggested by the Team's questions. In that case the design process would also have had to have been repeated. Clearly the testing of the practicability and general feasibility of alternatives should *precede* rather than follow their evaluation.

We do know, because this was the *raison d'être* for having a Regional Study, that differences of opinion existed between local authorities in the Region on where the future urban development should be located. The Team was right to include in the final short-list of alternatives a wide range of alternatives. Although they themselves offered a recommended strategy to the Conference, as requested, the Conference and the general public could debate that strategy in comparison with the others which were also considered at the final evaluation stages.

This course of action was adopted. The debate did not take place within a framework of a public inquiry. Rather, documents were published and agencies and private individuals were encouraged to comment in writing on the work of the Team and its consultants. This they did and about a year later the preferred strategy appeared, reflecting these outside comments, in the *Report 1972*. The possibility existed for the Conference, as decision-takers, to arrive at a different conclusion from that of the Team, since at least four alternatives were open for debate. This appears to us to be a desirable feature of the plan-making process. In the event, Conference submitted to the Secretary of State an alternative which was essentially similar, in the long term at least, to the Team's recommendation.

7.9. CONCLUSIONS ON THE WEST MIDLAND REGIONAL STUDY

After publication of the *Report 1971* the evaluation consultants identified what they regarded as two important lessons to be learned from the Study planning process.[43]

---

[41]*Technical Appendix V, Evaluation 2*, pp. 117–19.

[42]The Team may have suffered from poor reporting of their endeavours on this point.

[43]*Technical Appendix V, Evaluation 2*, pp. 297–302.

(1) There were differences between the stated objectives of the Team and those of the evaluation consultants. The criteria for design were not therefore the same as those of assessment. This could possibly have led to the eventual acceptance of a preferred alternative which was not amongst the best of all possibilities.

(2) The Study was unnecessarily protracted. This was largely because the initial work of the Team was oriented too far towards plan design and not enough to plan assessment. Accordingly, cycles of iteration of alternatives were required to obtain a preferred alternative although they were not initially envisaged. Possibly the evaluation consultants were commissioned at too late a stage in the overall planning process.

We have seen that there were eight main cycles to the planning process. Greatest attention appears to have been given to the reduction of the eight coarse options to four, the four fine options to one, and then as iteration in search of an improved preferred strategy. In our view the time devoted to the cycle reducing the eight coarse options to four should have been slight, given that the Team were then going to go on to iterate to a solution after detailed analysis of the four wide-ranging options on the short-list. There is much discussion in the documents about objectives, measures, and evaluation at this coarse-options stage, yet nothing of substances appears to have been done. Nor, in our view, was much investigation of the relative merits of those eight options necessary. Many of them were similar in structure (if not in precise locations of development). Moreover, the intention at the short-list stage was to consider in detail alternatives virtually across the complete spectrum of design possibilities. It was only necessary to remove a few of the intermediary alternatives to arrive at the short-list, and no great analysis was necessary for that to be achieved.

The fifth strategy cycle was included after the short-list evaluation in order to assist the Team to understand the implications of the evaluation consultants' findings. If the main evaluation process, which was a cost–benefit analysis in this case, had begun at the outset of the Study, this cycle would probably have been unnecessary.

The design assumptions were tested in the evaluation consultants' work. The information provided was then used to generate further alternatives at the fifth, sixth, and preferred alternatives cycles, and then on to the preferred strategy of the *Report 1972*. To the extent that the Team were able to generate successively better alternatives in that way, the preferred strategy may well be generally advantageous. We do not know whether the Team have arrived at a "local optimum" plan rather than some more "global optimum", since assumptions made very early on about design forms in relation to the Conurbation were never really tested. Perhaps this is an area of concern of professional judgement; that it is a waste of time to investigate thoroughly some design assumptions because little uncertainty exists about their validity. This was probably true for the importance of the Conurbation in the West Midlands spatial structure of activities. Yet it would still appear to be true that the main focus of the design work was established without much evidence to substantiate it in the Study's initial phases.

The evaluation consultants attempted to determine the advantages and disadvantages of alternatives from the point of view of members of the community likely to be affected. Evidence was collected of the strength of community preferences. The Team also explicitly expressed their intention to propose a preferred alternative shown to be advantageous in terms of the overall public interest.[44] Once the evaluation consultants' findings were known, the Team were, subject to their interpretation of the adequacy of the evidence, willing to use them to generate further alternatives. In that way we may say that there is some evidence to suggest that the preferred alternative was shown to be advantaged for the community as a whole, at least from amongst the alternatives considered, and probably amongst the range of possible alternatives which could be generated at this point in time. The subsequent preferred strategy also had the benefit of public scrutiny and observations although it is difficult to judge whether the process of public comment on the Study document was effective.

Accordingly, in conclusion we may say that the planning process of the West Midland Regional Study probably led the Team finally to a demonstrably advantaged alternative. There were, moreover, many desirable features in the planning process adopted to reach that conclusion. Amongst these were the initial deliberations to obtain a universe of crude alternatives, the final iteration to a preferred option once a fairly good alternative had been identified, and submission to the decision-makers of a range of alternatives for choice, as well as a recommendation. However, in our view the time and resources utilized to reach that alternative could have been reduced or used more effectively. Thus the main lessons to be learned are that the process of evaluation must start at the very outset of studies, and that consistent and formal linkages between evaluation activities and other stages in the planning process must also be established at that time.

---

[44]*Ibid.*, p. 15.

CHAPTER 8

Sub-Regional Studies

IN THIS chapter we consider two of the first wave of sub-regional studies undertaken in this country, initiated by Richard Crossman as Minister of Housing and Local Government. They have been based on inter-authority co-operation, with the Ministry providing guidance on the terms of reference. Hence the terms of reference specified for the various planning teams were very similar. The planning exercises were of a traditional land-use type, the main components being population, housing, industry, employment, shopping, and transport.

NOTTINGHAMSHIRE–DERBYSHIRE (June 1968–September 1969)

The work of the Planning Team was ambitious in many respects and involved some important innovations such as the use of development potential analysis, although the published Report of the Study does not fully bring out the calibre and detail of what was accomplished.

Among the chief features of the work that we identify are the very wide range of alternatives that the Team attempted to investigate; the deliberate rejection of the use of the proposed evaluation criteria as an aid to design; and the importance given to practical problems of implementation.

8.1. PURPOSE OF THE STUDY AND TERMS OF REFERENCE

The Study was commissioned by the Local Planning Authorities of Nottinghamshire and Derbyshire[1] for the purpose of preparing a plan for the Sub-region as a framework for the formulation of their respective development plans. The authorities appointed an *ad hoc* Planning Team to undertake the Study, and exercised technical control over the Team through a management committee comprised of a number of their own members.

[1] The authorities concerned were Nottinghamshire and Derbyshire county councils, Nottinghamshire City Council, and Derby County Borough Council.

163

The terms of reference given to the Team were "to examine the needs and potential for [urban] development in the area, to define proposals for the location of the major land uses, including population, industry and employment, shopping and recreation, and to consider relationships between these components and transport". The Team defined their task in terms of finding the best way to allocate given amounts of population and employment and associated activities to alternative locations within the Sub-region. Whilst a number of alternative sets of forecasts were made of aggregate amounts of population, employment, and so forth, one particular set of these forecasts was used for design purposes.[2] But in addition to the allocation of land-use activities, there was the task of estimating the "interactions", principally traffic flows, likely to result from alternative patterns of urban development and from proposed improvements to the existing transport network.

In cases where local plans are likely to affect each other, there are clearly advantages in preparing a common strategic policy within which local planning may take place. Co-ordination between authorities helps in avoiding serious policy conflicts, and thereby helps ensure that the policies adopted are mutually practicable. For instance, two neighbouring authorities may wish to encourage the growth of employment opportunities and may in effect be competing for a fixed amount of new manufacturing employment that can be attracted into their combined areas. Ignorance and uncertainty about each other's proposals could result in the preparation of two plans each containing a proposal for the location of all these jobs. Clearly either one or both plans would be infeasible. In addition, a number of items of cost and benefit that would be external to one of the authorities, by virtue of being experienced by people outside its boundary, will become relevant to plan evaluation and decision-taking in a joint planning exercise. Hence, decisions are more likely to be in the widest interests of those whose well-being will be affected.

The attempt to formulate joint policies is therefore to be welcomed. There will be interactions across the administrative boundaries of the four local authorities, and these will be especially important in the area between the towns of Nottingham and Derby. It is important to note that although the City of Sheffield lies just outside the boundary drawn for the sub-region, the effects of proposals on the Sheffield area were examined, and this group of externalities influenced the strategy which the Team recommended.[3]

No time period was specified for the proposals. The Team were left to decide this issue and chose to concentrate on developments for the following twenty to thirty years. However, they stressed that the quantities of population, etc., contained in the strategies which they considered were not intended as targets to be achieved by a particular date. They were to be regarded as indications of the scale of proposed developments and the changes which would occur during implementation, and were only loosely related to future periods of time. In part this reflected the Team's concern with the process of urban development rather than the production of an

---

[2]It should be noted that the robustness of plans in relation to alternative sets of forecasts was analysed during the evaluations.

[3]Despite its interest this work was not documented in the Study reports.

end-state plan.[4] A. Thorburn, the former Director of the Study, has stressed this point:[5]

"...our whole object was to indicate the direction in which the planning authorities should progress rather than the destination they should seek to reach. Our evaluation process was designed to select the best direction knowing that future change would pre-empt the possibility of our ever reaching the destination postulated in the alternative being tested."

However, to facilitate analysis and for convenience of presentation, a specific date was attached to most numerical indications of scale. The year 1986 was chosen because it was considered to be sufficiently far ahead to provide a basis for long-term planning yet still within the limits of reasonably reliable employment and population forecasts.

The terms of reference did not indicate why it was the concern of government to control and promote urban and regional developments. The Team thought they should clarify this by stating those broad aims which in their view underlay such governmental activity, and which the local authorities concerned would use to judge the success or failure of their policies. The postulated aims were as follows:[6]

"(a) to secure a rapid rise in prosperity for all the people living in the Sub-region;
"(b) to achieve the best possible physical environment; and
"(c) to encourage the provision of adequate social and cultural facilities and a wide choice and variety of living, working and leisure activities, which are the necessary physical basis for a satisfactory way of life."

These, then, became the aims of the proposals that were recommended by the Team. They were very general and abstract, and the Team considered them probably applicable to all urban and regional planning studies. They can also be interpreted to embrace virtually all the welfare consequences that are likely to flow from planning decisions. The first may be said to relate to individuals' real purchasing power for goods and services offered on the market; the second to a wide range of public goods and externalities in production and consumption; and the third to the range of choice available to individuals. However, there was no indication that equity matters are relevant to planning decisions, which we know to be the case. Indeed, the Team did debate a number of issues concerning the fairness and justice of their proposals. Instances of this were their attempt to give some assistance to intermediate areas through proposed locations for new job opportunities, and their concern over the effect of new shopping centres on existing traders.[7] Thus, equity is an omission of some importance in the formulation of the high-level aims.

[4]It also reflected forecasting difficulties.
[5]Personal communication.
[6]Notts–Derby Sub-regional Planning Unit, *Report*, Nottinghamshire CC, 1969. para. 6.
[7]*Tabulated Tests for Stages II and III of the Strategy Testing Process*, Record Report 36, November 1969, para. 4.1.

The objectives for the strategy were regarded as possessing instrumental value in that their achievement was intended to result in the attainment of the high-level aims. Unlike these high-level aims, the objectives related to particular characteristics of the Study area. They were not, however, consciously deduced through considering the logical implications of the aims they were intended to achieve; they were, instead, formulated in the light of the information obtained from survey work.

In considering the strengths and weaknesses of the Notts–Derby Study it is necessary to appreciate the circumstances in which it was undertaken. Only thirteen technical personnel were employed full-time. In addition there was considerable pressure to produce a set of recommendations within a fairly short period of time, and only a very modest sum of £100,000 was spent on the Study. The full Team began work in June 1968 and completed their *Report* (containing their recommended strategy for urban development) sixteen months later in September 1969.[8] Finally, planning techniques and methodology have advanced a lot during the past six years, and the task facing the Team was virtually new. Although the Leicester and Leicestershire Study was in progress when they began work, nothing similar had been completed in this country.

8.2.   APPROACH TO THE STUDY

In asking the Team to define proposals for future urban developments, the terms of reference had in effect delegated the function of decision-taking to the planners. The Team were to decide on a set of policy recommendations with the elected representatives, of course, still being responsible for the formal choice. Thorburn recognized that the Team's advice was to serve as an input to the decision-taking of the authorities and was not simply a substitute for the decision. Accordingly, the recommended strategy was put forward for *discussion*. It was stated that discussion was needed:

"(a) so that the interests of all the organisations concerned with implementing development can be taken into account before any decisions are made;
"(b) so that the proposals can be properly related to national and regional policies and to more detailed planning;
"(c) because the opinions and value judgments which have influenced the proposals are matters requiring a consensus view from society as a whole, over and above the advice of professionals."[9]

In order to inform these discussions, the Team's *Report* attempted to justify their proposals by setting out those comparatively good alternatives that could be chosen and the reasons for their rejection. Much to the regret of the Team, there was virtually no public debate on the proposals following the publication of their work.

[8]The Team stayed in existence until May 1970. Following the work documented in their *Report* they investigated a number of issues of detail concerning their recommended strategy and some of the others which they had examined.
[9]*Report*, para. 95.

Political considerations exerted a major influence upon the Team's work.[10] In the Director's view the recommended strategy should command general agreement from the elected members of the four councils, for two reasons. Firstly, acceptance by all groups of elected members was necessary for implementation of the Team's recommendations. The Team aimed at a degree of support at least sufficient to get their recommendations adopted by the decision-takers. In their view there was little point in examining in detail or recommending strategies that stood little or no chance of being adopted. However, the Team did not passively accept the reactions of the elected members to their choice of strategies for detailed assessment and to their recommendations. They attempted to convince the members of the appropriateness of those choices, both indirectly through discussions with their Management Committee and through argument in their *Report*. The problem was viewed by the Team as one of reconciling the proposals they considered to be in the best interests of the community with political acceptability.

We agree that planners should not passively accept the views of decision-takers. But we would also argue that in design and evaluation attention should not necessarily be confined only to those alternatives likely to meet with the approval of decision-takers. Some politically infeasible alternatives may be superior to others in terms of their effects on community welfare, and planners should attempt to reveal any social benefits that will be sacrificed by their rejection. In this way members of the public may be made more aware of the implications of government decisions and be in a better position to pass judgement on the policies of their government.

We discuss later the emphasis on producing proposals capable of being implemented. Here it is enough to point out that the Team had to take account of the fact that the decision-takers were not the only group able to affect implementation. For proposals to succeed in this sense the co-operation and approval of other professionals besides those in the town planning departments were necessary. In addition, the press were influential, and the general public were in a position to delay and obstruct action by various kinds of protests and inquiries. Finally, Central Government exerted considerable influence via its power to sanction or withhold finance and in various informal ways.

The desire to secure the support of elected members also reflected the Director's intention to produce a strategy that was in the interests of as many groups as possible within the community. The Team were asked to give advice about planning policy, and in the Director's view the best advice was that which the community acting collectively preferred to follow, and the only valid test was whether the changes it would produce were in the general interests of those affected.[11] Although politicians (like others) act in a self-interested manner, they must, of course, be to some extent responsive to the preferences of constituents in order to gain and keep office. Since

[10]The following comments are based upon a personal communication from A. Thorburn and discussions with G. Steeley.

[11]A. Thorburn, The decision orientated framework for the study, in *Papers from the Seminar on the Process of the Notts–Derbys Sub-regional Study*, Centre for Environmental Studies, Information Paper 11, January 1970.

the views of the elected members partly reflect the interests of various groups within the community, the degree of support by members for the Team's recommendations gives a crude indication of support from the community as a whole.

In an attempt to find out whether the politicians were likely to regard proposals as acceptable, the Team decided that their principal recommendations should be agreed with the chief planning officers and other relevant chief officers of the commissioning authorities before they were presented to the politicians.[12] These officers would have been able in the discussions which took place to ascertain the views of council members on the Team's proposals. Accordingly, whilst no direct approaches were made to council members, in the event this was really unnecessary. We understand that the possibility of direct consultations with the members at various stages of the planning process was carefully considered.[13] The Team came to the conclusion that this would not be practicable for a number of reasons. Important among these was their view that it would lead to a complete loss of secrecy,[14] to a loss of their own credibility, and to the initiation of political manoeuvres designed to influence their recommendations.

For instance, tentative objectives for the strategy were formulated early on with the intention of sounding out the views of council members (through consultation with the Management Committee) on whether they were appropriate. But the members were unwilling to discuss them or to commit themselves until they knew the consequences of doing so. Only after examining the recommended strategy did they formally adopt the objectives or agree to their publication.[15]

Political pressures prevented the Team from giving much attention to a more direct method of ascertaining the degree of community support for their proposals, such as discussions with interest groups. Some indication of the likely degree of community support for various strategies could have been obtained if the Team had traced the incidence of advantages and disadvantages for different groups within the community. Although they did consider equity matters to be relevant to the decision, practical difficulties prevented attempts to determine which groups would gain and which would lose.

Methods of Evaluation Employed

The Team formulated a set of twenty-two objectives in relation to which the performance of alternative strategies was to be compared.[16] Three main investigations were conducted during the various evaluations that were carried out:

[12]This was also done for purposes of technical collaboration.
[13]A. Thorburn, in a personal communication.
[14]Unnecessary alarm would be created if the public knew of some of the unconventional alternatives being examined. It was also important to maintain secrecy in order to avoid blighting and financial speculation.
[15]A. Thorburn, 1970, *op. cit.*
[16]The objectives for the strategy are reproduced in Appendix I of this chapter.

(a) An analysis was made of the "development potential" of strategies.

(b) Estimates were made of the resource costs involved in the strategies.

(c) Answers were determined for a check-list of questions in relation to those objectives whose achievement could not be assessed on a quantitative basis.

Together these investigations provided an indication of strategy performance for nearly all aspects of the objectives that were examined. The only item which was considered but not dealt with by these investigations was that of the user costs of private travel. A traffic model was employed to provide information on this item.

With only a few exceptions, the strategies were not evaluated directly in relation to the objectives in the form they were specified. Instead, they were evaluated against a variety of criteria derived from the objectives. Most objectives were specified in very general terms, and in order to assess the effects of alternatives it was therefore necessary to break them down into their constituent items. It was these items against which the strategies were evaluated. No attempt was made to integrate the results of the evaluations into an overall index of objective achievement in the manner of Hill's goals–achievement matrix method. The presence of intangible objectives provided an obvious problem in this respect. But nor was an attempt made to establish valuations of the various items of development potential that would permit comparisons with the resource costs associated with urban developments. It was thought that this could not be done in any meaningful way. In considering the findings of their evaluated exercises the Team formed a subjective judgement when necessary of the relative importance of those two sets of items.

The now well-known technique of development potential analysis (DPA) was used to assess the prospective "attractiveness" of different strategies to occupiers of the proposed residential and industrial developments and to assess the effects of those proposals on existing residents. The use of this technique had been mooted before the Team began work, but they were the first to put it into operation. The purpose was not to determine the amounts of new development that were likely to take place at different locations within the sub-region but rather to determine the benefits that would be gained *if* developments were distributed about the sub-region in the ways envisaged in the strategies.

An area's potential for industrial and residential development was viewed as comprising a wide variety of factors known to be important in attracting firms or people to move into an area or to prosper if already established there. These were termed "attraction factors". Examples of those given in the *Report* are proximity to major communication centres and job-growth prospects. The analysis of a strategy's development potential involved identifying the attraction factors, establishing the strengths or relative importance of those factors, and measuring the presence of each factor according to some index. In this way information about the effects of alternatives on four of the twenty-two strategy objectives was provided (numbered (i)–(iv) in Appendix I).

The analysis of resource costs involved estimating the value of the amounts of resources that would be forgone by opting for alternative strategies. These resources were of two types: natural resources that would be displaced or made sterile by developments and those that would be used as inputs in establishing and operating the projects envisaged. Examples of the former were minerals and timber. The latter included resources that would be used to provide public utility services and those required to overcome physical obstacles to development, such as areas liable to subsidence or flooding (giving rise to additional structural costs). Estimates of resource costs enabled assessments of the effects of strategies on seven of the objectives.

There were quite a number of objectives which were not wholly or even partly susceptible to quantitative assessment. Instances of these were the organizational and institutional problems that might result from some forms of urban development and possible opportunities for clearance or improvement of obsolescent areas or derelict land afforded by proposed developments. A check-list of questions was devised to deal with these outstanding objectives. Whenever possible the questions were phrased so that a yes/no answer could be given or so that some simple proxy measure could be used. In most cases it was only possible to indicate whether the alternatives would result in an increase or decrease in the extent of objective achievement; that is, to indicate the direction of change only.

Finally, a comment on the relationship between the evaluations made and the time horizon of the proposals is in order. In the first two cycles of the planning process proposals were formally evaluated for the years 1976 and 1986, and the implications of likely longer-term developments were examined in an intuitive manner. The dates chosen for the evaluations during the rest of the procedure were 1986 and 2001.[17] Thus the proposals were formally assessed for only a very few stages of the prospective course of urban development of the Sub-region. But levels of objective achievement will be subject to variations throughout the period of proposed developments, and thus the comparative performance of strategies is also likely to vary throughout that period. Of course, it is often not practicable to evaluate alternatives throughout the period to which they relate. But the Notts–Derby Study, like most other recent planning studies in this country, can be criticized for not paying greater attention to this aspect of evaluation.

The Adopted Planning Process

In this section we first outline briefly the Team's procedure for identifying their preferred alternative strategy from the numerous possibilities which existed. This is done with reference to the various phases of design and evaluation activity that were worked through. We shall then describe in detail certain aspects of the Team's planning process.

An important and novel feature of the process of design and evaluation of alternative

---

[17]The *Report* stresses that the precise dates chosen for evaluation are not significant in view of uncertainties as to the future rate of population and employment changes and the emphasis placed on process rather than end-state planning.

strategies was its cyclic nature. Instead of proceeding in a traditional linear manner from the formulation of goals and objectives to the design of a range of alternatives, the assessment of those alternatives, and then directly to the choice of a recommended policy, the strategy finally put forward was based upon four main cycles of activity. In each of the first three cycles the following operations were undertaken in sequence:

(a) formulation of design ideas; that is, the principles upon which the alternatives were to be produced;
(b) the testing and evaluation of the designs;
(c) discussion of the findings of the evaluation exercise to provide a basis for the designs in the next cycle.

It must be emphasized that the procedure was *not* one of progressive elimination of a set of alternatives produced at the outset. Design activity began *de novo* at the beginning of each cycle, and was based on the evidence procured during the previous cycle. During the later stages this led the Team to examine some strategies previously considered to have little merit. A break between cycles of the kind described was imposed in order to "avoid the danger of cumulative error" which would stem from the unknowing selection of only moderate or relatively poor alternatives for further consideration—especially early on in the process.

The procedure involved moving from a general examination of the whole Sub-region, so as to indicate very broad areas considered most suitable for locating new urban developments, to an investigation of a number of precisely defined alternatives which were developed to the level of detail required for implementation.

The cycles may be outlined as follows.

(1) Twenty-one basically different alternatives were formulated. These were represented by generalized population and employment distributions. Following an evaluation, a number of broad geographic areas were chosen for more detail study.
(2) The search for alternatives was concentrated within those areas identified as a result of cycle 1. The intention was to assess as wide a range of alternatives as practicable. Six sets of proposals were formulated to represent a variety of possibilities. These were specified in a highly diagrammatic form. None of them was chosen from those initially produced; all were entirely new. At this stage transport, retailing, and other ancillary land-use activities were introduced. The evaluation exercise enabled the identification of a fairly large number of locations which seemed advantageous for new developments.
(3) The purpose of this cycle was to examine refinements of the most promising proposals considered during the previous cycle. Three alternative strategies were designed and evaluated. These were devised so that they represented the realistic extremes of concentrated and dispersed development, favourable and unfavourable prospects for economic growth, and variations in the amount of mobility of population and industry.

(4) The conclusions reached from the assessments of cycle 3 formed the basis for formulating the preferred strategy. This was produced by bringing together what were judged to be the best features of the previous three alternatives. It incorporated refinements of the population, employment and mobility assumptions of the previous cycle, and took particular account of land already committed for development. Tests of the strategy were made for internal consistency, and some required adjustments were then made to detailed quantities and locations of developments.

The approach to design adopted throughout was to explore as wide a range of different alternatives as possible within broadly defined areas of search. The designs were not based on an explicit consideration of the strategy objectives, but the geographical areas of the Sub-region upon which attention was to be focused were defined after considering the results of the previous evaluation exercise. After the first cycle, for example, attention was focused on areas which comprised about half of the Sub-region.

The main conclusions from the first cycle of design, testing, and evaluation were threefold:

(a) Growth was unlikely to be feasible outside the main urbanized part of the Sub-region, embracing Derby, Nottingham, Mansfield, Worksop, and Chesterfield. But a certain amount of new development should take place in the rural areas to ease the severe problems faced by their inhabitants.

(b) The least constrained sites for development lay on the old coalfield.

(c) A dispersed pattern of urban development, which was not examined initially, should be considered during the next cycle.

In the light of all this it was decided that during cycle 2 attention should be directed to the central, most densely populated part of the Sub-region. At the end of the second cycle the Team identified a number of fairly well defined areas where new urban development seemed most desirable, and which required more detailed investigation. The more important of these included a growth zone in the area around Alfreton, Sutton, Mansfield, and Kirkby; a smaller growth zone in the Chesterfield–Eckington area; and some peripheral extensions to Nottingham and Derby.

The conclusions drawn from the testing and evaluation procedures of the third cycle are not adequately documented. We are told only that those features of the strategies which depended on a high degree of population and industrial mobility and on a high level of government economic assistance performed best in terms of the strategy objectives, whereas those that were based on converse assumptions tended to increase problems of unemployment and long-distance commuting in the northern areas of the sub-region and of congestion in the towns of Derby and Nottingham.[18] We are also told very little about the following step in the

---

[18] *The Development of Strategy Proposals*, Record Report 31, February 1970, p. 9.

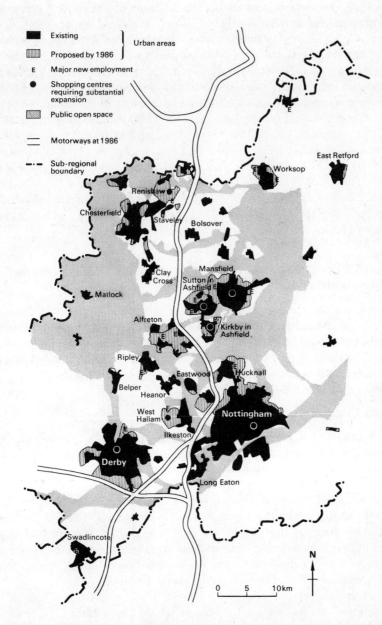

Existing ⎫
Proposed by 1986 ⎬ Urban areas

E   Major new employment

●   Shopping centres requiring substantial expansion

Public open space

Motorways at 1986

Sub-regional boundary

East Retford

Worksop

Renishaw

Chesterfield

Staveley

Bolsover

Clay Cross

Matlock

Mansfield

Sutton in Ashfield

Alfreton

Kirkby in Ashfield

Ripley

Eastwood

Hucknall

Belper

Heanor

West Hallam

Nottingham

Ilkeston

Derby

Long Eaton

Swadlincote

N

0   5   10km

FIG. 8.1. The recommended strategy. (Source: *Nottinghamshire and Derbyshire Sub-regional Study*, the strategy map, p. 50.)

Team's procedure, the combination of certain features of the cycle 3 strategies to form their preferred alternative (Fig. 8.1).

This account of the adopted planning procedure may have given the impression it was carefully thought out at the start of the Team's work. This was not the case. Rather, it was developed as the Study progressed. This was a deliberate choice taken by the Director and was made not as a result of any conceptual difficulties in devising a process but in order not to waste managerial resources. In his opinion, the gains from such an exercise would be small in view of the likelihood of wanting to alter course at certain stages in the light of experience and in response to unforeseen circumstances and advances in technique. (An example of the last factor was the innovation of DPA.) This runs directly counter to our own view, presented in Chapter 3, that for a fully effective planning exercise it is critical to establish the general approach and principles to be used for evaluation at the outset of a study. In the Notts–Derby Study those members of the Team who were preparing proposals sometimes had virtually no idea of how they were to be assessed.

8.3. EVALUATION IN THE PLANNING PROCESS OF THE NOTTINGHAMSHIRE-DERBYSHIRE STUDY

In this discussion we shall consider the collection of data for use during the evaluation exercises in passing rather than in a separate section, despite it forming a distinct stage in our model. Although it is desirable to start work on collecting this data as early as possible, in practice this work is often undertaken at many stages of a study, including the evaluation stage, as was the case with this Study.

Evaluation and Constraints

The Team formulated a fairly small number of constraints. These reflected a proper concern for the practical problems of implementation. Consideration was given to budget limitations and potential difficulties of an institutional and organizational nature.

A plan will obviously not be capable of realization if there are insufficient investment funds to undertake the various projects envisaged. Thus, if possible an estimate should be made of the size of the available budget. We are told that "It appeared from discussions with the County Treasurers that the availability of capital was unlikely to be a major obstacle to the implementation of development proposals".[19] Whilst guidance was obtained on financial feasibility, the planners were unable to arrive at any detailed and precise estimates of capital availability.[20]

Ten organizational and institutional problems which might hinder the realization of certain strategies or elements of strategies were identified. They arose from discussion with outside bodies as well as from discussion within the Team. Proposals

[19] *The Investment Project*, Record Report 25, December 1969, p. 2.
[20] *Ibid.*, p. 1.

were tested by considering a list of questions, devised to examine the potential problems. The following are examples.[21]

"Do proposals avoid direct conflict with the ideas, views and programmes of key individuals and institutions who are in a position to hold up implementation?

"Are the proposals likely to be reasonably economical in their demands on scarce administrative and professional skills regardless of how they are provided?"

Following conventional practice, the Team listed a variety of physical features within the Study area which would give rise to disadvantages in establishing new urban developments. These included items of ecological significance, landscape of high scenic quality, land liable to flooding, and high-grade agricultural land. Developments in areas where these were present would involve either loss of benefits by sterilizing or destroying productive resources, or additional construction costs, or damage to natural amenities. Physical factors should never be regarded as absolute restrictions upon development since it is always possible, at some cost, to overcome the obstacles presented.

Although the Team referred to these physical features as "constraints" on new development, they were careful not to treat them as absolute restrictions. It is true that during the first cycle of plan design use was made of the principle of locating developments in areas where physical "constraints" were minimal, but this was only one of six principles that were employed. By themselves, physical factors were never allowed to rule out parts of the sub-region completely. Even those physical factors considered to be of major importance (grade 2 agricultural land, grades 1 and 2 ecological areas and floodland) were not treated as inviolable in all circumstances.

As Jackson has noted, the specification of physical "constraints" in planning studies is "more an expression of reluctance to develop for some social, economic, or technical reason than a complete and irrevocable embargo".[22] However, opportunity costs of constraints, and thereby their validity, are rarely assessed. The Notts–Derby Team made a welcome departure from conventional practice. As well as rejecting the use of a sieve map to produce alternatives, except as one of a number of methods of producing some of the initial alternatives, they attempted to estimate the magnitudes of the disadvantages to which their "constraints" would give rise. The estimates produced were then used along with all other evidence obtained on advantages and disadvantages to aid in the assessments of development proposals.

Evaluation and Objectives

We shall consider three aspects of the strategy objectives:

(1) Whose interests they were intended to represent.
(2) The justification given for the Team's choice of objectives.
(3) The attention given to issues of equity.

---

[21]Record Report 36, *op. cit.*, para. 3.1.
[22]J. N. Jackson, *The Urban Future*, Allen & Unwin, London, 1972, p. 84.

There are two main reasons why it is important to know *whose* interests planning objectives are meant to represent. Firstly, decision-takers and others concerned in the process of decision-making will wish to know from whose viewpoint the proposals are being evaluated: for instance, are future generations and prospective in-movers included? Secondly, it is not possible to determine the incidence of gains and losses between different groups unless one knows whose interests are involved.

The strategy objectives were said to result directly from:

(a) the understanding gained of the factors limiting economic growth and of the social "needs" of the Study area's inhabitants;

(b) an appreciation of the area's physical environment and the desirability of conserving and improving it; and

(c) the desirability of ensuring that productive resources are not used wastefully.

The Study documents contain no explicit statement about whose interests the objectives represented. One of the high-level aims was concerned with the achievement of a fast rise in prosperity for all living in the sub-region. Presumably, then, the objectives were meant at least to reflect the interests of all *existing* residents. This view is supported by the Team's (unrealized) intention of obtaining general public agreement on a set of objectives before starting work on plan design and evaluation. Also, there is no indication that the interests of future generations or in-movers were to be excluded from the evaluations, although the Team should have made their principles clear. It is apparent that in formulating objectives the Team were not putting forward their own personal preferences nor those of the decision-takers. They did have regard to the wider interests of the community. It would appear, therefore, that the achievement of the strategy objectives was intended to lead to improvements in the well-being of those groups of individuals in the Sub-region who would be affected either beneficially or adversely by the proposals, regardless of whether they formed part of the existing community.

In the form in which they are specified, the objectives can be interpreted in terms of "sectoral" objectives. The objective to avoid the sterilization of mineral resources can thus be viewed as expressing the preference of people for more, rather than less, outputs of minerals and the goods which are produced from them. The conservation objectives relating to timber, agricultural land, etc., similarly reflect the preferences of those potentially affected.

Most of the objectives contained a number of distinct items of advantage and disadvantage. In order to assess the performance of plans in quantitative terms it was necessary to define these items. An example of this is the attraction factors that were employed in the DPA. Other examples are seen in the objectives: "To provide ample and attractive sites for housing for all socio-economic groups"; and "To provide good transport facilities." Attractive housing sites may be comprised of a large number of attributes, such as absence of noise and visual intrusion, pleasant views, or proximity to local shops. The qualities that go to make (public) transport attractive include frequency and speed of service, comfort in transit, and level of fares. If such objectives are to be used for evaluation the analyst should specify all constituent items. This is a matter of specifying each distinct sectoral objective. In view of their generality, it is not surprising that the plans were not evaluated in relation to the objectives as formulated but in relation to criteria derived from them. The criteria were thus a disaggregated statement of the objectives.

No evidence was collected or cited to show that the criteria were representative of the preferences of those potentially affected. Strictly speaking, this was a weakness since it is not possible for the validity of the objectives to be judged except intuitively. However, we know enough from past experience of studies and from casual observation to be able to say what people's direction of preference will be in relation to nearly all items of planning proposals that affect their well-being. That is to say, we know whether people prefer to have more or less of particular items such as accessibility to job opportunities, agricultural produce, and open landscape. The real issues surround the relative importance that people attach to such items.

It is difficult to ensure that objectives have been formulated for all items of consequence which are important enough to be worth investigating. It is difficult to anticipate all relevant consequences *in advance* of design, and one can never be sure that some important effects will not be overlooked during evaluation. In general, the consequences will not be discovered by chance; it is necessary to have some idea of what they are likely to be, so that one knows what to look for.

The Team did attempt to be comprehensive when they investigated items of advantage and disadvantage. The only test for this is to try to think of some items that might affect the well-being of the community and see if they have been included. We have not been able to think of any items of major importance that were left out of the evaluations.

We now turn to consider the attention paid to equity considerations. No objectives were specifically related to issues of the fairness and justice of proposals. But some attempts were made to identify and analyse problems of relative deprivation (or relatively low living standards) within the Sub-region, and some importance was given to remedying them in design and evaluation. The efforts made to help those with particularly severe difficulties indicate that the Team wished to give special importance to them in their choice of alternatives. For instance, high unemployment rates in the northern coalfield areas was seen as a major problem, and one recommendation was that there should be a "continuation of efforts to attract new jobs to the areas which already have serious employment problems". Other problems that were identified included the remoteness of some rural areas from service centres and large areas of poor quality housing in Derby and Nottingham. The evaluations took account of the likely degree of success in solving or reducing the severity of all these problems.

In addition, it was the Director's view that the incidence of gains and losses should not be overconcentrated in terms of different socio-economic groups. The aim of ensuring that as many people as possible were advantaged by the proposals reflected a concern with their general acceptability. Practical difficulties prevented quantitative estimates being made of the likely incidence of gains and losses for the groups affected. But a very crude indication was obtained of the distributional impacts through examining the effect of proposals on the various objectives. An attempt was made to ensure that as many as possible were attained to a satisfactory level (this was treated in the manner of an objective rather than a constraint). The reasoning here was that different objectives would be relevant to different groups (since not everyone would be affected by all the consequences of the proposals) and that different groups place varying importance on objectives held in common. Although the Team did not have precise definitions of what constituted satisfactory levels of achievement, the alternatives were examined with this general idea in mind. Data deficiencies prevented explicit trade-offs being made between the benefits that would result from a better distribution of gains and losses and those resulting from greater net benefits in the aggregate.

Evaluation and Opportunities

Here we use the term "opportunities" to refer both to the presence of conditions favourable for improving the well-being of the present and future community of an area, and to the scope for change to the existing pattern of urban and rural developments as a result of changes in population, employment, incomes, and so forth.

Attention was given to both these matters prior to the start of design. During some initial survey work the Team devoted a good deal of effort to identifying areas not yet urbanized where conditions were favourable for residential and industrial development. Examples were the presence of scenic landscape, the communication advantages of access points to the M1, and the reopening of the Nottingham–Mansfield–Worksop railway line. It was the opportunities for establishing new urban developments that were itemized as attraction factors and employed in the analysis of strategies' development potential. In addition, knowledge about the relative attractiveness of different locations was used as an input to the design process. For instance, one of the principles used during the first cycle of design was that of locating new urban developments "in areas where the opportunities were greatest". Thus, in both the design and evaluation work, attention was given to making the most of favourable environments as well as to those with problems and difficulties in establishing new developments.

Aggregate forecasts were made of likely changes in population, employment, incomes, etc., in order to provide some realistic limits for the designs. Although many alternative sets of forecasts were made, there was little variation among them. The Team formed the opinion that the differences in magnitudes were not significant for purposes of design and evaluation. The task was therefore reduced to one of finding the best way to distribute fixed amounts of increase in population, employment, and related activities around the Sub-region. For instance, the predicted increase in the resident population of the Sub-region was about 250,000 from 1966 to 1986 (very largely by natural increase). This represented the potential *scope* for new residential developments—not an inevitable increase. Planning controls could be devised to ensure that the resident population remained at its present level. But, instead of examining proposals to accommodate different amounts of additional population and employment within the predicted scope for increases, all strategies were designed with the same inputs of population and employment. This was done because the Team considered that to lose much of the natural increase in population through out-migration would cause major social problems. The migrants would tend to be young people of comparatively high ability. Labour shortages in key employment sectors and a high proportion of old among the population would result. It was considered that a loss of over half the forecast natural increase would be serious.

Evaluation and the Measurement of Plan Performance

Stage 5 of our general model of the planning process is concerned with the translation of the objectives, constraints, and opportunities into a form that will facilitate the design of alternative plans. The Notts–Derby Team deliberately rejected the formal use of strategy objectives during their design procedures. But, since they proposed to work through a number of cycles of design and evaluation, they began to devise the physical measures and the relative values to be used in the comparison of strategies soon after starting work on design.

We have already noted that a number of "criteria", derived from the objectives, were used in comparing the performance of alternatives. In this section we shall investigate the way in which these criteria were measured. The main quantitative comparisons of alternatives involved analysis of:

(a) development potential;
(b) resource costs;
(c) traffic congestion costs.

We discuss these three aspects in turn. Each factor considered relevant to the analysis of development potential was measured by an index, and each index was given a numerical weight to reflect its relative importance. The sum of the weighted indices was taken to indicate the total potential of a strategy. The indices that were used were simple and will have given only very crude indications of potential. For example, residents' accessibility to retail outlets was estimated by dividing the scales turnover for each retail centre by the distances from the centroids of residential zones. The way in which the indices were selected is poorly documented. But it would appear that in all, or nearly all, cases a highly subjective choice was made.

The weights placed on the attraction factors were certainly established subjectively. They represented a Team consensus based on judgements formed from their previous professional experience and impressions gained from their initial socio-economic investigations of the Sub-region. The Team could not be confident that their weights were valid. Some sensitivity analysis was therefore conducted to examine the effect of adopting different weights for the findings of the evaluations. At various stages of their evaluation work the weights were "substantially" varied. The weight applied to each attraction factor was varied upwards to a value of about twice the "best estimate" and downwards to a value of zero; these ranges were thought to include all plausible values. It is reported that the relative attractiveness of different locations as given by the results of the DPA were not much affected by the variations used,[23] which will have given the Team greater confidence in their findings. But, as with sensitivity analysis in general, there remained the difficulty of knowing whether those used were large enough to include the true valuations.

The Team recognized that their DPA had a number of limitations. They write: "The process of deciding which factors to measure, how to measure them, and the relative importance assigned to each was one involving considerable discretion and there is great scope for improvement and refinement."[24] It was suggested that the future development of the technique might begin with a more detailed consideration of the factors constituting potential, and that thought should be given to issues such as the degree of double-counting involved in the combination of separate indices and the necessity of employing different combinations of indices with alternative weightings. Essentially, it was argued that a more precise and accurate description of "potential" was wanted. Nonetheless, the Team rightly considered that "the mental discipline of carrying through a rigorous procedure of this kind is preferable to the informed guesswork which usually takes charge at this stage in the process of plan evaluation".[25]

It was pointed out that, in principle, the technique could be used to help generate plans as well as to evaluate them. But it was also emphasized that exclusive reliance on it would probably result in sub-optimal plans, since attractiveness did not incorporate any consideration of "needs"—by which was meant relative deprivations suffered by groups and their inability to express their strength of preferences. To deal with this, it was suggested that a "needs surface" should be devised to be used in conjunction with the potential surface as a guide to plan generation and evaluation. The Team's experience suggested that useful indications of "need" could be obtained from examining areas which are relatively lacking in potential on a *per capita* basis. They therefore devised an index of "inverse potential". This index was used during evaluation, but not for design purposes. The results of the "needs" test helped the Team to form a view about the comparative merits of their alternatives. It is interesting to note that the planners engaged on the Coventry–Solihull–Warwickshire Study incorporated equity considerations in their concept of development potential, thus integrating the Notts–Derby planners' notions of "potential" and "need" into one index.[26]

The resource costs of new developments comprised those involved in the supply of public utilities and those associated with overstepping physical "constraints" on new development. The former were estimated with little difficulty by the various

[23] *The Potential Surface Technique*, Record Report 38, undated, para. 12.

[24] *Ibid.*, para. 4. The measures of potential that were used are described in appendix I of this Record Report.

[25] *Ibid.*, para. 4.

[26] The C–S–W planners also advanced the application of the technique by giving greater attention to devising appropriate physical measures of the elements of potential and to establishing the relative importance of those elements.

servicing authorities. The latter were far more difficult to estimate, and comprised costs of additional construction and costs arising from the loss of natural resources.

In general it was not possible to estimate likely differentials of additional costs of construction on land liable to subsidence and so forth prior to more detailed specifications of locations and quantities of proposed developments. Such analysis was considered more appropriate to the level of structure plan preparation.

In estimating the loss of benefits from those natural resources which would be sterilized or destroyed by proposed developments, it was intended that notional costs per acre be applied to each type of resource affected. These costs were to reflect the value of the resources to the community. Market prices were considered to be an inadequate guide to these values, but the Team was unable to establish any better indications of cost. They relied instead on a simple areal quantification of "constraint violation" for each proposal. This involved estimating the amount in acres of each "constraint" used for new developments. It was stated that "By totalling [the areas of constrained land used for new developments] the performance of each strategy could be readily quantified and compared with that of the others".[27] But Thorburn has pointed out that in view of the implicit assumption that each constraint would be regarded as equally important, this summation was, in fact, avoided. We presume that a subjective judgement was made about the relative importance of the constraints.

Two main reasons were given for considering that data on market prices would be inadequate for making useful comparisons between losses of different resources.[28] Firstly, "reliance on current market values takes no account of future changes in public opinion concerning the value to be set on different types of resources". Secondly, "the value set upon, for example, agricultural land takes no account of its value as an everlasting asset, whereas the value set upon (say) mineral resources relates to exploitation on a 'once and for all' basis". We do not consider these to be valid objections to the use of market price data for establishing relative valuations. Public opinion is relevant only in so far as it is reflected in individuals' willingness to pay for goods that may be produced by a given resource. Market values reflect this through demand and supply schedules. Moreover, the market also reflects anticipations about future changes in the demand for goods produced by a resource, although these anticipations may not be accurate. Ideally, we would like to know how prices will in practice change in the future, but if this is too difficult to forecast it is necessary to resort to current prices. In addition, in itself it is of no importance whether a resource can be continually used for production or whether it is expended in the production process. In the case of an "everlasting" resource, its market value will approximate to the total discounted value of all future net revenues derived from its use, thereby taking account of its use over time.

A consideration of public transport was not thought relevant to the scale of analysis of the Study. But to determine differences in the efficiency of private

[27]*Physical Constraints and the Strategy Testing Process*, Record Report 34, February 1970, p. 1.
[28]*Ibid.*, p. 4.

transport proposals, use was made of a gravity-type model. Different private transport networks were proposed for the alternative land-use dispositions. The outputs of the model enabled the estimation of user travel times on those networks, which were used as proxies for total user costs. In the comparison of strategies, each of the major transport proposals were evaluated using data on user and construction costs. However, no attempt was made to investigate likely differentials for trip-end benefits, which is disturbing. Alternative land-use dispositions and transport networks will give rise to differences in the levels of accessibility for residents as between plans. Accessibility benefits are not necessarily correlated in an inverse way with the costs of trip-making which people experience. For instance, greater accessibility to central area urban facilities is likely to lead to higher levels of road congestion. Hence information about costs is useless for evaluation purposes without evidence as to likely benefits. Yet these benefits were not incorporated in any of the other measures employed for evaluating the strategies.[29] This is a very common feature of contemporary planning studies.

Admittedly, it is only very recently that sophisticated procedures for measuring accessibility benefits have been developed. However, some simple and fairly reliable methods do exist which could have been used to provide helpful indications of differences in net benefits. One such method, discussed earlier in Chapter 3, is to compute the differential travel costs required to reach a given number of opportunities, say number of job opportunities within reasonable commuting distance.

Evaluation and the Design and Testing of Alternatives

There were two main features of the approach to design that was adopted: the design of proposals began afresh at the start of each cycle in the light of the findings of the previous evaluation, and alternatives were specified in greater detail at each succeeding cycle. The main strengths of the Team's design work were the wide-ranging nature of proposals that were considered, and the willingness to reintroduce alternatives for evaluation that previously appeared to be disadvantaged. In this section we first comment on the strengths and then consider the main weaknesses of the design work. In our view the weaknesses were threefold: reluctance to use the evaluation criteria to aid the process of design; inability to assess a large number of the alternatives that were prepared owing to shortages of time and finance; and an over-reliance on urban development models in producing practicable alternatives.

It is clear that during the course of their work the Team examined alternatives with widely differing attributes. During the first cycle this was facilitated by the use of a number of contrasting design concepts and in later stages by the conscious attempt to explore as many alternatives as possible within the chosen areas of search. This had the advantage of reducing the likelihood of overlooking the preferred strategy through exclusive reliance on a particular set of design criteria.

---

[29]It should be noted that an inspection of the flows of traffic forecast for different transport networks gives (by itself) an ambiguous indication of net benefits.

In addition, the adoption of a cyclic design procedure made consideration of a large number of alternatives possible. Since alternatives were specified only in very general terms in the early phases, a great deal of effort was saved in their preparation. Until the third cycle the Team were concerned with only very broad areas of location and directions of growth for urban developments, and proposed amounts of populations and employments were only roughly quantified.[30]

The cyclic procedure also made possible another "short-cut" to considering alternative possibilities. This was the examination of a number of "strategic ideas" or elements of strategies, rather than strategies which were complete in themselves. It was a procedural device to economize on resources whilst permitting numerous issues to be investigated, and was used during the initial two cycles. At cycle 2, for instance, it was decided to combine certain features of some of the possible strategies in order to reduce the number for testing and evaluation. Each alternative produced for evaluation was comprised of a number of proposals. About thirty separate proposals were put forward. These were intended to represent extreme situations, so that the whole range of possibilities would be "considered". An illustration may help here. One of the alternatives examined at this stage was described as containing the following "strategy ideas".[31]

"Growth zone from Derby through Ilkeston to Nottingham.
Village expansion south and east of Nottingham.
Moderate growth of Mansfield–Alfreton area.
Growth point south of Staveley.
Moderate growth of Swadlincote."

The evaluation findings in each cycle led to a narrowing down of the number and size of geographical areas of search for alternatives. But parts of the Sub-region already rejected were not necessarily discarded from the rest of the design procedure. The Team recognized the importance of being willing to reconsider areas previously thought unfavourable in the light of subsequent information. Their understanding of the problems and opportunities for urban development and the relative merits of different policies was continually enlarged as data collection proceeded and as more refined evaluations were carried out.

We have noted that neither the strategy objectives nor the more detailed "criteria" for evaluation were used to guide the process of designing alternatives. Those produced during the first cycle were based on six different design concepts. These concepts are described in Appendix II of this chapter. Examples are to design so that new development would take place in areas where physical and organizational restrictions were minimal, and to design on the basis of a variety of geometric forms. Although some of these concepts were clearly related to the evaluation "criteria", and thereby to improving community well-being (e.g. the concept to

[30]This approach is valid because it is generally possible to discriminate between relatively very good and poor alternatives without considering their detailed characteristics. It is only necessary to know these when choosing between the few best alternatives.

[31]Record Report 31, *op. cit.*, p. 6.

locate development in areas with the greatest welfare problems), in all such cases the similarities are no more than coincidental.

The Study documents do not explain why the particular design concepts were chosen. A. Thorburn has recently clarified this for us.[32] The intention during the first cycle was to postulate a widely divergent set of alternatives as a basis for debate and subsequent investigation; these alternatives were to be produced in a random manner. In order to prevent any personal bias influencing the nature of the alternatives, it was felt necessary to design according to contrasting principles or "views of the problem" of design, and to get several individual Team members to prepare designs according to the same principle. The choice of principles was arbitrary, and Thorburn would not attempt to justify the ones used. Their only significance to the Team was that they should promote divergent thinking and therefore lead to widely different proposals.

The attempt to converge on the preferred strategy began after evaluation of the first cycle alternatives. The findings of the evaluation exercise at the end of each cycle were used to help focus attention on smaller areas of search.[33] (The degree of refinement of the evaluations was insufficient to suggest particular proposals.) As in the first cycle, the items of advantage and disadvantage and the proposed methods of measurement were not employed to aid design work. But, instead of making further use of the design concepts, members of the Team were asked to prepare designs according to their own views as to appropriate alternatives. Design proceeded on an intuitive basis. Again, a number of members each undertook the design process separately in order to reduce personal bias.

The attempt to design alternatives without directly using the criteria to be employed during their comparison was viewed by the Team as a strength. As we understand it, there were two main reasons for this view. First, their proposed evaluation criteria were tentative during the early phases and liable to modification in the light of subsequent investigations. In so far as they could not be sure that the evaluation criteria were "correctly" specified or were comprehensive in scope, good designs might have been overlooked by relying solely on them. It was therefore thought most important to use creative or imaginative approaches to design. G. Steeley has also argued that such approaches should be used because they allow the possibility of producing alternatives that are "conceptually superior" to those derived by rather "mechanical" procedures.[34]

It is, of course, never possible to be certain that proposed evaluation criteria are appropriate in all respects, and considerable doubt may surround the criteria in the early stages of a study. But an acceptable way of dealing with this problem of uncertainty is to recycle some of the rejected alternatives at later stages in order to test whether they are still inferior in the light of more sophisticated techniques of

----

[32]In a personal communication.

[33]Except at cycle 4, when the preferred strategy was formulated by combining elements of those considered at the previous cycle.

[34]In personal discussion.

measurement. We would not deny that creativity and imagination have an important role to play in plan design procedures. But we consider that some attention should have been given to designing alternatives with the principles and methods of evaluation in mind. In our view the Team overrated the dangers of what Steeley has termed "circularity of reasoning".

The second reason why the Team did not wish to rely upon the use of evaluation criteria for design was this. It was thought that one of the functions of the design work was to put forward some unconventional and seemingly unpromising alternatives which various persons and groups in the Sub-region were pressing for. Examples of "outside" ideas which were examined were proposals for a new town at Ollerton and a linear city stretching from Derby to Nottingham and towards the Wash. The Team seem to have been genuinely interested in exploring some of these proposals. In other cases, however, the only intention was to demonstrate their inadequacy, since it was obvious even without formal analysis that they were poor. In this way they could not be accused of ignoring others' ideas. Yet neither this aspect of the design process, nor the uncertainty surrounding the proposed evaluation criteria, constituted valid objections to attempts to link design and evaluation through the use of a common approach.

It was generally the case that the total number of alternatives which the Team wished to compare could not be formally analysed given the remaining time and finance. This was partly due to the programming of the work. For instance, it was realized during the first cycle that the time required to evaluate the twenty-one chosen alternatives was unexpectedly long.[35] The number, therefore, had to be reduced to twelve for the purpose of formal comparison. After the analysis of these twelve, the remainder of those initially selected were considered in an informal manner and a subjective judgement made as to the sort of conclusions that *would* have emerged from their evaluation. This judgement was based on the results of the evaluations already made and the degree of similarity between the various features of the alternatives. This was, therefore, an expedient short-cut, but its reliability must be open to some doubt. During the second cycle there were between twenty and thirty separate proposals or strategy "elements" that the Team wanted to evaluate, but due to shortage of resources they were unable to examine more than six plans. It was therefore decided to combine several of these different strategy elements in each plan.

---

[35]Forty-seven alternatives were actually put forward for consideration as the result of the initial design procedure. Many of these were very similar in character. To economize on the use of study resources it was decided to select a number of basically different alternatives (representative types) for initial assessment. The forty-seven proposals were examined for spatial similarities (i.e. with respect to the general pattern of location of population and employments), and thirteen groupings were identified, ranging from scattered growth throughout the Sub-region to complete concentration on one centre. Twenty-one of these were selected for assessment, care being taken to include members from each of the different groups. "Every effort was made to ensure that the rejected strategies did not include any which could be regarded as essentially dissimilar in spatial implications from those chosen" (Record Report 31, *op. cit.*, para. 10).

To conclude this discussion of the weaknesses of the design procedure we shall consider in turn the use made of the Garin–Lowry residential location model and the Lakshmanan–Hansen shopping model during plan design and assessment.

The Garin–Lowry model was used during each of the cycles to assess whether the spatial distributions of residential development and non-basic employment postulated in the strategies were "realistic"; that is, likely to occur in the manner proposed. Given the amounts and locations of new basic employment and the pattern of travel costs in the Sub-region, the model was run to investigate whether people would willingly choose to live in those areas designated for new housing, and whether additions to employment in industries serving local markets would take place in the specified locations. There are two difficulties with such a use of the model. Firstly, it does not consider all those factors relevant to people's choice of residential location; rent levels, for instance, are left out. Thus, some fairly strong other-things-being-equal assumptions are required for it to provide valid predications. Secondly, a pattern of locations that is initially judged to be infeasible *can* be realized by additional investments in transportation infrastructure or by different locations of basic employment. Indeed, we can use the Garin–Lowry model to explore the nature of controls and investments required to achieve some desired pattern of residential and shopping developments. The Team may have appreciated these two points. Yet, at the end of the first cycle of design and assessment they concluded from the output of the model that it would prove very difficult to depart radically from the established pattern of developments within the Sub-region, and they rejected a number of areas on this basis.[36]

The *Report* also states that the Garin-Lowry model was employed during the second cycle "to give more detailed indications of the *suitability* of particular areas of the sub-region for residential and service location"(our emphasis).[37] But, as with all other urban development models in current use, this model can only enable the planner to predict the way in which people will behave in certain circumstances. The model has no normative content; it is purely descriptive. Thus its predictions cannot provide a direct basis for policy prescription. There is no reason to suppose that the pattern of location of new residential development predicted by the model under one set of specified circumstances is to be preferred to some other pattern.

The shopping model was used from the second cycle onwards. This model forecast flows of expenditure on durable goods between residential zones and existing and proposed shopping centres, given the spatial distribution of consumers (and the amounts they spend on durables) and the pattern of travel costs. This set of forecasts was used for three purposes. One was to examine whether the new shopping centres proposed in the designs were likely to operate at the scale of activity envisaged, which provided a test of the operational feasibility of establishing new centres. This was done by comparing the predicted amounts of sales at each centre with its operating capacity. The comments made above on the use of the

[36]*Report*, para. 7.21.
[37]*Ibid.*, para. 7.29.

Garin–Lowry model apply here with equal force. Secondly, the data on predicted sales at existing centres were used as a basis for formulating proposals for amounts of floorspace that should be added to those centres. It was proposed that supply should be adjusted so that potential sales could be just realized at all established centres. This, of course, is not necessarily the best policy. Indeed, there is no reason for thinking that it would be. Another weakness was that no comparative assessments were made of the proposals contained in the different strategies. Murray and Kennedy[38] have pointed out that the output of the model can be processed to give information about mean cash flow distances, which would be useful in evaluating alternative proposals (assuming that information on benefits could also be obtained, which they do not discuss). But apparently this was not done.

A final point is that the model was used to investigate the effects of proposed new centres on current and future potential sales of existing centres. The findings helped the Team assess whether the proposed new centres were likely to be politically acceptable to the local authorities commissioning the Study.

Evaluation and Decision-taking

The work of the Study was geared to helping a decision to be taken by the members of the councils. The Director was very concerned that his Team should present their findings in a form that would most easily be understood by council members and that proposals should be put forward which they were likely to find politically acceptable and would be able collectively to agree. As a result, the *Report* was written expressly for those elected representatives responsible for taking the decision on the strategy. The issue of what technical matters to include and what to leave out and the level of detail of explanation and discussion were determined by this factor.

This effort to facilitate a positive decision was in itself commendable. However, it had the unfortunate effect of excluding any consideration of the wider process of public debate and appraisal of the proposals. The technical work was not written up in any detail in the *Report*; a brief summary only was appended to the main text. Detailed documentation was undertaken subsequently, but the resulting Record Reports have not been published and are not widely available. In addition, the *Report* did not explicitly state the important point that some groups in the community would inevitably incur significant losses whichever set of proposals are adopted, and that the decision was very much concerned with redistributional issues.

As a result, those groups and organizations in the Sub-region who had an interest in the decision found it very difficult to criticize and "interrogate" effectively the work that had been undertaken and the recommendations. It was difficult for them to answer the following kinds of questions: How far are the proposals in the general community interest? What features of the work leading up to the proposals are

[38]W. Murray and M. B. Kennedy, Notts/Derbys: a shopping model primer, *J. Town Planning Inst.* **57** (1971) 211–15.

technically sound and of a high standard and what features are not? Is the plan equitable? There was also widespread misunderstanding of the nature of the work carried out and, indeed, of the proposals themselves. Finally, the concern with political acceptance meant that there was no detailed investigation of policies which, despite meeting with political resistance, would nonetheless have been in the wider interests of the community.

8.4. CONCLUDING OBSERVATIONS ON THE NOTTINGHAMSHIRE–DERBYSHIRE STUDY

In conclusion we highlight the main features of the Study that have emerged from this review. Political considerations exerted a very strong influence on the approach adopted. Paramount importance was given to ensuring that the proposals put forward for adoption would meet with the general approval of the elected representatives. This mainly reflected the desire to get agreement between the four councils concerned so that a joint policy could be adopted and implemented. But it also served as a rough and indirect test of whether the proposals were likely to be in the general interests of the community at large. Attempts were made not only to judge the likely reaction of elected representatives to the various alternatives investigated, but also to convince them of the comparative merits of those alternatives which performed well in relation to the evaluation criteria employed. These features of the Study reflected the personal philosophy of the Director. To quote:[39]

> "From the outset the study was conditioned by a number of decisions made by myself which, for tactical reasons, have never been made public. The most important decision was that the principal study recommendations must be agreed with the chief planning officers and other relevant chief officers of the four authorities sponsoring our work before they were presented to elected members and the public. Without such agreement there would be no hope of the plan's being accepted by all four authorities. . . ."

The main drawback to this approach is that councils are more likely to be concerned with sectional interests than with the well-being of all groups in the community. In consequence their preferred alternative may well have appeared disadvantaged in terms of *total* social gains and losses. The approach also assumes that public debate and criticism cannot alter the dividing line between what is viewed to be politically feasible and what is infeasible, which is doubtful.

The Team deserve considerable credit for pioneering both a cyclic process of plan-making and the use of development potential analysis. Since they completed their work, growing attention has been paid both in the literature and in practice to developing cyclic planning procedures.[40] The advantages of such procedures are now

---

[39]A. Thorburn, Preparing a regional plan: how we set about the task in Nottinghamshire/Derbyshire, *J. Town Planning Inst.* **57** (1971) 216.

[40]For instance, D. B. Massey and M. Cordey-Hayes, The use of models in structure planning, *Town Planning Rev.* **42** (1971) 28–44; R. Gutch, *Goals and the Planning Process*, Oxford Polytechnic Working Papers in Planning Education and Research, No. 11, 1972.

beginning to be widely recognized. Others have also drawn on the Team's experience and have further refined DPA so that it may be used as a design technique as well as for evaluation. Despite certain technical difficulties of operation, it has proved a powerful method of ensuring that a manageable number of relatively good alternatives are fairly quickly produced for detailed assessment.[41]

In addition, the number and diversity of alternatives the Team sought to investigate were highly ambitious. However, for reasons of technical capability and resource limitations, they were prevented from formally analysing more than a few of them. In addition, over-reliance was placed on the use of urban development models in establishing the practicability of proposals. For instance, the Team used the forecasts of the Garin–Lowry model as a basis for judging which of their proposals for the location of residential developments were likely to be capable of implementation (although they did proceed with a few that did not conform with the model's forecasts). They took the view that it would be extremely difficult to influence the location of urban developments away from the pattern that would emerge from the interplay of market forces. But it does not seem to have been appreciated by all members of the Team that the forecasts given by urban development models depend on given assumptions about a range of variables such as the proposed locations of new manufacturing employment, which are subject to planning policy.

COVENTRY-SOLIHULL-WARWICKSHIRE (September 1968–May 1971)

In this review of the C–S–W Study we find that whilst the planning process was well designed, with considerable attention paid to consistency between plan generation and evaluation and to the efficient use of time and resources, the approach to plan evaluation was weak in a number of respects. The most important of these was the lack of serious attempts to obtain empirical evidence in support of the strategy objectives and the physical measures and values used for evaluation.

8.5. PURPOSE OF THE STUDY

The Study was undertaken by an independent Team under the direction of a Steering Group comprised of officers of the three sponsoring authorities. The Team's task was to advise the councils on a "strategy" to be adopted for the urban and rural development of the sub-region from the present time to near the end of the century.[42] This was to indicate a broad pattern of major land uses, including (*inter alia*) the future location of major residential developments, major shopping and employment centres, areas for rural conservation, and transportation network proposals (motor-

---

[41]In addition to its use on the C–S–W Study, it has recently been employed for design and evaluation purposes on the West Central Scotland Plan. West Central Scotland Planning Team, The evaluation of spatial strategies for 1981, unpublished paper, 1972.

[42]See terms of reference given by the clients, in C–S–W Sub-regional Study Team, *Study Management*, Supplementary Report 7, May 1971, pp. 83–84.

ways, main roads, and railways). Precise boundaries of land uses and transport route alignments were not to be indicated.

The purpose of the strategy was to provide an agreed broad framework within which the respective local planning authorities could formulate their detailed plans. It was intended to serve as a bridge between planning considerations at the regional scale and the structure plans of the LPAs. As we discussed earlier in this chapter, a major advantage of a common framework is that it makes possible the co-ordination of local policies and, by avoiding serious conflicts, helps to ensure that the various local policies are all capable of implementation.

Perhaps the most important reason for setting up an independent Team was that the LPAs could not agree among themselves as to the appropriate location of new urban developments within the sub-region. They hoped that an independent investigation would enable them to resolve satisfactorily their differences. As a result members of the councils were not involved in either the administrative or technical work of the Team.[43]

Work began in September 1968 and the Team completed their investigations about twenty-nine months later, in early 1971. Their final report,[44] containing a summary of their work and a description of their recommended strategy, was made available simultaneously to members of the councils and the general public in May 1971. During most of the time up to and including work on the design of alternatives, the Team was comprised of eight full-time planners; after this it reached a peak strength over a period of three months of ten full-time planners. In total, about £87,000 were employed on the Study, a similar amount to that spent on the Leicester and Leicestershire Sub-regional Study, and not far short of that spent on the Notts-Derby Study. The recommended strategy was accepted by all three councils in November 1971 as a basis for structure planning in the Sub-region.

8.6. APPROACH TO THE STUDY

The councils were, of course, formally responsible for taking the decision on the strategy to be adopted. However, since the Team was specifically directed to recommend to the members a strategy which in their view was best, they had to perform the function of decision-taking. It was therefore not sufficient for them to produce and present evidence on the advantages and disadvantages of possible strategies. Deciding on the preferred alternative will have involved members of the Team in debate over the correct interpretation of the evidence they produced and about the reliability and comprehensiveness of that evidence.

The Team decided that their proposals would relate to the period from the mid 1970s until the early 1990s, but it was emphasized that a proposed strategy and the situation envisaged for the early 1990s are only stages in the long term development

[43] *Ibid.*, para. 8.
[44] C–S–W Sub-regional Study Team, *The Report on the Sub-regional Planning Study*, Coventry City Council, 1971.

of the Sub-region. Owing to the time required for implementation, it was considered unlikely that the strategy could have any significant impact on developments until about 1976. Difficulties in forecasting was the reason given for not framing proposals for beyond the early 1990s. A single year, 1991, was chosen for assessment of the relative merits of the alternatives, although a tentative population forecast was made for the middle of the next century and its implications for residential development were pointed out in order to give the Study a long-term perspective.

The Team were strongly aware of the advantages of pre-planning the entire plan-making process, drawing on advice in this respect from those then working on the Leicester and Leicestershire Sub-regional Study. Accordingly, they gave considerable attention at the outset to formulating their approach. A proposed study programme was presented to the Steering Board in June 1969, nine months after work had begun.[45] In that document the Team clarified their view of their task; they put forward the basic criteria by which they were to judge the relative merits of alternative strategies; and they outlined the planning process to be adopted— indicating the tasks to be carried out and their approximate sequence, the nature of the surveys and data to be collected, and the modelling and forecasting techniques to be used.

The importance of ensuring consistency of effort throughout the planning process was recognized and stressed. Emphasis was placed on devising a systematic procedure for examining and comparing alternative possible strategies that might go some way towards achieving the objectives specified for the strategy. Consequently an attempt was made to integrate evaluation and other related work, particularly design, as closely as possible. In addition, the evaluation of alternatives was to be "comprehensive" in that the strategy objectives were intended to relate to all those consequences of the strategies which the Team considered significant in arriving at their recommendation. The main purpose of their work was viewed as being "to demonstrate how alternative strategies might perform in relation to each of the objectives [formulated for the strategy], and how the recommended strategy would best resolve conflict between objectives and was the most satisfactory framework for change".[46]

Evaluation Methodology

The emphasis placed on objectives and comprehensiveness of plan assessment did not, however, dictate the evaluation method to be used. In the event the Team decided to base their procedure for evaluating alternative strategies on Hill's goals–achievement matrix method. The GAM was adapted in two respects to suit the circumstances. Firstly, no attempt was made to divide the community into incidence groups and to determine the gains and losses which would accrue to each group from

[45]This is set out in Supplementary Report 7, *op. cit.*, appendix A.
[46]*Report*, para. 2.16.

the adoption of alternative proposals.[47] Thus it was not possible to deal with equity considerations in the evaluations (except by way of an objective to help areas of declining industry). Secondly, the method was used to compare the effects of proposals for a number of sectors of planning activity including transportation, housing, agriculture, and retailing. This extended the analysis further than was considered valid by Hill at that time. He had argued that it should be restricted to investigating single-sector projects and effects.[48]

As we have noted in Chapter 5, Hill has given little guidance in his writings on the critical questions of: Evaluation from whose viewpoint and according to what principles of assessment? He nowhere states explicitly whose objectives and values are to be taken into account, nor how the measurement of the welfare effects of proposals should be approached. The C–S–W Team therefore had no established principles to guide them in their evaluation work. They had to formulate and agree upon a set of principles which they considered appropriate. The principles they chose to adopt are regrettably not clearly stated in their published reports and are very difficult to discern from a reading of those reports alone.

Consideration was given to using social cost–benefit analysis, both as conventionally practised and within a planning balance sheet framework. But a goals–achievement evaluation[49] was carried out "because it was more suitable to the nature of the Study and not as a second best to a cost–benefit assessment". Two main reasons were given for preferring the goals–achievement approach,[50] neither of which appears convincing to us. One was that a full social cost–benefit analysis (SCBA) would have involved putting monetary values on objective achievements, including non-market items that are difficult to measure and value, such as beautiful landscape and accessibility to job opportunities, and "public reaction has shown the difficulty of putting a convincing price on barely tangible factors". As the Team appreciated, money is used in SCBA simply as a convenient common unit for expressing relative values. If the Team's statement about the public reaction to money valuation is true, it will hence be true for *any* procedure which assigns relative values to items of advantage and disadvantage.

The other main reason for not using SCBA was that "In the circumstances of this Study, we could see no conceptual advantage in putting a price on the intangible to compare with the tangible, rather than weighting the tangible to compare it with the intangible". As an alternative to assigning monetary values to those non-market and

---

[47]In the initial phase of the Study, however, the Team envisaged that they would determine the gains and losses for specific incidence groups. This intention was dropped when it was found that the work involved would have added about 40 per cent to the Study budget (personal communication from U. Wannop).

[48]On this point see the discussion in section 5.2.

[49]The Team termed their method "objectives–achievement evaluation", but the difference is purely terminological.

[50]See C–S–W Sub-regional Study Team, *Evaluation*, Supplementary Report 4, paras. 1.19–1.21. It should be noted that the Team did not object to the principles of SCBA. They simply thought that methodology less appropriate than the GAM in the case of their particular study.

intangible items in their evaluation, the Team chose to assign numerical points to them, i.e. notional units of value. However, they did recognize that in SCBA the money value placed on an item simply represents the value to individuals of that item relative to other items, and thus money performs the same function as a notional unit of value such as points. They both serve to express disparate items in common terms to facilitate choice between alternative proposals, and both rely on the ability of the analyst to determine the relative values of those items. Therefore the "weighting" of a *tangible* item (either by the use of points or money units) in order to make it comparable with an *intangible* item involves an identical operation to weighting the intangible item to make it comparable with the tangible. The resulting relative values should be the same whether one transforms the units of measure used to describe the intangible (e.g. number of Norman churches to be displaced) into those units used to describe the tangible (e.g. tons of wheat), or vice versa. It does not alter the nature of the valuation process whether, in order to achieve comparability, one acts upon the intangibles or the tangibles. Thus a points-weighting procedure of the sort advocated by Hill, and as used in the Study, can do no more than the valuation procedures employed by SCBA. The real problem is trying to find out what the relative values of the tangible and intangible items really are.

The former Director of the Study, U. Wannop, has said in private discussion that for the purpose of weighting objective achievements he preferred the use of numerical points to money because it would have been *too difficult* to determine the money value of all items in the Team's evaluation. Yet if the relative values of the items under consideration can be estimated, then they can always be expressed (and legitimately so) in money units; and if they cannot be estimated it will simply not be possible to employ any units of value.

I. Turner, a former member of the Team, has also argued that in practice the results of an evaluation which employs "points" or other notional units of value instead of money will be more easily understood by both the public and those responsible for taking decisions. In his view the officers and elected members who read their *Report* before approving the recommended strategy found the results of their evaluation exercises easier to grasp than conventional SCBA, and he considers that by comparison the misunderstanding and confusion which followed the publication of the Roskill Commission's analysis supports his view.

Turner has put forward a possible explanation for thie difference. He suggests that there might be feelings of guilt associated with money, and argues that elected members and officers respectively do not like being regarded as mercenary and materialistic. An evaluation in monetary units induces this feeling of guilt which they try to suppress when talking about the quality of the environment and other non-market aspects of planning proposals. In his view, the use of non-money units avoided this problem of conflicting perceptions.[51]

In our view it should be fairly easy for the layman to understand what the monetary values in a SCBA mean. A difference of, say, £1000 between two

---

[51]These points were made in a personal communication.

alternative schemes can be understood in relation to combinations of goods or items of value which are equivalent in worth to that sum of money. We consider it much more difficult for the layman to understand what is meant by a difference of, say, 1000 numerical "points". The points only relate to the particular objectives adopted for the plan; they preclude comparisons with other items of value, such as those goods secured through market transaction.

Planning balance sheet analysis was thought to offer no advantages over goal–achievement analysis. Whilst noting that the former method had been used to measure advantages and disadvantages to different groups in the community, which was seen as its strength, the Team pointed out that both methods facilitate the inclusion of the distribution of gains and losses.

The Adopted Planning Process[52]

In brief outline the planning process adopted by the Team was as follows:

(1) Forty-two alternative strategies produced by means of development potential analysis.
(2) These alternatives reduced to three by a process of synthesis, to which a "trend" strategy was added.
(3) These four alternatives were evaluated. After some sensitivity analysis, this led directly to the selection of the preferred strategy.

Prior to starting work on formulating strategies for assessment, the Team decided on their approach to evaluation. Subject to modifications in the light of experience as the Study proceeded, decisions were made concerning the objectives to be used in determining the advantages and disadvantages of alternatives, the indices for measuring the magnitudes of objective achievements, and the relative valuations to be used in comparing levels of achievement of different objectives. The purpose of deciding on these matters early on was to enable the Team to achieve consistency between their design and evaluation procedures. The principles and measures to be used for evaluation were incorporated into the design process as fully as was possible.

In their reports the Team state that without consideration during the design process to the way in which the alternatives were to be assessed, a vast number of possibilities would have had to be generated in order to ensure the inclusion of the optimum (or near-optimum) plan. They also stressed that even if it were possible to have evaluated rigorously an enormous number of alternative development patterns, that would have been a grossly inefficient approach. The aim was to arrive at a short-list of alternatives fairly quickly and be confident that the best possibilities were included.

The Team rejected traditional approaches to design, such as those based on

---

[52]The major stages of the Study are illustrated in fig. 2 of Supplementary Report 7, *op. cit.*, and are also set out in fig. 2.1 of *Report* in the form of a flow diagram.

geometric concepts of urban form and growth (giving rise to linear cities, satellite developments, star-shaped cities, growth corridors, and so forth), or those based on the sieve-map technique. The weakness of such methods is that they either proceed without reference to the criteria to be used in evaluation or, in the case of sieve maps, make use of only some of the relevant criteria to the exclusion of all others.

The objectives and the measures and relative values proposed for evaluation were used in a direct manner in the strategy generation process. These evaluation criteria were used to produce information about the comparative attractiveness of different parts of the Sub-region for new urban development. The whole of the Sub-region was divided into zones (each 5 kilometers square), and the attractiveness of each zone was assessed by measuring its potential performance in relation to a number of the planning objectives.[53] Potential levels of objective achievement were estimated and (after these were normalized) the valuations were applied to the scores of achievement. The resulting set of weighted scores were then summed to give a single index of potential performance for each strategy. Thus each zone was given a composite index of "development potential" which indicated its overall suitability for new urban development. The results of this exercise were represented by contours of development potential, which together formed a development potential surface. It should be noted that in calculating a zone's development potential, regard was paid to fulfilling some of the constraints which had been formulated earlier.

This procedure was repeated a number of times, using a large number of different sets of relative values or "weights". Each set gave rise to a different surface of development potential. The Team then identified those areas which had consistently high indices of potential for the different sets of values used, and these were grouped to form three alternative strategies. After some subsequent detailing, these— together with a so-called "trend" strategy—were the alternatives considered at the evaluation stage. The "trend" strategy was based on an extrapolation of past changes in the amount and location of urban developments within the Sub-region, and was an attempt to show the implications of a continuation of past policies for future residential development. It was assumed that the objectives of the LPAs and the relative importance attached to their achievement had been reflected in those developments permitted in the past.

The four strategies put forward for evaluation related essentially to proposed developments within the Sub-region from the mid 1970s to the early 1990s. They are illustrated in Fig. 8.3. But as we have noted, the relative advantages and disadvantages of these strategies were assessed for one year only (1991). With complex planning proposals at the Sub-regional scale, the presumption must be that differential levels of objective achievement as between strategies will vary significantly over about fifteen years or more. Yet no attempt seems to have been made to estimate the time profile of differentials to provide additional guidance as to choice.

---

[53]Not all of the objectives were used. It was felt that it was either impracticable or unhelpful to incorporate six of the total of twenty objectives. In addition, those that related to flexibility formed part of a separate study.

The evaluation of the alternatives for objectives relating to flexibility was undertaken as a separate exercise. This was done because the Team found it too difficult to determine the value of achieving the various dimensions of flexibility, which they identified relative to the value of achieving the other strategy objectives.

For all these other objectives, levels of achievement were estimated and, after being normalized, these were weighted by an agreed set of relative values to produce a combined index of plan performance. The sensitivity of the findings of this evaluation were examined in relation to those objectives about whose value there was most disagreement among Team members. To do this, use was made of those valuations suggested by individual members, which were said to represent their own "professional judgements" of the relative importance of the achievements of the various objectives.

The strategy which was ranked first (strategy 904) achieved that position not because it performed best on all objectives, or indeed on very many of them, but because it consistently performed relatively well. It was equal first on three of the sixteen objectives and outright first on two others. By contrast, the strategy which was ranked second overall (strategy 902) obtained three equal firsts and *five* outright firsts.

The analysis of flexibility showed that strategy 904 was to be preferred outright on two of the four flexibility objectives and jointly preferred on another. Although it only obtained second place (to strategy 902) for the remaining objective, the Team took the view that its disadvantage in this respect was not sufficient to outweigh its net advantage on other counts. It thus became chosen by the Team as their preferred strategy (Fig. 8.2).

8.7. EVALUATION IN THE PLANNING PROCESS OF THE COVENTRY-SOLIHULL-WARWICKSHIRE STUDY

Evaluation and Data Collection

If data collection starts early in the planning process it will speed the evaluation exercises and will allow the best possible evidence to be used in assessing alternatives. This will help to ensure that the study is not unduly protracted and is satisfactorily completed within the prescribed time. We comment here on the *procedural* aspects of data collection and the degree of "completeness" of the data employed in the Team's evaluation matrix.

To their credit, the Team gave considerable thought at the outset to the sort of data which would be required for evaluation. They were able to do this because of the early decisions on the objectives to be used in evaluation, the approach to their measurement and valuation, and the scope and detail which were required of the recommended strategy. The devising of a suitable range of objectives early on meant that these were more or less in their final form when work began on design. This applied also to the measures and relative values of objective achievements. In

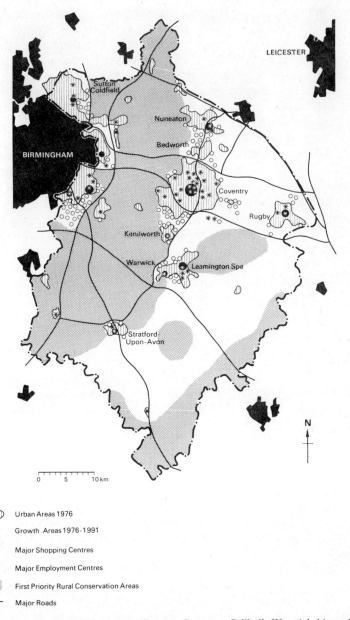

FIG. 8.2. The recommended strategy. (Source: *Coventry–Solihull–Warwickshire, a Strategy for the Sub-region*, fig. 1.2, p. 3.)

addition, the Team were able to use much of the information produced during the analysis of development potential in the comparison of strategies.

The evaluation itself took only four months, and although the Team in some cases had to make do with second-best data (for instance, in estimating the loss of mineral deposits through the siting of new development), sufficient evidence was produced for them to form a view as to the preferred alternative with confidence. They were able to measure the extent of achievement for all the specified objectives, and to place relative values on levels of objective achievement for all except those concerned with flexibility—a topic which has as yet been little explored.

However, the speed with which the evaluations were completed and the comprehensiveness of the information collected was only partly due to the early attention given to data requirements. Another important influence was the nature of the procedures used for establishing the objectives, measures, and values. The Team formed their views on these matters by almost exclusive reliance on their previous professional experience; that is to say, without obtaining more than a minimal amount of independent evidence by which to substantiate their judgements. For instance, the only direct empirical evidence on the preferences of the various groups in the Sub-region was obtained from a questionnaire survey of existing residents. Only 160 households were included in the sample; the estimated population of the Sub-region for 1970 being a little over one million.

Evaluation and Constraints

Since it is usually impossible *a priori* to determine the opportunity costs of laying down a particular constraint, a planning team should avoid the use of any constraints other than those which are really necessary. The Team formulated eight "essential objectives" by which to assess alternative strategies. For a proposed strategy to be admissible for selection it had to "fully attain" each of the essential objectives. These therefore acted as constraints on choice between possible alternatives.

Although the terms of reference contained a number of directives, there were no constraints as such on design solutions. However, one of the directives required that the Team "must take a realistic view of the resources likely to be available nationally for capital investment". Clearly, any strategy would not be feasible if the capital funds required for implementation were lacking. The Team made some attempt to estimate the amount of national capital which would be available for the strategy, and, as a result, specified a budget constraint for highway planning of £89 million for that part of the Sub-region lying outside the Birmingham conurbation. Unfortunately, they were, in general, unable to forecast the amount of capital funds likely to be available in the main fields of expenditure—housing, sewerage, and town centre redevelopment in addition to transport. This was largely due to the relatively short periods to which treasurers gear budget allocations and the difficulty of determining the shares of public and private expenditure on housing and town centre redevelopments.

The other seven constraints were not required by the terms of reference, and were self-imposed. Four stemmed from the Team's forecasts for 1991 of resident population, employment opportunities, and the demand for residential accommodation. They concerned the following:

(a) Providing sufficient land to accommodate the forecasts of potential increases in population and employment, at specified space standards and with supporting public services.

(b) Ensuring that there will be neither substantial labour shortages nor substantial rates of unemployment within the Sub-region.

(c) Providing a specified amount and quality of future dwellings.

A total of 1,410,000 people and 563,000 jobs formed common elements in all strategies. Thus no differences in levels of objective achievement which would result from different assumptions about future growth rates were examined. Yet, as they admit, no one rate of population or of employment growth was *inevitable*. The Team's forecasts represented the potential for urban growth which was consistent with the density standards chosen by them. These densities may be well below those which would occur in the absence of planning controls; that is, the density standards adopted may have restricted the demand for housing, labour supplies, retail facilities, and so forth below their full potential levels.[54] If this was so, then a reduction in densities would have implied a faster rate of future urban growth. Thus the levels of demand giving rise to urban growth were endogenous to the strategies.

The requirement that the recommended strategy must provide sufficient land for given amounts of residential accommodation and employment opportunities really resulted from population and employment growth aims. The Team did not, however, attempt to justify the particular growth rates which they specified.

They based their urban density standards on what they thought people within the Sub-region will be likely to demand in the future. Their assumptions about densities conditioned the amount of total urban growth which could be realized. Supposing that the specified densities *were* the most appropriate ones, why then did the Team aim to achieve the largest increases in population and employment consistent with those densities? On this matter their reports have only this to say: "The answer to the question—Why Growth?—is that the sub-region's economic and social well-being depends upon it very considerably; it is a consequence of the country's choice to increase its population and its economic growth."[55] However, a national policy of growth does not dictate that population increase and industrial development take place in any particular areas of the country; and it is not necessarily a good thing for the existing or the potential future residents of the Sub-region that planners try to achieve a high rate of urban growth in their area.

[54]Whether the forecasts of natural population increase, for instance, will be realized is dependent on how easy it will be for young couples to find suitable housing in the Sub-region, and this will itself be influenced by the rate of residential developments. The alternative for them is, of course, to move elsewhere; and that would have secondary consequences for the level of industrial and commercial activity.

[55]*Report*, para. 1.20.

The other three constraints not yet mentioned were formulated in similar terms to the strategy objectives in that no minimum acceptable levels of attainment were specified. They are:

"To locate all new development so as to protect flying operations at airports and the safety of residents." (But how much protection, and what degree of safety is an acceptable minimum?)

"To conserve sites of architectural, historical and ecological significance." (No interference whatsoever?)

"To give the public the greatest opportunity for recreational use of land, particularly suitable and appropriate for that purpose."

The constraint relating to public safety zones may be regarded as the expression of a planning standard, since safety standards are widely used in planning practice. But it is difficult to view the constraint relating to conservation as reflecting standards, and even more that relating to recreational opportunity. In general, it is difficult to explain why these constraints were not included in the set of ("discriminatory") objectives. Recreational and ecological considerations, for instance, would not seem to merit special treatment as opposed to those of residential environment or firms' accessibility to labour supplies. Losses associated with the former items may legitimately be traded-off against gains associated with the latter. This is denied if recreation and conservation aims must be attained to the fullest possible extent. If, on the other hand, the acceptable level of attainment is somewhere below what is possible, then by implication no value is given to increments above that minimum level, which is unrealistic.

It has been suggested to us by a former Team member that these aims were included among the "essential" objectives because they did not provide any basis for discriminating, spatially, between urban development strategies, at the level of generality of the Study.[56] However, since the total amount of urban growth envisaged in the strategies was determined without consideration being given to conservation, recreational opportunities, or safety, it seems difficult to justify the constraints except in so far as their fulfilment *would be* affected by alternative spatial dispositions of population, employment, and so forth. If, for example, differential degrees of conservation would not exist or would not be discernible given the level of generality of the strategies, then the issue of conservation would not be relevant to the evaluation of those strategies.

The main criticism of the constraints which the Team formulated is that they prevented an examination of the effects of alternative amounts of urban growth on the levels of achievement of the strategy objectives. A former member of the Team has argued that it was necessary to have common assumptions about the scale of urban growth built into all alternative strategies because if the "quantities" had varied between strategies it would not have been possible to assess them on a

[56]J. M. Shaw, in a personal communication.

comparative basis. We recognize that there are often severe practical difficulties involved in evaluating plans that contain, say, differential levels of capital investment or amounts of population and employment. Yet, in principle at least, there is nothing to prevent a satisfactory evaluation being made. The Brighton Urban Structure Plan Team, for instance, evaluated alternative strategies with a radical difference in the level of future residential populations within their Study area.[57] The scale of future urban developments was considered an issue of major importance in the evaluation. To make the evaluation comparative, assumptions were made of the net benefits which potential in-migrants would experience if they chose to continue living outside the Brighton area.

Evaluation and Goals and Objectives

Four very general and abstract "goals" were formulated for the strategy. These were as follows:

Type of Goal	Statement of Goal
"Social and Economic:	Balance and prosperity in the sub-regional economy and the greatest social welfare.
Environmental:	The best living and working environment throughout the sub-region.
Choice:	The greatest choice of opportunities.
Flexibility:	The ability to adapt to change whilst ensuring that social and economic advancement is maintained."

A goal was defined as "an idealised end state of the social, economic and physical environment, towards which the plan must strive, but for which no test of fulfilment can be applied". It was the goals which were thought to provide the ultimate justification for the recommended strategy.[58]

In this sense the goals may be regarded as the basic principles governing the formulation of the strategy objectives. They were intended to be universally applicable to urban and regional planning, regardless of the particular problems. Like the formal criteria of welfare economics, they represented supposedly non-controversial value judgements; that is, ones to which everyone or virtually everyone would subscribe. An objective was defined as "a specific statement about the physical world, derived from a goal for which the degree of attainment is measurable". Thus it was claimed that the objectives were *"derived"* from a

---

[57]Brighton Urban Structure Plan Team, *Report on the Evaluation of Alternative Strategies*, Brighton County Borough Council, December 1971.

[58]"We saw the purpose of the strategy as being to help [the community of] the sub-region towards certain goals which were seen as the ultimate achievements of a social, economic and physical environment" (*Report*, para 3.2).

consideration of the goals.[59] This implies that they were either formulated by a process of logical deduction or that, on an intuitive level, the goals suggested possible objectives. It is very difficult to determine which of these two processes of derivation operated.

At this point it is important to note three characteristics of the objectives. Firstly, they were valued apparently only in so far as their achievement would raise the level of attainment of the postulated goals. If this is so, the relationship between the goals and objectives is hierarchical. Secondly, it follows that each objective should be consistent with the attainment of one or more of the goals. Thirdly, the evidence relating to the likely extent of objective achievements was that used to select the preferred strategy. There was no discussion of the extent to which thereby the goals were achieved. Thus we may interpret the objectives as being particular elements of the goals; a given objective would therefore form *part* of one of the goals rather than having a separate existence from the goal itself.

In this section we first comment on the consistency between the goals and objectives of the strategy and the apparent degree of overlap between the goals. Following this we consider three issues in relation to the use made of objectives. The most fundamental of these is the basis on which the Team decided on the relevance of possible objectives. Here we shall investigate whose interests the strategy objectives were intended to represent. Secondly, we comment on the evidence which the Team put forward in order to justify their particular selection of objectives. Finally, we comment on whether the objectives, as formulated, enabled the Team to obtain a clear indication of the welfare effects of alternatives.

It is very difficult when reading the published reports to determine whether the objectives are consistent with the attainment of the goals. Terms such as "social and economic balance", "social welfare", and "environment" have no universally agreed meanings, and are used in a variety of ways by planners. The general notions behind goals such as to achieve "the greatest choice of opportunities" or to achieve "the greatest social welfare" may be fairly well understood. But without knowing the precise meaning to be attached to them one cannot with any confidence derive or deduce more specific and detailed aims from them. Unfortunately, there is virtually no discussion in the reports about what meanings the Team themselves attached to the goals.

These goals also appear to overlap considerably. For instance, under the heading "Social and Economic" is the goal to achieve "balance and prosperity in the sub-regional economy and the greatest social welfare"; and under the heading "Environmental" is found the goal of achieving "the best living and working environment throughout the sub-region". Presumably, the living and working environment was not thought of as an economic or a social factor. Similarly the goal under

---

[59]For instance, the objectives relating to the goal of providing inhabitants with "the greatest choice of opportunities" concerned the following: choice of housing sites for those seeking new homes, choice of jobs for workers, choice of labour for firms, the opportunity for all residents to obtain employment, range of available shopping facilities and ease of access to those facilities, and choice of transport routes and modes.

"choice," which was to achieve "the greatest choice of opportunities". But both choice and environmental considerations can be given a socio-economic interpretation. For example, the range of goods and services available in the market and the variety of public goods supplied to the community depend upon production decisions of private and public enterprises. Moreover, in terms of traditional consumer demand analysis, an individual is likely to move to a more preferred position if confronted with more, rather than fewer, alternative bundles of goods, or opportunities, from which to choose.

If, on the other hand, we ignore the labels given to the goals (in order to avoid semantic difficulties), it must follow that by differentiating these goals a good living and working environment and choice of opportunities are valued because they achieve something other than an increase in "welfare". This is very dubious. Indeed, it is difficult to think of what that "something" could be. The purpose of public agency planning should surely be to improve the welfare of the community by making its members better off in some sense than otherwise. This involves trying to reduce their disadvantages or costs and increase the magnitude of the benefits they enjoy.

The strategy objectives were decided upon by the Team, although they were developed with help from outside sources. Unfortunately, the reports nowhere state explicitly *whose* interests were taken into account when setting objectives and thus *whose* interests the objectives are intended to represent. This is a serious weakness, making it difficult for the decision-takers to tell whether the evaluation was comprehensive in relation to the community affected and why some possible objectives were disregarded. Why, for instance, were residents' costs of access to rural recreation facilities and the linkages between industrial and commercial establishments (e.g. by way of shipments of goods) not considered relevant? Perhaps potential differences between strategies for these items were too small to be worth taking into account, or perhaps they were simply overlooked—we cannot say.

There are a number of possibilities as to whose interests or preferences the objectives were meant to represent. They might have been the Team's hypotheses about the preferences of those individuals likely to be directly affected by the different strategies; or merely abstract notions about the kind of environment that the strategy should achieve, without formal consideration of the preferences of those potentially affected. Further, the objectives might have represented the preferences of members of the Planning Team. And there are other possibilities. From subsequent discussions between former members of the Team and others[60] it is clear that they were meant to represent the interests of those individuals who were likely to be directly affected.[61] The Team probably thought that this would be

---

[60]Such as the seminar held at the Economist Intelligence Unit, London, in January 1972, at which U. Wannop spoke on the topic of setting goals and objectives at the regional level.

[61]In formulating the strategy objectives the Team may not have been *consciously* attempting to specify the preferences of members of the community for the likely items of consequence of the proposals (i.e., having conscious regard to likely welfare effects), but their work may be interpreted in this way.

obvious. But these particular principles of evaluation are too important to be left unstated, no matter how obvious they may seem to those undertaking a study.

The Team collected some empirical evidence to support their choice of objectives. Initially, information about local policy issues and opinions on the proper aims of planning for the Sub-region was obtained. The sources included Central Government; members and officers of the commissioning planning authorities; development plans, reports and council minutes of those authorities; and items of local news and editorial opinion columns in local newspapers. But the only direct evidence came from the findings of a public opinion survey in which respondents were asked (among other things) whether or not they considered it important that the strategy should attempt to achieve the postulated objectives, and to add to that list of objectives any other which they personally thought important. The evidence was of limited usefulness since the only groups surveyed were those *then* existing within the Sub-region. The former Study Director now considers that more attention should have been given to the formulation of strategy objectives. Specifically, he would recommend that the public should be much more directly involved in the process.

The strategy objectives may certainly be viewed as essentially similar in form to what we term "sectoral" objectives, although the particular groups of individuals or "sectors" are not actually discussed or listed. For example, the objective "To locate new development so as to conserve areas of high landscape value" may be interpreted as expressing the objective of existing and new residents regarding countryside of high scenic quality. Other things being equal, they will prefer the existence of more beautiful countryside to less. Similarly, "To locate new residential development in areas of high environmental potential" may express the preference of new residents for various types of local amenity. All of the other objectives used for the evaluations may also be viewed in a similar way. The objectives relating to the flexibility of the strategies are no exception. Greater ability to adapt to unforeseen circumstances means that, if events do not occur as expected, the costs incurred by various groups in the community will be correspondingly lower. Those costs will themselves relate to particular items of preference, e.g. to the range of available job opportunities. "Flexibility" in itself, however, will not constitute an item of preference.

The Team's objectives were really categories of sectoral objectives. Each of them embraced a number of distinct items of preference having a common characteristic. In the case cited above of locating housing in areas of high environmental potential, a number of different amenities may be distinguished—for instance, recreational open space, pleasant views, and quiet. Some other objectives are more specific, but in general they, too, involve more than one item of preference. Hence, in order to facilitate the use of the strategy objectives for evaluation, the Team usually had first to specify their constituent elements. Measures had to be devised for each element, and the estimates of strategy performance were then combined into a composite index of objective achievement. Thus in order to obtain a clear indication of the welfare effects of their proposals, the Team had to specify their objectives in greater detail.

Evaluation and the Measurement of Physical Effects

The extent of achievement of an objective was assessed using a "performance criterion" or index.[62] The performance of strategies was assessed in two stages. Firstly, levels of achievement were estimated on the basis of what were considered to be the most likely out-turn of future events. After this the "flexibility" of strategies was assessed, which dealt with the ability of strategies to perform well under a variety of plausible future circumstances. To do this four objectives were employed, each relating to a different aspect of plan flexibility. The analyses undertaken in the first stage (dealing with the bulk of objectives) were described as "effectiveness" tests to distinguish them from the flexibility tests.

Here we are primarily concerned with the suitability of the indices of performance which were used, and whether they were checked against empirical evidence of how the individuals affected perceive the phenomena in question. But we also comment on the use made of a normalization procedure to express scores of objective achievement on a percentage scale.

It was necessary to convert the different physical measurements to a common scale since the relative values of objective achievements had been established without reference to the units of measure.

The choice of a physical measure of achievement is important since it can affect the ranking of plans with respect to the objective and thereby the ranking and choice of plans themselves. In devising their indices of effectiveness, the Team first determined some of the items of preference comprising each objective. Separate measures were devised for each aspect identified and the measures were then combined into a composite index. For instance, landscape quality was subdivided into various types of land use (farmland, woodland, heathland, built-on land, etc.) and allowance was made for the visibility of different areas from surrounding parts. However, it was generally the case that no evidence was presented to support the particular form of the indices employed. In this respect there was a significant lack of justification.

An example is afforded by the objective: "To locate new development so that there is the greatest possible choice of housing sites available to residents seeking new homes." A large number of aspects of choice were identified. These included the variety of spatial distribution of housing sites (number, size, and shape of different locations) and a number of specific characteristics of residential areas thought to be significant determinants of choice. This latter group included (*inter alia*) the socio-economic character of the area, noise, and air pollution levels, access to jobs and shopping facilities, and choice of mode of transport. Measures were devised for each one of the component attributes the Team had specified, but no evidence was produced as to their relative importance in giving variety of choice. Simply, percentage levels of achievement for each strategy were calculated for each attribute in turn and the *mean* taken to represent the overall level of objective

---

[62]There was one exception to this. Two separate criteria were employed for the objective concerning the ability of a plan to perform well in spite of possible changes in social values.

achievement. Implicitly the best possible level of achievement of, for instance, access to jobs was given an importance equal with that for access to shops and with choice of transport, which, from casual observation alone, seems absurd. The chosen characteristics of "choice" also made it unlikely that the selected index was satisfactory, for choice was defined in terms of the degree of mix of different types of housing site characteristics available and in terms of spatial distribution of housing locations. It is of little use, however, to have a wide mixture of types of sites if everyone wants one particular type. The Team may have recognized this, but it would seem that the actual pattern of consumer preferences was not taken into consideration. It is also difficult to see why measures of spatial dispersion, fragmentation, and compactness of the pattern of new residential development were incorporated into their index of choice. It seems more realistic to think of the differential benefits of choice as associated with the costs to consumers of securing an alternative bundle of housing attributes similar in type to their most preferred bundle.

Another interesting example of the Team's process of measurement is given by the objective "To locate new development so that the loss of workable mineral resources is kept to a minimum". This objective was measured by the criterion of the area of each mineral deposit sterilized by new development in each strategy expressed as a percentage of the total area of the mineral deposit within the Sub-region, summed for all minerals. We are told that this criterion was a proxy for the value of the mineral deposits *in situ*, and that it was used because information could not be obtained on many of the factors affecting the costs of extraction and shipment of the minerals nor on the depths of the mineral deposits.[63] We are not arguing here about data availability but about principles of measurement. The percentage area of mineral-bearing land taken for development is an unsuitable measure of the costs of sterilization, since it is the absolute amount of a mineral which is foregone that is important and not its proportion of the total amount available. The Team's simple summation of the percentage amounts of mineral-bearing land to be displaced by new developments implied that the smaller the total quantity of deposits of a given mineral within the Sub-region, the more valuable was a unit of that mineral relative to a unit of other minerals. This implicit assumption is likely to be quite misleading. In addition, it was at variance with the Team's statement that they treated "each economically important mineral as being . . . of equal importance to all other minerals".[64]

Independent evidence could have been obtained quite easily and cheaply to support the validity of the measures adopted for many items in the analysis, although it appears that this was not done in most cases—for instance in measuring the loss of

---

[63]Thus, there were no data that the Team could produce on the prices which operators might be willing to pay for rights of extraction of the minerals, which could have been used as an indication of the value of the minerals to society. The minerals under consideration were coal, marl, sand and gravel, and road stone.

[64]Supplementary Report 4, *op. cit.*, p. 243.

good quality farmland and the environmental potential of prospective new residential areas. Furthermore, the evidence should be clearly set down so that the decision-takers and others can judge the reliability of the measures and thus the quality of the analysis. It is normal to use evidence so that debate can be facilitated. In general, the Team only set down their *views* as to the indices that should be employed. We cannot debate these; we can only agree or disagree with them.

As we have mentioned, the extent of achievement of each objective was generally expressed on a percentage scale. The upper and lower limits of this scale represented the Team's estimates of the best and worst possible levels of achievement, given existing conditions. Relative values were established in relation to these hypothetical levels of achievement and without reference to the various units of measurement to be employed. Given this procedure, unless levels of achievement were estimated on some normalized scale the findings of an evaluation would have depended upon the nature of the units of measurement used, which is clearly undesirable. However, contrary to what some former members of the Team seem to imply, it is not necessary to normalize scores of objective achievement in order to undertake a comparative evaluation. To compare alternative plans which have disparate items of advantage and disadvantage, it is only necessary to determine the relative valuations of the items.

The estimates of best and worst possible achievement levels were derived from an analysis of development potential. For each zone of the Sub-region levels of objective achievement were calculated on the assumption that all its available land would be taken for new development. The total amount of new land required by the strategy was known. For a given objective the lowest level of achievement which a strategy could obtain was given by summing the scores of those zones which performed least well for that objective, and the highest level by summing the scores of those zones which performed best. This procedure was satisfactory for fixing zero per cent achievement levels and for fixing 100 per cent levels for negatively valued objectives, such as to minimize the amount of high grade agricultural land taken for development (in this case 100 per cent achievement was given by the smallest possible reduction to the existing amount of such land). However, the procedure was far less satisfactory for establishing the 100 per cent levels of positively valued objectives such as those concerned with firms' accessibility to labour supplies and consumers' accessibility to shopping facilities. In these cases a zone's potential achievement level depended upon assumptions about the location of *future* amounts of population and employment and investment to be made in transport facilities. These elements of a strategy would materially alter the existing pattern of accessibility to opportunities within the Sub-region. There does not seem any obvious and acceptable way of resolving this difficulty. In the event the Team estimated the 100 per cent achievement levels for their accessibility objectives by using information on the location of population and job growth as envisaged within the strategies themselves; the precise method of estimation is, however, rather difficult to follow.[65]

[65]Supplementary Report 4, *op. cit.*, pp. 322–4.

The difficulties in establishing hypothetical best and worst levels of objective achievement can be avoided if the valuation process is undertaken *after* the strategies have been prepared and estimates made of their physical effects. This obviates the need to convert measures of achievement into a standard scale before assigning relative values. The measures can be transformed directly into units of common value. In our view it is far better to establish the physical differences between plans first and then to assign relative values to those differences than to get embroiled in vague and hypothetical notions about maximum and minimum possible achievement levels and the value of the best possible level of item A compared with that of item B.

We turn now to consider the Team's approach to assessing the "flexibility" of the strategies put forward for evaluation.[66] Flexibility was viewed as "the capacity of a plan to cope efficiently with uncertainty about the future". Whilst there is general agreement among planners about the broad meaning of flexibility, the identification and measurement of its various dimensions is a very recent area of investigation.[67] A number of planning studies prior to that of Coventry–Solihull–Warwickshire have included a consideration of certain aspects of the flexibility of alternative plans during their evaluation exercises, but degrees of plan flexibility have been examined in a largely qualitative manner with the use of subjective judgement to reach conclusions. The merit of the Team's approach lay in the attempt to measure the degree of plan flexibility quantitatively. The measures which they devised enabled a more formal and precise comparison of the differences between plans for certain elements of flexibility.

Flexibility is not wanted for itself, but only for the relative ease of adaptation to unexpected future circumstances that it allows. The value of having some flexibility in a plan must be that the disadvantages arising in unexpected circumstances will be lower than otherwise. These disadvantages will consist of costs falling on particular people within the community, and a greater amount of flexibility will mean that these costs are potentially lower.

The tests of flexibility were rightly regarded as part of the formal evaluation exercise. Whilst the bulk of the tests of objective achievement (i.e. for objectives 1–16) dealt with the Team's view of the "most likely" circumstances during implementation, the tests of flexibility were concerned with variations in those which, if they arose, would worsen an alternative strategy in relation to others.

Two types of "flexibility" may be distinguished within the Team's analysis. One is the built-in capability of a plan to adjust or adapt actively to changes other than the "most likely" during implementation. Elements of the plan itself produce potential responsiveness to change. This may be provided by built-in redundancy, such as reserve road lanes or areas of land to which no activities are allocated and which

[66]The analysis of flexibility was undertaken in co-operation with the Local Government Operational Research Unit.

[67]Existing approaches to the analysis of plan flexibility are reviewed in G. F. Blundell, The role of flexibility in planning, unpublished MPhil thesis, University of London, 1972, ch. 3.

would not be used in the expected course of events. Another instance is flexibility of plant and infrastructure; a bus system is more flexible than a railway system. In accommodating unexpected changes, ease of adaptation may be thought of in terms of the consequent reduction in prospective levels of objective achievement, which will constitute the cost penalties of a strategy. Comparisons between alternative plans must therefore be based on measures of the penalties arising from lack of flexibility. These penalties may take the form of additional resource costs required to accommodate unexpected change, or reduced levels of benefit in the case of non-resource objectives.

With the second type of flexibility, a plan is flexible if it remains advantageous compared with other alternatives in a variety of circumstances. No *changes* to the plan as envisaged are assumed to take place. In this case one needs to measure the responsiveness of a plan's levels of objective achievement to changed assumptions about the future. This is conventionally known as sensitivity analysis. The Team's analysis did not differentiate between these two types of flexibility, which we think unfortunate since they are conceptually distinct.

Here we are concerned with the general nature of the measures used. Two of the tests dealt respectively with the capacity of a strategy to adapt to increases of population and employment which are faster or slower than the "most likely" growth rates and with its capacity to permit short-term readjustments to cope with sudden unexpected events. The first test used an index which comprised both estimates of the departures from the strategy performance (or "effectiveness") scores, and the proximity of proposed new growth to spare capacity assumed to be available in large existing settlements. It would seem that in this index there are elements of ordinary sensitivity analysis in addition to elements of adaptability as such. The other test was confined to adaptability. An index was employed which comprised measures of accessibility to job opportunities and choice of transport mode and route.[68]

A third test examined the extent to which it was necessary to change the relative values which the Team had established and applied to levels of objective achievement in order to alter the order of preference of the strategies. This comprised a conventional sensitivity test. The greater the change required to upset the rank order, the more confident the Team could be that the set of values they used was a sufficiently close reflection of community values to make no difference to their recommendation, and that their choice of strategy would not be affected by possible future changes in community values.

The final test concerned the ability to switch from a given strategy to one or more of the other strategies put forward for evaluation once implementation had begun. Each strategy was measured, appropriately, by an index of "interchangeability" based on the number of geographical zones of proposed new development common between one strategy and all the others. The objective of retaining the option to change over to other strategies was probably intended to relate to the desirability

---

[68]This relied on the assumption that short-term adjustment of activity patterns would be aided by greater job accessibility and choice of transport.

(other things equal) of being able to keep open the options for future development by deferring commitment. However, as formulated, it merely implied a desire for similarity between alternative strategies. The degree of similarity between strategies is not a useful indication of ability to adapt; in fact, it indicates quite the opposite.

Future events may make the chosen plan undesirable compared with other possibilities, so that the ability to switch to some other course of action is desirable. Accordingly, we should determine for each strategy the ease of switching to other courses. But little advantage is gained if one can only switch to a plan which is very *similar* in content. Switching will be easiest between two virtually identical plans, yet the advantage will be minimal. The measure devised by the Team took no account of this. They should, instead, have attempted to measure the relative costs of switching to different alternatives, irrespective of the degrees of similarity.[69]

Evaluation and Relative Values

We shall investigate four aspects of the relative values used in the comparison of strategies:

(a) the principles that governed the way the values were determined;
(b) the nature of the evidence collected in support of the values;
(c) the problem of allowing for diminishing marginal utility of increments in the level of achievement of a given objective;
(d) the use of notional units of value.

The process of establishing the relative values of objectives for use in evaluation was termed "weighting". Each member of the Team was asked to allocate a fixed number of points (or a notional budget) between the strategy objectives (except those relating to flexibility), so as to indicate the relative value that should be attached to their achievement. Thus the greater the number of points which a particular objective received, the higher its relative importance was deemed to be. In order to derive a single set of "weights" from the views of all the members of the Team, a mean value was calculated. In calculating this mean the "weights" assigned by each member were adjusted to reflect the length of his professional experience which was used to indicate ability to make the appropriate judgements.

The Team frequently point out that the values which they established represented their *professional judgement*, based on their own experience as planners, on the relative importance of the objectives. But this in itself is not very illuminating. As with the case of strategy objectives, the reports do not explicitly state *whose* preferences were deemed to be relevant. It is possible to argue from scattered statements in the reports that the Team tried to indicate how they thought potentially affected members of the community would value the achievement of the objectives.

---

[69]The appropriate use of the test which the Team adopted would have been in determining the optimum sequencing of developments through time.

But the absence of any explicit statement of the principles of valuation is a significant drawback to the Team's published material. It is difficult for the reader to understand what the Team were trying to do, and thus to appraise the quality and scope of their work.

U. Wannop has confirmed that in assessing the achievement of the objectives it was the values of the people who would be affected which were viewed relevant and not those of others, such as the decision-takers or the Planning Team.[70] Another former Team member, M. Shaw, while agreeing that the Team attempted to identify community values, holds the view that, unconsciously at least, the Team's valuations tended to reflect their *own* preferences rather than those of the persons affected.[71]

As indicated earlier, the only direct evidence as to the values held by different groups in the community came from a questionnaire survey of opinions of existing residents within the Sub-region. From those objectives put forward by the Team, respondents were asked to identify the five which they personally considered of greatest importance. The findings were intended to provide a rough check on the Team's subjective assessments.

How useful were the findings for this purpose? Firstly, opinion and attitude surveys are not in general a reliable method of obtaining information about people's values. Evidence as to people's values is usually better obtained by observing behaviour in making choices, either in real life or in some kind of experimental situation. It is difficult to state one's preferences reliably unless faced with a concrete situation. Also, there are invariably difficulties associated with the motivations of respondents to such surveys. Respondents are often led to answer "strategically" and mask their true preferences in expectation of being able to obtain the benefits of a scheme without having to bear part or any of their share of the cost. This is illustrated in the attempts which have been made by economists to determine the prospective benefits to members of society through the provision of public goods. Furthermore, those who stand to gain or lose little by the decision on alternatives will have little incentive to take care in answering.

It is also far from clear how the C–S–W questionnaire was to be interpreted. For each objective respondents were asked to indicate whether they considered that (a) every effort should be made to achieve it, (b) some effort should be made, or (c) whether achieving it was unimportant. They were then asked to rank what they considered the five most important objectives in order of preference. However, no guidance was given on how it was proposed to measure the objectives, nor were respondents asked to compare specific levels of achievement. Thus they were being asked to rank objectives *in the abstract*, which is a meaningless exercise. It is

[70]Personal communication.

[71]There was little or no socio-economic bias in the views of the Planning Team. Indeed, their views were correlated lowest with the "professional" category of respondents to the public questionnaire. We have been inclined to interpret this as an indication of a consciously disinterested approach. But Shaw has commented: "I feel more inclined to interpret it as reflecting a common educational background which laid stress on egalitarianism rather than materialism, and the case for social justice..." (personal communication).

difficult to make sense of such a question as: Do you consider the objective to conserve attractive landscape to be more or less important than that of providing a wide range of job opportunities?

If respondents took the questionnaire seriously, they might themselves have thought up notional levels of achievement, or thought up likely units of measurement, in order to give sensible answers. In the former case it is possible that respondents had in mind the highest levels which could be attained by different strategies, thus being consistent with the Team. However, it would be most unlikely for everyone to have the same ideas of what could be attained. If, on the other hand, respondents resorted to measurement units, it is virtually certain that different measures will be selected. There are many different and intuitively reasonable ways of measuring each of the objectives. The Team attempted to achieve consistency of interpretation during their own interviewing, but it has been confirmed that the questionnaire was interpreted differently by the respondents.[72] It is difficult to see what meaning could be given to the findings of the survey.

Aside from all this, it was not legitimate to compare the public's weights with those postulated by the Team, since the former were based on information about the *ranking* of objectives. Ranking objectives is obviously a far cruder and less reliable method of determining the relative values placed on their achievements than that of assigning cardinal numbers. The use of alternative questionnaire formats were considered which, in principle, could have given a valid indication of the preference *intensities* of members of the public. The results could therefore have been used directly in evaluation, instead of at best providing a rough check on the Team's weights. One of these formats was based on the allocation of a quota of points between objectives (i.e. the procedure adopted by the Team themselves), but it was rejected because of the additional time and finance involved.

Even if a points-weighting procedure had been used by members of the public, there were three other features of the survey which conditioned the use of the findings. Probably the most important of these was that only existing populations within the Sub-region were surveyed. Their interests in the proposals are likely to have been diametrically opposed to occupiers of future new developments. Of course it is often impossible to identify future residents, and therefore to survey many of those who will be affected. However, some allowance should have been made for the likely values of such persons.

Secondly, it was quite unreasonable to expect the public to be capable of answering accurately a number of the questions. They would not have had enough information to be able to say, for instance, what the loss of a given amount of good quality farmland (or of a given amount of, say, coal reserves) was worth relative to, say, a specific improvement in their residential amenities. This is a case of the wrong type of question being asked. For the objective cited relating to loss of farmland, the question should have been phrased in relation to the loss of particular types and amounts of *foodstuffs*. That is, in each case the Team should have asked the public

---

[72]I. Turner, in a personal communication.

about the values they place on *final* goods—goods they consume rather than resource inputs or any intermediate goods.

Thirdly, the size of the sample was small; only 160 households were interviewed. Any conclusions drawn about the values of the community at large will therefore have been subject to considerable margins of error.

Despite the fact that for many objectives there were sizeable differences between the valuations which the Team had postulated and those derived from the results of the public opinion survey,[73] the Team felt that no changes to any of their valuations were warranted. Had there resulted differences in the overall ranking of plans from the use of the two sets of values, the Team would have chosen that strategy which performed best according to the weights they put forward. This presumably reflects a scepticism about the reliability and meaning of the questionnaire answers.

We turn now to discuss the fact that in assigning values to the objectives, the Team made no allowance for likely reductions in the amount of satisfaction, or utility, associated with successive increments of achievement of a given objective. One value only was assigned to each objective. This was intended to reflect the relative importance of a maximum level of achievement attainable in the circumstances. For instance, the values given to an objective a and an objective b indicated the value of the highest possible level of achievement of objective a relative to the highest possible level of achievement of objective b. However, the same relative values were assumed to apply for all other levels of achievement below these maxima. This implies that for each objective the marginal utility to be obtained from successive unit increases in achievement was constant. This runs counter to the conventional behavioural postulate of economics that the more of a good an individual consumes, the less he will value a marginal increment relative to his consumption of other goods. Thus, other things being equal, the value he places on additional unit amounts of residential quietness relative to, say, a given increase in job accessibility will fall as the total amount of quiet increases. It will be seen that the Team should have specified a number of different weights for each objective, each weight to represent the relative value given to increments at different levels of achievement.

We may represent the Team's weights in diagrammatic form, as shown in Fig. 8.4, using the case of just two strategy objectives for simplicity of exposition.[74]

A specific weight P is assigned to objective a and another weight Q is assigned to the other objective b. A fixed weight was applied to all percentage changes in the level of achievement of a given objective. Thus successive marginal changes were valued equally for each objective. The total utility to be derived from a particular level of achievement of one objective, say at C, relative to the other is given by the percentage score multiplied by the weight. For objective a this is given by the area $OCDP_a$, and for objective b by the area $OCEQ_b$. If we know, for example, that the ratio between the weights P and Q is equal to $3:4$, it follows that an individual will

---

[73]See Supplementary Report 4, *op. cit.*, table 5.7, p. 78.
[74]The analysis may easily be extended to include the case of a large number of objectives.

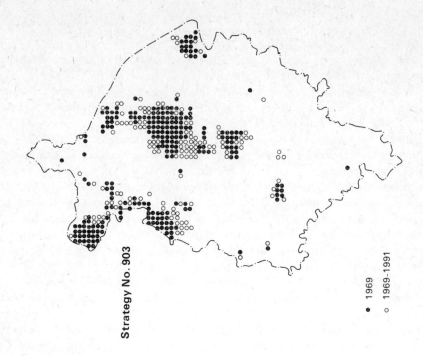

Strategy No. 903

• 1969
○ 1969-1991

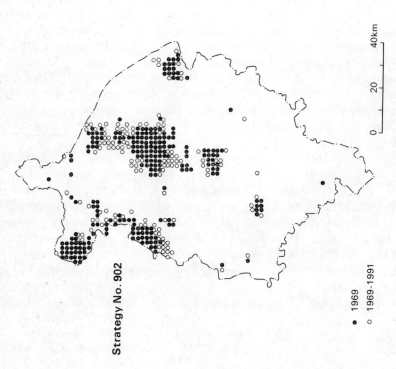

Strategy No. 902

• 1969
○ 1969-1991

0   20   40km

214

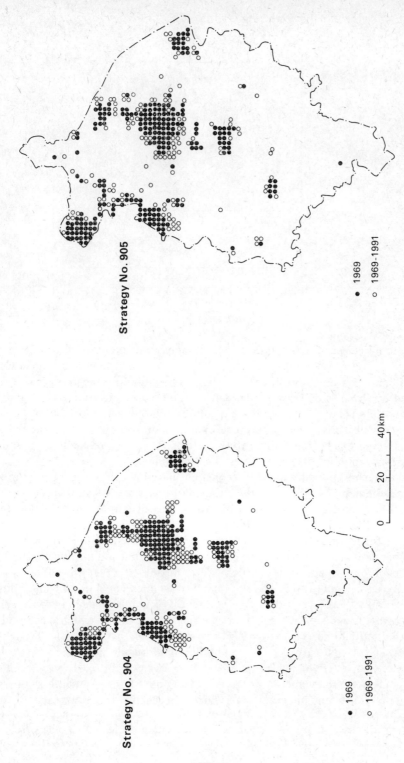

Strategy No. 905

Strategy No. 904

● 1969
○ 1969-1991

● 1969
○ 1969-1991

0   20   40km

215

FIG. 8.3. The short-listed strategies. (Source: *Coventry–Solihull–Warwickshire, a Strategy for the Sub-region*, figs. 1.13–1.16, pp. 17 and 18.)

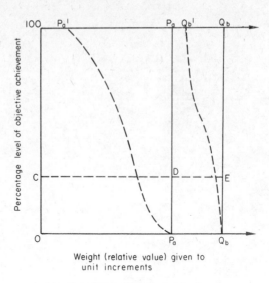

FIG. 8.4. The weighting of objectives.

be indifferent between receiving three percentage points increase of objective *b* and receiving four percentage points increase of objective *a*. The conventional assumption of items of value (or objectives) possessing diminishing marginal utility is illustrated by the broken lines in Fig. 8.4. Unit increases of objectives *a* and *b* are valued less than previous unit additions, and the relative amounts of utility obtained from the two objectives may therefore change from one level of achievement to another. P_a^1 and Q_b^1 lie somewhere to the left of P_a and Q_b respectively; whilst the curves are monotonic, they are not necessarily linear.

Since the Team implicitly assumed constant marginal utility for given increments in the achievement of any objective, the marginal rates of substitution between increments associated with different objectives were also assumed to be constant. In our example above, the rate of substitution of increments in the achievements of objective *a* for increments of objective *b* was in one case *constant* at the ratio 4 per cent to 3 per cent. This, of course, gives rise to straight line indifference curves.[75]

The Team employed values which were meant to be representative of the community as a whole rather than a variety of values for different individuals or groups. We may therefore draw up the community's indifference map for alternative combinations of levels of achievement of objectives *a* and *b* which was implied by the adopted valuations. This is as Fig. 8.5 shows.

The strategies put forward for evaluation will result in a set of alternative combinations of levels of achievement of objectives *a* and *b*. The locus of these combinations of achievement levels is analogous to the production possibility frontier used in economic analysis, which represents the boundary of output

[75]In consumer demand theory indifference curves are drawn convex to the origin, indicating a diminishing marginal rate of substitution of one good for another.

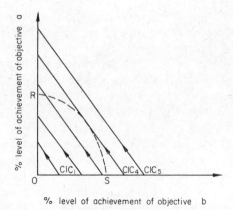

FIG. 8.5. Community indifference map.

possibilities with given resources and the current state of technology. A possible locus of objective achievement levels is depicted by the broken line *RS* in Fig. 8.5. If faced with alternatives on this line the community would maximize its utility by choosing that combination of achievement levels where it touches the highest indifference curve—in this case where it is tangential to CIC_4.[76] The Team assumed constant marginal utilities as a way of simplifying their analysis, and thus side-stepped the arduous task of having to specify values for all plausible levels of achievement for all strategy objectives. Although it would not have been possible to obtain sufficient empirical evidence about the values of such a range of achievement levels, this particular difficulty would not have arisen since the Team were willing to *guess* community values. Nonetheless, the task would have been very time-consuming.

The problem of placing values on a number of small as well as large changes in levels of objective achievement is, of course, common to all evaluation methods. In practice this problem is rarely tackled, either in urban and regional planning or in other fields such as health or education. In social cost–benefit studies, for instance, the assumption is conventionally made that changes in outputs are insufficiently large to affect prices in the various "markets" considered. However, if the Team had waited until the strategies had been prepared and their physical consequences assessed, the task of allowing for changes in marginal utility would have been less severe.

Finally, we consider the ability of notional as opposed to real units of value to give a reliable indication of changes in the satisfaction of individuals' wants or, in other

[76]The locus of objective achievement levels could take a number of different forms. For instance, instead of being concave to the origin, it could be a straight line sloping downwards from left to right or a curve convex to the origin. These two possibilities would reflect the presence of conflict between the achievement of different objectives. Complimentarity between objectives would be represented by a curve or line sloping upwards from left to right. In the C–S–W Study the actual form of the locus will have varied as between different pairs of objectives.

words, changes in individuals' utilities. We contend that if the analyst is concerned with establishing an indication of the utility or satisfaction to be obtained from the achievement of a set of objectives, a valuation procedure which employs notional units of value (as with the Team's "points-weighting" procedure) is inferior to observation of how individuals allocate their income and wealth between items in their day-to-day behaviour. For convenience we term these two procedures "points-weighting" and "money-weighting" respectively.

Assume that decision-taking is to be guided by the principle of choosing that plan which provides the greatest increase in aggregate satisfaction for all individuals affected. In practice we have to make do with measures which provide an *indication* of the satisfaction to be derived from particular items, since we cannot observe satisfaction directly. We wish to avoid a situation in which the evaluation exercise leads to the choice of an "inferior" plan as preferred, where an inferior plan is defined as one that is less advantageous in relation to one or more other plans in terms of the aggregate amount of satisfaction which it yields.

Both the points-weighting and money-weighting procedures employ a willingness to pay criterion; that is, the value of an item is indicated by the alternatives which an individual would willingly sacrifice in order to obtain that item. Our argument for the superiority of a money-weighting procedure rests on the proposition that the greater the number of other items of value with which a given item is to be compared for valuation purposes, the more accurate will be the indication obtained of the amount of satisfaction yielded by it. To know that item A is valued three times as highly as item B and four times as highly as item C is superior information to knowing only that A is valued at three times item B. The extra comparison gives a more accurate notion of the value attached to A. Hence, it is more difficult to draw inferences about satisfactions if only half a dozen items are compared than if a hundred are involved. We may observe large differences in the relative values of the half-dozen items and conclude that the ones most highly valued give rise to large amounts of satisfaction. But if these items all have a low value in relation to the hundred or so items, we suspect the opposite.

We suggest that the willingness to pay criterion is most useful when the greatest possible number of items of value are used to establish the values of those items associated with the planning proposals. Given a certain number of items to be valued, we are saying that their values should be established with reference not only to each other but also to a range of other items which are not associated with the planning proposals. This is so with a money-weighting procedure, but not with points-weighting one. In the latter case the procedure dictates that the individual must exhaust his entire budget of points among that set of items (or objectives) under consideration. Although an individual must allocate all his money income and wealth, the range of items open to him is virtually unlimited. His choices cannot be restricted to those items relevant to the comparison of the proposals, since he does not receive income specifically for making relative valuations of certain items. Instead, we observe the way he allocates his disposable income among all items of choice available to him, including those items which may be relevant to the evaluation (such as time savings and a quiet residential environment), and others (e.g. hot meals and clothes). The values he places on items included in the evaluation will reflect the amounts of satisfaction he obtains from them in relation to the satisfactions to be obtained from all other items which he may consume.

We have argued that a points-weighting procedure suffers from the fact that values are determined with respect to a restricted set of choices. However, if a commonly encountered item, such as a foodstuff or a car, is included in the list of planning items, this weakness may be overcome. We know how cars are valued in relation to many other items, and can therefore use that information to express the values of the planning items in terms which relate to other items. That a car is not actually relevant to the proposals themselves is immaterial. In the C–S–W Study an item like this could have been added to the list of strategy objectives in the public questionnaire. Moreover, if two or more such items had been added, the Team would have had a means of assessing the reliability of the respondents' answers, since the relative value of, say, a particular type of car and a particular footstuff would already have been known.

Evaluation and the Design and Testing of Strategies

In this section we consider two principal questions. First, could the Team be confident that the alternatives which they prepared included the "best" of all possibilities? This is a matter of consistency between their approaches to design and evaluation. Second, were the strategies, as put forward for evaluation, feasible in relation to constraints already formulated?

The Team stressed that the "process of generating alternatives and synthesising a limited number of realistic alternatives for detailed testing was itself a considerable part of the evaluation process". They recognized that the selection for comparative assessment of certain possible strategies from the whole range which existed would itself necessarily involve making comparisons, if only implicitly. Accordingly, they attempted to use the principles of their proposed method of evaluation in order to guide the process of generating alternative proposals.

As we have mentioned, the technique of development potential analysis (DPA) was used to try to achieve a high degree of consistency between the generation of alternatives and their subsequent comparison. This was an imaginative and sophisticated approach to design and involved some developmental work by the Team. They built on some of the recent attempts to rationalize the process of design in urban and regional planning.[77] The development potential technique had been used previously

[77]See, for instance, M. Batty, *Systematic Design Method in Spatial Planning: Some Suggestions*, Centre for Environmental Studies, London, June 1969; G. Chadwick, *A Systems View of Planning*, Pergamon, Oxford, 1971, Chapter 12.

by the Notts–Derby Study Team as an aid to their evaluation exercises, but it had yet to be used (in Britain, at least) for design purposes.[78]

However, in using this technique two main design possibilities either had to be specially allowed for or rejected at the outset. These were a new or expanded town solution and a low density spread of urban development throughout the Sub-region. Both of these were examined and rejected prior to the formal design work. The Team satisfied themselves that neither possibility would offer any overall advantage. A number of reasons are put forward in the Study documents, although little formal analysis seems to have been undertaken.[79] For instance, it was said that a new town solution would have necessitated a major relocation of industry within the Sub-region, been relatively expensive in terms of infrastructure, and been unlikely to receive Central Government support. In undertaking their DPA, the Team did not neglect the potential of any particular part of the Sub-region. No matter how intuitively unpromising a zone might have seemed, it was, nonetheless, systematically examined against each of the objectives used to assess suitability for development, and a quantitative estimate made of its potential. We have noted earlier that whilst the objectives were still provisional at the design stage, their formulation changed very little before being finalized for evaluation purposes. It follows that the best alternative (according to the Team's criteria) would be produced by combining those areas of the Sub-region with relatively high indices of development potential, providing the following conditions were met.

(a) In computing the indices, use was made of all those objectives likely to give rise to significant variations in potential between zones.
(b) Allowances were made for likely changes in the indices of potential between the present and the mid 1970s, the date for the start of strategy implementation.
(c) Allowances were made for the likelihood that the implementation of the strategy would itself significantly influence, say, residents' accessibility to retail facilities, and in this way affect the indices of potential.

Only ten of the total of twenty strategy objectives were employed in computing the indices of development potential. A variety of reasons are given for the omissions. In some cases it was not possible to obtain satisfactory data at the design stage (e.g. in relation to the loss of workable mineral deposits); in other cases the level of achievement depended on the location and amount of future development which would be undertaken (e.g. disturbance to existing residential development caused by new roads, and those objectives relating to flexibility), or they were very closely related to other objectives and therefore left out. The last reason noted does not seem valid. If it is thought legitimate and desirable to include two strongly

[78]However, its use in design had been suggested by the Notts–Derby Team and had been developed in a preliminary fashion by J. Forbes. Notts–Derby Sub-regional Planning Unit, *The Potential Surface Technique*, Record Report 38, undated; J. Forbes, A map analysis of potentially developable land, *Regional Studies* 3 (1969) 179–95. At the time, the C–S–W Team were not aware of Forbes's paper.
[79]*Report*, paras. 4.13–4.32.

interdependent objectives in evaluation, then in order to achieve consistency they must both be incorporated into the design process. Apart from this, the fact that certain objectives could not be incorporated into the analysis meant that one or more other techniques might have been used to advantage in designing alternatives.

We suggest that, if practicable, an examination should have been made of the *implications* of the ten remaining objectives for those particular strategies which were generated by the development potential technique. It might have been possible to examine the implications of these remaining objectives by producing an "extreme" strategy for each. In each case the aim of these strategies would be to attain the maximum possible level of achievement of one of the objectives. Since interactions between objectives could be ignored, this would be a fairly simple exercise in most cases. Achieving the maximum choice of housing sites, for example, depended on a dispersed pattern of urban development and a high variety of site characteristics within different urban areas. The Team could have used the data from their preliminary appraisal of the Sub-region, and from subsequent work on the topic studies and forecasting, to indicate differences in site characteristics (such as environmental quality and accessibility to job opportunities). The design problem would then have involved optimizing on the two items of dispersal and the attributes of the sites. It should have been possible to produce a strategy which was relatively good (if not optimal) in this respect. The location of developments in that strategy could then have been compared with those produced by the development potential analysis in order to see whether modifications should be made to reflect considerations of housing choice.

The purpose of this exercise would only be to see how the initial set of strategies might *themselves* be modified to reflect the desirability of achieving the other objectives. In this way the initial strategies would hopefully be improved in terms of overall advantage. It is not intended that the extreme strategies should be formally compared either with each other or with the initial strategies. In addition, the extreme strategies need not be designed in as much detail as the recommended strategy, since they are not to be evaluated. We recognize that in practice it might prove very difficult to realize what kind of design adjustments are implied by the extreme strategies. They certainly would not always be obvious; strategies are defined in terms of a spatial distribution of land uses, and objective achievements do not vary predictably over space.

The Team did investigate the degrees of change in the zones' indices of development potential that were likely to occur between 1969 and 1991 (the year taken for evaluation purposes). The strategies had been produced on the basis of the potential surfaces computed for 1969, and it was realized that modifications might be necessary in the light of prospective changes to those surfaces over time. For instance, decisions about the location of new job opportunities in the strategy could have a significant effect on indices of residents' job accessibility–opportunity. The 1969 surfaces were revised to take account of changes in the amount and location of population and employment growth, both up to the mid 1970s when implementation of the strategy was to begin and afterwards as a result of implementation itself.

However, it was considered that no modifications to the strategies were required in the light of these revisions. In view of the relatively large increases in populations and employments which were envisaged in the strategies, this is somewhat surprising. The resident population was expected to increase by 27 per cent between 1971 and 1991 and employment by 23 per cent over the same period.[80] Together these estimates implied an increase in the built-up areas of the Sub-region from 14 to 19 per cent.

Forty-two alternatives were produced for consideration. These were quickly reduced to three by a process of "synthesis". Since the alternative patterns of development contained high degrees of similarity, there was a strong efficiency argument for assessing a few basically different alternatives in depth, rather than a far less thorough assessment of a large number of alternatives, many of which would be very similar. Accordingly, the strategies were reduced by grouping them according to physical similarity and formulating one representative strategy from each group, to be put forward for evaluation. Alternatives within each group were not simply eliminated. Instead, each representative strategy was comprised of those zones which had relatively high indices of potential and which were common to a large number of the alternatives within the group. This procedure was better than simple elimination, for it gave preference to retaining those zones that appeared attractive under a variety of assumptions about relative values, compared with those which were less robust in this sense.

We must conclude that in general the adopted design procedure was an efficient one. It enabled the Team to narrow down fairly rapidly the whole range of possibilities to a few which could be assessed in a comprehensive manner during the rest of the Study. By using their evaluation criteria in design the Team were confident that they had identified a range of alternatives which were good in relation to other possibilities and included the best of all possibilities.

However, one respect in which the design procedure seems to have been rather inefficient was the large number of different sets of relative values which were employed. There were forty-two sets, generating forty-two different alternatives. A number of these represented the views of planners outside the Team who were connected with the Study.[81] When put beside their own, the Team took these views to reflect the amount of doubt that existed about the values which should be employed. But although the Team's own views on values were tentative, the differences represented *disagreement* between themselves and other groups of planners, not the Team's own doubts.

The remaining sets of values used for design were derived by giving special importance to the interests of particular groups within the community, such as the members of the National Farmers' Union. For this purpose greater or lesser emphasis was given to objectives concerning conservation, residential environment,

[80] *Report*, table 7.1, p. 92.

[81] These groups included the Team's liaison officers in the three commissioning authorities, the Team's transportation consultants and other planners concerned in some way with their work.

accessibility, transport, and choice. A large number of permutations were used and a strategy produced on the basis of each permutation. The Team went through this exercise in order to demonstrate they had considered these "partisan" alternatives and indicate why they had not been selected as preferred. In view of this, we suggest that it might have been sufficient for the Team to point out to such groups that they were basing their choice of strategy on a concept of the public interest, and that since special pleading was inconsistent with that approach there was no need for them to investigate partisan alternatives. The former Study Director does not share this view. He considers that it was necessary to be seen to assess partisan alternatives in order to demonstrate that the Team were being fair to the various interests concerned, and to convince those groups that their own preferred alternatives were not superior to others which the Team viewed to be beneficial for the community in general.[82]

We fully agree that it is not enough to simply tell groups that their particular interests have been fairly dealt with while working behind closed doors. In our view, however, an account of the thinking behind the design work, and the reasons for ignoring certain kinds of alternatives, should normally be sufficient to show whether proper account has been taken of all groups. We also think that it will often be interesting and informative in considering equity issues to debate alternatives which favour particular groups. However, the Team was unable to investigate equity issues for reasons mentioned earlier, and so the partisan strategies were not formulated for this purpose.

Turning now to strategy feasibility, only two of the eight constraints specified were considered useful in generating spatial patterns of urban development. Nearly all the others were treated as quantitative inputs to the strategies (e.g. total amount of employment to be provided). These therefore formed common elements of the strategies, and the task of feeding them into the designs was simple. As a result, there was little need to test the feasibility of strategies with respect to constraints prior to evaluation.

Evaluation and Decision-taking

We comment on three aspects of the decision-taking: documentation of the Team's work, choice criteria, and the use made of the flexibility tests.

The adopted plan-making process and the details of the technical work have been very fully and clearly written up by the Team in their reports. This will have greatly helped the decision-takers and others with an interest in the decision to understand and appraise the Team's work and recommendations.

In putting forward alternatives for evaluation, the Team were only interested in ones which were likely to perform relatively well in relation to the evaluation criteria. They had been specifically asked to select a preferred strategy themselves, which they did. But, as far as the Team knew, the decision-takers may well have had

[82]Personal communication.

rather different criteria in mind in making their selection. Hence, it might have been helpful if the Team had prepared some strategies (at the level of detail required of the recommendation) which were deliberately designed to perform relatively poorly according to their own evaluation criteria.

We now consider the use which the Team made of the results of the flexibility tests in selecting their preferred strategy. The Team did not intend to assign values to the measurements, since they could find no evidence about the relative importance of the various dimensions of flexibility they were considering. Short of guessing at the appropriate values, the best that could be done was to rank the strategies in order of preference on each of the four tests and then to inspect the rankings for dominance. This the Team did, and found that strategy 904 (which had highest weighted index of achievement in relation to the non-flexibility objectives) performed best on three of the tests and second best on the other one. The fact that this strategy was inferior to another strategy for one of the tests meant that no conclusion as to its overall position could be drawn from the findings of the evaluation alone. However, instead of recognizing this and making a subjective judgement as to whether the net advantages of strategy 904 were sufficient to outweigh its disadvantages on the one flexibility test, the Team proceeded to sum its rank scores for the flexibility tests and to compare the flexibility of the strategies on the basis of those scores.[83] It is not legitimate to sum ordinal rankings, since it implicitly assumes both that the differences between plans for a given test are of equal value and that the value of these differences are identical for all tests. These assumptions were clearly unrealistic.

8.8. CONCLUDING OBSERVATIONS ON THE COVENTRY–SOLIHULL–WARWICKSHIRE STUDY

The adopted planning process had some very good features. The most notable was the effort made to achieve a high degree of consistency between the activities of design and evaluation by employing the strategy objectives and their proposed measures directly in the strategy generation process. Design and evaluation were regarded as part of a single exercise to narrow down the area of doubt as to the optimum strategy. The Team fully appreciated that design activity itself involves judgements about the relative merits of possibilities which are rejected or deliberately ignored. Accordingly, they sought to ensure that only inferior alternatives were excluded from those put forward for evaluation.

The Team also made some important innovations. They extended the use of development potential analysis so that it could be employed as a highly effective design tool. It enabled them to consider an enormous number of possible strategies and within a short period of time to produce a few that appeared to be relatively good in terms of their evaluation criteria and which could be compared in depth, given the time and resources available. In addition, attempts were made to assess quantita-

[83] *Report*, table 5.16 (p. 78) and para. 5.66.

tively the differential capacity of alternative strategies to adjust to unforeseen circumstances. This was an advance upon the conventional practice of, at best, an informal and discursive treatment of plan flexibility.

Considerable attention was paid to the efficient use of study time and resources. Instances of this are the rejection of expensive urban modelling procedures as a means of establishing the detailed allocation of land-use activities within the strategies put forward for evaluation, and the design of a traffic model in the light of evaluation data requirements.

The approach adopted to evaluation did, nonetheless, have important weaknesses. These mainly concern the Team's lack of any serious attempts to obtain direct empirical evidence to support their choice of objectives, and associated physical measures and valuations, used in evaluation. Their decisions here were based almost entirely on past professional experience. The Team were attempting to ascertain the differential effects of the strategies for all potentially affected persons within the community. Yet their only source of direct evidence of community preferences was a public opinion survey. That evidence was an unsatisfactory basis for evaluation for a variety of reasons, not least because respondents were asked to assign importance to objectives in the abstract. In addition, the Team do not appear to have recognized the importance of checking proposed physical measures of achievement against evidence of their suitability for indicating welfare effects.

Investigation of the adopted approach to evaluation suggests that the Team had regard to the *principles* of social cost–benefit analysis. However, the differences between what they did and what a cost–benefit analyst does in practice amounted to differences in kind rather than of emphasis. Not only was little effort made to obtain evidence of preferences, the evidence which was obtained related to stated rather than observed preferences. Thus the objectives and their valuations had no behavioural validation.

APPENDIX I

OBJECTIVES FOR THE STRATEGY IN THE NOTTINGHAMSHIRE–DERBYSHIRE STUDY[84]

(i) To encourage a location of population which will provide a labour market in which a choice of jobs is ensured.

(ii) To provide attractive sites for offices, research establishments, warehouses, and institutions in proper relationship with the environment, labour supply, and the communications network.

(iii) To provide ample attractive and substantial industrial sites conveniently located for the supplies of labour.

(iv) To promote policies which have the effect of encouraging the growth of firms.

[84]Reproduced from *Report*, paras. 33 and 93.

(v) To provide ample and attractive sites for housing for all socio-economic groups.
(vi) To provide good transport facilities.
(vii) To encourage the efficient and convenient distribution of shopping, social, cultural, and recreational facilities.
(viii) To improve the appearance of the Sub-region.
(ix) To provide an environment which is adaptable in character so that it can accommodate changes in the requirements of society.
(x) To promote policies likely to encourage the conservation, improvement, or renewal as appropriate, of the existing urban environment.
(xi) To promote policies likely to ensure that new urban areas are attractive, convenient, safe, and healthy.
(xii) To conserve good agricultural land and encourage full utilization of its potential.
(xiii) To conserve land used for growing timber.
(xiv) To avoid sterilization of mineral resources.
(xv) To conserve land of high landscape value.
(xvi) To reduce air pollution.
(xvii) To avoid siting development in foggy locations.
(xviii) To conserve water resources and eliminate water pollution.
(xix) To reclaim or tidy up derelict land.
(xx) To conserve areas of high natural history interest.
(xxi) To prevent wasteful use of land.
(xxii) To keep down construction and operation costs, particularly of roads and services.

APPENDIX II

CONCEPTS USED DURING THE FIRST CYCLE OF
DESIGN IN THE NOTTINGHAMSHIRE-DERBYSHIRE STUDY

The six design concepts were as follows:

(1) "Development in areas with the greatest welfare problems"

Strategies based on this concept were intended to alleviate a variety of problems which had been identified during the early survey and analysis work. Instances of these problems have been given in the review.

(2) "Development in areas where the opportunities were greatest"

By "opportunities" was meant the presence of conditions favourable to attracting new industry and population into the Sub-region, and thus they related to achieving the maximum growth of industrial output and residential development. As one would expect, strategies based on this concept tended to be in contrast to those based on welfare problems.

(3) "Development in areas with the greatest potential for future growth"

This concept was very similar to that of (2). The main difference lay in the time period considered. Alternatives based on "potential" were generated by reference to the pattern of development potential that was estimated to obtain at about the time of the Study, whereas this concept involved the anticipation of future events.

(4) "Development in areas where physical and organisational restrictions were minimal"

The intention was to design alternatives that paid maximum regard to costs resulting from the presence of physical factors and organizational problems. These were initially treated as absolute constraints, and development was restricted to comparatively small areas. Those "constraints" viewed to be least important were then removed successively to provide additional options.

(5) "Development employing ideal urban spatial forms"

Like the sieve-map technique, this is a traditional way in which planners have generated development proposals. Various ideas were investigated, including corridors of growth, linear growth, joined ring of towns, and grid-based development.

(6) "Development following trends"

Some very similar alternatives were generated by projecting past trends in the direction and form of urban growth. These were intended to enable the implications of the continuance of past planning policies to be explored.

CHAPTER 9

An Urban Structure Plan Study: Brighton

(March 1970–March 1974)

In this chapter we review the work which has recently been undertaken on the preparation of a "strategy" for the urban development of the Brighton area from the mid 1970s until the end of this century.

The adopted evaluation procedure is very similar to that of the Coventry–Solihull–Warwickshire Study, but the Brighton Team incorporated evaluation within their planning process in a far less effective and efficient manner. This is most disappointing, especially as they undoubtedly attached great importance to evaluation. The consistency between the requirements of the Team's method of evaluation and the work undertaken at other related stages of their planning process was generally weak. In particular, no explicit attempt was made to use the objectives and their associated physical measures and valuations in the process of generating alternative strategies.

9.1. BACKGROUND

The Study was set up by the local planning authorities (LPAs) of Sussex[1] for the purpose of preparing an urban structure plan for the coastal area from Lancing to Seaford. The area is about 20 miles long and extends inland for a distance of between about 2 to 4 miles (Fig. 9.1). At present there is an almost continuous strip of urban development along the coastline; the rest of the area consists very largely of the South Downs. The planning strategy contains broad proposals relating to the future growth of populations and employments, the location of major land uses (such as housing, industry, shopping centres, and recreation), and transport infrastructure. The Study documents stress that the eventual structure plan is intended to provide a general policy framework for future development and use of land rather than a detailed and precise statement of future land use, and to be a guide to development through time rather than a plan for a fixed date.

---

[1]The authorities concerned were Brighton County Borough Council, West Sussex CC, and East Sussex CC.

The LPAs appointed an *ad hoc* Team to undertake the technical work and to recommend proposals for adoption. In addition three committees were set up to facilitate the preparation of the plan, as follows:

(1) A Joint Advisory Steering Committee, consisting of certain elected members of the LPAs concerned.
(2) A Consultative Committee, consisting of the members of (1) together with a member from each of the urban and rural district councils in the Study area.
(3) A Technical Committee, consisting of the planning officers and surveyors of the LPAs.

These committees existed for consultation and to give guidance to the Team during the various stages of their work. The main function of the Steering Committee was to give the policy views of the councils on alternative courses of action at critical points in the planning process. The evaluation procedure involved the progressive elimination of alternative plans, entailing three separate evaluation exercises. Policy guidance was therefore important when the results of each evaluation exercise were produced and a decision required as to which of the alternatives should be retained for further consideration.

A two-stage planning procedure was adopted by the commissioning authorities. A formal decision was first reached on a preferred strategy for development, and these proposals were then detailed to the level required of the plan. "... the preferred strategy is no more than a concept which is representative of its type and will need to be refined during the preparation of the Structure Plan. There is scope for manoeuvre in regard to the population, employment structure and the broad

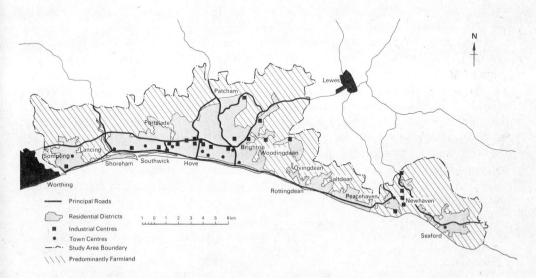

FIG. 9.1. Study area: present urban structure. (Source: *Brighton Urban Structure Plan, Report 1, Physical Environment*, fig. 5, p. 15.)

disposition of land uses without departing from the principles of this strategy."[2] The Team began their work in early 1970 and at the time of writing had submitted their recommendations concerning both the land use and transport elements of the strategy for urban development.[3]

We shall consider the work of the Team leading up to their choice of a preferred *strategy* (focusing largely on the land-use aspects). Because of timing we are unable to deal here with its subsequent elaboration to the level of detail required of the structure plan, a draft of which was submitted to the Steering Committee in November 1973.

9.2. THE TEAM'S APPROACH TO THE STUDY

Evaluation Methodology[4]

The Team used evaluation both to assist their decision on the strategy to be recommended to their Steering Committee, and to assist the council members in deciding whether that strategy or some other should be implemented. The Team recognized that formulating objectives by which to determine items of comparative advantage and disadvantage, and measuring the extent to which alternatives will attain the objectives, are tasks central to any "respectable" evaluation methodology. They also stressed that the evaluation exercise should be regarded as a "learning process"; the objectives and their associated physical measures and relative values should not be regarded as fixed and final from the time of initial formulation. Rather they should be open to modification and refinement in the light of experience gained during any part of the planning process. The Team regarded this open-minded attitude as basic to their evaluation methodology.

It was decided to base the evaluation procedure on Hill's goals–achievement matrix (GAM) method. As we have noted earlier, Hill provides the planner with a framework for comparative assessment, but does not specify the principles which should govern the evaluation. The Team therefore had to decide for themselves *whose* objectives and values were to be taken into account, and the approach to be adopted in measuring the magnitude of objective achievements. Unfortunately, no reasons are given in the Study documents for choosing to use the GAM method, although it was indicated that the planning balance sheet was seen as the principal alternative. It was also contended that fundamentally there is little difference between these two methods, although there was no written discussion on this matter.

---

[2]Brighton Urban Structure Plan Team (BUSPT), *Report on the Evaluation of Alternative Strategies*, December 1971, para. 4.2.

[3]*Ibid.*, and BUSPT, *Transportation Strategies*, September 1972.

[4]Our comments on this are based on BUSPT, *Working Paper on Evaluation Methodology*, unpublished, undated.

The Adopted Planning Process

In arriving at the preferred strategy, the Team's planning process consisted of three main phases:

(1) Twenty-one land-use variants were designed at a very low level of detail and tested and evaluated in a preliminary manner. Seventeen of these alternatives were considered to be impracticable. The remaining four formed a short-list.
(2) The short-listed alternatives were specified in greater detail. These were subjected to a more rigorous evaluation, leading to the selection of one of them as the preferred land-use strategy.
(3) Four basically different transport proposals were formulated in relation to the chosen land-use strategy. They were evaluated and one of them selected for recommendation.

Although the Team began with a fairly small number of land-use alternatives for purposes of initial *assessment*, at the very outset they formulated nearly one hundred strategies. These were designed as "broad concepts" on the basis of four major policy variables:

(a) the main economic activities of the Study area;
(b) the amounts and general locations of new urban developments;
(c) the balance of investment between private and public transport;
(d) the location of major roads to serve the predicted east–west traffic movements.

Each of the strategies consisted of a different combination of these variables. Since each variable could take a large number of different forms, it was considered necessary to limit the number of variants to a few representative types. Nevertheless, the combination of variants formed a total of eighty-four strategies, which was considered too many for each to receive the necessary amount of analysis. It was therefore decided to examine the transport policy variables after the evaluation and decision on land-use alternatives. This reduced the number of alternatives for initial investigation to twenty-one.

These twenty-one land-use alternatives were evaluated in relation to a set of objectives for the structure plan. The purpose of the preliminary evaluation was to reduce these quickly to a short-list of relatively good alternatives. The four short-listed alternatives were specified as diagrammatic land-use distributions instead of "broad concepts" as in phase (1).

The preliminary evaluation had the following main features. A separate evaluation of the strategies was carried out by each member of the Team. Levels of objective achievement were estimated using measures that individual members considered suitable. Thus different members will probably have used different methods of measurement. The estimates obtained were converted to a percentage scale performance; zero was used to represent the worst possible level of performance and one hundred to represent the best possible level. In establishing relative valuations of the achievement of different objectives each member used his own judgement, based on his professional experience and there will thus have been differences between members. The individual results were then compared and alternatives eliminated by a process of Team discussion.

Thus formal assessments were made of the twenty-one alternatives, but those assessments were largely subjective. The procedure also seems wasteful of man-power since prior agreement on the measures and values of objective achievements would have obviated the need for separate evaluations.

The detailed evaluation of the four short-listed alternatives differed from the preliminary evaluation in two main respects. Firstly, it was based on agreed views among the Team as to the appropriate measures of achievement. Secondly, the valuations employed were derived from a survey of public opinion about the relative importance of the different objectives;[5] they did not just represent the Team members' views in the absence of empirical information.

Alternative transport proposals were formulated in the light of the main transport "problems" which had been identified through survey work.[6] These problems primarily concerned increasing congestion on the existing road network (especially in the town centre of Brighton and on the principal east–west routes which run through the built-up area between the Downs and the sea) and increasing environ-mental costs imposed by vehicle users.

The rising levels of road congestion had seriously affected the performance of bus services as well as having raised the costs of private travel. In the Team's view there were two basic alternative ways of dealing with the problems identified:

(a) apply measures of restraint to reduce the use of private vehicles, especially in the central area of Brighton, and to promote the use of bus and rail services;
(b) increase highway capacity by improvements to existing roads and the con-struction of new roads.

Two alternative proposals were formulated to reflect these respective policies of restraining and promoting the use of private transport, and two further alternatives were formulated with respect to a road network based on alternative locations for a new east–west distributor.[7] These alternatives were combined to form four basically different sets of transport proposals, which represented alternative strategies.

The effect of the strategies on the transport-related objectives for the plan was assessed separately by each member of the Team. Achievement levels were indicated by a percentage score. The resulting scores for a strategy were averaged for each objective and the valuations obtained from the public opinion survey then applied to the average scores and summed to give each strategy an overall score of objective achievement.

[5]The results of the survey of public opinion on the objectives were not available at the time of the preliminary evaluation.

[6]BUSPT, *Transportation*, Survey Report 12, July 1972.

[7]Regardless of the emphasis to be placed on public transport, it was considered that additional road capacity should be provided for east–west traffic within the Brighton, Hove, and Portslade area.

In the rest of this review we shall concentrate on the process of arriving at a preferred land-use strategy; transport aspects will be considered only in passing. Nearly all of the points we wish to make can be related to the land use aspects of the Team's work. However, the separation of the land use and transport aspects of the Team's work requires some comment. The decision to separate them was made to save time and resources and to reduce the task of evaluation to manageable proportions. It is well known that the location of land-use activities is strongly influenced by the pattern of travel costs, but it appears that no allowance was made for such interaction at the strategic level. Clearly the Team considered that the broad disposition of land uses for a given strategy of urban development was not likely to be materially altered by the choice of a road network, but there is no discussion of the matter in the Study documents. The amounts of population and employment growth envisaged in some of the alternatives considered were substantial; the residential population, for instance, was in some cases envisaged to increase from a present level of about 340,000 to 460,000 by the end of the century. There do not seem to exist any *a priori* grounds for supposing that the broad location of activities would *not* be materially affected by basically different transport arrangements. The question therefore arises as to what extent the recommended transportation and land-use strategies are consistent with each other. As far as we know the Team have not investigated this issue.

The first aspect of the adopted planning process we shall discuss is the Team's approach to the design of alternatives; the other is the degree of consistency between the "preliminary" and "detailed" evaluation exercises undertaken on the land-use strategies.

The evaluation criteria were not employed in a direct way in the design procedures. As we have noted, the initial twenty-one land-use alternatives were generated by the use of a number of planning variables, i.e. the main elements of the plan which could be affected by local authority planning activity. A preliminary set of objectives for the structure plan had been agreed upon prior to the start of design work and the general approach to evaluation had been established. But the Team had not then devised the measures of objective achievement nor determined the relative importance to be assigned to the objective achievements. Hence it was not possible for them consciously to design alternatives that were likely to be relatively good in terms of the evaluation criteria to be adopted. Whilst it was possible to design proposals that would increase existing levels of attainment of given objectives, such as those "to conserve good agricultural land" and "to encourage the growth of manufacturing industries", the existence of conflict between objectives prevented the use of some kind of optimization procedure. That would have necessitated comparisons between levels of objective achievement.

The objectives for the structure plan may have exerted some influence on the particular *form* of the planning variables used in design. For instance, the variable relating to the amount and location of new urban developments took forms that reflected contrasting policies of conservation and growth. These policies themselves were consistent with the attainment of a number of objectives. Conservation-related objectives included those "to conserve attractive countryside and areas of natural history interest", and "to conserve good quality farmland". The objectives relating to growth included those "to encourage the development of regional service centre facilities" and "to encourage the provision of homes for people who do not work locally and for retired people".

The thinking behind the Team's design procedure is not fully explained in the Study documents. It is nowhere stated whether they would like to have employed the objectives together with their measures and values in a formal manner in producing the designs. Although certain of the alternatives can be *interpreted* as attempts to achieve the objectives for the plan, it is doubtful that the Team had those objectives consciously in mind. The use of different emphases on the three main "economic functions" of the Study area in generating alternatives supports this view. Six of the seven possible functional variants put forward simply represented significant increases in the importance of one or of two of the functions relative to the others, and the other possibility represented a continuation of the functions' present relative importance.

It was the Team's intention to produce a range of basically different alternatives for examination. They were strongly aware of the limitations that time and manpower placed on the number of alternatives which could be usefully analysed and evaluated. By generating widely different alternatives they ensured that some relatively good plans would be included initially. In addition, they indicated that they were prepared to use the results of the evaluation exercises to design further "hybrid" strategies by combining elements of those previously examined. Features of the most promising alternatives could be combined to form new and hopefully superior strategies.

In the event, however, no attempts were made to generate further alternatives in this way, for the stated reason that "It was considered unnecessary to re-cycle the evaluation process to test hybrid growth strategies as the results show clearly that no better [performance] scores would be obtained".[8] This is somewhat surprising, as the likelihood of including the optimum of a vast number of possibilities among a few chosen without the guidance of the evaluation criteria was remote.

It is clear that the criteria used to compare the initial twenty-one and the four short-listed land-use strategies were not wholly consistent. We appreciate the need to adopt relatively crude criteria in order to focus attention quickly on a few relatively good alternatives. But it is vital that the evaluation is based on the same principles, and that the less-refined criteria are sufficiently close to those used subsequently to indicate correctly the alternatives which are relatively poor and those which are relatively good. The set of objectives employed were identical in both evaluation exercises, but the measures and values were different.

In the preliminary exercise a number of different measures were used to assess the achievement of each objective, whereas one agreed measure was used for each objective in the subsequent evaluation. We do not know to what extent the various

[8]BUSPT, *Report on the Evaluation of Alternative Strategies*, December 1971, para. 3.11.

preliminary measures differed from one another and from the measures employed subsequently. But different *approaches* to measurement will have been adopted during the two exercises. This may well have given rise to significant inconsistencies. In general, there are a variety of intuitively plausible ways of measuring given objectives, and so the choice of measures by individuals will probably differ considerably. Any inconsistencies in approach could have been eliminated, or greatly reduced, if Team members had agreed on one set of measures for use in the preliminary evaluation.

The values used in the preliminary evaluation were an average of the Team members' views on the relative importance which would be assigned to objective achievements by those individuals in the community whose well-being would be affected. These values represent subjective judgements in the absence of empirical evidence. However, in the main, they differed comparatively little from those obtained from the subsequent public opinion survey. Each of the fifteen objectives used for evaluation was given a numerical score from zero to ten to indicate its relative importance, and nearly all differences (as between the two cases) in the average scores obtained were less than 1·6.

The issue here is whether a similar ranking of the initial twenty-one alternatives would have resulted from the use of valuations derived from the public survey, which was considered by the Team to give a more accurate indication of community preferences than their own judgements. Although differences between the two sets of valuations were comparatively small, they *might* have led to a different short-list. As no details of the preliminary evaluations have been released, this is not possible for us to determine.

In principle, it would have been better if, for the preliminary evaluations, the Team had used values based on *some* empirical evidence of community preferences. A pilot survey of public opinion could have been made for the purpose. Guessing at the values of others is hazardous, and little reliance can be placed on valuations arrived at in such a manner.

9.3. EVALUATION IN THE PLANNING PROCESS OF THE BRIGHTON STUDY

Evaluation and Constraints

A total of six constraints were employed.[9] Two were concerned with ensuring that the strategies were consistent with national and regional planning policy, and practicable with regard to economic, social, and technological considerations. Although it is not clear what was meant by a strategy being economically and socially feasible, these particular constraints are unexceptionable as they stand.

The other four constraints were concerned respectively with providing particular levels of public utility, health, welfare, and education services; ensuring the

[9]*Ibid.*, appendix 1.

improvement or replacement of all dwellings below the standard considered unfit for human habitation or potentially so; providing sufficient land to meet the housing demands of the design population; and ensuring low rates of unemployment or low excess demand for labour in the Study area. The first two of these constraints may be justified in terms of principles of social policy: no matter what gains may accrue to others, it may be argued that government agencies should ensure that no individuals involuntarily fall below some specified minimum standard of living. The provision of land for housing was a direct input into the design process and formed elements of the strategies put forward for assessment. The scale of future increases in resident population varied considerably between strategies, and therefore this constraint of land provision really reflected alternative aims for the amount of future urban development in the Study area. Finally, the constraint relating to the under- and over-supply of labour was not required because the method used to predict future growth in employment opportunities and population contained the assumption that in practice the demand for and the supply of jobs would adjust in such a way that virtual full employment would exist.[10]

In general, therefore, we would not take exception to the Team's constraints as they are specified. However, the precise meaning given to them is not described in the Study documents. For example, they do not state the levels of quality of public services that the Team considered acceptable, nor is there a definition of a "socially feasible" plan. Thus, it is not possible to debate whether the minimum standards required of the plan were appropriate.

The importance of the constraints is illustrated in the assessment of the twenty-one initial land-use strategies. Seven of these strategies involved high density development and large-scale redevelopment in and on the edge of existing urban areas. In the Team's view, high density residential development would have resulted in certain social problems due to overcrowding and lack of privacy, and was socially unacceptable. (The nature of the social problems was not discussed.) Thus, a third of all the alternatives considered were rejected as a result of this residential feature alone.

Evaluation and Goals and Objectives

Following what has now become common practice,[11] a two-level hierarchy of aims were formulated. The higher-level aims ("goals") were abstract and very general statements considered to have a more or less universal validity and application, and therefore relevant to nearly all planning studies. The lower-level aims ("objectives") were particular statements relating to housing, transportation, landscape, and so

[10]BUSPT, *Employment*, Survey Report 5, January 1971.

[11]See, for instance, in addition to the Notts–Derby and Coventry–Solihull–Warwickshire studies reviewed here, Milton Keynes Development Corporation, *The Plan for Milton Keynes*, 1970; South East Joint Planning Team, *Strategic Plan for the South East*, HMSO, London, 1970; South Hampshire Plan Advisory Committee, *South Hampshire Structure Plan: Draft Document for Participation and Consultation*, Hampshire CC *et al.*, September 1972.

forth, and were formulated with regard to the nature of the Study. The objectives were seen as steps towards the attainment of one or more goals; they are thus means rather than ends in themselves, and thus possess instrumental, as distinct from intrinsic, value.

The "objectives" formulated for the plan were of two types. One type represented a set of aims which had to be fully attained in order for a strategy to be admissible for selection. Rather confusingly, they were termed "mandatory objectives"; we have dealt with them in our discussion of constraints. The other type were termed "discriminatory objectives" and represented objectives proper in that no minimum acceptable levels of attainment were specified. They were used as a basis for judging *between* strategies.

Plan evaluation was undertaken with respect to the achievement of the objectives which the Team established and not to the higher-level goals. It was not possible directly to assess the extent of goal achievements because they were formulated in very general and abstract terms. For evaluation it was necessary to specify the goals in greater detail, since measurement depends upon a precise description of the relevant phenomena. The objectives should be regarded as component elements of the goals.

We first comment on the nature of the goals formulated for the structure plan and their apparent degree of overlap, and then go on to discuss a number of aspects of the "discriminatory" objectives which the Team employed in their evaluations.

Three goals were postulated for the plan:[12]

"Economic prosperity
The achievement of a balanced and prosperous economy.

"Social Satisfaction
The achievement of the greatest possible social satisfaction in regard to the availability, standards and choice of housing and social facilities and the opportunities for a full social life.

"Physical Environment
The creation of a high quality environment for all activities."[13]

The division of goals into these three separate categories is unnecessary and tends to be confusing. Aspects of the physical environment, for instance, are important only in so far as they affect the activities and well-being of *people*. It is therefore artificial to divorce them from other aspects of planning proposals which affect people, such as the availability of job opportunities and the provision of recreation facilities. It is true that beautiful landscape and other aspects of the physical environment are not subject to market transaction, and as a result are not reflected in

---

[12]These are given in the Team's *Working Paper on Evaluation Methodology*.

[13]The Team point out, rightly, that there may exist a large number of such goals that contribute to a person's well-being. They only listed those which they considered would be influenced by structure planning.

calculations of the national product. However, like all other items which are valued by individuals (either positively or negatively), they may be given an economic interpretation and form the subject of analysis according to economic principles.[14] The fact that some items of value are traded in the market place and others are not is due partly to the different supply characteristics of goods and partly to historical accident.

The division between "economic prosperity" and "social satisfaction" also appears artificial. Items commonly regarded as "economic" are valued for their ability to satisfy the wants of individuals; and the satisfaction obtained by a society from elements of a plan represents no more than an aggregation of the satisfactions of its individual members. It also follows that since the well-being of individuals is affected by the degree of choice afforded by the availability of facilities, the opportunity to choose may also be subject to investigations of a social cost–benefit nature.

We shall consider in turn the following issues in relation to the objectives formulated for the plan and used in the evaluations:

(i) Whose interests are the objectives intended to represent?
(ii) Was suitable evidence collected to support the Team's choice of objectives?
(iii) Do the objectives serve to enable a clear indication to be gained of welfare effects of proposals?

Unfortunately the Study documents do not discuss whose interests were to be taken into account in establishing the objectives. All we are told is that the goals purport to be those held by "society". We may presume that the objectives were also deemed to be held by society; but this raises a number of questions. Were the interests of all members of society taken into account or were certain groups of individuals excluded? And, in particular, was the evaluation made from the viewpoint of existing residents only or of all future residents in the Study area including in-movers and unborn generations? There is nothing to suggest that the Team deliberately wished to disregard any persons of groups potentially affected. Nevertheless, the governing principle should have been stated, since otherwise it is difficult for the decision-takers and members of the public to judge the quality of the evaluation in terms of what it was intended to achieve.

The only empirical evidence collected about the objectives of persons who would be affected by the proposals was that derived from the questionnaire survey of public opinion. Respondents were presented with a list of tentative objectives for the plan and were asked to indicate whether any of those objectives was of "no importance" to them, and to note any objectives not included on the list and which they thought should have been included. Despite the fact that only existing residents were surveyed, these seem to be useful checks on the relevance and completeness of the Team's set of objectives. But there are difficulties that need to be borne in mind when analysing the results. For instance, the public may not fully be aware of the

---

[14]E. J. Mishan, *The Costs of Economic Growth*, Staples Press, London, 1967.

factors which structure planning can or cannot influence, and therefore may be unaware of the range of potential consequences. They might refrain from suggesting additional objectives because they think they are not within the scope of the plan. In addition, the public have little or no motivation to think hard about possible omissions.

We shall now consider whether the objectives were formulated in a way that facilitated the assessment of welfare effects. We have presumed that the objectives used in the Study were intended to relate to the preferences of those directly affected, and that it was thought that achieving the objectives would produce welfare gains.

Ten of the plan's fifteen objectives may be interpreted either as single sectoral objectives or as combinations of sectoral objectives. For instance, one of the objectives was "To conserve good quality farmland". This can be interpreted in terms of the preference of residents for more rather than less agricultural produce (since greater yields are obtained from high quality land, other factor inputs being held constant).

The other five objectives for the plan were formulated in terms of specific planning *policies*. Instances of these are:

"To encourage the growth of manufacturing industries;

"To encourage the provision of homes for people who do not work locally and for retired people.

"To develop the public transport system as an effective alternative to the use of the private car in congested areas."

These objectives were no doubt meant to be instrumental in making people better off. For instance, the growth of manufacturing industry will (other things being equal) lead to an increase in job choice and employment for local residents. Policy objectives are, however, one step further removed from gains in welfare than sectoral objectives. They may result in welfare gains by going some way towards achieving the sectoral objectives. The main problem with their use is that it is difficult to determine the extent that achievement of a policy objective is likely to improve people's welfare. We may measure the achievement of the policy objective to encourage the development of manufacturing industry in terms of the number of additional job opportunities created for local residents, but it is difficult to know how to interpret the results. A greater choice of job opportunities is valued primarily because it reduces the costs of search and transfer incurred by a worker in changing his job. Hence in measuring associated benefits there will be a number of items to be taken into account. The location of the new jobs in relation to residences will be of considerable importance; so, too, will be the probability of workers choosing or being forced to change their employers.

It is not surprising, therefore, that the measurements of the policy objectives of the Brighton Plan provided no indication of the likely effect of the proposals on the well-being of the community. For example, the objective concerning homes for commuters and retired persons was measured in terms of the number of new residences likely to be provided for them. A number of tests were devised for the purpose, such as the availability of suitable sites for commuter residences by distance from nearest railway station and the attractiveness of the local residential environment.[15] No indication is given of benefits which commuters and retired people would experience by living in the Study area, nor by how much different strategies might make them better off. The objective in relation to public transport was measured by the likelihood of being able to develop bus and railway services of sufficient quality to compete with the use of the private car. Again, no attempt was made to calculate the differences in benefit to users resulting from different levels of public transport services.

Evaluation and Opportunities

It is helpful in delimiting the search for practicable possibilities if, before design work begins, limits can be established on the potential rate and scale of future urban developments. This the Team did. Forecasts were made to represent the range of possibilities open to the planning authorities should they decide, on the one hand, severely to restrict future developments and, on the other, to encourage as much growth as feasible in population, employment, and associated activities. The data were a direct input to the designs.

The amounts of urban development which can take place is largely dependent upon the number of additional job opportunities created in the basic sectors of employment. If their potential increase is fully encouraged by the release of land for industrial and housing development, the estimated population potential for the Study area is an increase of about 120,000 by the end of the century. In contrast, the minimum increase in population was taken to be 34,000, estimated as the largest increase consistent with preserving the existing high quality of the urban environment.

Objectives should be formulated in relation to opportunities for making acceptable states of affairs even better as well as in relation to "problems". In addition to benefits resulting from the solution or amelioration of problems, there are benefits to be gained if such opportunities can be realized. It may also prove very costly to solve problems or to reduce their severity, which may give a comparatively low *net benefit*. The team developed the objectives for the plan from the results of their initial survey work and after considering the experience of other recent UK planning studies. Whilst the surveys did reveal a number of problems, they also enabled the Team to identify factors which in general contributed to the well-being of the area's residents—for instance, the availability of job opportunities and the level of provision of retail and cultural facilities. The objectives were not developed

[15]BUSPT, *Growth/Function Strategies, Objectives Achievement Account 1*, undated.

with specific reference to problems. Whilst they were consistent with problem-solving they were also directed to going beyond this; they were directed to improving welfare generally.

Evaluation and Physical Measurement

A number of performance "criteria" were established for each objective, and in each case one or more "tests" were employed to indicate the extent to which those criteria would be met. The criteria devised for each objective represented various items which would affect its level of achievement. In some cases these items were components of the objectives themselves. But in other cases they were the factors considered to *cause* a change in present levels of achievement. The tests represented the way in which it was thought the various items could best be measured.

Those cases in which objectives were broken down into constituent items are illustrated by the objective "To conserve attractive parts of the urban area and features of historic and architectural interest". In evaluating transport strategies, three criteria were employed for this objective. They concerned disturbance to buildings of architectural or historic interest, the amount of townscape intrusion, and disturbance to features of archaeological interest. It will have been necessary to make comparisons between the measures of these three items in order to assess the achievement of the objective itself. This process is nowhere discussed in the Study documents, nor is there evidence which indicates what the relative importance of the constituent items might be.

The objective "To retain in existing areas and encourage in new areas the physical and social individuality of different districts" illustrates the other approach employed, where the causes of objective achievement were examined. That objective was assessed in relation to six criteria. Two of those criteria were the likelihood of physical or social disruption of existing districts and the loss of "green wedges", for which a number of tests were employed. For the former criterion, tests were used to give estimates of the prospective population increases in both absolute and percentage terms. The loss of "green wedges" was assessed by the number of land units in such areas which would be displaced by building developments, and the number of land units which would be partly displaced or affected by externalities. The criteria mentioned related to the causes of a change in an area's physical and social individuality, and the tests were measures of likely strength of these causal factors. Unfortunately, the Team give no indication of how they estimated the consequent levels of objective achievements from this evidence on causation.

Furthermore, the Team did not in general give reasons for selecting particular measures in preference to others which were intuitively plausible. Evidence of the degrees to which they correlated with people's perceptions of the phenomena may have been collected, but in only a few cases (e.g. for noise nuisance) is any evidence cited.

Evaluation and Relative Values

The issue concerning us here is whether the evidence of community values was sufficiently reliable for evaluation purposes. This will be considered in relation to two matters:

(1) the suitability of the questionnaire used to survey public opinion; and
(2) the groups of people surveyed.

The valuations used in the comparison of the four short-listed alternatives were derived from a questionnaire survey of public opinion. Respondents were presented with the list of proposed planning objectives and asked to indicate the relative importance which they personally attached to them by assigning to each a numerical score from zero to ten. They were asked to give a score of ten to that objective which they considered to be of "greatest importance", and then to compare all other objectives with that one and score them accordingly. It was thus clear that the Team were seeking *relative* valuations. It should be noted that a zero score would indicate either that the objective was considered to be of no importance, or that the respondent's direction of preference was opposite to that implied by the objective. The answers of all respondents were averaged out to give a mean score for each objective, and those scores were then used for evaluation purposes.[16]

Asking respondents to score each objective in relation to a maximum total of points is perhaps a slight improvement on one of the procedures adopted by the Coventry–Solihull–Warwickshire Study Team, in which respondents were asked to allocate a *total number* of points between the objectives. The Brighton Team's procedure was probably easier, since iterative adjustments to an initial assignment are likely to be fewer and will be simpler to carry out (although there is a greater danger that the respondent will misunderstand the intention and give high scores to all objectives).

Nonetheless, the approach used is open to four main criticisms. As we discussed these at length in our review of the C–S–W Study, we deal with them here briefly. Firstly, it is meaningless to assign relative values to objectives in the abstract; that is, without reference either to proposed units of measurement or to specific levels of achievement. It is only possible to state one's views on the relative importance of, say, "providing the greatest possible space and privacy in and around the home" and "conserving attractive countryside" if unit quantities or levels of such provision and conservation are defined. Other things being equal, it is obvious that the higher the level of achievement of a particular objective, the greater the value which a respondent will place upon it in relation to the achievement of other objectives. Hence, giving sensible answers would have involved respondents in thinking up units of measurement or developing their own notions of the relevant levels of

---

[16]In evaluation, the estimated levels of objective achievement were multiplied by the numerical scores (i.e. relative values) of the objectives, and the resulting totals were then summed to give an overall level of performance for each strategy.

objective achievement. Almost certainly, this would have meant widely different assumptions between respondents.

Secondly, despite the fact that alternative strategies would result in differential changes in the levels of objective achievement, respondents were asked to specify one value only for each objective. In comparing plans the Team applied only one value to the various levels of achievement of an objective. This implied constant rather than diminishing marginal utility from additional unit increases to levels of achievement. However, from our observations of the way consumers allocate their income between goods we know that this will not be so.

Thus, if values are to be determined before plan consequences are known, to ask respondents simply to specify one particular value for each objective is not sufficient. Values should be specified for a number of different levels of achievement of each, the limits being governed as far as possible by the prospective consequences of the plans under preparation. It is better, however, to wait until the plans have been designed and their levels of objective achievement have been estimated before trying to obtain values. It will be far easier for respondents to trade-off objective achievements, since the number of comparisons will be greatly reduced and the achievement levels will represent the actual choices available. When the Team issued the questionnaire the public were not confronted with the alternative strategies and their likely effects for the objectives, presumably because their work was not sufficiently advanced at that stage.

Thirdly, the "points-scoring" procedure is unsatisfactory in making allowance for differences between individuals in their intensity of preferences. When asked to express preferences, individuals are confronted only with the particular set of objectives for the plan. As a result two people may give identical relative values to the same achievements of particular objectives, but obtain very different amounts of utility. However, if we establish their preferences by observing the way in which they allocate their income and wealth between all items available to them, including those outside the sphere of the planning proposals (such as meals, visits to the cinema, and clothes), the true differences in utilities would show up better.

Finally, as in the C–S–W Study, the questionnaire was issued only to existing residents in the Study area. In using the results no allowance was made for the likelihood that their relative values would be markedly different from those of prospective in-movers. It is hardly surprising that respondents gave relatively high scores to those objectives concerned with conservation and the maintenance of the quality of the physical environment. The five top ranking objectives (from a total of fifteen) were:

"To keep to a minimum noise, pollution and danger from traffic and other sources;

"To conserve attractive countryside and areas of natural history interest;

"To secure visually attractive surroundings for living, working, recreation and travelling;

"To conserve good agricultural land;

"To provide the greatest possible space and privacy in and around the home."

Broadly speaking, these objectives conflict with a substantial growth in population through in-migration, the amount of which will depend upon growth in job opportunities and the rate of new residential development. The potential numbers of in-migrants over the next thirty years is high, and would result in an increase of about 30 per cent in the present number of residents.[17] But substantial net in-migration cannot take place without reductions in the achievement of objectives oriented towards minimum amounts of new urban development. Existing interests in the Study area stand to lose considerably from policies aimed at achieving a high rate of urban growth.

The interests of potential in-movers will be largely opposed to those of existing residents. These in-movers would no doubt derive much benefit from living close to extensive open countryside and from other features which existing residents seek to preserve. However, as a group, additional urban growth will make the Brighton area more attractive to them. Other things being equal, the greater the amount of new residential development, the better the chances of a prospective in-mover obtaining suitable accommodation within his price range; and, unless he moves with his current job, the greater the range of available job opportunities the better off he will be.

Unless the Team were concerned solely to protect and further the interests of those currently living in the Study area, no matter what the consequences for those intending to move in, the questionnaire survey by itself was an inadequate basis for establishing community values.[18] Valuations based only upon the views of existing residents are unjustifiable. It is, of course, difficult to identify prospective in-movers, but some assumptions as to their present locations could have been made and the questionnaire given to a sample of people in those towns thought likely to supply future residents. If this was impracticable the Team could, for example, have made an intuitive estimate of the values of in-movers; they were, after all, willing to guess at community values in their preliminary evaluation exercise.

Evaluation and the Design and Testing of Alternatives

In putting forward a set of alternatives for evaluation, the designers must select a manageable number from the whole range of possibilities that exist. As we have noted, the Brighton Team chose to examine a few alternatives representing a wide range of different types of plans which were generated with little regard to the evaluation criteria. We consider, firstly, whether those alternatives were sufficiently wide-ranging to have included one or more courses of action which were very good

---

[17]Owing to the high proportion of elderly people in the local population, the rate of natural increase has been negative during the recent past. Predicted increases in population rest entirely upon prospective in-movers.

[18]P. Hall has brought attention to this weakness in commenting on the Team's evaluation of land use strategies. See Planning, *New Society*, 10 February 1972, pp. 291–2.

compared with all possibilities. We shall then discuss the use made of the six constraints that were formulated.

The variables employed in generating the land-use strategies were the balance between the main economic activities of the Study area and the extent and direction of future urban growth. To what extent were these two factors varied in the designs? The main economic activities of the area were taken to be those of service industries selling to those living both within and outside the Study area; manufacturing industry, with markets largely outside the Study area; and the provision of a pleasant residential environment for commuters and retired persons. The relative importance of these activities was varied in seven ways.[19] One alternative was to retain their current relative importance; the rest of the alternatives were formed by "substantially" increasing the importance of one or two of the activities relative to the others. Unfortunately, we are not told what orders of magnitude are implied by substantial changes in relative importance.

Three variations in the extent and direction of urban growth were investigated. Two of these represented the maximum feasible growth in population and employment by the end of the century, i.e. an additional 117,000 residents and 48,000 jobs. Of these two high-growth variants, one involved high-density redevelopment within existing urban areas and some new high-density development on the edges of certain coastal towns; very little of the Downs would be built upon. The other high-growth variant provided for growth by new medium density development on the periphery of existing coastal towns; large areas of the Downs and other countryside would be built upon. The third variant reflected a conservation policy, aiming at the minimum estimated growth rates of 35,000 additional people and 17,000 additional jobs by the end of the century, with new housing and industrial developments located very largely within the existing built-up areas.

These three variants are strikingly dissimilar in both the amount and location of future urban development. Over three times as much population growth and nearly three times as much employment growth was associated with two of the variants compared with the other. Although they each represent an extreme policy, in between these extremes will lie a number of other variants which are also significantly different. They also warranted inclusion.

We must conclude that since only two growth assumptions were involved in the twenty-one land-use strategies, a number of basically different proposals have not been examined. In itself this throws considerable doubt on whether that strategy finally selected as preferred did approximate to the best of all possibilities.

We now turn to the use made of constraints during plan design and testing. If plans can be designed to be consistent with any constraints, the efficiency of the planning process may be greatly increased, effort being saved on searching out and elaborating impracticable alternatives. The Team did attempt to incorporate their constraints into the design process, but were only partly successful in doing so.

Three of the six constraints employed were in effect *elements* of the strategies

---

[19]The importance of an activity was measured by its associated number of jobs or population.

themselves. These related to the public provision of certain facilities, such as water supply, to meeting the demand for different types of housing of the design population and to ensuring a certain minimum standard of housing throughout the Study area. It was fairly easy to build these particular constraints into different strategies (although this was not successfully achieved for housing demand in the concentrated growth strategies). One of the other three constraints was fulfilled automatically as a result of the population and employment forecasting procedures. The other two presented some difficulties. They involved a clarification of what was entailed, firstly, by economic, social, and technical feasibility, and, secondly, by the design of alternatives within the context of national and regional policies.

The consideration of existing policies at the regional and national levels is of some interest. The Team were concerned that their strategies were developed in accordance with the proposals given in the *Strategic Plan for the South East* (*SPSE*) which had then been published, although it was awaiting acceptance by Central Government as the basis of regional policy. Particular regard was paid to the admissible amount of population growth in the Study area and to the admissible amount of new urban development on the open countryside of the South Downs.

The Team were doubtful whether the amount of population increase envisaged in their maximum growth alternatives was consistent with the scale of new urban development and population growth envisaged in the *SPSE*, which proposed populations for the Sussex coastal area as a whole (610,000 by the year 2001) but not for that part comprising the Brighton Study area. However, a *pro rata* adjustment of the *SPSE* figure gave an end-of-the-century population level of 395,000 for the Brighton area compared with the Brighton Team's maximum estimate of 460,000. The Team recognized that the *pro rata* figure was valid only as a very crude order of magnitude, since the *SPSE* did not state the appropriate spatial distribution of proposed populations. They also pointed out, rightly, that the *SPSE* does not in any case give a definitive view on future population growths. Regional proposals may be modified in the light of experience gained in preparing local plans. One of the functions of planning at the local scale is to test the desirability of certain elements of higher-level plans by examining the opportunity costs of adhering to those plans.

The Team's treatment of the issue of development on the South Downs also reflected the view that regional proposals should be regarded as modifiable in the light of local investigations. Despite the fact that the South Downs was one of the areas of landscape designated for conservation in the *SPSE*, the Brighton Team decided to put forward for evaluation one strategy based on maximum growth in population and employment, involving considerable displacement of Downland through the outward expansion of existing built-up areas. The purpose of this was to demonstrate the likely advantages and disadvantages of pursuing such a policy. This was commendable. The Downs should not be treated as an absolute restraint on urban development, since *a priori* it is not possible to determine the benefits which will be foregone. It is, however, surprising and unfortunate that, having made a comparative assessment of the outward growth strategy, the Team gave as one of the reasons for rejecting it the fact that it "may in any case not be acceptable in the context of the *SPSE* ".[20] That should not have been an argument against recommending the strategy.

All of the twenty-one initial land-use strategies were tested for their feasibility with regard to the constraints and for internal consistency (i.e. the mutual compatibility of their various elements). There are two points of interest here. Firstly, despite the fact that many of the alternatives were judged to be impracticable as envisaged, it appears that they were all subjected to a comparative assessment in terms of objective achievement. The Team, it seems, carried out testing and evaluation concurrently, as one exercise, instead of completing the tests before starting the comparisons. A waste of study effort therefore occurred at this stage.

Secondly, after testing, only four of the twenty-one initial alternatives were considered practicable. The seven growth strategies involving high-density developments all violated the constraint of meeting the demand for dwellings of different types; in addition, high-density residential development as the norm for the next thirty years was thought socially unacceptable. Three of the outward-growth strategies would result in the establishment of more industrial activity than was compatible with regional policy. Seven more strategies were eliminated because they contained incompatible elements (three of these were based on outward growth and four on restricted growth). For instance, the maintenance of (or an increase in) the relative importance of manufacturing activity was considered to be incompatible with a policy of restricted growth because the pressures for expansion beyond the limits proposed for development would become too intensified. Three of the remaining four feasible alternatives were variants of a conservation policy. The range of choice open was thus highly restricted.

Evaluation and Data Collection

The Team nowhere state that they encountered difficulties through lack of evaluation data in arriving at the preferred land-use and transport strategies. This is supported by an inspection of their summary tables of results for the evaluation of the short-listed land-use strategies and the transport strategies, and the associated objective achievement accounts[21] showing the scores obtained for the tests of objective achievement.

However, the fact that the Team completed their evaluations in a manner they considered satisfactory was not because of early attention to data requirements. Rather, it was because they were quite willing during their preliminary evaluations to use subjective judgements in establishing the objectives, physical measures and valuations, and in estimating levels of objective achievement; and in the later evaluations to rely on the use of a simple opinion questionnaire to give empirical data on community preferences. Questionnaire surveys may be a poor method of eliciting

---

[20]BUSPT, *Report on the Evaluation of Alternative Strategies*, December 1971, para. 3.10.
[21]BUSPT, *Growth/Function Strategies, Objectives Achievement Account 1*; and *Transportation Strategies, Objectives Achievement Account 2*, May 1972.

people's preferences, but they will always give results which can be fed into an evaluation exercise! In addition, it appears that there was virtually no attempt to check the validity of the physical measures used to assess levels of objective achievement.

Evaluation and Decision-taking

The council members were involved at three critical points during the Team's planning process. The Team put forward for their consideration a chosen short-list of land-use strategies after the preliminary assessments of the initial set of alternatives, and subsequently put forward chosen strategies for land use and transport. In each case council members made a decision on the Team's recommendations, via the Steering Committee, in the light of the findings of the evaluation exercise. This procedure has helped to ensure that the structure plan which the Team will finally put forward to the councils for adoption will meet with agreement.

Obtaining the agreement of councils at those stages when the number of alternatives was being whittled down did produce gains in the efficient use of time and resources. But the technical work was written up in a way which will have made it difficult for the Steering Committee to judge the soundness of the Team's recommendations. The procedure and findings of the preliminary land-use evaluation are very poorly documented. A discussion of this part of the Team's work takes up only a page and a half of their evaluation report. In addition, for none of the evaluation exercises is there an appraisal of the quality and scope of the evidence produced on the comparative advantages and disadvantages of the alternatives.

9.4. CONCLUDING OBSERVATIONS ON THE BRIGHTON STUDY

The strategy which the Team recommended to their Steering Committee, and which was subsequently accepted by the councils as the basis for the structure plan, is one of severely restricted growth in population and employment. Since the valuations of objective achievements were based on the views only of *existing* residents within the Study area, this choice of strategy is hardly surprising. Current members of the community have a strong interest in maintaining the *status quo*, and the views of council members will tend to reflect existing interests. If allowance had been made for the likely preferences of potential in-movers it is doubtful whether a restricted growth strategy would have emerged from the evaluation findings as preferred.

There are some additional reasons why the recommended strategy is not the best, or even a good, strategy compared with other possibilities. Some of these arise from the way the Team's evaluation methodology was incorporated into their planning process. The two most important of these are as follows. Firstly, the evaluation criteria were not used to guide the process of generating alternatives. No attempt was made to determine empirically the preferences of the community before work began on the initial design of alternatives. Moreover, although when design work was under way a tentative set of objectives had been established, those objectives were not consciously employed in the design process. Secondly, only two different rates of growth of urban developments were examined. Fourteen of the initial twenty-one land-use alternatives represented conservation strategies; they were variants of a policy of greatly restricting new urban development to maintain the present "environmental quality" of the area. The other seven alternatives represented variants of a policy to accommodate the maximum feasible increases in populations and employments. There were obviously a large number of basically different alternatives within these two extremes which it would have been desirable to assess.

The Team did not think it worth while to design further land-use strategies in the light of their evaluations. Yet, since only four practicable alternatives were examined out of a very large number of possibilities, and since these were selected without using the evaluation criteria, it is highly unlikely that the truly preferred strategy was included among those evaluated.

CHAPTER 10

A New Town Study: Irvine

(September 1968–January 1971)

An interesting feature of the Irvine Study is that an optimization technique was employed to aid the design, phasing, and evaluation of alternative plans. Despite the obvious theoretical attractions of employing some type of optimization procedure in plan-making, such an approach has rarely been used in practice in the United Kingdom. The Study also provides a fairly recent example of the preparation of a new town plan, a task which has confronted a number of post-war planning teams.

The process of arriving at a decision on the preferred plan (which is currently being implemented) extended over a period of five years and was comprised of two main phases. The first consisted of the preparation of a broad plan for urban expansion, and the second a major review and revisions to those proposals leading to the adoption of a structure plan by the Development Corporation. The process began with a study in the spring of 1965 by Hugh Wilson and Lewis Womersley, who acted as consultants to the Scottish Development Department. Their proposals for urban expansion (the Wilson proposals) led to a designation order, which was confirmed in November 1966. There was then a two year lapse before the Development Corporation were appointed and had recruited a nucleus of staff. Further planning data collected during this time, and the preparation of sub-regional proposals, stimulated a major revision of the Wilson proposals. The process of revising those proposals and elaborating them to the level of detail required for implementation took a further two years, being completed in early 1971.

In this discussion we are interested in the second main phase of the planning process; that is, from the decision taken by the Development Corporation in September 1968 to review the Wilson proposals through to the finalization of the proposed structure plan. It may be helpful first to briefly describe the Wilson proposals and outline the events which led to the decision to review them.

250

10.1. BACKGROUND

In November 1963 a White Paper was published which proposed that the Irvine district (Fig. 10.1) be developed as one of Central Scotland's growth areas.[1] As discussed earlier in our review of the Grangemouth/Falkirk Study, the purpose of these growth areas was to relieve problems caused by the presence of declining industries, which included high unemployment rates, and to improve conditions of overcrowded and poor quality housing. The areas defined were considered to offer particularly favourable prospects for employment growth and were chosen as being potentially the best locations for industrial expansion. The Irvine district was viewed to be one of two "growing urban areas where further industrial and housing development is possible on a considerable scale",[2] and it was stated that "If suitable arrangements can be made with the local authorities concerned, the Government do not rule out the designation of a fifth Scottish new town in the Irvine area".[3]

In December 1964 the Scottish Development Department (SDD) commissioned Wilson and Womersley to prepare a plan to provide for an expansion of population of about 55,000 in the vicinity of Irvine and Kilwinning. Provision was to be made for major land uses, including housing, employment and shopping, and for traffic

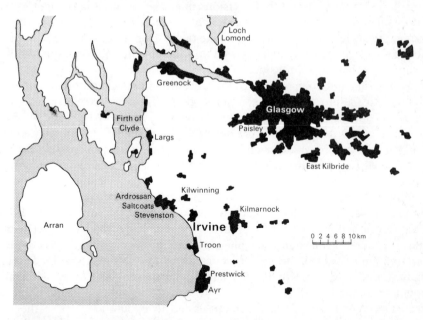

FIG. 10.1. Regional settlements. (Source: *Irvine New Town Plan*, fig. 3.1, p. 34.)

[1]Scottish Development Department (SDD), *Central Scotland: A Programme for Development and Growth*, HMSO, Edinburgh, 1963.

[2]*Ibid.*, para. 106.

[3]*Ibid.*, para. 109.

movements. The consultants were asked to submit an interim report by the end of May 1965, outlining their proposals.[4]

The proposals contained in the report produced by Wilson and Womersley (the Wilson report) were briefly as follows.[5] New population was to be concentrated in a wide arc 15 km (9 miles) long and 8 km (5 miles) wide lying to the east of the existing town of Irvine. The new developments took form of a series of residential and industrial districts placed along a major communications spine, designed for both public and private transport. The development was very flexible in form and could accommodate various amounts of population growth.

Following discussions between the SDD and the local authorities concerned, a draft designation order was issued in February 1966 which, after some minor modifications, was confirmed in November of that year. Although the Irvine Development Corporation was appointed in June 1967, it was not until the autumn of the following year that they had established a nucleus of technical staff and therefore in a position to begin work.

The Corporation was formally responsible for organizing and supervising the final planning and the construction and management of the new town. On their appointment they went back to Wilson and Womersley for advice on possible revisions to the plan. The Corporation felt that revisions might be required in the light of recent surveys which had revealed the existence of extensive areas liable to mining subsidence; this was not apparent at the time the Wilson proposals were prepared. In addition, a sub-regional study had been set up following the Wilson report, and a plan for the area was then under consideration.[6] This plan was to provide a context for the planning of Irvine and Kilmarnock. In the Corporation's view the Wilson plan could be modified to fit into the proposed sub-regional framework whilst retaining the planning concept on which it was based. However, whilst Wilson and Womersley agreed that changes to their plan were desirable, they argued that it was not possible to modify it in a suitable manner and at the same time retain their original planning concept. They convinced the Corporation that a new approach to designing the new town plan was required.

In addition, it should be noted that the Corporation had two major criticisms of the Wilson proposals. Firstly, that it ignored the potential of the run-down harbour and the underdeveloped beach and foreshore. It was thought that this area would be suitable for major entertainment and recreation developments. Secondly, the Corporation (and the local authorities) considered that the plan involved too much destruction of property in Kilwinning. These points were to be taken account of in subsequent planning work.

Wilson and Womersley were recommissioned to update and revise their initial

[4]The reason given for requesting an early interim report was that Government urgently needed information to form the basis for short-term decisions. But we are told no more than this.

[5]See H. Wilson and L. Womersley, *Irvine New Town: Final Report on Planning Proposals*, HMSO, Edinburgh, 1967.

[6]This study was undertaken by the Ayrshire Joint Land Use Working Party. The Corporation were actively involved in its preparation.

plan and were aided, as previously, by Jamieson and Mackay on highway and traffic aspects. In addition, PA Management Consultants and the Israel Institute of Urban Studies were commissioned to undertake some evaluation work. Whilst these two groups of consultants worked in liaison with the professional staff of the Corporation, there was hardly any direct contact between them; they really worked separately throughout the Study. PA and the Israel Institute assessed plans given to them by the Corporation; some of these were produced by the Corporation's own staff, whilst others, it would appear, were based on the work of Wilson and Womersley. But the methodology of the evaluation consultants was not used to assist Wilson and Womersley in their work; the latter used their own approach to plan assessment.

Two reasons may be suggested for this lack of integration of effort. First, the evaluation consultants' method of appraisal had not been used before in the United Kingdom and was unfamiliar to the Corporation. Its use was regarded as experimental, and until it had been tested it may have seemed most sensible to run two approaches in parallel. Second, Wilson and Womersley were sceptical about the suitability of the evaluation consultants' methodology, and were probably unwilling to place much reliance on the evidence about the advantages and disadvantages of plans that it would generate.

In this review we are largely interested in the way that the evaluation work of PA and the Israel Institute was fitted into the decision-making process of the Corporation. We refer to the work of Wilson and Womersley only in so far as it throws light on this.

10.2. APPROACH TO THE REVISION OF THE WILSON PROPOSALS

Methodology Used by Evaluation Consultants

PA and the Israel Institute used a formal method of analysis to evaluate alternatives. They based their work on an optimization model which utilized linear programming. The model was developed not just for use in finding the best of a given set of alternatives, but also for searching out all feasible possibilities and, in the same operation, selecting the optimum of those identified. But, as we shall see, it was used in a restricted way, namely, only indirectly for design purposes.

The evaluation consultants persuaded the Corporation that the use of an optimization model might enable them to produce a better plan more quickly and accurately than by traditional methods. The possibility of using an optimization procedure was mooted towards the end of 1967, and proposals for evaluation work were submitted to the Corporation in August 1968. Work on the evaluation followed soon after, and was completed towards the end of 1969.

It was claimed that the model used was able to perform four main functions. First, to be capable of identifying the efficient plan within a given set of constraints; that is, identifying the plan which maximizes the value of the objective function subject to meeting the constraints imposed. The efficient plan would be selected from the range of all possibilities that exist. A second function was to identify the best of a range of plans selected for evaluation. A third was to analyse the shadow prices of the constraints; that is, the change in the value of the objective function as a result of a marginal relaxation of any constraint. (For a given constraint, the resulting difference in value may be thought of as the marginal opportunity cost of having to meet it.) The final main function was to give guidance on the most suitable phasing of developments over time.

The objective function of the model, containing the preference criteria and their respective weights, was based on the principles of social cost–benefit analysis. The criteria represented concepts of costs and benefits relevant to those whose well-being would be affected by planning proposals.

The model was in fact restricted to a consideration of factors relating to the location and density of housing and to the effects of plans on the occupiers of existing and proposed residential developments. It was limited in this way not because it was thought that residential occupiers were the only persons of importance. The scope of the model simply reflected the nature of the items of difference between the plans put forward for evaluation. The plan for the new town was to consist of proposals for the future amounts and locations of populations and employments, the location of the town centre, and investments in transport facilities. However, the alternative plans prepared were virtually identical in all respects except for the location of the town centre and housing. Although the model would not pick up all items of difference between these plans, it is clear that the effects on residential occupiers should be the focus of attention. This suggests that the model used in the Study was devised with knowledge of the nature of the plans to be evaluated and their likely differences. That is, it was devised to meet the particular evaluation problem at hand.

The objective function of the model had two parts.

(1) The market value of all housing in the plan,[7] less:
    construction costs;
    site development costs;
    opportunity costs of the land.
(2) The value of travel time saved compared with a postulated alternative plan based on the Wilson proposals.

It will be observed that the accessibility attributes of housing location were separated from all other attributes. It should also be noted that the benefits from the physical attractiveness of the local environment were only considered during the final application of the model. Presumably, it was thought that differences for this item would show up only in fairly detailed investigations.

Although the evaluation consultants pointed out in their report that "The construction of a meaningful welfare function which correctly reflects the weight of

---

[7]The value of housing for both rent and sale was assessed in terms of its free market value, since rents normally charged do not reflect the true value of housing to the community.

each of the preference criteria is a complicated problem which no social scientist will claim to have solved", they did claim that their model was adequate for use on this Study.

The evaluation model was first used to compare the effects of six alternative outline plans, prepared by the Corporation. No use was made of it during this design exercise, which is surprising since linear programming is normally used to identify the optimum solution straightway. It was used to determine the welfare value of each of these outline plans, the results being presented in tabular form with the plans ranked in order of performance. One of them was selected for further consideration, and after substantial revisions to it had been made by the Corporation, the model was used to compare the revised version with the initial six alternatives. The model was then used to analyse the shadow prices of each of the constraints under which the chosen plan had been prepared in an attempt to find the optimum. After estimates of these shadow prices had been made, the Corporation agreed to relax some of the constraints and to use the model further to reallocate housing between different areas in order to produce the efficient plan within the new set of constraints. Following this, the model was used in making a sensitivity analysis to find the extent to which it was possible to relax each constraint without altering the preferred choice of plan. Finally, the costs and benefits of alternative phasings of residential development were estimated, and the findings used to establish a recommended programme for implementation.

The Planning Process of the Corporation and their Evaluation Consultants

We turn now to the procedure followed by the Corporation and their evaluation consultants in making use of the cost–benefit model. We shall first outline the planning process very briefly, and then discuss certain of its aspects in detail. The process followed may be understood in terms of three main cycles, each cycle being comprised of the design of alternatives, their evaluation, and either the selection of proposals for further consideration or the making of a recommendation.

Cycle 1

Six alternative land-use/transport plans were designed and compared, leading to the choice of one of these for further consideration, namely, "alternative plan 3". The Wilson proposals formed one of these alternatives.

Cycle 2

Plan 3 was extensively revised in the light of new information and subsequent events. This in effect became a new plan. It was then compared with the initial six alternatives and found to be preferred, and hence provisionally adopted. This was termed Interim Revised Outline Plan (IROP).[8]

---

[8]Wilson and Womersley's work was incorporated directly into this IROP; indeed, it was essentially a result of their efforts. After this point, however, they were no longer involved in the Study.

Cycle 3

The IROP was developed in greater detail and some subsequent modifications made to it. The modified version of the IROP was compared with its initial version and found to have a higher welfare value. In the light of this, it was put forward as a recommendation to the Corporation. This plan differed in a number of respects from that ultimately adopted (Fig. 10.2).

The alternative which was chosen for further consideration during the first cycle was *not* the one which was ranked first on the basis of the results of the cost–benefit analysis (CBA). The chosen plan had a net welfare value of £28 million but this was £2·3 million lower than the value of the top-ranking plan, "alternative plan 5". Plan 5 owed its overall advantage to its superiority on one of the three items listed in the findings of the evaluation,[9] these outweighing its disadvantages on the other two items. However, it was not rejected because of doubt over the reliability of the findings for its item of advantage. Rather, it was rejected for reasons associated with the location of the town centre, which were not highlighted by the CBA because of the limited scope of the model.[10]

The plan chosen at the end of the first cycle (plan 3) was then revised for two reasons. First, in the light of new information on mining conditions and the release of further land for development. Second, and more important, it was revised to conform with sub-regional planning proposals. The revisions made to plan 3 were considerable and the resulting plan is best regarded as essentially a different plan. The differences between the initial and modified versions of plan 3 can be seen by referring to Figs. 10.3 and 10.4. Figure 10.3 shows alternative plan 3 as initially prepared. This is based on locating new residential and industrial developments around an oval-shaped communications route. Most of the residential developments are located on the east side of the communications route alongside its north–south section, and much of the industry is located alongside the parallel north–south route in the west (although this is more difficult to generalize about). Figure 10.4 shows the considerably modified version of that plan. It will be seen that the emphasis was shifted from a north–south location to an east–west location, with developments lying predominantly to the east of the proposed Irvine By-Pass, extending towards Kilmarnock. This modified version of plan 3 has great similarities with the sub-regional proposals put forward by the Ayrshire Joint Land Use Working Party. Although it is not explicitly stated, it would appear from the Study documents that the cost–benefit model was not directly used to help modify plan 3.

The IROP was compared with the initial six alternatives and found to have a net welfare value equal to plan 5, which was the top-ranked of the initial plans. Of these two, the Corporation preferred the IROP, because in addition to its computed welfare value "the Corporation subjectively considered it the most promising".

[9]See, PA Management Consultants and the Israel Institute of Urban Studies, *Irvine New Town Planning Study*, 1969, p. 90.

[10]It was thought that the town centre as located in plan 5 would have serious commercial disadvantages.

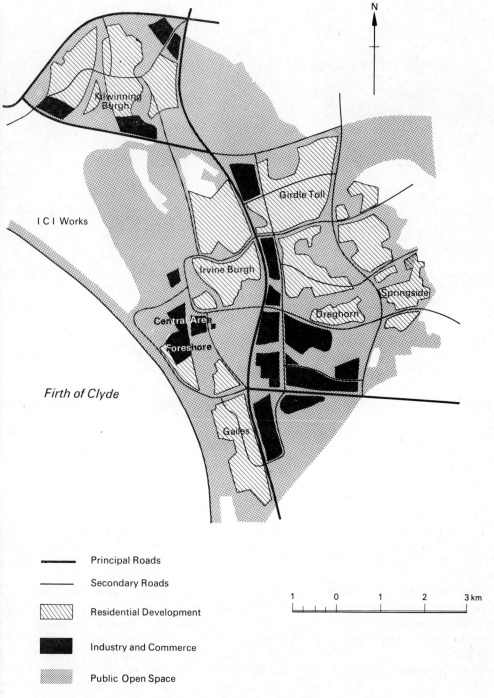

N

I C I Works

Kilwinning Burgh

Girdle Toll

Irvine Burgh

Springside

Central Area

Dreghorn

Foreshore

Firth of Clyde

Gailes

—————— Principal Roads

——————— Secondary Roads

Residential Development

Industry and Commerce

Public Open Space

1 0 1 2 3 km

FIG. 10.2. The plan adopted by the Irvine Development Corporation. (Source: *Irvine New Town Plan*, fig. 1.5, p. 22.)

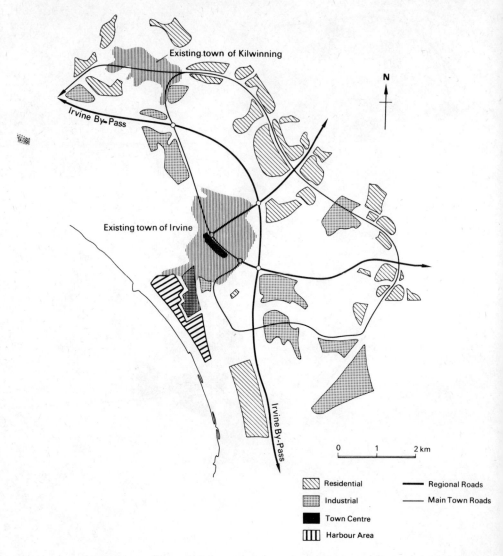

FIG. 10.3. Alternative plan 3. (Source: *Irvine New Town Planning Study*, fig. 3, p. 21.)

Regrettably we are told no more than this, but we may surmise that again the reasoning concerned the location of the town centre.

At the start of the third cycle, the IROP was formulated at the same level of detail as the earlier Wilson proposals. It required further elaboration in order to meet the requirements of the structure plan. In addition, however, it was found necessary to revise it in the light of up-dated planning information and further analysis of the shadow prices of constraints. In the light of data on the latter, some of the constraints were relaxed and changes made to the housing locations. The revised form of the IROP was found to have an improved welfare value of over £2 million.

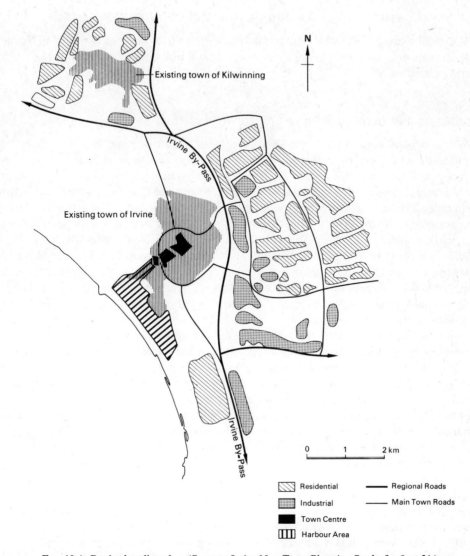

N

Existing town of Kilwinning

Irvine By-Pass

Existing town of Irvine

Irvine By-Pass

0 1 2 km

Residential	——	Regional Roads
Industrial	——	Main Town Roads
Town Centre		
Harbour Area		

FIG. 10.4. Revised outline plan. (Source: *Irvine New Town Planning Study*, fig. 9, p. 31.)

To conclude this discussion of the planning process, the main strategy adopted for identifying the optimum alternative was to design a few fairly good alternatives and to select one of these as the preferred plan. A secondary feature was that during the process of narrowing down the range of alternatives initially prepared, it was necessary to develop one or more in greater detail; that is, to the level required for implementation. In addition, this procedure was characterized by continuous improvements to planning data and, during the first two cycles, by the formulation of planning proposals for the sub-region. This meant that considerable revisions were necessary to the new town proposals.

10.3. EVALUATION IN THE PLANNING PROCESS OF THE IRVINE STUDY

We shall examine the way evaluation was related to a number of other planning activities where the principles of evaluation should influence the nature of the work to be carried out.

Evaluation and Determination of Constraints and Opportunities

We consider constraints first, and comment on three matters: the type of constraints which were employed, their importance, and their validity.

It appears that there were two constraints given to the planning teams at the outset of their work. One of these was the SDD's directive to the Corporation to provide for a specified increase in the future population of the Study area. The other concerns the boundary of the Study area itself. The boundary which was drawn in the designation order, following the submission of the Wilson proposals, was very similar in extent to Wilson and Womersley's chosen area of search and embraced the area covered by the Wilson proposals. This boundary to the designated area appears to have acted as a definite constraint on searches by the Corporation.

In preparing their initial alternatives, the Corporation also made use of many physical features of the Study area in order to limit the areas of search for new developments. These were thus also treated as constraints on development. In general, these physical constraints adopted were the same as those put forward in the Wilson report, modified as necessary by the Corporation in the light of further information on physical factors. The Study area was divided into land not available for development, land unsuitable for development, and land suitable for development. Unavailable land included existing built-up areas, areas of outstanding landscape or historic interest, existing public open space, and land scheduled for gravel extraction. Unsuitable land included certain old mining areas, peat bogs, land liable to flooding, and land steeper than 1 in 15. Restrictions were also imposed on some of the remaining land by the presence of old mine workings and the load bearing capacity of the soil; and in some cases a tighter constraint was imposed on allowable land gradient—for instance, industry was located only in areas which, among other things, had a gradient of less than 1 in 30.

All of the constraints formulated which rendered land either unavailable or unsuitable for development could have been overcome at some cost. They would be valid if this cost is greater than any benefits to be gained from violating them. Indeed, the shadow prices of these constraints were estimated by systematically relaxing each one and computing the resulting change in a plan's welfare value. The shadow price of a given constraint indicated the maximum cost of improving the land which was justified. Wherever the cost was lower than the shadow price the evaluation consultants rightly recommended that the constraint in question be relaxed.

The application of physical constraints meant that there was little "suitable" land available for industry and housing over and above that which would be required by the forecast land-use requirements. For instance, only about 400 ha of land were deemed suitable for industrial development and virtually all of this would be required to provide additional jobs for new residents. This testifies to the importance of the constraint on the total area of search. The Corporation may have felt that the boundary had been drawn far too tightly, although no indication of this is given in the Study documents.

A large number of planning constraints were incorporated into the cost–benefit model. These may be divided into two categories for our discussion: those relating to non-quantifiable items and those relating to quantifiables. The former were required in order to make the model operational, but the latter were not, and should have been incorporated as items of cost and benefit in the objective function. The effect of transgressing them would have shown up in differences in the computed welfare values. There were only two constraints in this category—on phasing (which concerned the number of additional households in the new town at the end of each stage of implementation) and construction of dwellings (concerning land of "suitable" gradient, and load-bearing capacity). It appears that the opportunity costs of fulfilling these constraints were not estimated, and thus we do not know their practical importance.

The proper way to deal with the non-quantifiables is to examine the shadow prices of each at different minimum levels of attainment and to then form a judgement as to what extent it is desirable to forge their achievement for gains in the achievement of other items. All of the constraints on non-quantifiables were examined in this way during each of the three cycles of the planning process, with particular regard being paid to their estimation in the last cycle. For instance, during the last cycle it was found that the greatest improvement in the welfare value of the objective function would result from relaxing the constraints on population location. The removal of these constraints led to an improvement in the welfare value of the IROP of about £5 million.[11] As a result of this, some changes to the constraints were agreed with the Corporation.

We turn now to opportunities and the scope for change in the scale of future urban development. Since a given population increase was specified for the new town, there was little room for manoeuvre except in the structure of employment and the amount of commuting in and out of the Study area (affecting the amount of new employment opportunities). But the Corporation chose to use common employment assumptions, reflecting their aim to provide employment for all in-movers.

Evaluation and Formulation of Objectives

Two main groups of objectives were employed during the revision of the Wilson proposals. One of these was comprised of those objectives specified for the plan by the Corporation, as set out in their major report.[12] The other group were implicit in

[11] The shadow prices of the population constraints are given in PA Management Consultants and Israel Institute of Urban Studies, *Irvine New Town Planning Study*, 1969, appendix 4A, table 2.

[12] Irvine Development Corporation, *Irvine New Town Plan*, 1971, para. 8.13. The objectives are listed in the appendix to this chapter.

the variables used in the objective function of the cost–benefit model. In this section we comment on the suitability of the Corporation's objectives for evaluation purposes and examine in what way the objective function of the cost–benefit model related to them.

The planning objectives specified by the Corporation were essentially identical to those used by Wilson and Womersley in preparing their initial outline proposals. By adopting these objectives the Corporation preserved a continuity in the preparation of the proposals. Although the Corporation did not exist when the Wilson proposals were prepared, we must presume that the Corporation found the objectives then formulated to be quite acceptable.

As Wilson and Womersley had done earlier, the Corporation used a set of objectives to provide a design brief. They treated these objectives as a list of requirements which a good plan should fulfil, and attempted to prepare a plan which would meet all of them to some acceptable extent. They were particularly concerned during plan design with transport systems and with the interrelationships between transport, land use, and urban form. This is reflected in their planning objectives.

Four of the Corporation's eight objectives were concerned with traffic and communications. Three of these were based on what has been termed "instruments of design", instances of which are the concepts of an environmental area and a hierarchical road system. These concepts may be regarded as solutions to particular design problems. For example, one of the objectives stated that "The communications system must be based on a clearly defined hierarchy of roads and public transport routes. The main roads must be free from conflicting activities such as parking and servicing of buildings". This gives the designer a clear idea of what is required of the design of the communication system; and it aids him in his work by indicating the main characteristics of the design which would be preferred. The sectoral objectives underlying these design instruments were not spelt out, however. Although some of these may have been fairly obvious, this is an omission of some importance. In so far as the designs were intended to have regard to community welfare, the intended welfare effects should have been explicitly stated so that those participating in the decision process could readily appreciate what the designs were intended to achieve.

Nevertheless, these design instruments may be justified in the following way.[13] There are a number of obvious traffic system design features which will create a good physical environment or improve an existing environment in a number of respects. But because the creation of a good environment is not costless it is necessary to be able to quantify and value various environmental attributes in order to formulate sensible guidelines for design. At present we require a good deal more research before we are able satisfactorily to appraise environmental characteristics for the purpose of plan-making. However, in the interim practicable approaches have to be adopted, and a number of "instruments" of design may be helpful for this purpose. For instance, the concept of an environmental area may be justified by the

[13]The following points are taken from K. M. Gwilliam, Traffic and towns: an overview, in G. D. N. Worswick (ed.), *Uses of Economics*, Blackwell, Oxford, 1972, 204–23.

idea that some land uses are more sensitive than others to particular aspects of the physical environment and by the placing of a high value on not adversely affecting those sensitive land uses.

The idea of establishing a hierarchy of different classes of roads is another case in point. Our present environmental problems arise partly from trying to use the same type of road for all our travel requirements. A hierarchy of roads is a useful way of contributing to environmental improvement through the separation of conflicting functions. The use of the hierarchical concept is a means of avoiding the need to re-examine recurring aspects of common problems (a technique frequently adopted in architecture). It is a means of incorporating into our designs the existing knowledge on certain generally experienced problems. A third case in point is that of specifying minimum design standards. This may be regarded as a reasonable second-best approach in the absence of information on variations in costs and benefits.

Of the remaining four of the Corporation's planning objectives, three of them may be viewed as sectoral objectives (nos. 1, 6, and 7). The other objective (no. 8)—that there should be a "satisfactory balance" of population in relation to age groups, family structure, and employment—was a case of what we have termed a policy objective. The purpose of this objective was to avoid undue strains on the use of community facilities or the commitment of high expenditure.

None of these four planning objectives were described in terms of factors to be either maximized or minimized but rather, as we have noted, as requirements to be met. No impression is given in the Corporation's report that trade-offs between objectives were to be established and used for evaluation.

We turn now to the relationship of the cost–benefit variables to the planning objectives. We have noted these variables earlier in our discussion of the evaluation methodology in section 10.2. None of the variables were explicitly mentioned in the list of planning objectives, although constraints on congestion and attributes of the physical environment were reflected in objectives 2 and 5. The objectives were formulated independently of the cost–benefit model, and it is clear that not all of the variables employed in that model were reflected in the objectives relating to housing.

Evaluation and Design of Alternatives

The Corporation put forward five new alternative designs which were to be compared with each other and with the Wilson proposals. The purpose of including the Wilson proposals was presumably in order to demonstrate that the new designs were actually superior. Each alternative contained proposals for the location of industry, housing, and the town centre, and for the main road network. The new designs retained the Wilson principle of a major communications spine and environmental housing areas,[14] but the land-use allocations were substantially

---

[14]The concept here is that put forward in the Buchanan Report: Ministry of Transport, *Traffic in Towns*, HMSO, London, 1963.

modified. The land-use changes arose not from changes in the purpose and objectives of the plan but rather from the existence of new geological and mining information. It appears that the designs were prepared using the same basic requirements for the plan and the constraints as were used in the preparation of the Wilson proposals.

There were very few major differences in the design characteristics of the new alternatives. The plans were very similar or identical with respect to industry and transportation. There was said to be very little "suitable land" for industrial development, and the plans contained identical quantities and locations for industry except for "alternative plan 9" which had one industrial area omitted. The main road network was the same in all plans except for small differences in road alignment in "alternative plan 10". There were some small differences in the location of new housing areas, these arising in an area lying about 2 miles north-east of the existing Irvine town centre. Although the new town centre was in each case located on or adjacent to the communications circuit, their spatial positions did vary somewhat. However, in the case of four of the five new designs the locations of the town centre were within 2 miles of each other on the eastern side of the circuit; the other plan (alternative plan 3) had its town centre on the site of the existing centre.

Unfortunately, we are not told the way in which the five new alternatives were produced except that great reliance was placed on the use of physical factors and constraints. The location of industry was thought to be heavily constrained by geological, soil and mining conditions. Some of the areas of land identified for industrial development in the Wilson plan were no longer considered suitable, hence new areas for industry had to be found. These were located on areas free of constraints, but the amount of unconstrained land was only just sufficient to accommodate this development. It is not clear why alternative road networks were not formally considered. We must presume that the design reflected some informal evaluation of alternatives and represented what the Corporation considered to be the most suitable network. Likewise there are no reasons given for the differences in the location of residential areas, and no justification for ignoring other possibilities. Adjustments to the location of the town centre were thought necessary because in the Wilson plan it was not well "integrated" with the new developments.

The question arises as to why a cost–benefit model was not used to aid the design process during the first cycle of plan-making. The model which was used contained variables relating exclusively to the location and intensity of housing, and therefore a more comprehensive model would have been required for this purpose. The Israel Institute had at the time developed a model which they regarded to be generally applicable to searching out optimum urban and regional plans,[15] and presumably they would have been willing to use that model on this Study. The Corporation might have resisted such a suggestion, for two reasons at least. First, because of scepticism about the suitability of the model. Second, it might have involved them in undue

[15]H. Ben-Shahar, A. Mazor, and D. Pines, Town planning and welfare maximization: a methodological approach, *Regional Studies* **3** (1969) 105–13.

expense on data collection and running the model, and involved a highly time-consuming procedure.

After selecting one of the five new plans for further consideration (alternative plan 3), a fundamental change occurred in the Corporation's thinking. This stemmed from the results of the continued work of the Sub-regional Planning Team. Their detailed proposals for the Sub-region showed an emphasis on residential and industrial expansion in an easterly direction from Irvine and westwards from Kilmarnock. This contrasted markedly with the Corporation's alternatives, in which future developments were to be located on a north–south axis. As a result, during the second cycle of the planning process, major changes were made to the location of industry and housing and to the transport network of plan 3. The reasons why the Corporation wanted their plan to conform with the sub-regional proposals is not clear. There is no discussion in the Study documents as to the merits of the sub-regional proposals.

The cost–benefit model was not used to help this process of modifying plan 3 in the light of sub-regional proposals. Its only use as a design aid was during the work of revising the IROP at cycle 3. Here it was used to reallocate residential land and population in the light of new planning data.

Evaluation and Measurement of Advantages and Disadvantages

The evaluation consultants claimed that the cost–benefit model assessed alternatives in terms of the welfare effects of plans for society as a whole. We shall now consider whether the model was able to give a valid indication of changes in social welfare. We shall do this by examining in turn each variable of the objective function.

The market value of housing was intended to relate to all attributes besides that of any differences between plans in accessibility benefits. It is not possible to say whether the estimates made were reliable, but by definition they would contain no allowance for consumer surpluses. There is now some evidence (from the Third London Airport investigations, for instance) to show that this element of benefit is in general likely to be substantial for existing residents. No information was collected separately on this issue, however.

Turning to site development costs, estimates were made of the costs associated with local distributor roads, sewerage, and site-levelling. It is stated that no estimates were made of the costs of the supply of water, gas, electricity, and telephone services. These items were omitted because their costs were "borne by other private oriented bodies". But this is no reason for excluding them from a cost–benefit assessment. The supply of public utilities will involve the use of resources, and these costs must be counted in regardless of the type of development agency by which they are financed.

It was assumed that all unbuilt-on land which was not allocated for future development would be retained for agricultural use. Unfortunately, we are not told how the value of agricultural use was determined.

It was stated that accessibility benefits were reflected in the value of time saved in daily travel for various purposes. Estimates were made of the time spent in travel by families in each socio-economic group in each traffic zone, and values then applied to the travel time differentials. The differentials between plans in the value of time spent travelling were used as the sole indicator of differences in net accessibility benefits. Now the costs associated with making journeys of particular types will have varied with the location of the town centre and with the location of housing *vis-à-vis* other land uses. It is clear that a reduction in the cost of making a given trip will result in a benefit to travellers. But it is not necessarily the case that reduced costs of travel will result in a reduction in total travel costs which are actually incurred. This follows from the observation that reduced travel costs will lead to an increase in trip demand. If the price elasticity of demand is greater than one, the total costs which travellers incur will *rise* as the cost of travel falls. Thus the model might have given both incorrect quantitative estimates of differences in net accessibility benefits and have led to a plan being considered disadvantaged for this item when it should have been credited with an advantage.[16] Furthermore, the correct approach to measuring these accessibility benefits would have been to take account not only of the pattern of travel costs but also of trip-end benefits. For this purpose some accessibility index could have been employed, some examples of which were discussed earlier in chapters 3 and 6.

Surprisingly, no mention is made in the Study documents of the methods used to calculate the value of time savings to residents. The Corporation themselves point out that the report of PA and the Israel Institute is very thin on explanation and justification of methods used to calculate both travel times and values.[17] The welfare values of the plans were particularly sensitive to differences in travel time savings. For instance, the improvements made to the IROP very largely reflected such differences; the savings amounted on average to six minutes per family per day. Some may object that this amount of time saving is too small to be of any significance. But it must be remembered that the conventional valuations of time savings have been derived from studies of commuter behaviour where the modal choices involved differences of this order of magnitude—not large time differences. In addition, the figure of six minutes is an average over the whole population, not just those who would actually experience savings. (We also understand that the estimates of journey times were subject to margins of error owing to the crude nature of the designs.)

No mention is made of the capital costs of road provision which will have varied between the Wilson proposals and the other five alternatives initially put forward by the Corporation. This is an omission of some significance, although it is not possible to say how significant. In addition, any differences in the access of industries to labour supplies were ignored. In this case the differences were probably too small to be worth taking into account.

---

[16]The procedure used in the Study to estimate accessibility benefits would only be valid providing the demand for travel is perfectly inelastic, which will never be the case in practice.

[17]Irvine Development Corporation, 1971, *op. cit.*, appendix 5.

Some of the weaknesses in the model just mentioned could have been overcome fairly easily; for instance, the costs of supply of public utilities could have been determined reliably from consultation with the relevant bodies, and a simple and cheap procedure used to give an indication of any differentials in trip-end benefits. Others, such as the measurement of householder surpluses, were more difficult to deal with, however. This brings us to a general point about the use of formal social welfare functions in plan-making. Their specification and application involve a number of severe practical and conceptual difficulties. A very considerable amount of data are needed on welfare variables and the preferences of individuals (or groups) potentially affected. The total costs of collecting this data will invariably be high and, given the conventional size of study time and resource budgets, are likely in practice to prohibit the consideration of a number of consequences of proposals. Those items which cannot be measured in the particular circumstances of a study will have to form constraints if the social welfare function is to be operational. Also, since distributional consequences will usually be of relevance to the decision, the costs and benefits have to be traced through to those who will ultimately suffer and enjoy them. There are formidable technical difficulties in this tracing of incidence; these have proved insurmountable in nearly all major planning studies (given available resources). Furthermore, a truly comprehensive social welfare function should include a set of equity weights to reflect normative judgements about the social desirability of alternative distributions of costs and benefits between different groups. These judgements are the prerogative of decision-takers, but they will rarely if ever want explicitly to make known their views on equity matters.

These difficulties are magnified if a social welfare function is used as an optimization tool. This use is certainly intended by the Israel Institute for the more comprehensive model they have developed, mentioned earlier.[18] However, the function that the authors suggest should be maximized seems unduly restrictive, and in most planning situations would give only a partial indication of changes in social welfare. The objective function consists of the total demand prices for all building less construction and demolition costs for new ones, and less all costs associated with the provision and use of communications infrastructure and capital. Although the authors point out that only decision-takers can determine optimality criteria, they nevertheless claim that this function is generally valid for planning.

Evaluation and Decision-taking

There were three main planning teams engaged on the Study (including the Corporation's own team), all of whom contributed inputs to the decision on the final plan. Since our interest lies with the way that the cost–benefit evaluations were incorporated into the planning process, we shall comment on the way that the work of PA and the Israel Institute was related to the decisions taken by the Corporation.

[18]H. Ben-Shahar *et al.*, 1969, *op. cit.*

The Corporation adopted some of their evaluation consultants' recommendations, but they modified or rejected others. For instance, the evaluation consultants recommended that previously proposed development in the east of the Study area should be eliminated. This did not accord with the planning proposals for the Sub-region and the expansion of Irvine on an east–west axis. In addition, their proposal to restrict development at Kilwinning to that already committed was at variance with the Corporation's wish to continue the current housing programme for areas within and adjacent to that town. Whilst such considerations cannot be fed into a quantitative analysis of social welfare, they could have been specified as constraints in the cost–benefit model. This implies that closer co-operation was needed between the decision body and their consultants.

The Corporation were satisfied that the cost–benefit model was capable of providing a sound basis for evaluation, although we have noted that it did have some basic weaknesses. However, they did not think that the model was suitable for refining particular aspects of alternatives, nor that by itself it could establish how development should be phased (since no account was taken of the demand for different types and sizes of housing for various mixes of socio-economic groups). The Corporation's other main reservation was that the value of travel time was based on the income of a family's main wage earner. As a result of this they thought that "an undue emphasis had been placed on socio-economic groupings", since the wages of high socio-economic groups would lead to high values of travel time compared with lower socio-economic groups. Since willingness to pay is influenced by income levels, and the distribution of families by income did vary between plans, this is a fair point.

Finally, the evaluation consultants' reasons for their selection of items of difference between plans is poorly documented in their report, and there is very little explanation of the methods of measurement.

10.4. CONCLUDING OBSERVATIONS ON THE IRVINE STUDY

The initial intention of the Corporation was to modify the Wilson proposals, mainly to take account of new planning information which had been gathered in the two-and-a-half-year period since those proposals were first put forward, and of the sub-regional studies then underway. The approach adopted was to design a few hopefully good outline plans, and then to select the best of these as the basis for preparing the more detailed urban structure plan. Whilst the Corporation favoured the use of a formal evaluation model, the link between the design and evaluation work was very weak. The design of initial alternatives proceeded with reference to a list of requirements which the plan should fulfil. Whilst these requirements may have been based on considerations of community well-being, they certainly differed from the items of social cost and benefit in the evaluation model, and they were not stated in terms of intentions to promote or curtail, respectively, social benefits and costs. Although the evidence produced by the cost–benefit model was used in some measure to assist the process of refining designs, its use in plan design was extremely limited.

This inconsistency between the objectives implicit in the cost–benefit model and the planning objectives employed by the Corporation is of obvious importance. If, during their design work, the Corporation had made use of those concepts of social costs and benefits incorporated in the model, markedly different kinds of alternatives might have emerged. Admittedly that model was of limited value for design, since it took account only of consequences of the location and intensity of residential developments. However, as noted earlier, a more comprehensive cost–benefit model had been developed by the Israel Institute for the purpose of generating the optimum of all possible plans.[19] We are not told why the Corporation rejected the use of this model for purposes of producing an optimum plan, but it may have reflected doubts about the possibility of specifying a valid social welfare function, and of being able to represent all relevant factors in model form. If they did have such reservations it would have been interesting to run it as an optimization model and then to compare the welfare value of the plan produced with the values of others under investigation. Yet despite its very restricted use so far (involving less than 10 per cent of the total budget devoted to preparing the new town plan), the model can be used to help update the plan in the light of future events and changes in planning objectives and constraints. Here some experimental use could be made of it in future design work.

In the event, however, the most important influence on the Corporation's thinking seems to have been the work of the Sub-regional Planning Team. The publication of their proposals during the course of the Study led to a number of basic changes in the form of the design which was then under consideration (i.e. alternative plan 3).

APPENDIX

THE DEVELOPMENT CORPORATION'S OBJECTIVES FOR THE IRVINE NEW TOWN PLAN[20]

1. The planning strategy must be sufficiently flexible in terms of land use and communications to allow for growth and to compensate for the uncertainties of long-term forecasting arising from changes in social, industrial and commercial requirements, and to provide a structure that will function efficiently at all stages of development.

2. The communications system must be designed to integrate all forms of transport. There must be a regard to a high level of car ownership and usage, and the plan must allow for the development of an efficient public transport system from the outset not only for those who need it, but to provide an alternative choice for private car users.

---

[19]*Ibid.*
[20]Reproduced from Irvine Development Corporation, 1971, *op. cit.*, para. 8.13.

The communications system must be based on a clearly defined hierarchy of roads and public transport routes. The main roads must be free from conflicting activities such as parking and servicing of buildings.

3. Land uses with high traffic generation should be dispersed to achieve the maximum balance of peak traffic flows. This applies particularly to industrial sites and other major employment centres.

4. Pedestrians and fast-moving vehicles do not mix and thus there should be the maximum degree of segregation that can be economically achieved throughout the town with a separate, direct, well-defined and attractive footpath system linking the residential areas with the schools, shops, other community facilities, work places and recreation areas.

5. The development should be based on a series of environmental areas from which extraneous traffic is excluded. These should be based on a maximum walking distance of about 0·5 km to primary schools, shops, public transport and other facilities.

6. As far as possible building should proceed comprehensively, area by area, to cause the minimum inconvenience to residents.

7. The town should have a coherent structure which can be easily appreciated by those who live in and visit it and satisfactory relationships achieved between built up areas and open spaces. The new development should be carefully related to the existing.

The programming of the development must be arranged to ensure that at each main stage of development, a part of the town is established that would support a reasonable range of facilities.

Any necessary re-development to ensure comparable standards in the existing town or integration between new and old should be phased into such a programme.

8. There should be a satisfactory balance of population in relation to age groups, family structure and employment to provide a sound basis for the development of the town at all stages of its growth, particularly at the second generation period.

CHAPTER 11

A Major Project: Third London Airport

(June 1968–December 1970)

The deliberations of the Roskill Commission on the Third London Airport were distinguished by the very clear and logical process by which recommendations were arrived at. The Commission adopted five cycles, from the definition of a "universe" of possibilities to a short-list of four sites, and then directly to a recommended alternative. One particularly important feature was that the evaluation criteria were determined at the outset of the process and were then used consistently throughout.

11.1. BACKGROUND

The eventual recommendation by the Roskill Commission of Cublington as the site for the Third London Airport in preference to Foulness led to considerable controversy. This controversy, coupled with the fact that the Government eventually decided in favour of Foulness against the Commission's recommendation, has obscured many interesting and original features of the process by which the Commission reached its recommendation. In this chapter we discuss some of the main features of this process. It does not cover the ground of the many critiques of the Commission's work which have mainly concentrated on the treatment of measured items in the Commission's Research Team's evaluation; intangibles in the decision; important issues affected by the decision but outside the Study terms of reference, and on the validity of the Commission's conclusion. In this chapter any reference to these topics is restricted to those cases illustrating a feature of the site selection process itself.

One might say that the setting up of the Commission was a result of public outcry over an inadequate process of site selection. The arguments against the decision to locate the airport at Stansted were largely motivated, and strongly supported, by the fact that the Stansted decision was not shown to be in the general public interest. There was no formal evidence to suggest that the alternative possible sites to Stansted which were considered had been rigorously investigated, with all factors for and against them, in comparison with Stansted, taken into account in the decision. Much of the work behind the selection of Stansted was undertaken in

271

secret. Even under the impact of severe criticism, the authorities were unwilling to produce evidence in support of their decision. In the minds of many people this suggested that they were unable to produce satisfactory evidence.

Accordingly, the Roskill Commission was under a strong obligation to undertake its work according to a set of procedures which could not be generally criticized by the public for being unfair, unjust, or inefficient. The terms of reference of the Commission indicated a strong commitment to public participation. This took two main forms: firstly, the Commission published voluminous documents which would clearly lead to debate; and, secondly, there was to be a very lengthy final public inquiry at the fifth stage of the deliberations. The Commission's objective was to adopt a planning process which was rational and which would be seen to be so. As they said, "the need for both public participation and for the establishment of confidence in the proposed procedure has now been accepted".[1]

Such a procedure would need to be efficient in the sense of moving smoothly from the initial deliberations and stated approach to the final conclusions, which in this case were to take the form of the recommendation and presentation of the *Report*. The Commission should manage its allotted time and resources to the maximum advantage in arriving at its preferred option, and in producing the supporting evidence. We must, then inquire into the Commission's allocation of its resources to see whether work was unnecessarily duplicated, or whether areas of investigation seem to have been omitted, or to judge whether emphasis was correctly placed on the various activities of generation and evaluation of alternative airport possibilities.

In addition to the managerial efficiency with which the Commission undertook its task, we may also investigate the consistency of its site selection process. By this we mean the extent to which the principles and measures which were used to assess the relative advantages and disadvantages of proposals were also used to aid their generation. There are clear advantages to be gained from integrating the activities of data collection, objectives determination, design, testing, and evaluation, rather than seeing them as discrete and independent activities. Complete integration of evaluation criteria into the planning process is never possible for two reasons; firstly, because of the necessary time-lag between the design of alternatives and obtaining full information about their likely consequences, and, secondly, because of the usual complex interrelation between items of advantage and disadvantages in planning proposals. Nevertheless, it is possible to assess the extent to which the Commission achieved consistency in its generation and evaluation attempts.

Accordingly, in this chapter we shall try to review the Commission's achievements according to these two main criteria—the efficiency of the whole process and the consistency of the approaches at various stages. More specifically we shall refer to the evidence used to reject airport alternatives prior to the short-listing of four sites for detailed consideration, and the evidence that rejected alternatives which might subsequently have appeared advantaged. We shall discuss whether the mix of sites

---

[1]CTLA, *Report*, HMSO, London, 1971, para. 3.3.

included in the short-list was defensible and consider the effort devoted to the generation of evidence on key items of advantages or disadvantages. We shall review the resources devoted to the analysis of the short-list sites in relation to those devoted to the Commission's other activities. We shall also look for any procedures which the Commission consciously decided not to follow in its adopted site selection process.

As our primary focus of attention is on the role of evaluation in the planning process, a few words on the Commission's view of evaluation will assist the discussion. Whereas their terms of reference stated that the Commission was to include amongst its investigation the undertaking of a cost–benefit analysis (CBA), the Commission nevertheless made it clear that they appreciated that different approaches to the assessment of proposals are possible. They referred to the "market approach" and to the "planning approach" as possibilities that had been suggested to them.[2] By the planning approach the Commission meant the identification of socially desirable aims (such as the conservation of the countryside) and then the application of aesthetic and cultural standards to achieve them. This might be called the "goal"–achievement approach to plan evaluation. The task of overcoming problems to a given standard is identified with the achievement of the stated objectives. In the context of the location problems of the Airport, this approach might have involved the establishment of various criteria as constraints on the search for a site, and then finding sites which conform to those criteria. In contrast, in the market approach (to use the Commission's terminology) attention is focused more on positive increments in the well-being of members of society. This would be similar to our sectoral objectives approach to evaluation, whereby advantages and disadvantages of proposals to particular individuals or groups of individuals (sectors) are identified and measured. Of the two possibilities suggested to the Commission, CBA clearly comes closer to the market approach. It purports to include a comprehensive list of consequences of proposals which affect the well-being of members of the community. It approaches the measurement of those advantages and disadvantages according to the recipients' relative valuation of these consequences. In any event, a distinguishing feature of the Commission's overall procedure was the extensive collection and use of cost–benefit evidence.

We have already expressed our preference for using sectoral objectives in evaluation and our preference for the conventional cost–benefit approach to measurement. Accordingly, we concur with the Commission's view of the value of evidence provided within a cost–benefit framework of analysis. They laid great emphasis on the value of cost–benefit in assisting their decision by providing information and a framework for that information. Interestingly, the Commission saw the form of analysis as helpful to their short-list selection of alternatives as well as to the selection of their preferred alternative from the short-list.[3] Where we may differ with

---

[2]*Ibid.*, para. 2.9.
[3]*Ibid.*, para. 3.13.

the Commission is on its selection of particular items for assessments of alternatives at preliminary stages of its investigation, where comprehensiveness of coverage of items is impracticable, and on the measurements of particular items of cost or benefit.

The principles of assessment of alternatives and the practical approach to certain important items were set down in advance of the evaluation exercises in the *Proposed Research Methodology*.[4] This document provided the necessary foundations for the detailed work to follow. It was commendable not only as a clear statement of intent but also because it demonstrated that the Commission and its Research Team had thought through the approach to evaluation at a comparatively early stage in their deliberations. The Research Team acted as the Commission's planning team in the sense that they were to generate some of the alternatives, to detail those alternatives into a suitable form for further investigation, and to produce evidence as to their relative merits and demerits. The Commission retained the role of decision-makers both in the selection of alternatives for more detailed investigations and the final recommendation. However, the Research Team's role as planning team was not complete. Firstly, in the initial investigation of site possibilities, the Commission invited others, e.g. the Ministry of Housing and Local Government (as it then was) and Dr. Seeley (of the London School of Economics) as well as the general public to suggest possible site locations. Secondly, the Commission did not rely upon only the work of the Research Team for evidence of the comparative advantages and disadvantages of alternatives. Indeed, the purpose of the inquiry at the final stage of the Commission's deliberation was to allow others to present evidence which might have conflicted with that of the Research Team or which might be additional to that already collected. But only in these two minor respects were the Research Team fulfilling a role which was slightly different from that of the planning team of a local authority or as part of a planning study.

The Commission were decision-makers within their own study, and could decide which alternative site (and the timing of its development) to propose. In that context we would hope to find that they showed a logical progression from the universe of possibilities to the determination of their own preferred option. We shall debate whether this progression was clear and efficient. Nevertheless, the Commission's role was limited to the making of a recommendation. The Government retained the right to decide on what action to take. Clearly an autonomous Commission might have different choice criteria from an elected government. Accordingly, whilst the Commission had an obligation to recommend it also had a duty to submit to the ultimate decision-makers' evidence about other alternatives which they might well prefer. This task is clearly difficult since the Government's choice criteria are never likely to be made known in advance or even to be made clear in the final event. We shall try to assess how well the range of short-list alternatives were likely to satisfy this requirement.

[4]CTLA, *Papers and Proceedings*, vol. VII, part 1, HMSO, London, 1969.

11.2.   THE COMMISSION'S SITE-SELECTION PROCESS

There were five discernible cycles to the process of arriving at a preferred alternative plan. Taking the number of site alternatives considered at each cycle, they were: firstly, the *78* coarse alternatives; they were reduced to *29* alternatives which were then eventually reduced to *15* alternatives; the 15 alternatives were then reduced in number to the *4* which were the subject of the final inquiry; *1* of the 4 alternatives was then submitted by the Commission to the Government as its recommendation.

The initial number of 78 alternatives concealed further options, since clearly within the vicinity of a site many variations in runway alignments and precise location of facilities are possible and many different operating arrangements feasible. Strictly speaking, each variant represents a new alternative. It is certainly true that the Commission continually searched for new and superior designs at each of the sites under investigation. In this sense new alternatives were being generated throughout the deliberations. Nevertheless, no new search for site areas was undertaken after the identification of the initial 78 possibilities. The principal distinguishing characteristics of subsequent cycles was the collection of additional information about the social and economic consequences of operating an airport from the site areas. The Commission and its Research Team undertook work according to a variety of distinct stages at each of their cycles of activity. Such stages include data collection, plan design, testing, and evaluation. Nevertheless, the emphasis of the stages after the initial generation of alternatives was on design detailing and on the collection of evidence for evaluation.

The Commission's terms of reference, like the terms of reference of many planning studies, constrained the search for alternative development possibilities. In the case of the Commission this was a four-runway airport for traffic serving airports in the London Region.[5] The practical consequences of these constraints were twofold. Firstly, the preferred solution could only be preferred within these constraints and need not necessarily be preferred of all possibilities. This was more an area of concern for the Government than for the Commission, so long as the Commission felt that their terms of reference were acceptable. Secondly, the time and resources devoted to the particular activities of seeking out desired alternatives would clearly differ, given these constraints, from a situation where no constraints existed. Their problem was to ensure rapid focus upon a manageable problem. Nevertheless, from Fig. 11.1 it will be seen that the Commission did not have too narrow a view of the geographic limits of its area; certainly it looked wider than the London Region even though most passenger origins and destinations in the United Kingdom for airports in the London Region are, not surprisingly, located in the London Region. Yet many of the 78 initial site possibilities are in the Midlands.

The public were invited to suggest alternatives at the outset, and an "open" invitation presumably existed for them to do so subsequently. They did not know

[5]Official Report (Commons), 20 May, 1968.

FIG. 11.1. Location of sites. (Source: Commission on the Third London Airport, *Report*, appendix 5, fig. 2, p. 184.)

what range of sites the Commission had in mind at any of its stages prior to the short-listing. Indeed, the 78 alternatives were not published until the *Report* stage and the recommendation to the Government. But the *Proposed Research Methodology* was published early on, and this gave interested parties an insight into the general direction of the Commission's thinking. If, at the early stages, any interested parties had felt motivated to generate evidence in support of a particular proposal for eventual presentation to the Commission, they were free to do so, and some did do so, for example, in support of the various Foulness schemes.

After stage I (when the Commission invited suggestions from the public) and up to stage V (the final public inquiry) the Commission considered that the planning process was their total responsibility. In defence of this view they stated that debate on the alternatives would have prolonged the proceedings unnecessarily.[6] They were capable of considering the options and were reasonably confident that no outstanding possibilities had been overlooked since they had the benefit not only of their own investigations but those of any parties prepared to submit them. In the Commission's view, public participation was best concentrated on suggestions of options and detailed consideration of the critical issues surrounding the short-list sites. The argument about possible delays caused by greater public involvement in the intervening stages is compelling. The Commission were appointed to generate and sift evidence about options. But it is inevitable that great emphasis is placed on the ability of anybody placed in similar circumstances. They had to select a short-list of alternatives from the universe of possibilities available which not only represents a *wide range* of possibilities in themselves, since clearly the purpose of the participation at the final stage would be to discuss essentially different alternatives, but also to pick *uncontentiously superior alternatives from each of the various sets of possibilities.*

To illustrate this, the Commission's process was broadly according to the method of Fig. 11.2. On the left-hand side we have the full spectrum of 78 alternatives. At the second cycle alternatives drop out and the remainder may begin to form identifiable clusters where distances apart within groups (in terms, say, of some concept of net cost differences[7]) are slight compared with distances between groups. This is

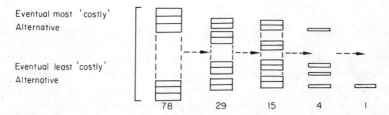

FIG. 11.2. Alternatives at each cycle.

[6]CTLA, *Report*, para. 3.7.

[7]Throughout this discussion we shall assume that differences between alternatives can be measured in cost terms as benefits of the schemes are broadly similar for all 78 possibilities.

accentuated at subsequent cycles until a preferred alternative is selected. Of course it does not follow that an alternative once rejected need never again be considered. In the Commission's process rejected options were closely inspected prior to the short-list in the light of new evidence, particularly at the stage immediately prior to short-listing; but "looking back" went on formally throughout the process. The problem is that we do not know where in the spectrum of costs the alternatives are located at the start, nor do we know the ultimate decision-maker's choice criteria (which need not be least cost as we have defined and measured it). We hope, therefore, to include in the final short-list of four alternatives at least one which is at, or close to, the least cost (as we have defined it), plus other alternatives which the decision-makers may prefer to choose. If the public are not involved in the process prior to the short-list stage of 4, the Commission must adopt some rules for ensuring that amongst the 4 short-listed ones are those (or alternatives close to them) which the public would want to debate.

Figure 11.2, at its right-hand side, also suggests that the Commission needs to be fairly confident that its preferred alternative is close to the preferred of all 78 possibilities. Given their time constraints, especially in the light of the necessary but lengthy final public inquiry, they ruled out iteration in search of a better alternative after the inquiry. Thus they had to ensure that the alternative at or close to the global optimum was in the short-list. The necessary safeguard was the generation of more information at the 29 and 15 alternatives cycles than would have been necessary had iteration been feasible after short-listing (when the best information would be available), plus a strategy which minimized the risk of omitting alternatives which would later be shown as desirable.

Presumably the only true test of the Commission's ability to select sites for the short-list would be to subject all 78 possibilities to the same intensive scrutiny as was given to the short-listed 4, but this is not a practical possibility. But if the detailed information generated at the short-listing stage had thrown up surprises, in so far as differences emerged between options which were significantly different from prior expectations, that would have presented a strong case for further iteration. The evidence suggests that the Commission, at least, were not substantially upset by the evidence at the stage V hearings.

The Coarse 78 Alternatives

The Commission's first task was to find a suitable list of four-runway airport sites. At the outset very little could be said about the relative merits of sites. Moreover it was important to include some alternatives which, from what little was known, would not appear very advantaged. There were two reasons for this. Clearly further evidence may emerge later which justifies their earlier inclusion. Secondly, eventual decision-making criteria were not known; hence many possibilities needed to be explored. Obviously *all* possibilities could not be explored, but consideration of a wide selection was possible. But in the absence of measures of difference between sites, how should the term "wide" be interpreted?

One obvious possibility was to interpret a wide spread of alternatives spatially. To some extent the Commission did this by including at least one alternative in each general locality within its total area of search. The density of sites varied across the study area, with far more to the north of London than to the south. The other interpretation of width of range was in terms of different organizations' views as to possible sites, when the Commission asked different people to suggest sites to include on the short-list.

Crude and loosely drawn criteria were adopted to select alternatives from this long list. No alternatives were allowed within 30 miles of Heathrow Airport so as to avoid "excessive" air traffic control problems; and other criteria for noise, landscape, and slope characteristics were also used to make the initial search manageable. One critic later suggested that, according to the eventual evaluation criteria at the short-list stage, a site right in the centre of London, possibly on a Royal Park, would have appeared as preferred. This claim was not made wholly in jest, although little evidence was provided to justify it. Certainly no alternatives were included on artificial islands in the sea away from the coast and none in the London built-up area.

Given that no investigation of new site areas was expected after compiling the long list, were any of the initial constraints on search drawn too tightly? Without subjecting alternatives outside the constraints to formal evaluation we will never know for sure; we will never know whether relaxing the initial noise constraints would have yielded payoffs in terms of enhanced accessibility, or even whether the amenity criteria would have been better met by locating the facilities, as we have suggested, on an artificial island in the North Sea. But it does seem plausible to suppose that some "back of the envelope" calculations were made to test the reasonableness of sites outside the constrained area of search. The Commission must have considered all the possibilities put to it by the public and agencies with an interest in its deliberations, and undoubtedly some of them must have been in these localities. The subsequent thoroughness of the Commission's search would suggest that no really interesting alternatives were overlooked in the preparation of the long list.

The Medium List of 29

The 78 initial alternatives represented a fairly comprehensive coverage of seemingly feasible alternatives. These had to be reduced to more manageable numbers. Why did the Commission not go straight from the 78 to the short-list of 4? Having decided on a medium list of 29 and a reduced medium list of 15, what was required of the alternatives on those lists and did the Commission's alternatives meet those requirements? No clear answer emerges in the *Report* as to why the Commission decided on its medium lists, although the reason for including sites on the lists is stated. But clearly, as the Commission proceeded with its task, more information about alternatives came to light. In order to combine the need to wait for additional information with the necessity to make selection tasks more manageable, the Commission introduced these intermediary cycles. In the absence of full information, the medium list must display characteristics similar to the list of 78 alternatives. That is, it would have to include a wide range of alternatives to avoid the risks of exclusion of sites of good potential at later stages and also to meet requirements for a wide mix of alternatives to be submitted later for public debate.

The medium list sites were not as "spread" geographically as the 78. Figure 11.1 shows that most of the 29 alternatives were grouped close together in areas to the north-west, north, and north-east of London. This is surprising unless there were grounds for supposing that small geographical distances between sites would lead to potentially large cost differences. In fact preliminary estimates of surface access, noise and air traffic control costs, and to some extent site preparation costs, did suggest that cost variation might be significant within the spatial clusters of alternatives which were chosen. Nevertheless, *a priori* it was surprising to find no sites at all in the outer regions of the initial search areas and only one site to the south of the Thames and its estuary. This indicates that the Commission began to think that some criteria were of sufficient importance to rule out large numbers of alternatives from further consideration.

The selection of the 29 sites was carried out using a very coarse filter (to use the Commission's terminology) in contrast to the finer filters employed later. In the main the coarse filter at this stage involved three criteria: surface access which, it was presumed, might have the largest potential inter-site differential; defence, which might have proved a "fatal flaw"; and noise, the most "popular" of the controversial issues and also likely to have large cost differences. "Judgement" was also used on other matters, such as urban and regional planning, although at this stage in their deliberations there could be no way of knowing the likely differences between sites to make any one of these many possible factors of relevance to the decision.

There had been little past experience of full comprehensive evaluations of alternative sites for airports in contrast to other studies where knowledge based on the experience of previous similar studies may allow the Study Team to focus on likely items of importance at an early stage. This might well justify the fact that the Commission chose to adopt criteria for which it was "easy" to obtain some crude cost measures of sites differences rather than selecting the most important criteria.[8] In fact, noise, defence, and surface access always appear amongst the most important items in the Commission's work. Nevertheless, urban and regional planning issues may have been seen by them to dominate at the time, for subsequently the largest item in the research budget was devoted to examining this issue.

After the initial selection of the 78 alternatives the Commission adopted a flexible attitude to alternatives which were rejected or accepted at subsequent cycles. Thurleigh, one of the alternatives in the final short-list of 4, was actually rejected in the selection from 78 to 29. It was brought back into the reckoning at the end of the medium-list cycle after scanning rejected alternatives in the light of additional information.

[8]T. Kitchen, The generation and coarse evaluation of alternatives in regional planning: a case study of the work of the Roskill Commission, *J. Roy. Town Planning Inst.* **58**, (1972) 8–12.

We have already noted the Commission's wish to use cost–benefit procedures at the preliminary stages of their activities as well as in the short-list assessments. The Commission chose to measure the differentials for the limited criteria between sites by the same assessment principles as they were to use in their final evaluation. The reliability of the physical measures (e.g. the number of people affected by noise nuisance) and their relative values (the relative value of noise nuisance compared with surface access advantages) were suspect at this early stage in the collection of evidence. This limited reliability and the range of criteria adopted, differentiated the early evaluations from those to follow. Nevertheless, the Commission were consistent in their *approach* to evaluation.

The Commission toyed with the concept of cost contours.[9] Costs were being determined for a number of criteria over a fairly wide variety of sites, and accordingly it was possible to draw up contours on the map for each cost item and overlay maps to obtain some ideas of composite costs. This is similar to the development potential surface adopted in some regional and sub-regional planning studies. Indeed, the development potential surface technique may be considered as a crude, uncosted, version of cost contours. The Commission could then have identified areas appearing to be relatively advantaged yet not represented by airport sites on their list. They decided not to take this approach very far. The main objection was that the surfaces were not "well behaved"; costs for selected items were found to vary markedly over short distances. The development and noise costs, for example, appeared to depend very critically on location.

Nevertheless, a spatial cost–contours approach seems to have been the way the Commission viewed its selection task, even though it did not formally extend its quantitative analysis far in that way. In selecting alternatives one (Silverstone) was included, which would probably otherwise have been ruled out because of a "geographic gap" on the map of sites to the north-west of their region. A similar view was taken later relating to the "Essex Gap", where, on the selected criteria of choice, no sites would have existed. Again the Commission thought it necessary to take a wider view than the evidence immediately before them at that stage. They wanted to maintain a spread of options. The main dimension to risk aversion and keeping options open was seen as spatial, although, as we have seen, there were clearly a number of gaps to the south of London which the Commission did not feel it necessary to fill. This was probably due to the apparent importance of passenger access in the airport system, where costs of access were much lower in the north of London than in the south. If a high correlation existed between large cost variations on a few items and particular localities, then it was right to attempt to include sites within all of those apparently low-cost localities. However, a risk-aversion strategy should still have required the inclusion of some apparently high-cost sites at this stage, not because of high cost *per se* but rather because in a wide-ranging sensitivity testing they might be preferred if one or more items were seriously incorrect in costing. It could be argued that the coastal and estuarine sites (e.g. Foulness, Dengie Flats, or Sheppey) filled that role. But these were all within one cluster of sites.

[9]CTLA, *Report*, para. 4.10.

Another apparently high-cost cluster might also have been included for contrasting items of disadvantage relative to the coastal cluster.

It should be recorded that in addition to the costed items the Commission obtained qualitative advice on air traffic control and rejected some alternatives because of possible conflict with activities at Heathrow and Gatwick airports. Although they were clearly interested in quantifying the effects of the sites, which we believe to be a commendable approach, the Commission were clearly not confident, because of data limitations, that such an approach could provide sufficient evidence for choice at this stage. Nevertheless, we have no idea of the shadow prices of air traffic control constraints and the reasonableness of such prices.

The analysis and sifting of the 78 alternatives was undertaken by a process of pairwise comparisons of sites, and then the rejection of sites for which other alternatives demonstrated dominance. It would appear from inspection of Fig. 11.1 that members of the Commission were beginning to perceive clearly the nature of the differences between sites, even at this early stage.

The Reduced Medium List of 15

The 29 medium-list alternatives were themselves then subjected to cost studies on five main criteria: surface access, defence, air traffic control, site preparation, and noise. The number of measures has increased, but, again, there is no explanation for their adoption.

As more information was collected by the Research Team, more sophisticated assessment procedures became possible. The Commission certainly felt that their estimates of cost differences between sites on the medium list were superior to those given in the comparisons of the 78 alternatives.

Now the assessment according to this expanded list of criteria in the *Report* (table 2, appendix 5) indicated that for one item, namely surface access, the differences between sites appeared much more significant than for any other criterion. This finding arose from the work of the Research Team. The Commission were not allowing surface access to dominate the differentials, as Kitchen has suggested,[10] but this item seemed to be giving the greatest differentials between the sites included in the assessment. There would be no reason for concern over this finding, *a priori* and certainly no grounds for ignoring or underplaying the item just because it seems, at first attempts at evaluation, to be important, as Kitchen seems to imply in his criticism of the Commission's approach. But a number of considerations are raised by the emergence of this item as dominant in the initial exercises.

Estimation of surface access costs depended on two sets of uncertain assumptions: the modelling of passengers' trip-making behaviour to airports, in which the Research Team relied on a gravity model as a basis for predicting passenger allocations to airports by mode, and assumptions for passenger travel costs, and especially for the value of time spent travelling. Both of these sets of assumptions

[10]Kitchen, 1972, *op. cit.*

proved to be contentious, and led to controversy at the public inquiry stage. Yet no independent research effort was devoted to analysing passenger demand to airports, and none given over to support the value of travelling time estimates used by the Research Team, which were based on estimates obtained from various previous studies made of other kinds of travel behaviour, principally commuting behaviour.[11] In defence it could be argued that gravity models are frequently used in modelling travelling behaviour in many situations, and also that much independent research had gone into establishing values for time wasted travelling, if not specifically travelling to airports. The Research Team may have then been better employed on research into other items. Indeed, they did later undertake their own research into other uncertain items in the evaluation, such as displacement costs of residents at the airport sites and noise-nuisance costs. But in view of the apparent significance of the early surface access findings it is surprising that there was no effort at all to verify the estimates. Others could have carried out this work of course, since the *Proposed Research Methodology* outlined the approach the Commission was going to take. But that possibility hardly defends the Commission's decision not to research as many contentious items as possible.

The circumstances of the airport location could certainly have been such as to make an item, possibly surface access in this case, more important in the differentials between sites than all other items put together. We may debate the accuracy of the cost figures, but nothing in principle stops one item being the most important in the differentials between sites. Kitchen correctly points out that the Commission did, at this stage, consider surface access to be of such significance; but why should they not do so, since all the evidence pointed that way? The Commission considered that the most promising looking sites at this stage were grouped in the northern and north-western sector of their region, where accessibility is best. There were five "most promising" sites in this category out of the 15 on the reduced medium list. However, what is surprising is to find that, in the short-list, three of the four sites were taken from this group of five. This is surprising because it presumes sufficient knowledge about alternatives at that early stage to strongly suspect the preferred alternative to lie in that narrow area of search. True, Foulness was also included to test the presumption. But to include Foulness alone as the contrast to the other three seemingly similar alternatives has the appearance of a risky selection strategy. Perhaps in order to be confident that one had minimized the risk of overlooking alternatives seen later as good, only two of the front-running alternatives at the medium-list stage should have been included in the short-list but combined with two distant alternatives. Indeed, the case of the "Essex Gap" indicated that the Commission were aware of these risks, for during the medium-list deliberations they did retain one site there (Good Easter) as a potential contender for inclusion in the short-list despite its comparatively low ranking in the crude analysis. Good Easter,

[11]M. E. Beesley, Project selection and social welfare, in G. D. N. Worswick (ed.), *Uses of Economics*, paper presented to Section F (Economics) at the 1971 annual meeting of the British Association for the Advancement of Science, Blackwell, Oxford, 1972, pp. 199–203.

"appeared otherwise to be a favourable area for consideration".[12] Moreover, the eventual inclusion of Foulness in the short-list testifies that the Commission were, to some extent at least, adopting a risk-averting selection strategy. This must be so, since Foulness did not appear very promising according to the cost estimates made at this stage either. Indeed, it was apparently inferior to Good Easter.[13] Why then was it included in the short-list?

The Commission felt the need to include a coastal site, "if the work at subsequent stages were to comprise a sensible range of alternatives and allow the major locational advantages of sufficient range of sites to be tested".[14] They saw a *coastal* site as offering the main alternative to *inland* sites which, on current considerations, looked generally more promising. They therefore selected three of the better-looking inland sites and the best-looking coastal site, which seemed to be Foulness although they also considered nearby Southminster. Now the coastal characteristic of Foulness offers promise only in relation to selected items of advantage or disadvantage. The Commission clearly thought that an apparently advantaged alternative on the uncertain grounds of urban and regional planning should be included in the short-list, despite heavy disadvantages on other grounds, such as access and construction costs. Certainly the Commission were aware that Foulness, on "general issue of town and country planning", might have advantages, but it was a topic area they had not yet managed to explore in detail; and accordingly they suspected that it might prove worth while to include it. There was nothing greatly attractive about a *coastal* site *per se*, without these particular advantages. But the Commission might well have sought out at least one other site with apparent advantages on seemingly less important criteria, even if it meant going back to the initial 78 alternatives. This seems particularly relevant in view of the narrow cost differences between the three short-listed inland sites at the medium-list stage, and, indeed, between those sites at the eventual conclusion of the study (although they could not be sure about the cost differentials until the end of their deliberations). If the three inland sites were close together, why did the Commission need three for inclusion in the intensive final analysis? The main reason seems to be that the Commission were concerned to find the "global optimum" site directly, without iterations and searches after the short-listing stage. They had, at that medium-list stage, formed a fairly clear view of where such a site was to be found and, it would appear, only completely unforeseen evidence would lead them away from the area to the north or north-west of London. They wanted to be fairly sure that the site eventually selected in that sector of their region would be close to the best possible site there. Accordingly they included as many of the promising alternatives as they could in the short-list.

If this view was correct, then Foulness really was "bogey for the course", and one or two less extreme risk-averting alternatives might have been more appropriate, say in the Essex Gap or nearer the Midlands. Risk-aversion strategies do not necessarily

[12]CTLA, *Report*, para. 4.25.
[13]*Ibid.*, appendix 5, table 3.
[14]*Ibid.*, para. 4.34.

imply finding completely different design *concepts* against which to test the most promising ones. Perhaps Foulness was included partly through pressure from the media, although that seems unlikely. Possibly at the stage prior to short-listing, members of the Commission were divided about where the preferred alternatives were to be found, and one or more members thought that Foulness offered the best location. The possibility of necessary compromise cannot be ruled out. Foulness could have been included even though some members thought it not the best option but only an acceptable one, given the feelings of other members of the Commission. Whatever the truth, it does seem to be clear that most of the Commission had, prior to short-listing, formed an opinion that the "best" site was somewhere north or north-west of London and that Foulness was in as the only test of that notion.

The Short-list of 4

We shall not consider the concluding stages of the Commission's deliberations at length since this aspect of its work has been given much attention elsewhere and is well documented. We shall limit ourselves to a few observations about the evidence produced in support of the 4 alternatives.

The evidence produced by the Research Team and its consultants was almost exclusively within the framework and according to the assessment principals of a comprehensive CBA. We have already noted our agreement with this general approach so long as the analysis is comprehensive and attempts are made to trace the incidence of the resultant costs and benefits. Incidence is necessary in order that the equity issues may be debated along with the magnitudes of the cost and benefit items. Although attention focused on the overall magnitudes of the cost and benefit items, and the Commission's publication of the Research Team's findings were by item (rather than by incidence group), incidence analyses were undertaken at the final inquiry stage[15] although difficulties encountered in tracing through the repercussions of the projects on various groups inevitably limited these exercises. They suggested that there were no serious equity issues other than the problems of heavy *per capita* losers through displacement of population and imposition of noise. This arose from inadequate arrangements for compensation and could reasonably easily be rectified before the opening of facilities, given a political will. Thus the Commission may not have considered it necessary to delve more deeply into the incidence effects.

The Research Team kept to the principles and procedures they had outlined in their *Proposed Research Methodology*. By and large the inputs obtained from various consultants to the Research Team (e.g. the agricultural experts) were also within this scheme. However, this was not the case for one fairly important aspect of the development proposals—the urbanization consequences of the airport. Two consultants were appointed to study these and they undertook their own evaluation

---

[15]N. Lichfield, Cost–benefit analysis in planning: a critique of the Roskill Commission, *Regional Studies* **5** (1971) 157–83.

exercises on alternative urbanization possibilities at each site.[16] Their studies were not within the Research Team's cost–benefit framework. This may have been unimportant in itself so long as the consultants undertook a comprehensive coverage of the wider social costs and benefit of the urbanization patterns. However, when it came to the point of placing the urbanization consequences of the four sites into the overall comparison, such evidence as was produced on the relative merits of the proposals was not consistent in form or content with the evidence on noise nuisance, accessibility, and the other factors in the Research Team's CBA. One suspects that there would be significant variations in the costs and benefits to users and others as a result of new developments (especially in the light of regional planning controversies in South East England), yet the final summary cost–benefit tables contain no reference to this at all, partly, one suspects, because the requisite evidence had not been produced. Perhaps this demonstrates the difficulties of integrating the working of two teams when one is acting in a capacity of a consultant to the other. The Commission's task was to ensure that the two consultants produced evidence that the Research Team could use. It would appear that they were not very successful.

There was consistency between the final evaluations and the evaluations at the 78 list and medium-list stages; here only the list of criteria and the quality of the evidence differed. This aspect of the work clearly resulted from the fact that the same Research Team undertook all of this evaluation endeavour. Most of the participants at the public inquiry were prepared to offer evidence according to the same general format. Most people were prepared to criticize the Research Team's exercises in the same broad terms as the Research Team had themselves used and were anxious to present conflicting evidence of the same general kind for the Commission to use to form its view as to the desirability of the sites. It should be pointed out, however, that the Commission did make strong representations to those proposing to give evidence to it that it would look more favourably on that kind of evidence than on "negative critisism". Witnesses clearly had an incentive to comply with the Commission's wishes, although in our view this was desirable. Even those critics who found the exercises strained in their attempt to evaluate disparate items of advantage and disadvantages in common units of relative value were nevertheless of the opinion that physical measures of advantage and disadvantage on members of the community should be made.

The evidence produced was, in so far as it was possible to tell, comprehensive in its coverage. All costs and benefits resulting from the comparison of the 4 sites as envisaged were taken into account. Indeed, the public inquiry ensured that it was so, since had the Research Team overlooked certain items or certain evidence, the general public could bring that fact to the Commission's attention, and, indeed, for a few items, did this. Moreover the Research Team and others undertook fairly extensive sensitivity analysis on their findings, some of them according to the formally stated wishes of the Commission itself, especially in relation to assumptions about the contentious values of time spent travelling and noise-nuisance costs. Of

[16]CTLA, *Papers and Proceedings*, vol. VIII part 1, HMSO, London, 1970.

course, if much uncertainty exists for selected items one cannot be sure that the range over which the sensitivity analysis is conducted is wide enough. Nevertheless the Commission had before them the results not only of the Research Team's best estimates of cost and benefits (and also the best estimates of cost and benefits of other participants at the inquiry), but also estimates resulting from variations about those values. The evidence was about as extensive as it could have been, given the limitation pointed out earlier that fundamental research on some key issues had not been undertaken, or was inadequate for this purpose.

Accordingly, the recommendation made by the Commission could be based on fully comprehensive evidence on the social advantages and disadvantages of the alternatives. They were not limited to the findings of the Research Team since expert evidence was given at the inquiry which was also consistent with the Research Team's approach to the evaluation. It was then possible for the Commission to form their view as to the desirability of the alternatives, given this comprehensive evidence, and to submit that recommendation with the evidence to the Government.

The Government operates under constraints quite different from an independent Commission. It must take into account in its own decision, "the interests of a small group of politically important and wealthy people".[17] A Commission need not and most probably would not want to give such groups special weight in its own recommendation. It can give freer reign to its views on which alternatives are in the wider public interest. *A priori*, a government is far more likely to have a constrained and limited view of the public interest. Government as final decision-takers may also have disagreed with the Commission over the interpretation and reliability of evidence, and that could have led to a different view as to which was preferred. In this example the fact of the matter was that the Government did disagree with the majority of the Commission. To us this gives clear and substantial demonstration of the need for two requirements to be met by the end of a planning study. Firstly, the range of alternatives subjected to detailed investigation must be comparatively wide in scope. Secondly, comprehensive and essentially comprehensible evidence must be provided for people to appraise the alternatives for themselves. Both these requirements were met in the case of the CTLA.

11.3. SUMMARY OF FINDINGS

Many features of the site selection process adopted by the Roskill Commission were exemplary. Their approach has contributed greatly to the advancement of planning practice. There was clarity of purpose and procedure at each cycle, and each of the cycles represented a step in a logical progression towards the making of a recommendation. A consistency of methodological approach to the assessment of alternatives was maintained throughout the cycles, and that approach was itself

---

[17] A. A. Walters, Investment in airports and the economist's role. J. F. Kennedy International Airport: an example and some comparisons, in J. N. Wolfe (ed), *Cost Benefit and Cost Effectiveness: Studies and Analysis*, Allen & Unwin, London, 1973, p. 40.

commendably based on attempts to trace the full welfare consequences of proposals in the form of the CBA. Linkages between evaluation exercises and other aspects of the study, such as the initial generation of alternatives, the collection of data, and the decisions made to include alternatives at each subsequent cycle, were clear and well developed. The Commission did not find it necessary to take more time than they had originally intended to form their recommendation, thinking it important to keep to their time budget, and doing so despite the voluminous work load. In view of the breadth of material covered and the efficiency of the documentation of the study, this signifies the managerial competence of the Commission, its secretariat, and the Research Team.

Accordingly, finding fault with the Commission's process may seem somewhat invidious. Yet there are aspects of the Commission's process which deserve critical mention for their relevance to planning practice. Perhaps the most important is the principle which should guide the selection of alternatives at any one cycle for submission to the next cycle. At early stages, full information about the social consequences of proposals is not forthcoming. A strategy of selection must be adopted which attempts to minimize the risk of overlooking alternatives which, in the light of subsequent information, appear advantaged. Now there is no way we can know for sure which sorts of alternatives constitute the limits of the eventual distribution of alternatives by cost. Spatial variation in the development proposals are, in themselves, neither a cost nor a benefit. However, we may discover, or assume, that certain spatial variations are synonymous with interesting cost and benefit variations. This seems plausible. Indeed, the Commission's preliminary but undeveloped exercises with cost contours suggests they had a spatial conception of the problem. If that were so, we would be justified in criticizing the Commission for too rapidly focusing on alternatives within a comparatively narrow band of their region, from the north-west to the north-east and all at virtually similar distances from the centre of London. This they did at their very first cycle. True, estuarine sites were included, but they were the only sites which could be differentiated from the inland sites which, on the face of it, had similar locational characteristics.

Kitchen has expressed the view that too little time was devoted to the preliminary analysis of alternatives, and that the Commission limited its options too early on. Our view is that the Commission were right to move quickly to more detailed analyses of fewer alternatives but that the *range* of alternatives in spatial terms could have been wider. This point has relevance even at the short-listing stage. The Commission opted for three fairly close and, at that time, seemingly front-running alternatives in the inland sites, and only one "risk-averting" alternative in Foulness. In our view this was too soon to form a view on promising alternatives. The Commission should still have decided to include the widest range of options, keeping open possibilities in, say, the Essex Gap or nearer the Midlands. Their justifications for focusing on the inland sites at this stage could be expressed as the need to ensure they recommended a site close to the best site possible (the local optimum group) amongst the group of sites which were best (the global optimum group). Subject to the inclusion of Foulness in the short-list, they had prior to the short-list stage decided that a site broadly to the north of London at about 40 miles from the city centre would be the global optimum. Because of the necessarily limited range of evidence available at that stage, this view seems too premature even if subsequent evidence did justify it. Again, Kitchen's view is that too little time was devoted to the pre-short-listing stages. In our view the Commission's preferred course would have been to go on to iterate to a final recommendation after evaluation of the short-list. We would concur with Kitchen only if subsequent iteration were ruled out. We believe that a new search for alternatives in the light of the extensive evaluation of a few on the short-list is the best safeguard for ensuring that an alternative close to the true global optimum will be found. Naturally resurrection of a previously rejected alternative would have wide implications for public participation. It would require a reappraisal of the position of the public inquiry and would, of course, necessitate a restructuring of the allotted time and budget. Looking back would have added quite substantially to the overall time taken on the Study.

The Commission were able to identify early on most of the issues of measurement which were likely to prove contentious in the final reckoning. Noise costs, displacement costs, amenity losses, defence, and the nature of the surface access demand were amongst them. For some items the Research Team were able to undertake pioneering research work, albeit limited by the time available. For others, like defence, the Commission were able to obtain new insights into the interference that the airport operations might cause. But so much controversy raged at the final public inquiry about some items, especially the value of time spent by passengers travelling to the airport and noise nuisance, that it is doubtful whether the Research Team gave adequate attention to verifying the estimates obtained for inclusion in their CBA.

Yet we may argue forever about the results of the evaluation exercises; indeed, it is in part the function of evaluation to stimulate controversy about alternatives. But it is important that the alternatives which are subjected to evaluation, and to public participation, should be generated in such a way that we are reasonably sure that we have a set which is the best of the possibilities which may be considered. It is also important to ensure that the evidence collected is relevant to the comparisons between alternatives in that it is comprehensive and incorporates the very best of recent research into community preferences. Subject to the points we have made about the coarse evaluation procedures and the lack of a check by the Commission on the overall desirability of its preferred option from the full range of alternatives considered, the Commission's site-selection process should in our view be considered as a pioneer of advanced planning practice.

PART III

Implications for Planning Procedures

Introduction

PRINCIPLES and practical considerations of two topics have dominated our discussions: the organization and management of particular planning studies and the assessments of alternative planning options. Principles were discussed in Part I. Practicalities were investigated in our inspection of case studies in Part II. In this final part we try to bring together our main findings. We do this by focusing on what, in our view, has been desirable practice and what has been misguided or wasted effort. From examples illustrating desirable planning practice we are able to formulate recommended procedures for the management of future studies. Part III is composed of one chapter.

CHAPTER 12

Recommendations for Short-listing Procedures and the Assessment of Options

THIS chapter is divided into three main parts. Principles and guidelines for the short-listing of options are followed by a discussion of the influence of various practical circumstances which affect the planning process. A concluding section offers some final recommendations about the organization and structure of the planning process, and the nature and role of evaluation within it.

12.1. SHORT-LISTING PROCEDURES

Planning decisions must involve the explicit consideration of alternatives. The planning process leading to the decision should result in a set of "good" or "interesting" alternatives for detailed investigation and debate at the short-list stage, arrived at in an efficient manner. The aim is to reduce the universe of possibilities to these few interesting ones as cheaply as possible. Time and effort devoted to designing and evaluating alternatives that are actually inferior should obviously be minimal. The difficulty lies in ensuring that the preferred alternatives are not unwittingly omitted from the short-list while not including the "uninteresting" ones. A balance between keeping a range of options open at successive cycles and the effort of detailing and evaluating those options must be correctly maintained.

Whatever the planning problem, a countless number of possible options exist. In practice, planning teams typically consider up to about a hundred distinct alternatives in their preliminary investigations. This seems to be sufficient to cover distinguishing characteristics between feasible alternatives. Not all undertake formal definition of each essentially different alternative, even in crude terms; for instance, the Notts–Derby Team initially considered twenty-one generalized population and employment distributions, and the Irvine Team considered only six outline plans in the first cycle. But those which did, such as the Grangemouth/Falkirk Study Team and the Commission on the Third London Airport (CTLA), appeared to find no advantage in investigating more than a hundred options.

Most studies worked towards a final short-list, normally of three or four. Some investigations went beyond the evaluation of the short-listed alternatives. The Notts–Derby and West Midland Regional Study teams went on to iterate, respectively, to a further one and to several superior alternatives.

Whether or not the study teams identified a large number of alternatives representing, for all practical purposes, their selection from the universe of options, or a smaller number of crude alternatives representing their starting point, they had to decide how to reduce the options. This seemed to involve two different kinds of problem with which we will deal in turn: how to choose between the various options and how wide to keep the range of options in so doing.

On the first point there seemed to be a large number of possible approaches which ranged between two extremes. The first was successive reduction by a cyclical process. This approach needed a decision on the number of cycles to adopt between the starting point and the short-list, and on the allocation of time and resources in these cycles and in each of the intermediate stages of the planning process.

The other approach is a successive re-definition of one basic option, or possibly of a few widely different options, by marginal adjustments towards the apparently preferred-of-all possibilities. Such a process also involves cycles and management decisions about their number and the time and resources for each. None of our case studies illustrated this kind of planning process in its pure form, although the Irvine and part of the West Midland studies come closest. The Irvine Study demonstrated an attempt which used a linear programming optimization model, with an objective function based on concepts of social costs and benefits. If the model had been used as a tool capable of producing the preferred option directly, only one cycle would have been required (although that would conceal the number of stages used in the optimizing algorithm). However, the model was used in a restricted way, primarily for evaluating a limited range of plans.

Marginal adjustments to a basic design were used in the latter four cycles of the West Midland Regional Study. Having determined an essentially good design solution, according to their particular criteria, from a wide range of alternatives to a short-list of four, the Study Team then reverted to this second type of process of successive incremental movements towards a preferred alternative.

It is not really surprising that the latter planning process was less attractive to planning teams than that of successive elimination (and greater design detailing) of a range of alternatives. A process of adjustment to a basic design will be efficient only when the study team are confident that they have a fair starting design, one which would be close to the eventual choice if all possibilities were open and known to the decision-takers. This will only be the case for studies with antecedents involving much information-gathering and the creation of general expertise. Possibly it will not be tenable even then. Normally it will only be used at the concluding cycles of a study.

It is necessary, moreover, to take into account the distinction which we have stressed between decision-*makers* and decision-*takers*. The decision-makers are the individuals and groups who are able to influence the decision. This, potentially at least, includes any member of the general public in most major planning decisions. The decision-takers are those with responsibility for the decision. Decision-makers will have widely divergent preferences and will attempt to convince decision-takers of the virtues of these. The debate leading up to the decision requires a short-list of options. If only one option is available, or a group of essentially very similar options, then there can be no useful debate, and an essential obligation of the planning team, to increase public awareness and participation in the decision, will not have been met. Unless most feasible courses of action are considered formally at some time during the plan-making process, we cannot be confident that the best alternative, which would be our ultimate choice, has not been excluded.

In discussing the Irvine New Town Study (Chapter 10), several further objections were raised to this "special case" of an incremental search for superior options, using an optimization procedure, such as linear programming. There is the problem of specifying an appropriate social welfare function. This is fraught with conceptual difficulties, the most intractable of which concern the incorporation of equity considerations. The planner as an analyst or technician can offer no conclusion on the relative importance of changes in the well-being of different groups in society, and so far no acceptable general method of discovering decision-takers' views on equity matters has been devised. Hence we do not know how to value alternative distributions of gain and loss in terms of some social welfare function. In addition, an enormous amount of data is generally required, relating to socio-economic and physical characteristics of the study area, the kinds of advantages and disadvantages which will be associated with alternatives, and community preferences. The costs of collecting these data are likely to be great. In some cases it may also prove impossible to obtain reliable evidence on the values placed on certain items of advantage and disadvantage by those potentially affected. These items will therefore have to be specified as constraints in the model if they are to be included at all. The generated solution will then be optimal only if the constraints have been fixed at the level where the costs of transgress are just greater than (or equal to) the benefits to be realized. Finally, there are the costs associated with the actual search for the preferred solution. In complex planning problems the advent of computers has enabled these costs to be kept within feasible limits, but they are still likely to take up a sizeable proportion of the study budget.

Regarding the manner in which study teams have reduced the numbers of alternatives down to a short-list of three or four, two essentially different approaches emerged when we considered the case studies in Part II. On the one hand, the teams tried to maintain a wide range of options throughout the cycles. For example, the Notts–Derby and West Midland study teams both kept options in their short-list which were almost as far apart in terms of their spatial and welfare differences as the extremes on their initial list. In contrast, the CTLA approached the short-list by trying to focus on the most likely area of search for the preferred option (according to their own choice criteria). Three of their four short-listed options were close together in both spatial and welfare terms and, hopefully, close to their global optimum—their choice if all relevant facts were known. Only the fourth and widely different alternative, Foulness, was available to test the desirability of the other three.

The Notts–Derby Team started with 21 basically different alternatives, and the CTLA with 78. Each then had two subsequent cycles to the short-list: Notts–Derby from 21 options to 6 and then to 3; CTLA from 78 sites on their long-list to the medium-list (of 29 initially and then 15 possible sites) and then to the 4 on the short-list. In neither case were alternatives rejected outright; indeed, both teams re-introduced rejected alternatives as new information came to light. Both left open the possibility of generating new options at any of the cycles. They specified and evaluated options in greater detail and precision in moving from one cycle to the next. There is little point in attempting precise and detailed evaluation of broad outline plans, for logically the results can only be used to indicate their approximate worth in terms of objective achievements. Similarly, in order to avoid unnecessary design effort, the use of coarse and fine evaluation techniques should be accompanied by increased detail of the designs.

The main distinction was that in the case of the CTLA it was not intended to proceed with a cycle or cycles of generation and evaluation after the short-list, whilst the Notts–Derby Team did intend to iterate to their recommended option after the short-list evaluations. Accordingly, the latter were not required to find the general "locality" of their preferred option prior to short-listing; they could put most of their evaluation effort into the short-list cycle, confident of subsequently finding the best plan (in their view). The CTLA's approach required them to be confident that one of the short-listed options was the best, or at any rate very nearly so, of all possibilities (again, in their view). This meant that in order to distinguish between the initial set of 78 alternatives, the Study's principal evaluation effort must precede the short-listing cycle. The evaluation of the short-list would therefore focus sharply on detailed differences between three essentially very similar options.

The Notts–Derby Team were bringing together both types of planning process— that of successive elimination of options and that of marginal adjustment in moving from one cycle to the next. Combining these two approaches clearly had important implications for the work to be undertaken at each cycle in their process and the types of alternatives considered, and also for the time and resources devoted to particular activities of plan generation and evaluation.

In our view this approach of the Notts–Derby Team, which was also employed by the West Midland Team, is the most appropriate one if practical circumstances (to be discussed below) allow it. The study team must submit a range of alternatives for debate; this they do with their short-list plus any subsequent alternatives which they then generate. Yet the study team must convince themselves that the option put forward as their own recommendation is the one which is, in their view, the best in the interest of the community at large. By iterating to a preferred option the main evaluation effort may be left to a late stage in the planning process, the short-listing stage, when the fullest range of data and evidence about the options has been assembled. Only with this evidence can the study team be confident in assessing the overall desirability of the strategies it may generate. In contrast, in the CTLA Study the short-list had to contain the desired global optimum alternative, or one very close to it. Any subsequent search for a better alternative was ruled out. In the case of the Notts–Derby Study, the short-list had to contain alternatives which were each quite different and each, in some respects, close to a local optimum alternative. The true global optimum from the Team's viewpoint could be found after the collection of detailed evidence about the welfare effects of all these short-listed proposals.

There is a further managerial requirement of some importance in studies like that of the CTLA, where there will be no post short-listing iteration. Proportionally less time is available for preliminary cycles and data gathering, and the study team must embark on the final cycle at about the middle phase of its deliberations. In contrast, where subsequent iteration is possible the final design and evaluation cycle need not be reached until the virtual termination of the study. Since the maximum amount of information about the welfare effects of options will inevitably be available at this concluding stage, the CTLA's position is clearly the more risky; their choice must be made from eggs in only one basket.

12.2. CIRCUMSTANCES AFFECTING THE CHOICE BETWEEN PLAN-MAKING STRATEGIES

Study teams are not completely free to decide on their planning processes and the organization of their studies. They are externally constrained in practice, e.g. by the institutional environment of their study, and particularly by the nature of the decision-making arrangements. In some cases decision-takers may work in consultation with the study team and directly influence the planning process, whilst in others their presence may only be latent until the conclusions of the exercise. The approach will be influenced to the extent that the terms of reference dictate the broad kinds of alternatives to be made available to the decision-takers at the study conclusions. It will be affected by the level of decision-making involved, e.g. if high-level policy decisions which are effectively unalterable impinge on design possibilities. Some of the options are closed if a final public inquiry is to be held.

In addition there are technical matters to consider, including manpower resources, the financial and time budgets, and the familiarity of the team with the type of problem or the study area.

We now consider these issues in the light of the case studies and try to draw some general conclusions.

The Institutional Environment

The study team's terms of reference will define the study boundaries and constraints. In the case of the CTLA the terms of reference went further, and specified that social cost–benefit analysis techniques were to be used in assessing alternative sites.

To what extent should study teams be bound by the terms of reference? The CTLA case is illustrative. Many observers thought that the search for and timing of a four-runway airport site was an incorrect specification of the real problem. The first task, in this view, was to draw up a supra-plan, a National Airports Plan, within which a new four-runway airport might or might not fit. Others felt that the given terms of reference were too constraining in defining the problem as one of searching for a site to cater for the growth of traffic using existing airports serving the London area. We saw, in Chapter 11, that the Commission certainly interpreted this aspect of their terms of reference widely and looked at sites well outside the Region. But the issue remained of whether the right problem was being investigated.

Clearly the study team has at the outset to be reasonably convinced of the suitability of the terms of reference. If there is strong feeling that they are incorrectly or inadequately specified, then the study may not get off the ground. But in general this issue will not come to a head until some information about possible options and their effects has been collected. We can see no objection, in cases where a team feel they are unnecessarily and unduly constrained by the directives given, to asking the client to justify them. If they are unsatisfied with the response, the team could usefully point out the implications of adhering to the constraints set by deliberately overriding them in generating and evaluating some of their initial alternatives. The evidence produced by evaluation of the social costs of the constraints could then be presented to the client for consideration.

The Brighton Study provides an instance of testing a higher-level policy constraint. The South Downs were designated as a conservation area in the Government-endorsed *Strategic Plan for the South East*. One of the strategies formulated by the Brighton Team involved large-scale displacement of Downland by residential and commercial developments. The comparative advantages and disadvantages of this alternative were then assessed (although these assessments were not based on concepts of social costs and benefits).

Another instance of the assessment of the opportunity costs of a constraint is provided by the West Midland Team, although the constraint in this case was not formally specified. The Team were not instructed to keep substantial urban development proposals clear of the designated Green Belt around the West Midland Conurbation (which had no statutory force at the time). Nonetheless here, as well as in other regions, there was a strong presumption that the Green Belt should be kept largely free from major new developments. Yet the Team chose to design some alternatives with developments in the Green Belt area, and one of the options explicitly considered was a highly concentrated one. Their intention was to assess the social costs (if any) of the Green Belt "constraint". They were free to do this and, it must be supposed, were wise to do so since their eventual preferred strategy did incorporate a number of proposals located on the periphery of the Conurbation. It was for the decision-takers then to assess the evidence supporting these proposals, which departed from the presumption of Green Belt preservation.

In our view it is acceptable to assess the "shadow prices" of such constraints. Obviously, only a small part of the planning effort can be devoted to the design and evaluation of plans which consciously breach constraints, but it may prove instructive to know what we forego in restricting ourselves to predetermined areas of search. This situation can arise where proposals depend substantially upon decisions made, or about to be made, on other plans or policies either at a higher or lower level. Circumstances may dictate that studies are carried out in this untidy way. For example, the West Midland and Coventry–Solihull–Warwickshire (C–S–W) studies were undertaken at broadly similar times and covered planning problems which were highly interdependent, since the latter Study was concerned at a sub-regional scale with issues that the former was considering at the regional level.

The way the study is to be concluded is important in deciding how to structure the planning process. Three main possibilities emerged from our investigation of case studies. The study may effectively finish with a public inquiry, which debates a short-list, as in the case of the Third London Airport. Having heard all the evidence on the alternatives, including that produced by its own Research Team, the Commission then proceeded to consider the options' relative merits. It published its recommendation, together with all the points made for and against the options by the various participants at the inquiry, for the decision-takers to arrive at their choice. Most of the structure-plan studies will similarly conclude the phases prior to decision-taking with an examination in public.

Alternatively, the study may simply finish with the publication of the study documents, which may contain the study team's own stated preference. In this situation the study team has no way of knowing how members of the public view its preference apart from any opinions obtained as evidence at the evaluation stage. The C–S–W and Grangemouth/Falkirk studies had this type of conclusion, both teams disbanding on publication of the documents. The debate then necessarily continues in an unstructured and informal way, and the decision-takers must obtain the views of various interested parties as best they may.

A third possibility is that the study team invite comment and criticism from the public without being obliged formally to defend their work. We encountered two varieties of this in the West Midland and the Notts–Derby studies. At the end of its short-listing deliberations and the iteration to a preferred alternative, the West Midland Team published its various documents including a short "popular" version of the main report. Instead of holding an inquiry, the Team invited comments on its proposals from anyone or any body interested. Comments were received from over a hundred different sources, mainly in writing. During the interim period the Team conducted their own further work. Their efforts, plus the evidence provided by these comments, were used to generate a final preferred strategy, which was published about a year later than the previous documents. The decision-takers are then in a position to consider this alternative in the light of public comment on all the short-listed and subsequent alternatives. In this way the study team can clearly obtain public reaction to their designs without the intense scrutiny which a public inquiry affords, if carried out in the manner of the CTLA. But it must also be accepted that the comment received may not be as thorough or perceptive as that obtained under formal inquiry conditions, with the possibility of intensive examination of witnesses.

A similar procedure was adopted by the Brighton Urban Structure Plan Team.

Following publication of their main study documents and detailed recommendations, they invited comments from any interested persons or organizations. But, in addition to a general invitation to comment, the Team distributed a questionnaire which sought the public's views on any matter relating to the proposed plan. Further commendable features were the use of exhibition techniques to put across the proposals and the use of local radio to obtain publicity and public reaction. When this public participation exercise is completed, the Team will make any necessary modifications before submitting their proposals to the Secretary of State.

Of these three types of conclusion, the public inquiry presents special difficulties for the team. An inquiry such as that at stage V of the procedures of the CTLA is not meant merely to be a vehicle for the receipt of ideas and suggestions from the public. This could only be true of the partial participation exercises of the West Midland Team. The function of an inquiry is to go deeper and to involve the public in the final recommendation subjecting all the options to detailed scrutiny. Accordingly, if the study team, following such an inquiry, were to use its evidence to generate one or more subsequent alternatives, then logically these too should be the subject of an equally intensive scrutiny. The prospect of two (or more?) inquiries per study, both lengthy and expensive to prepare and to run, is daunting. So the prospect of a closing public inquiry may effectively rule out any subsequent work on the search for even better alternatives than those on the short-list. Moreover, the expense involved may even lead to a smaller number of alternatives for the short-list as compared with the number that the study team could themselves generate and evaluate.

Where there is to be a fairly extensive public inquiry without any further searches for better options, the implication for the planning process is that the alternatives on it should already have been subjected to greater detail of investigation than otherwise. As was the case with the CTLA, the study team must be even more confident that one of the alternatives will be their global optimum. This requirement, coupled with the probable necessity for fewer options on the short-list than the study team might conceivably manage to analyse in the absence of an inquiry, presents a serious difficulty. They require more than one option in the locality of their global optimum because they are not sure, prior to the inquiry, which one will eventually be preferred. They also have to put on the short-list quite different alternatives from those in the region of their preferred options in order to promote the debate and to allow for possible disagreement over the virtues of their own choice. The public inquiry requires many alternatives, some close to the study team's global optimum and some further afield, if the result of the debate is to be sensible and yet concerned with only a few options.

If iteration to a preferred alternative is feasible after the short-listing stage (which will normally be the case when no public inquiry is required, but also if sufficient time is available), then the main evaluation effort can be reserved for the short-list. Otherwise the evaluation must be sufficiently thorough prior to short-listing to ensure that the main distinguishing characteristics of groups of alternatives are already identified. The West Midland Team were able to maintain a wide range of options on their short-list without substantive evaluation at their preliminary and coarse-options cycles because they could go on to design better options still at later cycles. This gave them the best chance to assemble good evidence of social advantages and disadvantages, since evaluation was to come relatively late in their process. In comparison, the C–S–W Team were not able to undertake design work after their short-list, possibly because their Study was of shorter duration than that affecting the Region as a whole. In their planning process alternatives were reduced from forty-two in number to four, from which they selected their recommended option. To this extent they must have been less sure than the Regional Study Team that their recommendation was the best of all (or most) design possibilities.

But these two studies exemplify a related management issue, that of giving attention to evaluation early on in the planning process. The C–S–W Team gave considerable attention at the outset of their work to the definition, physical measurement, and relative valuation of the objectives for the strategy, which was carried out before embarking on design. They then incorporated their evaluation criteria and measures into the design process. As a result, each of their designs should by intention have shown advantages on selected criteria. Complete evaluation was still necessary because not all evaluation criteria can be fully taken into account in design, and objectives interact and conflict in complex and often unforeseen ways in the design process. But the essential advantages and disadvantages of their options should have been known to the Team in a formal, even quantified, way prior to their evaluation. This was not the case with the West Midland Team. They started with all possible design solutions (or a very large number of them), and whittled them down in number whilst maintaining their range of difference in spatial terms with only an intuitive understanding for the relative merits of options. They then used the evaluation at the short-list to provide information on the relative merits of these options.

Clearly the C–S–W approach is the more efficient. This Team was able to retain a full understanding of the implications of their designs throughout, whilst the West Midland Team were far less certain of the virtues of their options until the short-list evaluation. Nevertheless, in our view the West Midland Team's planning process was superior in going on to a better option than the best on the short-list through a process of iteration. Given time, the C–S–W Team could also have iterated to a better alternative. Their task would then have been easier than that of the West Midland Team since of options on their short-list they should have had one much closer to the best of all possibilities than did the West Midland Team.

A final external consideration to be discussed, and one which will affect the nature of the study team's planning process, is the role of the decision-takers. We have assumed so far that the study team is free to get on with the job of providing decision-takers with a set of alternatives with the comparative advantages tested, possibly with a recommendation. This applies when decision-takers or commissioning agents are genuinely interested in an independent team taking a fresh look at an old problem or exploring possible solutions to a new problem. This was true of the CTLA, if we consider the Commission and its entire Research Team as "The Team", and the Government as the commissioning organization. It seemed also to be the case for the C–S–W Team, who in their final report do not mention decision-takers as entering the planning process and where they had no involvement in the Study as far as we are aware. In this case the Study was probably motivated by a need to resolve conflicting opinions about future developments in the Sub-region, the decision-takers wanting the Team to be free to consider all possible policy options independently.

However, this lack of decision-taking involvement is by no means the norm. Many studies have either formal steering committees or *ad hoc* consultations with decision-takers. In the Brighton Study decision-takers entered the planning process at a number of stages, especially at the conclusion of each cycle. In this case the Team needed to decide the nature of the alternatives to be submitted for further consideration at the next cycle, and were obliged to agree these alternatives with the decision-takers. This approach is advantageous if the team can obtain a better impression of the kind of alternatives likely to be favoured by the decision-takers, which can then be among those included in the short list. It can also help to establish how the results of evaluation exercises should be presented.

But dangers arise from such involvement if it risks the exclusion of some kinds of alternatives because they may not appeal to the decision-takers; such alternatives may appeal to other groups in the community. As we have repeatedly stressed, we believe that study teams have professional obligations which on occasion extend beyond the particular interests of their commissioning bodies. A variety of interesting alternatives should enter the debate even if some are included which decision-takers may wish to suppress. Obviously, this requirement can sometimes make it difficult for a study team to preserve its independence.

It is our impression that the involvement of decision-takers in the planning process is likely to be less helpful to study teams the more informal and disguised are the arrangements and contacts, unless decision-takers happen to be as keen as the professionals to see an independent study undertaken. If decision-takers, who may themselves be in conflict on major policy issues, are able to obstruct or bring strong pressure to bear on the study team informally, the result will inevitably be a poor mix of strategies on the short-list or heavy delays in producing a short-list.

In the Grangemouth/Falkirk Study decision-takers did play a necessary role in what was a slightly unusual planning process. The Team worked on outline plans early on. Agreement was reached with the decision-takers as to the best broad plan to adopt. The subsequent part of the planning process involved the detailing of this option. Essentially two planning studies were concentrated into one.

Once the decision-takers have completed their task, one or other of the proposals has then to be implemented. We then move into stages 10 and 11 of the generalized planning process (Chapter 2), of plan implementation and review of planned developments through time. It does not seem to be material to the planning process whether these tasks are the responsibility, wholly or in part, of the study team undertaking the studies leading to the decision, as with the Notts–Derby and West Midland teams which stayed in existence, or is left to others, as in the case of the C–S–W and Grangemouth/Falkirk teams.

Familiarity with the Problem

The greater the familiarity with the problem at hand, and thereby the greater the expertise of the study team, other things equal, the less the time and resources required for initial surveillance. There are three aspects to this: familiarity with the types of planning issues; familiarity with the study area; and the quality of the research base to be used for generating evidence on the relative merits of alternatives.

The Third London Airport Study provides a good example. There was little previous evidence on the wider social costs and benefits of major new airport developments which could be used. A considerable amount of research and investigation was called for. To some extent the problem itself was novel. While there had been a long history of searches for sites, the manner of the search was new, for the evidence on alternatives had to be comprehensive. The study area was reasonably well known to airport investigators, but the research base on key issues of measurement was of mixed quality. Some items, such as the construction costs and air traffic control considerations, were well and expertly researched. Others, such as the accessibility of passengers to and from the airports in the possible airport systems, were only partly researched and partly lacking in a research base. Accessibility models of a number of types were readily available to the Team, even if these models had not been explicitly applied to airport systems. Travel cost parameters were more suspect, especially for the value of time lost in travelling, and the Team eventually relied on values generated by researches into predominantly commuting behaviour. Other items had been very poorly researched or no evidence existed at all; these items included the costs to residents of displacement at the airport sites and of noise nuisance in the vicinity of the sites. Here the Team found it necessary to undertake its own research studies.

With fairly novel problems it will be necessary to explore initially a wide variety of different possibilities—seventy-eight initial options in the CTLA case. Even when both the type of study and the study area itself are reasonably well-known, a wide range of initial options may be needed if the research base is poor. This was so in the West Midland Regional Study, which considered over a hundred diagrammatic variants of possible options initially. It is clearly sensible for the team to investigate all extreme solutions during the initial cycle of plan-making.

Familiarity with the problem and the ease of assembly of sound evidence on the relative merits of options will affect the speed of producing a short-list. Despite our observations above about the research base for some items, the Commission and Research Team in the Airport case thought themselves reasonably sure of the quality of the evidence for the critical items to produce a short-list after only eight months of their thirty-month study. Despite this speed they still needed to reduce options from seventy-eight in number to four on the short list, indicating a good deal of initial uncertainty. Clearly this was dispelled by the rapid receipt of information on key items of cost as the Study proceeded.

The greater the body of previous experience and research, the less the time that needs to be devoted to the early scanning and understanding of widely different alternatives. We have seen in the United Kingdom over the past decade a number of regional and sub-regional planning studies, some of which we have reviewed here. Future studies can draw on the experiences gained in these exercises. We now know a lot more about the interaction of accessibility benefits and congestion costs in large city-regions than at the outset, and the importance to many members of the community of high levels of accessibility. The main implications of concentration and dispersal as policies for the locations of populations and employment activities are now quite well understood.

Does the nature of the planning proposals have any influence on the planning process? We have in mind here the distinction between an individual project such as an airport and a development plan such as produced by a sub-regional study. (Sometimes this distinction is blurred, as in the case of the design of a new town.) In the case of an individual project there are three main elements to the decision: what kind of facilities to provide, where to locate them, and when to go ahead. In the case of a development plan, the team are dealing with a set of projects which will be functionally interrelated, often in complex ways. An additional dimension to the problem is thereby introduced. In the studies we have considered, teams working on development plans have simplified their tasks by assuming away one or more of the plan elements; either the precise nature of the developments, e.g. in terms of common house types and densities as between different locations, or in the scale or timing of developments, e.g. by considering ways of locating fixed totals of population and employment or assessing alternatives into the future without giving much attention to the accuracy of the phasing of developments over time.

However, the *approach* to systematic elimination of alternatives or to incremental improvements to a basic design does not seem to be affected by the nature of the proposals. True, the elements of the basic designs to be marginally adjusted for improvement will differ. The main element of the basic design of a major project like an airport will be location. At each possible fixed site area detailed refinements will take place—for example, through runway realignments, adjustments in locating associated urban development, and different operating procedures. Marginal adjustments to a development plan, such as that of the West Midland Study, will, because of interactions between design elements, involve simultaneous alterations in the locations of populations, employment activities, and concomitant developments. But there seem to be no important differences between types of planning proposals when organizing the planning process.

Resources Available for the Study

Clearly the size of the team's budget will influence the quality of the plan-making exercise and affect the amount of expertise that can be employed, the extent to which use can be made of data processing facilities, and research and information gathering. These constraints will critically affect the scope and depth of analysis of alternatives. With a small budget it may still be feasible to explore a large number of possibilities, but of necessity the designs may have to be very coarse and the evaluation measures crude. There is thus a danger that the findings of the evaluation exercises, particularly in the early cycles, may be misleading, and decisions about which alternatives to eliminate based on unreliable information.

An illustration is provided by the Notts–Derby Study, where the planners had to work within a very modest budget. It was one of the earliest sub-regional studies carried out in this country; the Team had very little in the way of relevant previous work to guide them. Four cycles of plan-making were undertaken, the initial concern being to explore as many different types of alternatives as could usefully be handled. In order to help to generate contrasting alternatives, members of the Team were asked to design options on the basis of a number of different concepts. As a result twenty-one coarse, wide-ranging alternatives were put forward for evaluation. Although these formed a small sub-set of the universe of possibilities (even at a low level of detail), they seem to have been sufficiently widely spaced for initial exploration. Designs in the second cycle were guided by the earlier evaluation findings. Here an interesting short-cut was used to enable the investigation of numerous issues thought to be of major importance. Each alternative was comprised of a set of proposals, relating to various issues, but the mix of proposals was deliberately kept unconstrained by considerations of internal consistency (or mutual compatibility), and the interactions between different proposals were therefore ignored. Following evaluation, some of the more promising proposals were then selected and, after some modifications were made to them, were combined to form three strategies proper for the short-list. The Team were unable to consider as many alternatives as they would have liked at this short-list stage, and so focused attention again on widely differing options. Finally, the recommended strategy was formed by combining elements from the three on the short-list.

The Notts–Derby illustration may be contrasted with the C–S–W Team's experience. Their time budget was also very tight. They were conscious of the need to restrict their work load to reasonable proportions by refraining from highly experimental and adventurous design and evaluation work. Accordingly, they did not attempt to trace the incidence of the social costs and benefits of their proposals whilst recognizing that, with more time, this would be a useful evaluation exercise for decision-making. They also rejected the use of expensive modelling procedures for detailing their strategies. But they did start from the viewpoint that the principles and measures used to assess designs should also be used, as far as was practicable, to help with their generation. Although time was short, they used much of it at the outset in devising their planning process, in particular their approach to evaluation and attention to consistency of effort between plan generation and evaluation. Their planning process was remarkably efficient in this respect.

Efficient as their procedure was, the C–S–W Team had no cycles after short-listing. Similarly, the CTLA, who had a very tight time, if not money, budget could have no cycles after short-listing without substantially more time. The West Midland Regional Study Team, by way of contrast, did have four cycles after the short-list. (Although their study lasted two years longer than that of the CTLA, and longer than the budgeted time, not all of that extra time was due to subsequent cycles.)

Where time and financial resources are severely restricted, and especially where little is known about the problem at the outset, it would seem that subsequent cycles to the short-list are the phases of the planning process that can most readily be dispensed with. These cycles are time-consuming and, if the study team are reasonably confident about options on the short-list, become a luxury. They involve searching at the margin for an alternative which is better than those on the short-list. If resources are severely limited the study team may not have been able to collect sufficiently fine evidence to distinguish in welfare terms between marginal variations on a basic design. Accordingly, the design alternatives which are considered should be widely divergent. If the approach of the C–S–W Team is followed, and evaluation criteria and measures are largely determined in advance of design, then the study team will have some understanding of the essential differences between the designs. They may end up with a short-list which does not contain the plan which is their global optimum, the one they would choose if they had all the information they could ever require at their disposal. But it should contain an alternative in the region of their global optimum and other plans which are also near the preferred options of groups with an interest in the decision.

12.3. SOME FINAL RECOMMENDATIONS

We have tried to relate our observations of planning throughout this book to the practical world of studies. Our observations on principles in Part I were made with our own awareness of the practical difficulties involved. Part II was concerned with identifying approaches of various planning teams, the way they have organized their planning process, and in particular with the work they carried out on evaluation. We have tried to show where, in the light of general principles set down in Part I, we think they went wrong and where they exhibited sound and advanced practice. In Part III we have tried to bring together some of these main themes, principally by comparing the activities of study teams. Suggestions and recommendations have therefore emerged at a number of places in the text. It would be quite inappropriate to assemble them all here. But in a few pages we try to summarize the main ones.

Our case studies exemplify both poor and commendable practice in the use of evaluation within the planning process and in the quality of the evaluation exercises themselves. The C–S–W and CTLA teams are to be commended on a number of grounds. Both teams started their deliberations by thinking about how they would assess differences between the designs that they would subsequently generate. They set down the principles by which differences were to be identified, and attempted to focus on what seemed likely to be the most important items of difference and on possible ways of approaching the task of their measurement. Both attempted consistency in their approaches to plan generation and plan assessment by generating plans based, as far as practicable, on information that would be systematically used to compare them.

Two practical problems prevent such complete integration of design and evaluation criteria. Firstly, we cannot always know what will be the most important items for consideration in plan evaluation, since differences between plans are not fully known until after possible options have been designed. Secondly, we cannot use measures to aid design at the outset if the first step is to collect evidence and assemble information to help with the evaluation. Such evidence will become more comprehensive and reliable as the study proceeds. Hence in both the CTLA and C–S–W studies some "intuitive" design work was inevitable at the start, guided by whatever early information was available, and then by the later information that was rapidly generated in subsequent cycles.

Other study teams started their endeavours with design. The West Midland Team, somewhat like the CTLA, started by identifying in crude or diagrammatic terms their "universe" of possibilities. We believe this approach to be acceptable, indeed desirable, so long as only very limited resources and attention are given to the design exercise. But the West Midland Team were, in our view, open to criticism in not also giving preliminary regard to the evaluation of options. Indeed, this was not given serious attention until the short-listed cycle. This inevitably lengthened the Study, the full implications of the designs being unknown until that late stage. In comparison, many of the important implications of airport sites at various locations in the southern half of Britain were known to the CTLA by the end of their first cycle. Virtually all of them were known prior to short-listing.

Of the cases we considered only the planners on the Irvine Study used a technique aimed at fully integrating design and evaluation, namely a linear programming model. This model was not used for optimization purposes. We are not sure if this was due to the money and time involved in making it fully operational, or whether there was doubt about its conceptual suitability.

All of the teams engaged in our case studies saw evaluation as the activity of comparing alternatives and providing information for the choice between them. However, they disagreed as to the type of information that was needed. Some, such as the Brighton Team, did not have welfare gains for the community explicitly in mind. In that Study five of the fifteen objectives could be identified as planning policies. Accordingly it is difficult, if not impossible, to draw conclusions from the evaluations or even to interpret the evaluation findings. There are no satisfactory measures of the achievement of planning policies without prior identification of which groups in society are going to gain or lose by them, and by how much, relative to other gains or losses.

Others, such as the Notts–Derby and the C–S–W teams, used objectives in their evaluations which could, possibly with some effort, be interpreted as sectoral objectives. That is, they were attempts to specifically identify ways in which members of society would be made better or worse off by the planning proposals. This is clear and logical in its approach. And yet the effort devoted to establishing evidence of the amount of benefit or loss was minimal. In the C–S–W example the Team, like those at Brighton, used a questionnaire to survey opinion of a small sample of existing residents. Both teams rejected the use of other evidence of community preferences. Their questionnaires were not comprehensive in covering population groups likely to be affected by proposals or in terms of the types of effects to be analysed. Indeed, the C–S–W Team realized that their survey of public opinion did little to help them or the decision-takers, and placed more reliance on their own views of the nature of community preferences. They fell back on their own judgements of the way in which objectives would be measured and, perhaps even more critically, of how they would be weighted, one objective relative to all others on their list.

In our view this is a quite unacceptable way to proceed with evaluation. It is perhaps legitimate to use professional judgement without formal evidence at the conclusion of the first cycle of the planning process, when formal evidence may be thin on the ground. But even in these circumstances this judgement may easily give an incorrect impression of the merits of options and may lead the team to make early decisions which could prove expensive later. There is no doubt that professional judgement is a way of providing "usable" results; it is easy to get something down on paper. Our concern, however, is with the quality of those results. To rely on professional judgement is to take the easy way out of a difficult problem, and one that must be faced up to. There are no grounds for supposing that planners, or any other group, can know the strengths of others' preferences, unless that knowledge is based on evidence, preferably hard evidence. This being so, the evidence should be set down for decision-takers to see. It is rarely incontrovertible: some may give it a different interpretation from others, some may believe it to be less reliable than others. Differences of opinion are bound to occur, especially for major planning issues. In the case of the C–S–W and Brighton studies no reliable empirical evidence was produced, and so it was impossible to debate the validity of the weights used by the teams.

In the C–S–W case the Team normalized all their physical measures of objectives on to a zero–hundred scale and then applied their weights to these scores in a grand evaluation matrix. The result was that the numbers in the matrix appear to lose all meaning to the reader. It becomes too difficult to discern why one plan is featuring better than another in the assessments, and therefore to judge the reasonableness of the results. Debate about the relative merits of options is stifled because one is unable to see a way through the assessments that the Team have made.

By way of contrast, the approach of the CTLA, as we have already noted, was exemplary. All their evidence on relative merits of their proposals was obtained from observation of behaviour and surveys of attitudes of the community; they did not use weights arrived at by hunch or guesswork, although they did, of course, have to interpret the evidence which they assembled. Like the Brighton and C–S–W teams they carried out some social survey work. The CTLA surveys were designed to provide evidence on specific issues; for example, the losses from displacement of residents and from serious noise nuisances were measured in units of relative value which could be readily understood. This evidence then fitted in, alongside other items of evidence obtained from other studies, to a table of results, the implications of which were all too well understood by the decision-takers! Indeed, a casual glance at the figures in the summary tables of the CTLA Study would have led to immediate recognition of the consequences for anyone interested in the decision. The units of assessment (money units) were easy to comprehend, and participants at the final inquiry were able to debate them fully and vigorously, even if there was much general disagreement.

Whether or not planning teams accept the conventional social cost–benefit approach to plan evaluation (as the CTLA did), their evaluations should be based on the preferences of people affected. They should utilize empirical evidence of the strengths of community preferences. Evaluations should be presented, with units of analysis and results in tables, which are at once comprehensive and comprehensible.

Turning now to the management of the planning process, in general the study team will have to commence their efforts with the coarse design of a wide range of options, especially when information on the type of problem or the study area or the research base for the evaluation is thin. These coarse designs should effectively cover the widest range of feasible possibilities and represent, for practical purposes, the universe of options. This universe of crude options would normally be reduced to a short-list by two or three cycles. This number of cycles appeared to be necessary to the study teams covered in our reviews. Then at each subsequent cycle the options should be specified in progressively greater detail.

Following the evaluation of the short-listed options, it is desirable that the study team go on to search for one or more superior designs by marginal adjustments to the best of those on the short-list. Only where time or resource constraints are particularly tight, or where the institutional environment will not allow it (e.g. when a public inquiry is to be held on the short-listed options), should the subsequent iteration for a preferred option be ruled out after short-listing. Those options found to be of interest after this iteration then join the other alternatives on the short-list for the decision-takers' consideration.

If there are to be one or two cycles of searching for and evaluation of options after the short-list with the fullest information at the study team's disposal, then the short-listing cycle must start about half-way through the planning process. This timing is needed simply to keep sufficient resources available for the fine evaluation of the short-list options and the subsequent search. Typically too little time is devoted to this fine evaluation.

Alternatives should be selected for the short-list because they are considered to be potentially the best (i.e. potential winners). In addition to those which showed up well at the previous evaluation exercise, given the assumptions and measurement techniques employed, potential winners are likely to include some which performed comparatively poorly overall but which had some interesting features. Such alternatives will be selected because of uncertainties surrounding the early evaluation findings, or for their appeal to some groups of decision-makers. The choice of the short-list alternatives should be based on considerations of both the overall magnitude of gains and losses and the incidence of those gains and losses between different groups. The decisions of the team about its own recommendation should also be based on these dual considerations.

If we presume that some insights *can* be obtained into the incidence effects of alternatives, despite our limited technical ability and the high costs of investigation, which particular patterns of incidence will be of most interest? This question is the proper concern of elected representatives. But they are not likely to reveal their true feelings on the matter. Moreover, in our view when elected representatives are able to offer advice during the planning process, the study team should not consider themselves bound to include only those types of options which the decision-takers might favour. Indeed, in major planning studies it is vital that a wider view of the issues is maintained than that likely to be taken by elected representatives alone. To this extent the study team will have to rely on their own judgement as to options of interest for the short-list. The use of their own judgement also applies to the alternatives which have considerable potential but also high uncertainty, because they seem to be favoured for items where evidence is especially limited.

In our view the short-list should contain at least four options, and one or more which is close to the study team's choice. It should contain others that diverse groups in society, including decision-takers, may consider to be most preferable or worthy of full debate; and those for which there are grounds to suppose some advantage will be shown from information to come to light during the fine evaluation.

Study teams may embark upon some design work in the initial phases of their study in order to obtain a feel for the possible *kinds* of design solutions which face them. They may also wish to identify in coarse terms the *range* of possible design solutions. But whether they embark upon such preliminary work or not, the initial phases of the planning process must, in our view, be used to set down the principles of evaluation and the broad approaches to be adopted eventually for measuring differences between designs. In short, evaluation must come first as well as last in studies which lead up to the decision. Strong links exist between evaluation and all the other main activities of plan-making. It is particularly sensible to generate designs with all possible awareness of the way in which they will be compared. It also makes sense to embark upon the collection of evidence for comparisons well before designs are complete. This seemingly obvious advice needs stressing since, with few clear and notable exceptions, planning teams have devoted too little attention to plan evaluation, or do not consider how they will assess options until it is too late for really effective evaluation.

By and large there has been a growing recognition of the important role of evaluation in the planning process and the need to think of evaluation requirements in the plan generation stages. Some of the case studies were exemplary in this respect. But there is still a need to base evaluation exercises in urban and regional planning studies on a clear set of principles, where advantages and disadvantages of plans are identified specifically with gains and losses to particular groups of people in mind. Coverage of the groups should be comprehensive. Findings should be presented by incidence groups if this is practicable, although we recognize the severe practical difficulties of tracing ultimate incidence given current techniques and costs of information gathering.

We cannot rule out the possibility of significant and maybe even revolutionary advancements in the principles and procedures of evaluation; indeed, this is something which we continue to look forward to expectantly. But nothing has occurred up to the date of writing to disoldge us from our view of the most appropriate approach to plan evaluation, which is based both on practical experience of undertaking planning balance sheet analyses as well as on the studies reviewed in Part II. This view we have tried to develop and justify in this book. Given the approaches currently at our disposal, we believe that in general comprehensive social cost–benefit analysis best meets our present evaluation requirements.

Epilogue

WE HAVE deliberately limited the scope of our discussions to the activity of urban and regional planning. We are aware that these kinds of major decisions must be seen in the contexts of wider planning processes. These contexts are continually changing and parallel changes in techniques of planning practice. So we should like to dwell for a few moments on three kinds of planning process alternative to the one on which we have focused attention; these are structure planning, corporate planning, and the monitoring of change. We touch upon these because we are aware of their importance in current practice and we believe that in general terms, although not in detail, what we have had to say is also relevant for them.

Speculation about the way structure plans will evolve has given way to evidence from the first examples to appear. This suggests that, despite claims to the contrary, they will probably constitute sophisticated forms of traditional land-use planning. Land-use and development proposals continue to form the main subject-matter of the exercise. However, structure planning is an example of techniques of plan generation and assessment showing rapid advance. The social implications of structure plan proposals are currently being more fully investigated by comparison with past traditional planning studies.

In our reviews of advanced planning practice we discussed only one case of structure planning *per se* because of the lack of suitable studies at the time of our research. But if in practice structure plans are to be essentially similar in form to past development plan exercises, then our discussions could well apply to the preparation of a structure plan. In so far as the content of structure plans subsequently moves beyond being largely oriented to development and land use, we would admit to the empirical difficulties of extending the analysis of their consequences, given the present sophistication of evaluation techniques. But what we have said in reviewing case studies does not, on the face of it, appear to be out-dated in the light of initial structure planning exercises.

Corporate planning presents us with a more difficult problem. Within the context of municipal government, growing recognition of the need for greater levels of interdependence between departments providing services, and an awareness of the

313

inefficiencies of traditional budgeting methods, suggest that a wider view of decision-making should be taken. This view is not limited to major decisions of strategic importance, but applies also to the day-to-day process of providing municipal services. Thus corporate planning involves a process of continuous decision-making across a wide variety of sectors rather than a "one-off" decision within one sector.

Urban and regional planning is, in a sense, wider in its view than corporate planning since it affects public and private agencies, although largely in the land-use and development sense. Corporate planning, whilst limited to the public sector, spans wider policies in housing, education, transportation, and so on. Accordingly, our investigations are less obviously relevant for those looking for guidance on how to incorporate evaluation into the corporate planning process.

However, some observations can be made. Corporate planning is being introduced into public sector organizations for wider community benefit and to assist in bringing greater rigour into decision-making in the provision of services for members of the community. This is entirely consistent with our view of planning and with our approach to evaluation and applies equally to day-to-day decisions or to decisions of strategic importance. In *principle* there is no inconsistency between our approach and that of corporate planners. However, it is true that in terms of technique only limited advances have been made in making evaluation exercises comparable between sectors, e.g. between education and medical services. In practice we must therefore accept that current evaluation techniques, and hence evaluation as an activity in the corporate planning process, may not be taken as far as we indicate is currently feasible for the urban and regional planning process. This may not be very serious. Corporate planning is being only tentatively introduced into municipal government organizations, and it is unlikely that full integration of government services will be achieved within the next five to ten years. Hopefully evaluation techniques will develop alongside the maturing of corporate planning procedures.

We must admit to having made very few observations about the process of making on-going decisions within either the areas of corporate management or of town planning, such as in terms of development control. Strategic decisions differ from day-to-day decisions in the extent of their importance. Clearly the amount of information which it is worth while to collect about the consequences of strategic decisions will be greater, and greater resources will be allocated to its gathering. Accordingly the roles of plan generation and evaluation, and of information collection, will differ in scale, and in practice these scale differences will probably amount to a difference in kind. The organization of an on-going planning process is likely to be very different from that of a strategic planning process.

We would suggest again that there is nothing inconsistent with our *view* of evaluation of strategic proposals and the information required to make on-going decisions. It is necessary to have evidence of the wider social consequences that will result. To this end information systems should exist which can provide those responsible for day-to-day decisions with some evidence of these social effects.

Such evidence should be not unlike the sorts of evidence we suggest is required for comprehensive evaluations of strategic proposals.

Development control is one instance of the role of monitoring change. Another is the recording of events to assist in periodic consideration of whether modifications to policies and prospective projects are necessary or desirable. In this case one must not only consider the accuracy of forecasts regarding the nature of developments processes, but in addition the effectiveness and costs of the adopted policies and projects. This in turn means considering their *actual* welfare effects in contrast to their *predicted* welfare effects on which plan evaluation prior to implementation was based.

We believe that no inconsistencies exist between suggestions made here, in the context of strategic urban and regional planning, and suggestions which we would have made about these other planning processes, had we considered them. This belief requires substantiating, of course. Perhaps discussion of the role of evaluation in these other planning processes would be a fruitful area for further research.

Working Papers Prepared During The Research Project

1. Hypothesis and Aims of the Research Project and Method of Study, by N. LICHFIELD and P. KETTLE (March 1972).
2. The Planning Process, by R. M. SARLY (March 1972).
3. Evaluation in the Planning Process, by M. WHITBREAD (May 1972).
4. Urban Development Models and Plan Evaluation, by M. HILL (November 1972).
5. The Planning Process of the Commission on the Third London Airport, by M. WHITBREAD (March 1973).
6. Measurement in Evaluation, by M. WHITBREAD (January 1973).
7. A Comparison of the Planning Balance Sheet and the Goals–Achievement Matrix Methods of Evaluation, by P. KETTLE (November 1972).
8. The Use of Cost–Benefit Analysis for Plan Evaluation: A Rationale, by N. LICHFIELD and M. WHITBREAD (August 1972).
9. A Discussion of the Irvine New Town Study, by P. KETTLE (March 1973).
10. Evaluation in the Planning Process—The Case of Accessibility, by M. WHITBREAD (June 1972).
11. A Critique of the Coventry–Solihull–Warwickshire Sub-regional Planning Study, by P. KETTLE (December 1972).
12. A Review of the Brighton Urban Structure Plan Study, by P. KETTLE (January 1973).
13. A Review of the Notts–Derby Sub-regional Planning Study, by P. KETTLE (March 1973).
14. A Discussion of the West Midland Regional Study, by M. WHITBREAD (March 1973).
15. A Critique of the Grangemouth/Falkirk Regional Survey and Plan, by H. I. McKAY (December 1974).

Name Index

Subject Index

Questionnaire surveys 211–13, 225, 242, 247, 308

Ranking 103
REAL experiment 107
Regional studies 126–62
Residential location model 186
Resource costs 55, 180
Resources, available for a study 305–7

Safety standards 200
Scotland 63
   central, White Paper on development in 127
Sectional interests 10
Sectoral objectives 27–9, 106, 137, 176, 204, 262, 263
Shopping model 110–15, 186
Short-listing of options 294–8
Sieve-map technique 195
Skelmersdale 50
Skopje 64
Social cost–benefit analysis xv, 8, 11, 12, 55–8, 65–7, 78–9, 103, 124, 145, 152–4, 158, 159, 192, 193, 225, 254, 256, 265, 268, 273, 288, 298, 312
Social mix 5
Social policy 236
Social satisfaction 237, 238
Society as an entity 5
Stansted 271
Stevenage Public Transport Study 35
Strategic Plan for the South East 14, 28, 246, 299
Strategies, circumstances affecting choice of 298–307
   flexibility of 208–9, 224
Structure planning 228–49, 313
Sub-regional studies 163–227
Swanley Study 74, 80

Terms of reference 298–300
Third London Airport 9, 11, 13, 21, 35, 37, 42, 50–1, 67, 70, 74, 94, 271–89, 294–309
   associated urban development 38
   background 271–4
   site-selection process 275–87
     coarse 78 alternatives 278–9

medium list of 29 279–82
reduced medium list of 15 282–5
short-list of 4 285–7
summary of findings 287–9
Threshold analysis 56, 64, 126, 138–41
Traffic model 115–18, 149–50, 154, 169
Traffic noise 99–100
Transformation functions 89–90
Transport 181–2, 232, 262, 269
Transport and Road Research Laboratory 107
Travel benefits 43–4, 117, 150, 182, 266, 267
Travel costs 44, 115–18, 150, 266
Travel demand function 117
Travel time valuation 266

Urban development models 109–19

Valuation and evaluation 4–5

Warsaw optimization method 64
Warsaw Urban Region 64
Wealth, transfers of 108
Weighting of objectives 210, 213
Welfare xvi, 3–6, 10, 25, 30, 33, 83, 87, 94, 141, 159, 239, 262
Welfare test 3, 65, 66
West Midland Conurbation 144
West Midland Regional Study xvi, 8, 13, 14, 118, 143–62, 295–308
   background 143
   coarse options cycle 145, 148, 149, 157–9
   conclusions on 160–2
   evaluation in the planning process 154–60
   fine-options and subsequent cycles 145, 151–4, 156
   idealized strategies 146–7
   initial cycle of plan-making 146
   planning process, detailed 146–54
     outline 145–6
   preferred alternative 145, 146, 151, 153, 160
   reports 143, 156
   Study Team 144
   traffic model 149–50
"Willingness to pay" criterion 69–72

THE URBAN AND REGIONAL PLANNING SERIES

Other Books in the Series

CHADWICK, G. F.
A Systems View of Planning: Towards a Theory of the
Urban and Regional Planning Process (Volume 1)

BLUNDEN, W. R.
The Land Use/Transport System: Analysis and Synthesis
(Volume 2)

GOODALL, B.
The Economics of Urban Areas (Volume 3)

LEE, C.
Models in Planning: An Introduction to the Use of
Quantitative Models in Planning (Volume 4)

FALUDI, A.
A Reader in Planning Theory (Volume 5)

COWLING, T. M. & STEELEY, G. C.
Sub-Regional Planning Studies: An Evaluation (Volume 6)

FALUDI, A.
Planning Theory (Volume 7)

SOLESBURY, W.
Policy in Urban Planning: Structure plans, programmes and local plans (Volume 8)

MOSELEY, M. J.
Growth Centres in Spatial Planning (Volume 9)

SANT, M.
Industrial Movement and Regional Development: The
British Case (Volume 11)

Other Titles of Interest

CLOUT, H. D.
Rural Geography

JOHNSON, J. H.
Urban Geography, 2nd Edition

The terms of our inspection copy service apply to all the above books.
A complete catalogue of all books in the Pergamon International Library
is available on request. The Publisher will be pleased to consider
suggestions for revised editions and new titles.